"Brandon Crowe has already made significant contributions to our understanding of the person and ministry of Christ. Now he places us further in his debt with *The Lord Jesus Christ*—an outstanding exposition that is as readable as it is comprehensive. Dr. Crowe brings to his task the skills of a fine biblical scholar who is also sensitive to the history of doctrine. In addition he writes with a clear sense of the importance and value of systematic theology in its explorations of the deep logic of the biblical testimony to Christ. All this is combined with deeply thoughtful application for today. While wide reading and careful scholarship underlie every page of *The Lord Jesus Christ*, it is written in a style that is accessible to anyone willing to join Professor Crowe in his journey through Scripture and theology. It will be instructive to students and hugely stimulating to preachers and teachers, and it should delight any thoughtful reader. Indeed, it belongs to the special category of literature famously described by Francis Bacon: 'Some books are to be ... chewed and digested.' These pages simply increase our admiration for Dr. Crowe's gifts and our debt of gratitude for the particular gift he offers us in this study. The Lord Jesus Christ is to be treasured—and so is this wonderful book about him."

SINCLAIR FERGUSON
Chancellor's Chair of Systematic Theology, Reformed Theological Seminary

"We have here the solid and clear communication of orthodox doctrine, in a way that combines careful attention to the biblical texts and to the history of doctrine."

VERN S. POYTHRESS
Distinguished Professor of New Testament, Biblical Interpretation, and Systematic Theology, Westminster Theological Seminary

"While Brandon Crowe writes as a professor of theology on the glorious locus of Christology, one also detects—praise God!—a pastoral element at work in this book. In *The Lord Jesus Christ: The Biblical Doctrine of the Person and Work of Christ*, Crowe brings together a range of skills to produce a book that highlights some of the best elements in a good systematic work—namely, both an accurate history of key questions and a biblical-theological emphasis that brings a richness to the work. I could see this work as a helpful tool for students of theology, but it may indeed have a wider use for those serious about learning more about the Lord Jesus Christ."

MARK JONES
pastor, Faith Vancouver Presbyterian Church

"Here is a solid, readable, faithful Reformed Christology. Comprised of three sections—biblical, historical/dogmatic, and practical—the book provides a clear introduction to the person and work of Jesus Christ. Crowe's joy in 'the abiding grace of Jesus Christ' is manifest on every page."

MATTHEW LEVERING
James N. Jr. and Mary D. Perry Chair of Theology, Mundelein Seminary

"As the author asks, 'Can we ever have too much of Christ? Can we ever think of him too often?' Focusing broadly on the biblical witness to Christ, the dogmatic development of Christology, and the application of both to the life and ministry of the church, Crowe's work is clear, profound, and far reaching. His work refreshingly displays both precision about Christ and warmth of devotion to him, as the author makes a solid case for Jesus' person and work in ways that give readers a valuable compendium of a multi-faceted Christology. The precise intertwining of exegesis, systematic theology, and devotion makes this one of the best recent books on Christology that I have read. It is solid, thorough, and readable."

RYAN M. MCGRAW
Morton H. Smith Professor of Systematic Theology,
Greenville Presbyterian Theological Seminary

"Brandon Crowe has produced a substantial systematic statement of Christology for our day, uniting exegetical rigor, historical sensitivity, and theological profundity as well as igniting proclamation and mission by giving the church plenty of fuel for our highest end: knowing Jesus Christ."

HARRISON PERKINS
pastor, Oakland Hills Community Church (OPC)

"Brandon Crowe's *The Lord Jesus Christ* is an exciting development. Not only is it the first published volume in a very promising new theological series, it is an accessible yet comprehensive Christology that covers both the person and work of Jesus Christ. Crowe's approach is in the tradition of Bavinck and the best of the Reformed theological tradition that seeks to give careful attention to the whole deposit of revelation in Scripture in its natural unfolding while also synthesizing theological reflection. One of this volume's many strengths is the exegetical skill Crowe brings to christological texts, which, in turn, provides freshness to his theological insight and contemporary application. This Christology is a confessionally Reformed one and rightly catholic in its scope through Crowe's firm grasp on the history of christological reflection from the early church to the present. Whether you are a theological student or simply desiring to go deeper in your knowledge of the Lord Jesus Christ, I highly commend this book to you!"

D. BLAIR SMITH
associate professor of systematic theology, Reformed Theological Seminary

BRANDON D. CROWE

(PhD, University of Edinburgh) is professor of New Testament at Westminster Theological Seminary in Glenside, Pennsylvania, and author of *The Last Adam: A Theology of the Obedient Life of Jesus in the Gospels* and *The Hope of Israel: The Resurrection of Christ in the Acts of the Apostles*.

THE LORD JESUS CHRIST

THE BIBLICAL DOCTRINE OF THE PERSON AND WORK OF CHRIST

WE BELIEVE

STUDIES IN REFORMED BIBLICAL DOCTRINE

We Believe is a series of eight major studies of the Christian faith's primary doctrines as confessed in the Nicene Creed and guided by the Reformed tradition. In each volume, trusted authors engage a major creedal doctrine in light of its biblical-theological foundations and historical development, drawing out its spiritual, ethical, and missional implications for the church today.

1

One God Almighty

The Biblical Doctrine of the Triune God

2

Maker of Heaven and Earth

The Biblical Doctrine of Creation and Providence

4

For Us and for Our Salvation

The Biblical Doctrine of Humanity and Sin

5

He Will Come Again in Glory

The Biblical Doctrine of the End

6

The Giver of Life

The Biblical Doctrine of the Holy Spirit and Salvation

7

He Spoke through the Prophets

The Biblical Doctrine of God's Self-Revelation

8

One, Holy, Catholic, and Apostolic Church

The Biblical Doctrine of the Church

THE LORD JESUS CHRIST

THE BIBLICAL DOCTRINE OF THE PERSON AND WORK OF CHRIST

WE BELIEVE: STUDIES IN REFORMED BIBLICAL DOCTRINE

VOLUME 3

JOHN MCCLEAN AND MURRAY J. SMITH, SERIES EDITORS

BRANDON D. CROWE

The Lord Jesus Christ: The Biblical Doctrine of the Person and Work of Christ
We Believe, edited by John McClean and Murray J. Smith

Lexham Academic, an imprint of Lexham Press
1313 Commercial St., Bellingham, WA 98225
LexhamPress.com

Print ISBN 9781683597162
Digital ISBN 9781683597179
Library of Congress Control Number 2023930836

Lexham Editorial: Todd Hains, Claire Brubaker, Lynsey Stepan
Cover Design: Joshua Hunt
Typesetting: Anna Fejes, Abigail Stocker

Ἰησοῦς Χριστὸς ἐχθὲς καὶ σήμερον ὁ αὐτὸς καὶ εἰς τοὺς αἰῶνας.

Jesus Christ is the same yesterday and today and forever.

Hebrews 13:8

The revelation made of Christ in the blessed Gospel is far more excellent, more glorious, and more filled with rays of divine wisdom and goodness, than the whole creation and the just comprehension of it, if attainable, can contain or afford. ... This, therefore, deserves the severest of our thoughts, the best of our meditations, and our utmost diligence in them. For if our future blessedness shall consist in being where he is, and beholding of his glory, what better preparation can there be for it than in a constant previous contemplation of that glory in the revelation that is made in the Gospel, unto this very end, that by a view of it we may be gradually transformed into the same glory?

John Owen, Works

For Cheryl

קָמוּ בָנֶיהָ וַיְאַשְּׁרוּהָ בַּעְלָהּ וַיְהַלְלָהּ

Proverbs 31:28

τὸ μυστήριον τοῦτο μέγα ἐστίν
ἐγὼ δὲ λέγω εἰς Χριστὸν καὶ εἰς τὴν ἐκκλησίαν.

Ephesians 5:32

CONTENTS

PART 2: DOGMATIC DEVELOPMENT

SERIES INTRODUCTION

Your word is a lamp to my feet
and a light to my path.
Psalm 119:105

The unfolding of your words gives light;
it imparts understanding to the simple.
Psalm 119:130

AN INVITATION TO CONFESSIONAL THEOLOGY

We Believe is a series of eight studies of the primary doctrines of the Christian faith as confessed in the Nicene Creed and received in the Reformed tradition. The series marks the 1700th anniversary of the Council of Nicaea (AD 325) by re-affirming and advancing the Church's confession.[1] The title of our series is drawn from the first words of the Creed—the single Greek verb Πιστεύομεν—which introduces what has become the classic confession of the Christian Faith. Since the Church's confession neither began at Nicaea, nor ended with its creed, *We Believe* examines the biblical foundations of the Church's faith, traces its development (especially in the Reformed tradition), and applies its truths to the worship, life, and mission of the Church today. Since true theology begins in prayer and worship of the God who has revealed himself, each volume opens with a theme prayer, shaped by Scripture and the Church's confession. Further,

1. For the history of the Nicene Creed, which received its final form at the Council of Constantinople (ad 381), see D. Fairbairn and R. M. Reeves, *The Story of Creeds and Confessions: Tracing the Development of the Christian Faith* (Grand Rapids: Baker Academic, 2019), 48–79.

since even the deepest truths of the faith need to be simply expounded so they can be clearly grasped and faithfully lived, each volume closes with a series of theses, which summarize the doctrine covered in the book. *We Believe* provides a comprehensive and integrated biblical, theological, and missional treatment of the major doctrines of the Christian faith.

BIBLICAL REVELATION

The Church's confession is rooted in and ruled by God's revelation in Scripture. The Scriptures are "the Word of God written" and "the rule of faith and life" (Westminster Confession of Faith 1:2). The first part of each study, therefore, is devoted to a fresh examination of biblical revelation.

Fundamentally, our studies are tethered to the text of Scripture, and each volume in the series includes expositions of the primary biblical texts which form the doctrine under consideration.[2] Moreover, since Scripture is the only "infallible rule" for its own interpretation (Westminster Confession of Faith 1:9), our studies seek to interpret Scripture by Scripture, initially by embracing the discipline of Biblical Theology.[3] We begin—where God's people have always begun—with the recognition that Scripture is God's inspired and authoritative Word. We proceed by tracing God's progressive revelation of himself and his purposes in the organically unfolding canon of Scripture, taking full account of its varied forms, while especially recognizing its fundamental, Christ-centered unity. This procedure is one we learn from Scripture itself. The Bible regularly claims that its revelation forms a single coherent narrative climaxing in the gospel of Christ, even as it also indicates that this narrative has many dimensions, and is revealed in a diversity of literary forms.[4] Faithful Christian readings of Scripture—from Irenaeus and Augustine to Calvin and Kuyper—have,

---

2. For convenience of reference, these biblical expositions are highlighted in text boxes. Several key biblical texts are important for more than one doctrine, but to avoid repetition, these are only treated once in the series.

3. We understand this discipline along the lines sketched by Geerhardus Vos in his 1894 Inaugural Lecture at Princeton Theological Seminary. G. Vos, "The Idea of Biblical Theology as a Science and as a Theological Discipline," in *Redemptive History and Biblical Interpretation: The Shorter Writings of Geerhardus Vos*, ed. R. B. Gaffin (Phillipsburg: P & R, 1980), 3–24; *Biblical Theology: Old and New Testaments* (Grand Rapids: Eerdmans, 1948), 3–18.

4. See, for example: Deut 26:5–11; Josh 24; 1 Sam 12:6–18; Pss 78; 105–6; 136; Neh 9:7–37; Acts 7; 13:13–43; Heb 11.

therefore, always recognized a fundamental unity within the rich diversity of Scripture—a unity which is conceptual (in that the Scriptures speak of the same God relating in consistent ways to the same created world), and narratival (in that the Scriptures narrate a single redemptive-history).[5]

In the first part of each study, then, we look for the organic unfolding of God's revelation from its seed form in the Garden of Eden (Gen 1–2) to its full flowering in the Garden-City of the New Jerusalem (Rev 21–22). As Augustine said, "in the Old Testament the New is concealed, in the New the Old is revealed."[6] So we read Genesis in the light of the Gospels, Exodus in the light of the Epistles, and Ruth in the light of Revelation. We follow the rich network of citations and allusions—the "inner biblical exegesis"—by which Scripture interprets Scripture.[7] We outline the primary biblical themes relevant to each doctrine—God's kingdom and covenant, God's creation and blessing, God's Son and people, God's Spirit and temple—together with their many related sub-themes, as they inform and shape the Church's confession. We use Scripture's own words and categories to trace the drama of redemption from creation to new creation centered on Christ.

Following this approach, we recognize that the Bible fundamentally structures its own unfolding narrative, and organizes all its major themes, around God's two primary covenants with Adam and Christ (Rom 5:12–21; 1 Cor 15:22). Reformed theology came to characterize these as the "covenant of works" and the "covenant of grace," confessing that, from start to finish, God has related to his people and his world by way of covenant (Westminster Confession of Faith 7:1–6).[8] Scripture thus presents each of the major post-fall biblical covenants—God's covenants with Abraham,

---

5. See C. H. H. Scobie, "History of Biblical Theology," in *New Dictionary of Biblical Theology*, ed. T. D. Alexander and B. S. Rosner (Leicester: InterVarsity Press, 2000), 11–20.

6. Augustine, Quaest. in Hept. 2: 73: *Novum Testamentum in Vetere latet, Vetus Testamentum in Novo patet.*

7. The phrase "inner biblical exegesis" was coined by M. A. Fishbane, *Biblical Interpretation in Ancient Israel* (Oxford: Oxford University Press, 1985). See further: G. K. Beale and D. A. Carson, eds., *Commentary on the New Testament Use of the Old Testament* (Grand Rapids: Baker Academic, 2007); G. K. Beale, *Handbook on the New Testament Use of the Old Testament: Exegesis and Interpretation.* (Grand Rapids: Baker Academic, 2012); G. E. Schnittjer, *Old Testament use of Old Testament: A Book-by-Book Guide* (Grand Rapids: Zondervan, 2021).

8. See esp. G. P. Waters, J. N. Reid, and J. R. Muether, eds., *Covenant Theology: Biblical, Theological, and Historical Perspectives* (Wheaton: Crossway, 2020); H. Perkins, *Reformed Covenant Theology: A Systematic Introduction* (Bellingham, WA: Lexham Press, forthcoming).

Israel, David, and the new covenant—as successive administrations of the single covenant of grace: the covenant which was first promised in the garden (Gen 3:15), climactically sealed by the blood of Christ (Matt 26:28 and Mark 14:24 with Exod 24:8), and which ultimately will be fulfilled in the new creation when the triune God comes to dwell with his people at last (Rev 21:3).[9]

Above all—and consistent with the covenant theology we have just sketched—we take Jesus's own word as our guide, and look for him, the Lord Jesus Christ, "in all the Scriptures" (Luke 24:27). Following Jesus and his apostles, we recognize that God "promised...the gospel...beforehand through his prophets in the Holy Scriptures" (Rom 1:3–4; cf. Luke 24:44–49; Gal 3:8; 1 Cor 15:3–5; 1 Pet 1:12). Christ himself—his person, his work, and his kingdom—is the climax and goal of the triune God's gracious plan to redeem his people and his world. Indeed, Christ is the very "substance" of biblical revelation (Col 2:17; cf. John 5:39; Rom 10:4; 1 Cor 10:4; 2 Cor 1:20; 2 Tim 3:15; 1 Pet 1:10–12). The grace of God in Christ was not merely foreshadowed and prophesied in the Old Testament; it was mediated in advance to the saints of old, by the Spirit, through the "promises, prophecies, sacrifices...and other types" given to God's people in that period (Westminster Confession of Faith 7:5–6). We therefore affirm that the Old Testament is *both* Christo-telic (in that it points forward to Christ as its goal), *and* Christo-centric (in that its types and promises really mediated God's grace in Christ, through the Spirit).[10] Thus, with John Calvin, we are right to "seek in the whole of Scripture...truly to know Jesus Christ, and the infinite riches that are comprised in him and are offered to us by him from God the Father."[11]

---

9. For the central covenant promise—"I will be your God and you will be my people" (or variations), see: Gen 17:7–8; 28:15; 31:3, 5, 42; 39:2–6, 21–23; Exod 6:7; 29:45–46; Lev 11:45; 25:38; 26:11–12; Deut 23:15; 26:17–18; 29:12–13; 2 Sam 7:23–24; 1 Chron 17:22; Ps 95:7; Jer 11:4; 24:7; 30:22; 31:1, 33; 32:38; Ezek 14:11; 34:24, 30–31; 36:28; 37:23, 27; Zech 2:11; 8:8; 13:9; Hos 1:8–2:23; Matt 1:23; 18:20; 28:20; 2 Cor 6:16; Rev 21:3.

10. See: P. A. Lillback, ed. *Seeing Christ in All of Scripture: Hermeneutics at Westminster Theological Seminary* (Philadelphia: Westminster Seminary Press, 2016); L. G. Tipton, "Christocentrism *and* Christotelism: The Spirit, Redemptive History, and the Gospel," in *Redeeming the Life of the Mind: Essays in Honor of Vern Poythress*, ed. J. M. Frame, W. A. Grudem, and J. J. Hughes (Wheaton: Crossway, 2018), 129–45.

11. From Calvin's preface to Pierre Olivétan's French translation of the New Testament (1534) in *Calvin: Commentaries*, J.Haroutunian and L.P. Smith, trans. and eds, (Philadelphia: Westminster Press, 1958), 70.

In thus seeking Christ in all the Scriptures, we find that later revelation in Scripture interprets earlier revelation in ways that are consistent with its original meaning; the later revelation shows the "true and full sense" (*sensus plenior*) in light of the fulfillment in Christ (Westminster Confession of Faith 1:9). The New Testament offers no radical reinterpretation, much less correction, of the Old, but unfolds the full meaning of God's inspired Word. As B.B. Warfield put it, the Old Testament is like a room "richly furnished but dimly lighted," such that "the introduction of light [from the New Testament] brings into it nothing which was not in it before," but "brings out into clearer view much of what is in it but was only dimly or even not at all perceived before."[12] As we read the Scriptures as the unfolding narrative of God's redemptive purpose, we learn to see, again and again, that Christ is the center and substance of the Scriptures, and so the center and substance of the Church's faith.

DOGMATIC DEVELOPMENT

The Church confesses not only what is "expressly set down in Scripture" but what "by good and necessary consequence may be deduced from Scripture" (Westminster Confession of Faith 1:6). The second part of each study in the *We Believe* series, therefore, is devoted to an account of the dogmatic development of the doctrine under consideration. Far from being opposed to each other, Biblical Theology and Systematic and Confessional Dogmatics actually need each other; there is a necessarily reciprocal relationship between the two.[13] While both disciplines deal with God's special revelation in Scripture, they analyze it according to different principles.

12. B. B. Warfield, "The Biblical Doctrine of the Trinity," in *Biblical Doctrines: The Works of Benjamin B. Warfield*, vol. 2 (New York: Oxford University Press, 1932), 141–42.

13. For reflection on the relationship between the two disciples in the Reformed tradition, see esp. Vos, "Idea," 3–24; J. Murray, "Systematic Theology," in *Collected Writings of John Murray, vol. 4. Studies in Theology: Reviews*, ed. I. Murray (Edinburgh: Banner of Truth, 1983), 1–21; R. B. Gaffin, "Systematic Theology and Biblical Theology," *WTJ* 38 (1975–76): 281–99. For review of these contributions and a constructive proposal, see M. Allen, "Systematic Theology and Biblical Theology—Part One," *JRT* 14 (2020): 52–72; "Systematic Theology and Biblical Theology—Part Two," *JRT* 14 (2020): 344–57. Note also. J. McClean, "Of Covenant and Creation: A Conversation between Systematic Theology and Biblical Theology," in *An Everlasting Covenant: Biblical and Theological Essays in Honour of William J. Dumbrell*, ed. J. A. Davies and A. M. Harman, RTR Supplement Series 4 (Doncaster: Reformed Theological Review, 2010), 187–227.

The primary organizing principle for Biblical Theology is history—the organic unfolding of God's work of redemption and his interpretation of the same in his inspired Word. The primary organizing principle of Dogmatics is logic—the rational organization of God's revealed truth. As Geerhardus Vos observes, while Biblical Theology constructs a historical "line," Christian Dogmatics constructs a logical "circle."[14] Thus, while Christian Dogmatics, including the Church's creeds and confessions, generally follow the redemptive-historical shape of biblical revelation, they self-consciously set that redemptive history within the reality of the triune God and his relations to his world as these are revealed in all of Scripture.[15] In the same way, while Christian Dogmatics fundamentally expresses itself using biblical language, it also employs extra-biblical language to summarize and synthesize biblical teaching, especially where Scripture uses a variety of expressions for the same reality, or where this is necessary to refute error.[16] Since "the Word of God is living and active" (Heb 4:12), the God-given language of Scripture remains primary. Faithful Dogmatics rightly recognizes what John Webster calls the "rhetorical sufficiency" of Scripture.[17] Indeed, since "the Old Testament in Hebrew ... and the New Testament in Greek" were "immediately inspired by God," the final court of appeal for all Christian Dogmatics is the words of Scripture in the original languages (Westminster Confession of Faith 1:8). Yet still, the same theological judgment can be expressed in a range of different conceptual and linguistic forms, and the faithful presentation and propagation of biblical truth sometimes requires extra-biblical expression.[18]

There is, moreover, a real history of doctrinal development to be traced through the ages of church history. As the very Word of the living God, the Scriptures possess an inexhaustible depth. As the Church reads and re-reads God's Word in an ever-changing world, we find that there is always more to confess regarding God and his ways in the world, and always more

---

14. See Vos, "Idea," 23; cf. Murray, "Systematic Theology," 9.

15. Cf. Allen, "Systematic Theology—Part Two," 355–56.

16. Cf. "Systematic Theology—Part Two," 355.

17. J. Webster, "Biblical Reasoning," in *The Domain of the Word: Scripture and Theological Reason* (London: T & T Clark, 2012), 131.

18. See D. S. Yeago, "The New Testament and Nicene Dogma: A Contribution to the Recovery of Theological Exegesis," *ProEccl* 3 (1994): 87–100. Compare B.B. Warfield's comments to this effect on the doctrine of the Trinity (Warfield, "Trinity," 133).

to celebrate in the depths of his "being, wisdom, power, holiness, justice, goodness, and truth" (Westminster Shorter Catechism 4). Herman Bavinck states it well:

> Scripture is not designed so that we should parrot it but that as free children of God we should think his thoughts after him...so much study and reflection on the subject is bound up with it that no person can do it alone. That takes centuries. To that end the church has been appointed and given the promise of the Spirit's guidance into all truth.[19]

As each generation has read the Scriptures, confessed the faith, proclaimed the gospel, instructed children, discipled converts, and refuted errors, the Church—under the oversight of its living Lord, and by the enabling of his Holy Spirit—has deepened in its grasp of biblical truth.[20] The Church has learned again and again that "the Lord hath yet more light and truth to break forth from His Word."[21] The foundational doctrines of God and Christ were fundamentally established in the Church's early centuries, and codified in the ecumenical creeds, such that they received only incremental refinements thereafter. Other doctrines, however, no less crucial to the life of the Church—for example, the doctrines of Scripture and authority—received considerable development in the medieval, Reformation, and modern periods.

Doctrinal development, however—at least where it can be considered faithful—never moves beyond Scripture; it only ever penetrates more deeply into its truth. Faithful Dogmatics is thus not the imposition of a foreign grid onto Scripture, but a complementary means of interpreting Scripture by Scripture. In doing so, we make use of sanctified human reason. For while the Fall has corrupted the human mind (Rom 1:21–23; Eph 4:17–18), that same mind is renewed in Christ and by the Spirit (Rom 12:2; 1 Cor 2:10–13; Eph 4:23), and as such can play the role of servant in the task of theology. Thus Francis Turretin helpfully distinguishes between revelation as the "foundation of faith" and reason as the "instrument of

19. H. Bavinck, *Reformed Dogmatics: Vol. 1—Prolegomena* (Grand Rapids: Baker Academic, 2003), 83.

20. The role of the Spirit in doctrinal development is helpfully emphasized by Murray, "Systematic Theology," 1–21, esp. 6.

21. G. Rawson, "We Limit Not the Truth of God" in *Leeds Hymn Book*, 1853, no. 409.

faith," which can serve to "illustrate" and "collate" biblical passages or arguments, to draw out "inferences," and to help assess whether various positions agree or disagree with what has been revealed.[22]

The Church has been at this task for nearly two-thousand years, and there is a great deal to be learned from the wisdom of the ages. For this reason, each volume in the *We Believe* series provides a survey of the historical development of the doctrine under consideration. In charting this development, we give the Church's creeds and confessions pride of place. For while Augustine, Aquinas, Luther, Calvin, Turretin, and Bavinck—among a host of others—have provided significant insight into biblical truth, the Church's creeds and confessions reflect the official teaching of the Church *as* Church or—perhaps better—the common teaching of the Church's elders, that is, the teaching of those appointed by the Spirit, and charged with guarding and promoting the apostolic gospel and, indeed, "the whole counsel of God" (Acts 15:1–35; 16:4; 20:27–28; 1 Tim 3:2; 5:17–18; 2 Tim 2:2; Titus 1:9).[23]

The Church's teaching is always subordinate to Scripture. Scripture is the magisterial authority, the "rule that rules" (*norma normans*); the Church's teaching is a ministerial authority, "the rule that is ruled" (*norma normata*). In the order of authority, "the Supreme Judge, by which all controversies of religion are to be determined, and all decrees of councils, opinions of ancient writers, doctrines of men, and private spirits, are to be examined, and in whose sentence we are to rest, can be no other but the Holy Spirit speaking in the Scripture" (Westminster Confession of Faith 1:10). At the same time, in the order of knowing, there is wisdom in beginning with the Church's confession. We rightly take the Church's teaching as our guide in reading, interpreting, and applying Scripture. We learn the truth from our elders as they teach us the truth from God's Word. This yields an iterative process: the Scriptures form our confession; our Scripturally-formed confession provides the lens through which we read

---

22. F. Turretin, *Institutes of Elenctic Theology*, trans. G. M. Giger, 3 vols. (Phillipsburg: P&R, 1992–97), §1.8.3, 6–7; 1.12.15.

23. See M. S. Horton, *The Christian Faith: A Systematic Theology for Pilgrims on the Way* (Grand Rapids: Zondervan, 2011), 211–18.

the Scriptures, and; our further reading of the Scriptures further refines our confession.[24]

We Believe stands unashamedly in the Reformed confessional tradition, and seeks to defend and advance it. There are, of course, significant differences between the various Christian confessions. While the whole Church receives the doctrine of the ecumenical creeds (the Apostles', Nicene, and Athanasian creeds, together with the definition of Chalcedon), the later confessions present divergent views on a host of significant matters. It is our conviction that the Reformed confessions, especially the Three Forms of Unity and the Westminster Standards, present the best—that is, the most fully biblical—account of Christian truth. That very tradition, however, has always aimed to contend for "the faith that was once for all delivered to the saints" (Jude 3) and has thus championed a kind of Reformed Catholicity.[25] Our approach in the *We Believe* series is therefore eirenic, and ecumenical. We write *from* the perspective of the Reformed tradition, but *for* the Church catholic.

Moreover, while the Reformed confessions of the sixteenth century are a high point in the development of the Church's doctrine, they are not the end point. The body of Christ will not "attain to the unity of the faith and of the knowledge of the Son of God, to mature manhood, to the measure of stature of the fullness of Christ" (Eph 4:13), until Christ fully unites us to himself by his Spirit, when he raises his people from the dead, and perfects us by his glorious presence (1 Cor 15:42–49; Phil 3:20–21). The bride of Christ will not be fully purified, "without spot or wrinkle," until the Lord returns and presents us to himself "in splendour" (Eph 5:27; Rev 21:2, 9). The city of God will not be complete until God himself comes to dwell among us in all his fullness and illumine us with his light (Rev 21:3, 22–23). A Reformed commitment to the creeds and confessions is, therefore, not an end point, but a stimulus to further biblical exposition and dogmatic clarification.[26] As a work in Christian Dogmatics, *We Believe* does

24. S. Swain, "A Ruled Reading Reformed: The Role of the Church's Confession in Biblical Interpretation," *IJST* 14 (2012): 177–93.

25. Horton, *Christian Faith*, 30–32. Cf. M. Allen and S. R. Swain, *Reformed Catholicity: The Promise of Retrieval for Theology and Biblical Interpretation* (Grand Rapids: Baker Academic, 2015); *Christian Dogmatics: Reformed Theology for the Church Catholic* (Grand Rapids: Baker Academic, 2016).

26. See Bavinck, *Reformed Dogmatics* 1, 31.

not merely aim to retrieve or to repristinate the Reformed tradition, but to constructively develop it, always under the authority of God's Word. If this series makes a modest contribution to the Church's pilgrimage to maturity in Christ, it will have achieved its goal.

TRUTH FOR WORSHIP, LIFE, AND MISSION

The Church's maturity in Christ involves far more than doctrinal faithfulness and clarity. The drama of redemption, which forms the Church's doctrine, aims ultimately at discipleship and doxology.[27] The third part of each study in the *We Believe* series, therefore, briefly considers the ways in which the doctrine under consideration shapes the Church's worship, life, and mission. While the discussion here is necessarily indicative rather than exhaustive, we aim to demonstrate how biblical doctrine creates a moral vision for all of life. This includes, at the broadest level, observing the way in which the particular doctrine provides the basis for biblical principles for Christian worship, life, and mission, whether these are given explicitly in the biblical text (e.g. Matt 7:12 the "golden rule"), or summarized from biblical revelation as a whole (e.g. "the sanctity of life").[28] It includes, more sharply, consideration of the way in which Christian doctrine grounds the moral law, summarized in the Ten Commandments, and further summarized in the two great commandments of love for God and neighbor (Westminster Confession of Faith 19.2, 5; see esp. Exod 20:1–17; Deut 5:6–21; Matt 22:37–40; Rom 13:8; Gal 5:14; Jas 2:8). It also includes, further, consideration of the wealth of biblical examples which illustrate—both positively and negatively—the wisdom of life according to God's law. Crucially, since Reformed theology has always emphasized the necessity of the work of the Spirit in enabling faith and renewing those who were lost in sin by uniting them to Christ, this section also considers the way in which each doctrine highlights the gracious work of God in enabling his people "to live and work for his praise and glory" (*A Prayer Book for Australia*).

27. For this alliterative summary—"drama, doctrine, doxology, and discipleship"—see Horton, *Christian Faith*, 13–27.

28. See J. Murray, *Principles of Conduct: Aspects of Biblical Ethics* (London: Tyndale Press, 1957), 78–140.

Each of the authors for the series subscribes to one or more of the major Reformed confessions, and shares the general approach to Scripture and theology we have just outlined. At the same time, each author has approached the task in their own way, and—within the rich agreement just sketched—there are differences between us at the level of detail. We have deliberately assembled a company of authors who are experts in either Biblical Theology or Dogmatics on the conviction that in the Reformed tradition scholars must have a facility in both, even while maintaining their own expertise. The books aim to show the necessary integrity of Biblical Theology and Systematic Theology, to introduce students to biblical-confessional theology, and to help enrich and expand Reformed theology, while serving as a resource and reference for pastors, elders, and thoughtful Christians. We're thankful to Lexham Press, and especially our expert editor Dr Todd Hains, for their partnership in this venture. Our hope and prayer is that these eight *Studies in Reformed Biblical Doctrine* might serve to ground the Church more firmly in the truth of God's Word, that together we might "glorify God and enjoy him forever" (Westminster Shorter Catechism 1).

Almighty God, you are enthroned on the praises of Israel,
and all nations will worship and glorify your name.
Grant us counsel, instruct us, and reveal yourself to us,
that we would enjoy and glorify you in heart, soul,
and mind in this life and forever.
Through Jesus Christ our Lord,
who lives and reigns with you
and the Holy Spirit, one God,
now and forever.
Amen.

John McClean
Vice Principal and Lecturer in Systematic Theology and Ethics
Christ College, Sydney

Murray J. Smith
Lecturer in Biblical Theology and Exegesis
Christ College, Sydney

PREFACE

Writing on the person and work of Christ is a daunting task. Who is sufficient for these things? I am not. And yet Christology stands at the heart of Christianity. As a professor called to teach at a Christian seminary and as an ordained minister of the gospel, I have been tasked with expounding the ineffable. Though the issues are mysterious, we can also take solace that Christ comes to us and meets us where we are, preeminently in the incarnation. Though I am acutely aware of my own inadequacies when explaining the wondrous glories of Christ, it is perhaps a greater danger to stay silent when the world is in such great need of faithful, biblical teaching on our only Savior.

The need is also great in the church. Can we ever have too much of Christ? Can we ever think of him too often? Christ is worthy of our most assiduous attention and most careful articulations.

The stakes are high; many have gone astray by failing to grasp Christology rightly.

I have therefore undertaken this project with both hesitation and alacrity. Combining the person and work of Christ into one volume is a challenge (many books focus on either the person or the work of Christ), but also reflects the proper biblical connection between the Savior and salvation, which must always be held together. It is not my aim to say anything substantially new about Christ and his work. I affirm the great creeds of the church, and my own ordination is based on the Westminster Standards as a faithful representation of the teaching of Scripture. Readers should expect to find in what follows a discussion of Christology that gleans heavily from the Reformed tradition, though as Robert Letham has noted, the

Reformed tradition in its best forms is consistently catholic[1]—an approach I hope to model as well. The Reformed creeds include extensive, faithful teaching on the person and work of Christ. And yet there is always more to say, even if the fundamental doctrines have long since been established. The doctrine of Christ must be engaged by each generation, though this must be done in conversation and conscious reliance on the best of the Christian exegetical-theological tradition.

I aim to provide an exegetical foundation for the doctrine of Christ and will highlight key themes throughout the section on the biblical witness, such as the role of the exodus and Christ as prophet, priest, and king. Even so, I will engage in both biblical- and systematic-theological discussion. This blending of approaches—if indeed it is necessary to call it blending—has a long history in Christian interpretation, and we do well to continue it today. Good systematic theology is robustly biblical, and sensitive biblical theology is both synthetic and canonically aware. As the discussions and references that follow will indicate, I am greatly indebted to many teachers, both past and present, who have shaped my understanding of the riches of Christology. However, given the catholicity of the tradition, it is not possible to identify the guiding source for every point I make. Here at the outset, I gratefully acknowledge my debt to so many who have shaped my understanding of Christology. Readers should be aware that—consistent with the whole *We Believe* series—I write from a Reformed framework, though my hope is that what I say will be profitable to those from other traditions as well.

I have sought both to uphold orthodox Christology throughout this volume and to provide fresh discussions of the issues. To this end, I interact with both contemporary scholarship and classic voices. At the end of each chapter I include a brief, annotated bibliography. Readers should not conclude that I endorse or recommend all these books. Instead, they reflect a range of perspectives on the issues covered in the chapter, even if I have reservations about some of the works. Comparing the bibliography to the footnotes in each chapter may give readers a sense for which works I find most helpful. Given the space restraints for this book—which is already much longer than originally planned—I have not been able to address

1. Robert Letham, *Systematic Theology* (Wheaton, IL: Crossway, 2019), 33.

every christological issue or engage every important primary or secondary source. This book must remain an introduction, though my aim has been to provide as thorough and user-friendly an introduction as possible, given the space constraints.

I am grateful to John McClean and Murray Smith for the invitation—and challenge—for a New Testament professor to write a book on a locus of systematic theology. Their feedback has proven quite valuable. Thanks to Todd Hains and the entire team at Lexham Press for their support and quality workmanship. I am grateful to the board of trustees, administration, staff, and colleagues on faculty at Westminster Theological Seminary for supporting and sharpening this project in various ways. My colleagues are consistent sources of information and wisdom. Thanks especially to Vern Poythress for reading the entire manuscript and making many valuable suggestions and to Todd Rester for sharing his time and expertise in Latin and his expansive knowledge of church history. Blake Franze read large portions of the manuscript and made many valuable suggestions, many of which I have fruitfully incorporated. Thanks also to Andy Abernethy, Greg Beale, Bob Cara, Stephen Coleman, Iain Duguid, Brannon Ellis, Sinclair Ferguson, David Garner, Mark Garcia, Jonny Gibson, Charles Hill, Ryan McGraw, Blair Smith, Gray Sutanto, and Chad Van Dixhoorn for serving as conversation partners and providing feedback of various kinds. Those who have served as teaching and research assistants while I worked on this book have supported its completion: James Beevers, Joe Fischer, Blake Franze, Michael Hunter, Jon Jung, Tyler Milliken, Pip Mohr, and Joel Sienkiewicz. Thanks to Donna Roof for tracking down a number of books and articles. I also benefited from insightful questions from and discussions with students at Westminster Theological Seminary. Thanks to James Beevers and Caleb Burkhart for preparing the indices.

I am grateful for my family. My wife, Cheryl, is a constant support and encouragement. She has done much in many ways behind the scenes to support the writing of this book; it is my privilege to thank her publicly. I also thank my children. My deepest desire for them is that they would always love, follow, and rest on the living Christ of Scripture. My parents and parents-in-law continue to provide encouragement and support, modeling Christlike love in many ways.

Though it typically goes without saying in acknowledgments, in this case I mention explicitly I write this book out love for Jesus Christ. This is not a book about an abstract idea or a dead figure from the past. This book is about the living Lord of lords who lives and reigns now. I therefore write with the prayer that what I have written will honor Jesus Christ and draw many to worship him. May Christ be exalted.

Brandon D. Crowe

ABBREVIATIONS

GENERAL

CSB	Christian Standard Bible
ESV	English Standard Version
LXX	Septuagint
MT	Masoretic Text
NA	Nestle-Aland, *Novum Testament Graece*
NIV	New International Version
NT	New Testament
OG	Old Greek
OT	Old Testament
pars.	parallels
SBLGNT	Society of Biblical Literature Greek New Testament
THGNT	Tyndale House Greek New Testament

ANCIENT JEWISH TEXTS

Dead Sea Scrolls

1QS	Rule of the Community
4Q44	Deuteronomy[q]
4Q175	Testimonia
4Q365a	Temple Scroll[a]
4Q521	Messianic Apocalypse
4Q524	Temple Scroll[b]
11Q13	Melchizedek
11Q19 21	Temple Scroll

Old Testament Apocrypha and Pseudepigrapha

1 Macc.	1 Maccabees
2 Bar.	2 Baruch
LAB	Liber antiquitatum biblicarum (Pseudo-Philo)
LAE	Life of Adam and Eve
Pss. Sol.	Psalms of Solomon

APOSTOLIC FATHERS

1 Clem.	1 Clement
2 Clem.	2 Clement
Did.	Didache
Diogn.	Epistle to Diognetus
Barn.	Epistle of Barnabas
Ign. *Eph.*	Ignatius, *To the Ephesians*
Ign. *Magn.*	Ignatius, *To the Magnesians*
Ign. *Trall.*	Ignatius, *To the Trallians*
Ign. *Rom.*	Ignatius, *To the Romans*
Ign. *Phld.*	Ignatius, *To the Philadelphians*
Ign. *Smyrn.*	Ignatius, *To the Smyrnaeans*
Ign. *Pol.*	Ignatius, *To Polycarp*
Mart. Pol.	Martyrdom of Polycarp
Pol. *Phil.*	Polycarp, *To the Philippians*

OTHER GREEK AND LATIN WORKS

1 Apol.	Justin, *First Apology*
2 Apol.	Justin, *Second Apology*
Ant.	Josephus, *Antiquities of the Jews*
Autol.	Theophilus of Antioch, *Ad Autolycum*
C. Ar.	Athanasius of Alexandria, *Oratianes contra Arianos*
Carn. Chr.	Tertullian of Carthage, *De carne Christi*
Cels.	Origen of Alexandria, *Contra Celsum*
Dial.	Justin, *Dialogue with Trypho*
Enarrat. Ps.	Augustine of Hippo, *Enarrationes in Psalmos*
Ep.	Gregory of Nazianzus, *Epistulae*

Epid.	Irenaeus of Lyons, *Epideixis tou apostolikou kērygmatos*
**Haer.*	Hippolytus of Rome, *Refutatio omnium haeresium* [*Authorship uncertain]
Haer.	Irenaeus of Lyons, *Adversus haereses*
Hist. eccl.	Eusebius of Caesarea, *Historia ecclesiastica*
Inc.	Athanasius, *On the Incarnation*
Inst.	Calvin, John. *Institutes of the Christian Religion*. Edited by John T. McNeill. Translated by Ford Lewis Battles. 2 vols. LCC 20–21. Louisville: Westminster John Knox, 1960
Inst.	Turretin, Francis. *Institutes of Elenctic Theology*. Translated by George Musgrave Giger. Edited by James T. Dennison Jr. 3 vols. Phillipsburg, NJ: P&R, 1992–1997
Leg.	Athenagoras of Athens, *Legatio pro Christianis*
Marc.	Tertullian of Carthage, *Adversus Marcionem*
Noet.	Hippolytus of Rome, *Contra haeresin Noeti*
Or.	Gregory of Nazianzus, *Orationes*
Paed.	Clement of Alexandria, *Paedagogus*
Pecc. merit.	Augustine of Hippo, *De peccatorum meritis et remissione*
Praescr.	Tertullian of Carthage, *De praescriptione haeriticorum*
Prax.	Tertullian of Carthage, *Adversus Praxean*
Princ.	Origen of Alexandria, *De Principiis*
Protr.	Clement of Alexandria, *Protrepticus*
SPT	*Synopsis Purioris Theologiae / Synopsis of a Purer Theology: Latin Text and English Translation*. Edited by Dolf te Velde et al. Translated by Riemer A. Faber. 2 vols. Studies in Medieval and Reformation Traditions 187, 204 / Texts and Sources 5, 8. Leiden: Brill, 2014–2016
Strom.	Clement of Alexandria, *Stromateis*
Syn.	Athanasius of Alexandria, *De synodis*
Trin.	Novatian, *On the Trinity*

MODERN WORKS

AB	Anchor Bible
ABD	*Anchor Bible Dictionary*. Edited by David Noel Freedman. 6 vols. New York: Doubleday, 1992

ANF	*The Ante-Nicene Fathers*. Edited by Alexander Roberts and James Donaldson. 10 vols. Repr., Peabody, MA: Hendrickson, 1994
BBR	*Bulletin of Biblical Research*
BC	Belgic Confession
BDAG	Danker, Frederick W., Walter Bauer, William F. Arndt, and F. Wilbur Gingrich. *Greek-English Lexicon of the New Testament and Other Early Christian Literature*. 3rd ed. Chicago: University of Chicago Press, 2000
BECNT	Baker Exegetical Commentary on the New Testament
BZNW	Beihefte zur Zeitschrift für die neutestamentliche Wissenschaft
CCSL	Corpus Christianorum: Series Latina
CCT	Contours of Christian Theology
CD	Canons of Dordt
COQG	Christian Origins and the Question of God
ESBT	Essential Studies in Biblical Theology
FET	Foundations of Evangelical Theology
HC	Heidelberg Catechism
ICC	International Critical Commentary
IJST	*International Journal of Systematic Theology*
JETS	*Journal of the Evangelical Theological Society*
K&D	Carl Friedrich Keil and Franz Delitzsch. *Biblical Commentary on the Old Testament*. Translated by James Martin et al. 10 vols. Repr., Peabody, MA: Hendrickson, 1996
LCC	Library of Christian Classics
LW	*Luther's Works*
LNTS	Library of New Testament Studies
NAC	New American Commentary
NICNT	New International Commentary on the New Testament
NIGTC	New International Greek Testament Commentary
NIVAC	NIV Application Commentary
NovTSup	Supplements to Novum Testamentum

NPNF[1]	*The Nicene and Post-Nicene Fathers*. Series 1. Edited by Philip Schaff. 14 vols. Reprint, Peabody, MA: Hendrickson, 1994
NPNF[2]	*The Nicene and Post-Nicene Fathers*. Series 2. Edited by Philip Schaff and Henry Wace. 14 vols. Reprint, Peabody, MA: Hendrickson, 1994
NSBT	New Studies in Biblical Theology
NTS	*New Testament Studies*
OTL	Old Testament Library
PG	Patrologia Graeca [=Patrologiae Cursus Completus: Series Graeca]. Edited by Jacques-Paul Migne. 162 vols. Paris, 1857–1886
PNTC	Pillar New Testament Commentary
PPS	Popular Patristics Series
ProEccl	*Pro Ecclesia*
PRRD	Muller, Richard A. *Post-Reformation Reformed Dogmatics: The Rise and Development of Reformed Orthodoxy, ca. 1520 to ca. 1725*. 2nd ed. 4 vols. Grand Rapids: Baker Academic, 2003
PTS	Patristisches Texte und Studien
RD	Bavinck, Herman. *Reformed Dogmatics*. Edited by John Bolt. Translated by John Vriend. 4 vols. Grand Rapids: Baker Academic, 2003–2008
SC	Sources chrétiennes
SJT	*Scottish Journal of Theology*
SNTSMS	Society for New Testament Studies Monograph Series
Them	*Themelios*
TNTC	Tyndale New Testament Commentaries
TOTC	Tyndale Old Testament Commentaries
TynBul	*Tyndale Bulletin*
VC	*Vigiliae Christianae*
WBC	Word Biblical Commentary
WCF	Westminster Confession of Faith
WLC	Westminster Larger Catechism

Works	Owen, John. *The Works of John Owen*. Edited by William H. Goold. 16 vols. Reprint, Edinburgh: Banner of Truth, 1965–1968
WSC	Westminster Shorter Catechism
WTJ	*Westminster Theological Journal*
WUNT	Wissenschaftliche Untersuchungen zum Neuen Testament
ZECNT	Zondervan Exegetical Commentary on the New Testament

A PRAYER FOR THE STUDY OF CHRISTOLOGY

"Open to me the gates of righteousness, that I may enter through them and give thanks to the LORD. This is the gate of the LORD; the righteous shall enter through it. I thank you that you have answered me and have become my salvation. The stone that the builders rejected has become the chief cornerstone. This is the LORD's doing; it is marvelous in our eyes. This is the day that the LORD has made; let us rejoice and be glad in it."

Psalm 118:19-24 ESV

Holy God: Father, Son, and Spirit,

We humbly ask for your help in studying truths that are too wonderful for us to comprehend.

Our Father, we thank you for sending your Son to redeem us when were under the curse of the law.

Lord Jesus, we thank you for coming to be our reconciliation and redemption; for living the life that we could not live; and for your glorious resurrection from the dead which assures us of eternal life.

Holy Spirit, we ask for your illumination, that we may understand the Scriptures rightly, and that we may benefit from the work of Christ by faith.

O God: as we seek to grow in our knowledge of christological doctrine, grant that we may also grow more and more in love for you and for our neighbors, that they too may grow to love more and more the glories of our wonderful Savior.

We offer this prayer through the mediation of Jesus Christ, our great high priest.

Amen.

INTRODUCTION

"WHO DO YOU SAY THAT I AM?"

CHRISTOLOGY AT CAESAREA PHILIPPI

WE BEGIN AT CAESAREA PHILIPPI (Matt 16:13–20; Mark 8:27–30; Luke 9:18–20). Jesus had been engaged in a powerful ministry of word and deed in and around ancient Roman Palestine, including Galilee, the Decapolis, Samaria, Syro-Phoenicia, and Judea. He had cleansed lepers, healed the lame, cast out demons, raised the dead, walked on water, and calmed a storm. He had forgiven sins and taught with authority no one had ever seen. He had rebuked Pharisees, Sadducees, and scribes, choosing instead uneducated men for his disciples.

Then, at Caesarea Philippi, the narrative focuses in on one of the most consequential questions in history. Jesus had gathered with his disciples near the cave said to be home to the Greek god Pan, which was more recently distinguished by a temple in honor of Caesar Augustus. Under the pall of these pagan powers, Jesus asked his disciples, "Who do you say that I am?"[1]

The disciples wrestled with the identity of who Jesus was (see Mark 4:41; Luke 8:25). Peter responded to Jesus's question: "And they said, 'Some say John the Baptist, others say Elijah, and others Jeremiah or one of the

1. For more on Caesarea Philippi, see Elaine A. Phillips, "Peter's Declaration at Caesarea Philippi," in *Lexham Geographic Commentary on the Gospels*, ed. Barry J. Beitzel (Bellingham, WA: Lexham, 2016–2017), 286–96; Bruce Chilton, "Caesarea Philippi," *ABD* 1:803–6.

prophets.' [Jesus] said to them, 'But who do you say that I am?' Simon Peter replied, 'You are the Christ, the Son of the living God'" (Matt 16:14–16).

Peter got it right. Even so, this brief encounter raises a host of issues.

First, Jesus referred to himself as the Son of Man. The meaning of this phrase is not self-evident. Is it a title? A circumlocution for "a man like me"?

Second, Jesus assumed the prophetic world of ancient Judaism. When the people proffered possible solutions to the conundrum of Jesus's identity, they suggested he could be John the Baptist, Elijah, Jeremiah, or one of the prophets. Jesus is indeed a prophet, but he is more than that. He is greater than the mighty Elijah, who himself ascended into heaven and who had just appeared on the Mount of Transfiguration. Jesus is greater than Jeremiah, the weeping prophet, who spoke of the destruction of Jerusalem and a new covenant. John the Baptist—though he leaned forward as though to help cast open the doors of the coming eschatological kingdom—was the final prophet of the old order, whom Jesus considered to be the greatest of all those born among women. Yet even the least in the kingdom of heaven is greater than John (Matt 11:11). How could this be? Answering this requires us to wrestle with Christology.

Third, Peter's answer identified Jesus as the Christ, the Son of the living God. Both these concepts also derive from the Old Testament. Christ means "messiah" and is one of the most profound, if rare, appellations for Jesus in the Gospels. He is the anointed one, the Son of David, who will bring deliverance. Additionally, Jesus is identified as the Son of the living God. That the true God is the living God distinguishes Israel's covenantal Lord from idols in the Old Testament. Jesus also spoke of his impending death and resurrection in Jerusalem (16:21), portraying himself as the suffering servant. This Messiah, this Son of the living God, was also the one who would suffer, die, and be raised. Again, the Old Testament precedents are crucial.

In sum, this key christological passage at Caesarea Philippi contains many of the elements that we must address if we are to understand Jesus rightly. And these only make sense if we understand their precedents in the Old Testament. Stated simply, if we want to understand New Testament Christology, we have to wrestle also with the Old Testament. For the Scriptures speak about him (Luke 24:25–27, 44–47; John 5:39).

THE CHRISTOLOGICAL QUESTION TODAY: IN THREE PARTS

"Who do you say that I am?" This is not a question relegated to the past; it is a question everyone must answer. Who is this man who healed the sick, cast out demons, raised the dead, and preached with authority? Who is this man who was rejected, crucified, and raised to new life? Who is this man who talked about himself in unique ways? My goal in this book is to help us answer this question faithfully in our own day. To do this, we will look at the evidence from a combination of angles.

Biblical Theology

In part 1 I provide a largely inductive approach to christological issues, following the contours of the biblical texts. I consider how key concepts begin early in Scripture and come to full bloom in the New Testament, noting elements both of continuity and discontinuity. I assume the inspiration and overarching unity of Scripture, which is particularly focused on the person and work of Christ.

I also give sustained attention to christological titles in the New Testament, but not exclusively so. It has long been understood that a focus only on titles is insufficient and can be myopic.[2] If we want to understand whether and/or how Jesus is the Messiah, focusing only on titles would cause us to miss the many ways that Jesus claimed to be the Messiah without using the term. The exigencies of Jesus's ministry seem to have required a certain opacity to his language, so that it was revealed to those with eyes to see and ears to hear. This is particularly true of the Gospels. The contours of the Gospel narratives—the way they are structured, the events that are included, how they are described, the pace of the action, and so forth reveal who Jesus is no less than titles. Further, sound exegetical method requires avoiding the word/concept fallacy. We should not conclude that a given word indicates the same concept in every context; neither should we conclude that the absence of a word indicates the absence of a concept. New Testament authors often communicate Christology even where no titles are used (e.g., Jesus calming the storm in Mark 4:35–41). Additionally,

2. See, e.g., Leander E. Keck, "Toward the Renewal of New Testament Christology," *NTS* 32 (1986): 368–70.

I will give attention to the role of the Old Testament in the New Testament, and often the New Testament echoes the Old Testament for christological purposes even where no titles are used. For indeed, many streams of Old Testament expectation coalesce in Jesus himself (see Ps 78:2 in Matt 13:35).[3]

With these caveats, I will nevertheless give sustained attention to the theme of sonship as a ballast throughout the Scriptures to provide continuity and as a landmark to keep the discussion calibrated. This is appropriate and fits well with the filial emphasis of the New Testament writers.

Dogmatic Development

IN PART 2 I ADDRESS christological issues from a dogmatic and systematic perspective. Here I will consider the historical developments of orthodox christological doctrine, along with the sorts of topics one might expect to find in a systematic work on Christology. These include the development of the church's creeds, the role of Christ as mediator of the covenant of grace, the two natures of Christ, the unity of Christ's person, the two states of Christ, and the atonement.

Here again it is important to understand how terminology will be used. Doctrinal precision requires the use of technical, theological terms, even terms that are not found in Scripture or that may be used differently from Scripture. It has long been understood that technical terminology is legitimate and useful to ensure clarity and precision.[4] For example, though the word "Trinity" is not found in Scripture, the doctrine is necessary exegetically. Further, technical terms are needed because often debates have centered on what the words of the Bible mean.[5] Thus, I will use technical terminology in part 2. To aid in understanding some of these technical terms, a glossary is included at the end of this volume.

Applying Christology

PART 3 ADDRESSES THE APPLICATION of proper Christology. Here I argue for the centrality of Christology to the gospel message and discuss implications of the person and work of Christ in a pluralistic world. Given space

---

3. See D. A. Carson, "Matthew," in *The Expositor's Bible Commentary*, vol. 8, *Matthew, Mark, Luke*, ed. Frank A. Gaebelein (repr., Grand Rapids: Zondervan, 1995), 321–23.

4. See especially Calvin, *Inst.* 1.13.3 (1:123–24); Turretin, *Inst.* 1.1.3 (1:1).

5. See Letham, *Systematic Theology*, 100.

constraints, these will be briefer, but are crucial inasmuch as they reflect the relevance of the christological question posed at Caesarea Philippi for life in the twenty-first, globalized century.

It is not overstatement to say that the question Jesus posed to his disciples at Caesarea Philippi is one of the most consequential questions in world history. More personally, it is a question we all must answer—and answer rightly. But it is not merely a private question; it is a question with implications for the world at large. To answer this question we turn first of all to Scripture.

PART 1

BIBLICAL REVELATION

1

THE SON OF GOD IN CREATION AND THE OLD COVENANT

HIDDEN PRESENCE

To provide shape and structure to our understanding of the person and work of Christ, we begin in the Old Testament. In this chapter I will consider the relevance of the Pentateuch for Christology through three primary lenses. First, I consider briefly the presence of the Son of God in the Old Testament, especially in creation. Progressive revelation means that more is known about the Son of God in the New Testament than in the Old Testament.[1] However, this does not mean that the Son is entirely hidden in the Old Testament. For indeed, the Son of God is the eternal and divine Son—the second person of the Trinity. He is therefore present and active in the Old Testament. To find the Son in the Old Testament is not necessarily to read the Old Testament inappropriately, though we must be aware of overreading the first Testament in a way that leaves no room for further revelation and organic development in the New Testament.

Second, I focus more specifically on the Old Testament theme of sonship. As eternal Son, Jesus Christ is the second person of the Trinity. Yet

1. Following the NT and confessional precedents, I will speak of the presence of Jesus Christ in the OT. This is because of the unity of the person: the Son of God is identical to Jesus of Nazareth; therefore, it is appropriate to speak of the presence and work of Christ in the OT, even prior to the incarnation. See, e.g., 1 Cor 10:4; Jude 5; WLC 31; Letham, *Systematic Theology*, 502 (following Aloys Grillmeier). I discuss this further in ch. 8.

as the incarnate one he is also the true human son, the true Israelite, and the true Davidic king. The category of sonship is thus a concise heading that subsumes much relating to the person and work of Christ.

Third, I consider a selection of other relevant themes that provide proper context and background for the work of Christ, including the exodus as a paradigm of redemption, Israel's sacrificial system (especially the Day of Atonement), and the persons and institutions of prophet, priest, and king.

These lenses must be related to the twin themes of creation and covenant. The Son was active in creation and before the fall of Adam, and he is also the Mediator of the covenant of grace who works redemption from sin. Though we can rightly speak of a "covenant" with Adam, much of my focus on covenant will be on the outworking of the single, postfall covenant of grace throughout the Bible.

THE SON OF GOD IN CREATION

Creation is a work of the triune God. It would be mistaken to think of a divine monad, or only one person of the Godhead, creating the heavens and the earth. God is and always has been Trinitarian. Further, all the external works of God (as Trinity) are undivided (*opera trinitatis ad extra indivisa sunt*). When Genesis says, "In the beginning God created the heavens and the earth," this describes the work of the triune God. Later, the Gospel of John alludes to Genesis 1:1: "In the beginning was the Word, and the Word was with God, and the Word was God. ... All things came to be through him and apart from him came not one thing which has come to be" (John 1:1, 3).[2] In John this creative, eternal Word is Jesus of Nazareth (see 1:14). While it would not be correct to say that *only* the Son created the world, it is proper to say that the Son created the world.[3]

If creation is the work of the triune God, this includes the creation of humanity in the image of God. In Genesis 1:26 God (אלהים) says, "Let us make man in our image" (see also 5:1). The plural here is not best taken as a "royal we" or as an address to the divine council. God did not employ the assistance

---

2. My trans. Here I do not follow the punctuation in the NA[28] Greek text (which places ὃ γέγονεν at the beginning of a new sentence), but I take ὃ γέγονεν with the sentence that precedes it.

3. See also Charles Hodge, *Systematic Theology* (repr., Peabody, MA: Hendrickson, 2008), 1:445.

of any created being in the creation of humanity, nor was humanity made in the image of angels. Creation was the work of God alone, as Scripture repeatedly emphasizes (e.g., Gen 1:1; Exod 20:11; Isa 40:28).[4] Instead, the plural "let us make man" may be a reference, however shadowy at this point in Scripture, to the triunity of God.[5] However we understand this particular passage in Genesis, the whole of Scripture makes it clear that creation was a work of the triune God, which means the Son of God was active in creation.

The creation of humanity in the image of God is further important in light of the incarnation of the Son, which came later.[6] The Son's taking a human nature demonstrates the organic unity of the whole person—body and soul—in the image of God.[7] Further, since humanity was made in the image of God, it is both possible and fitting for the Son of God to take a human nature in the incarnation. Herman Bavinck captures the matter pithily: "God could not have been able to become man if he had not first made man in his own image."[8]

The Son of God was present and active in the work of creation. But the Son's work is not limited to creation, for the Son is present and active throughout the Old Testament. This means that the Son is present and active in the old covenant—a topic that merits more extensive discussion.

THE SON OF GOD IN THE OLD COVENANT

The Old Covenant and the Covenant of Grace

The Son is the Mediator between God and humanity not only in the New Testament but already in the Old Testament.[9] Again the Gospel of John helps us understand the Old Testament. In John 1 the Son is identified as

4. See also Turretin, *Inst.* 3.26.4–5 (1:273–74).

5. See, e.g., Petrus van Mastricht, *Theoretical-Practical Theology*, trans. Todd M. Rester, ed. Joel R. Beeke (Grand Rapids: Reformation Heritage, 2021), 2:109–10, 500; Hodge, *Systematic Theology* 1:446; Samuel Maresius, *Theologiae elenchticae nova synopsis; sive Index controversiarum fidei ex Sacris Scripturis* (Groningen: Nicolaum, 1646), 1:3.1 (page 76).

6. It is common to see humanity made in the image of the *Son*, who is the image of God (e.g., Col 1:15; Athanasius, *Inc.* 11, 13–14; Letham, *Systematic Theology*, 364). Yet Bavinck argues that humanity—male and female—is made in the image of the *triune* God. See *RD* 2:554–55, 60; Nathaniel Gray Sutanto, "Herman Bavinck on the Image of God and Original Sin," *IJST* 18 (2016): 178–84.

7. Following *RD* 2:560.

8. *RD* 2:560.

9. *RD* 3:215.

the λόγος (= word; John 1:1, 14), which has long been understood in Christian exegetical tradition as a fitting way to refer to the mediatorial and communicative role of the preexistent Word of God.[10] Logos again points to the activity and mediatorial role of the Son of God already in the Old Testament.[11]

To speak of the old covenant immediately raises the question of what this phrase means. From one angle, "old covenant" is virtually the same as saying Old Testament, since "testament" historically has designated a covenant. This approach works. Another approach is to relate the old covenant to the redemptive covenant of grace introduced in Genesis just after the fall of Adam and Eve (see Gen 3:15).[12] Simply put, the covenant of grace refers to the provision of God whereby he offers life and salvation to sinners by faith in the work of a Mediator—Jesus Christ.[13] The Lord promised to redeem his people by the seed of the woman, who would emerge victorious over the seed of the serpent.[14] The one covenant of grace, in which the coming of the woman's seed is progressively revealed, is found both in the Old Testament and New Testament, though it is administered in various ways. All told, whether by "old covenant" we mean the Old Testament or the covenant of grace administered in the Old Testament makes little difference, since the Old Testament recounts the outworking of this covenant of grace from Genesis 3 onward.[15]

I devote most of my attention in this chapter to the Son of God in the context of the old covenant. I have already argued that the Son of God is really present in the Old Testament. In what follows I consider the biblical-theological, filial precedents in the old covenant that are

---

10. E.g., Justin, *Dial.* 127–128; Irenaeus, *Epid.* 12, 45–46. I discuss this further in ch. 6. See also Geerhardus Vos, "The Range of the Logos Title in the Prologue to the Fourth Gospel," in *Redemptive History and Biblical Interpretation: The Shorter Writings of Geerhardus Vos*, ed. Richard B. Gaffin Jr. (Phillipsburg, NJ: P&R, 1980), 59–90; Vern S. Poythress, *Theophany: A Biblical Theology of God's Appearing* (Wheaton, IL: Crossway, 2018), 207.

11. See *RD* 3:215–16.

12. See, e.g., WCF 7.3–5; WLC 30–34; WSC 20. The Reformed creeds referenced throughout this volume can be found in James T. Dennison Jr., ed., *Reformed Confessions of the Sixteenth and Seventeenth Centuries in English Translation, 1523–1693*, 4 vols. (Grand Rapids: Reformation Heritage, 2008–2014).

13. WCF 7.3; WLC 32.

14. The Latin Vulgate mistranslates this as the *woman* who will bruise the head of the serpent (*ipsa conteret caput tuum*, "she will bruise your head"), whereas in the MT it is the seed of the woman who will bruise the head of the serpent (הוּא יְשׁוּפְךָ רֹאשׁ).

15. See John Owen, *Works* 1:120–25.

more fully developed in later biblical texts, particularly with reference to Christ himself.

Sonship in the Old Covenant

TO UNDERSTAND THE CONTOURS OF the old covenant, and the biblical-theological theme of sonship, we start with Adam. Adam was not only created in the image of God, but is also identified as the son of God. In Genesis 5:1–3 Adam is said to be created in the image of God (דמות, 5:1), and in a similar way Adam fathered a son (Seth) in his own image (5:3). The implication is that just as Seth's image bearing entails sonship, so Adam's being made in the image of God entails sonship.[16] This point is made explicit in Luke 3:38, where Adam is identified as son of God.

Adam as Son of God

Sonship, therefore, entails image bearing. Since Genesis portrays God as the great king, then Adam's filial image bearing means that he was a royal son of God. He was called to rule over God's creation (Gen 1:28). Adam also had a task given to him: he was to serve in (עבד) and guard (שמר) the garden of Eden (2:15). These same Hebrew terms are used elsewhere for the tasks of priests (e.g., Num 3:7–8; 8:25–26; 18:5–6; 1 Chr 23:32; Ezek 44:14), and many have noted that the garden is portrayed as a temple.[17] These factors most likely mean that Adam is portrayed as a priest in the original created order. Likewise, Adam was entrusted with the word of God (e.g., Gen 1:28–30; 2:16–17), denoting the role of a prophet. From the beginning, then, we find in Adam a son of God who is portrayed as a prophet,

---

16. See further G. K. Beale, *A New Testament Biblical Theology: The Unfolding of the Old Testament in the New* (Grand Rapids: Baker Academic, 2011), 401–6; Stephen G. Dempster, *Dominion and Dynasty: A Theology of the Hebrew Bible*, NSBT 15 (Downers Grove, IL: InterVarsity Press, 2003), 58.

17. See further Gordon J. Wenham, *Genesis 1–15*, WBC 1 (Nashville: Thomas Nelson, 1987), 61, 67; G. K. Beale, *The Temple and the Church's Mission: A Biblical Theology of the Dwelling Place of God*, NSBT 17 (Downers Grove, IL: InterVarsity Press, 2004), 66–77; Bruce K. Waltke, *An Old Testament Theology: An Exegetical, Canonical, and Thematic Approach* (Grand Rapids: Zondervan, 2007), 255–56, 460, 741; Meredith G. Kline, *Kingdom Prologue: Genesis Foundations for a Covenantal Worldview* (Overland Park, KS: Two Age, 2000), 26–33; Richard P. Belcher Jr., *Prophet, Priest, and King: The Roles of Christ in the Bible and Our Roles Today* (Phillipsburg, NJ: P&R, 2016), 5–11; L. Michael Morales, *Who Shall Ascend the Mountain of the Lord? A Biblical Theology of the Book of Leviticus*, NSBT 27 (Downers Grove, IL: InterVarsity Press, 2015), 52–53; Brandon D. Crowe, *The Last Adam: A Theology of the Obedient Life of Jesus in the Gospels* (Grand Rapids: Baker Academic 2017), 64.

priest, and king.[18] The close correlations made between Adam and Christ in Scripture include the concepts of sonship and these three offices (or at least functions) of prophet, priest, and king. I will return to these three offices later in this chapter.

The task given to Adam will also help us understand the work of Christ. Adam was created upright and called to love and obey God fully. Yet he also had a goal of permanent eternal life before him, which required Adam's perfect obedience (WCF 7.2; 19.1). Adam was presented with a probationary test not to eat from the tree of the knowledge of good and evil (Gen 2:16–17). This test summed up all that was required of Adam.[19] The positive side of this negative command, though not stated explicitly, is that were Adam to have passed the test, he would have inherited eternal life (signified by the tree of life).[20] Because Adam failed this test, and thus failed to persevere in obedience in his sinless state of integrity, he forfeited his right to eternal life. This Adamic administration is often referred to as the covenant of works.[21] Though the term "covenant" (ברית) is not used in Genesis 1–3, the concept is present, and Hosea 6:7 likely does refer to a covenant with Adam.[22] That this is called the covenant *of works* does not mean that Adam could have autonomously earned eternal life. Nothing Adam could ever have done would have earned eternal life, strictly speaking—he was a created being who owed obedience by nature. Instead, the covenant of works teaches that Adam would have inherited eternal life because of God's goodness to grant this in the context of a covenant relationship.

Crucially, eternal life required Adam's perfect obedience. Once Adam failed, he could no longer meet the strict demands of the covenant of works. This is the context in which we first meet the covenant of grace in Scripture. The New Testament makes it clear that Christ did what Adam failed to do: obey God fully, thus attaining eternal life (see Rom 5:12–21). But Jesus had to do even more than Adam, for he had to overcome the disastrous

---

18. See *RD* 3:331; Benjamin L. Gladd, *From Adam and Israel to the Church: A Biblical Theology of the People of God*, ESBT (Downers Grove, IL: IVP Academic, 2019), 12–19.

19. Louis Berkhof, *Systematic Theology*, 4th ed. (Grand Rapids: Eerdmans, 1996), 215–18.

20. See, e.g., Augustine, *Pecc. merit.* 1.2; Turretin, *Inst.* 8.3.7 (1:575–76); Geerhardus Vos, *Biblical Theology: Old and New Testaments* (repr., Edinburgh: Banner of Truth, 1975), 27–29.

21. Other terminology includes "covenant of life," "covenant of creation," or "covenant of nature."

22. For a defense, see Crowe, *Last Adam*, 59–61.

consequences of the sin that Adam caused as well. The covenant of grace is not only a New Testament idea, but begins already from the time of the fall. Already the Son of God was Mediator and was active as prophet, priest, and king.[23]

Israel as Son of God THE NATION OF ISRAEL IS also identified as son of God in the Old Testament. The first explicit reference comes in Exodus 4, where Moses is instructed to tell Pharaoh: "Thus says the LORD, Israel is my firstborn son, and I say to you, 'Let my son go that he may serve me.' If you refuse to let him go, behold, I will kill your firstborn son" (Exod 4:22–23). Here Israel, enslaved in Egypt, is already identified as the LORD's firstborn son. The LORD wanted his firstborn son to be allowed to worship him freely, and the consequence of Pharaoh's disobedience was the death of his firstborn. The exodus became the paradigmatic act of redemption in the Old Testament, and the logic of the exodus leans heavily on sonship. Israel's identification as son of God underscores the deep, covenantal love that God has for his people (see Deut 1:31). He heard their cries for help and liberated them with a mighty, outstretched hand.

Israel's sonship also called for their obedience—in the context of covenant, love and obedience go hand in hand. This is evident when Israel comes to Mount Sinai, where the Mosaic covenant is instituted (see especially Exod 19–24). The logic of redemption, however, is clear that Israel's obedience did not save them. Rather, Israel was saved by the power and initiative of God. Yet those who are redeemed are called to obey God from the heart, and the Ten Commandments and other laws (Exod 20–23) showed Israel what it meant to obey. Sonship requires obedience. This logic is particularly clear in Deuteronomy, where Israel's call to obedient, covenantal sonship is one of the organizing features of the entire book.[24] Because Israel is son of God, they should obey God from the heart (see esp. Deut 8:5–6; 14:1–2). If Israel disobeyed, they would be turning their back on the covenant, and it would be as if they were no longer God's children (Deut 32:4–6, 18–20,

23. These two sentences follow Bavinck, *RD* 3:365.

24. On sonship in Deuteronomy, see Brandon D. Crowe, *The Obedient Son: Deuteronomy and Christology in the Gospel of Matthew*, BZNW 188 (Berlin: de Gruyter, 2012), 88–117.

43).[25] This emphasis on Israel's covenantal sonship, and the accompanying call to obedience, will be foundational for Israel's prophets. The exodus is paradigmatic not only for redemption but also for sonship, which entails both God's deep love for his people and his people's call to true obedience.

As son of God, Israel was a royal nation. This is implicit in Israel's sonship, especially in light of the Adamic precedent of sonship in Genesis 1–5. In a similar way, when the Lord delivered Israel from Egypt, he did so as the great king who saved a people and entered into covenant with them. As son of God, Israel was like Adam, a royal image bearer. This is also stated explicitly at Mount Sinai in a highly significant passage to understand the role of Israel: "'Now therefore, if you will indeed obey my voice and keep my covenant, you shall be my treasured possession among all peoples, for all the earth is mine; and you shall be to me a kingdom of priests and a holy nation.' These are the words that you shall speak to the people of Israel" (Exod 19:5-6; see also 1 Pet 2:9–10). Here, just after the redemption from Egypt, Israel was corporately identified as a kingdom of priests, denoting Israel's royal status as son of God, and as a holy nation. This priestly aspect of Israel's identity likely reflects their privilege to walk in close fellowship with the Lord, serving him, thereby mediating the knowledge of God to the surrounding nations.[26] Elsewhere it is clear that Israel was entrusted with the oracles of God (see Rom 3:2; 9:4), denoting a prophetic aspect to Israel's existence as well. In sum, Israel, like Adam, not only was son of God, but also is portrayed as prophet, priest, and king.

Despite the similarities between Adam and Israel, we must also take due note of differences between them.[27] Adam and Israel are not interchangeable. First, only Adam is the progenitor of the entire human race. Second, only Adam had the opportunity to inherit eternal life on the basis of perfect covenantal obedience, thus fulfilling the covenant of works. All Israelites were

---

25. Deut 32:43 presents a difficult textual issue. Departing here from the MT, the best reading is "his sons" (LXX, 4QDeut[q]), agreeing with the ESV, which translates this phrase "his children."

26. See, e.g., R. Alan Cole, *Exodus: An Introduction and Commentary*, TOTC 2 (Downers Grove, IL: InterVarsity Press, 1973), 153; Douglas K. Stuart, *Exodus*, NAC 2 (Nashville: Broadman & Holman, 2006), 422–23; Nahum M. Sarna, *Exodus*, JPS Torah Commentary (Philadelphia: Jewish Publication Society, 1991), 104; Brevard S. Childs, *The Book of Exodus: A Critical, Theological Commentary*, OTL (Louisville: Westminster, 1974), 367.

27. See also Crowe, *Last Adam*, 65–67.

fallen in Adam and in need of redemption from sin. Thus, the obedience of the Israelites could never be sufficient to meet the demands for eternal life. The Mosaic law given to them must be understood as part of the covenant of grace. In the New Testament Jesus is portrayed as the true Israelite and as new, faithful Israel. Yet even more fundamental to understanding the work of Christ is the identification of Jesus as the second and last Adam. This does not mean we must dichotomize sharply between Israel and Adam, but we must ensure that we do not miss the distinctions between Adam and Israel. Both Adam and Israel are called to covenantal obedience as sons of God, and both are described in terms of prophet, priest, and king.

The roles of both Adam and Israel in the Old Testament provide ample biblical-theological precedents for the sonship of Jesus. Adam is the first son of God. Israel as son of God dominates much of the rest of the Old Testament. Later the Davidic dimensions of son of God will swell. Even so, it is important to remember the Son of God's preexistence: he is the Creator who existed before Adam, Israel, or David. These biblical-theological dimensions of sonship find roots in the eternal sonship of the Second Person of the Trinity.[28] The sonships of Adam, Israel, and David anticipate the fullness of sonship manifested in the incarnation and are ultimately typological manifestations of the eternal, unchanging, ontological sonship of Christ.

ANTICIPATIONS OF THE WORK OF CHRIST IN THE PENTATEUCH

Exodus and Redemption

The paradigm for redemption in the Old Testament is the exodus. Geerhardus Vos puts the matter quite strongly: "The Exodus from Egypt *is* the Old Testament redemption."[29] Given the prominence of the exodus paradigm, an appreciation for the exodus is necessary to understand various dimensions of the work of Christ.

In the exodus, the Lord proved faithful to his covenant promises. In Genesis 3:15 the Lord promises to defeat the seed of the serpent by the seed of the woman. Later the world was preserved through Noah, which provided the context for the protection and flourishing of the coming seed

28. See, e.g., Bavinck, *RD* 2:272.

29. Vos, *Biblical Theology*, 109, emphasis original.

(Gen 6–9). The promised seed gains more specificity in the Abrahamic covenant (Gen 15; 17), where we learn that it is Abraham's seed that will be the means by which the entire world will be blessed (Gen 12:1–3). The Lord later told Abraham that his offspring would be as numerous as the stars in the sky (15:5), but they would also be slaves in a foreign land for four hundred years (15:13). This happened after Joseph, one of Abraham's great-grandchildren, ended up as governor in Egypt (42:6). Joseph not only saved Egypt in the midst of a great famine, but also provided a refuge for his estranged family (Gen 37–50). Yet, though the focus of these final chapters of Genesis is largely on Joseph, Jacob prophesied at the end of his life that it would ultimately be Judah who would rule over his brothers (49:8–12).

The book of Exodus begins with a list of the children of Jacob (i.e., Israel) who came to Egypt. True to the Abrahamic promise, the Israelites had grown into a great company of people (Exod 1:1–7; see Gen 15:5). Yet eventually a new pharaoh arose who did not know Joseph, and he feared the numerous Israelites (1:8–9). Thus Abraham's descendants were enslaved in Egypt.

This provides the context for the exodus. The exodus can refer to a range of related events, including the ten plagues, the Passover, the plundering of the Egyptians, the leading of the Israelites by cloud and pillar of fire, and the parting of the Red Sea, with the attending defeat of Pharaoh's army. Given the importance of the exodus for understanding the work of Christ, I list here eight ways the exodus serves as an Old Testament paradigm of salvation and prepares us for the work of Christ in the New Testament.[30]

First, the exodus provides objective deliverance from the bondage of sin. The Israelites were enslaved not only physically but spiritually. They were not free to worship God, as the goal of the exodus—that is, to worship the Lord—suggests (see Exod 3:18; 4:23; 5:3; 8:27). Put in modern terms, the Israelites were enslaved to the world in Egypt and liberated from this system of oppression in the exodus.[31]

---

30. Here I glean heavily from Vos, *Biblical Theology*, 109–21, though several of the points are my own.

31. Vos argues that the exodus also provided subjective deliverance from the power of sin, at least for some Israelites (*Biblical Theology*, 112). This is, however, difficult to quantify, especially given the role of the wilderness generation collectively as a warning against hard-heartedness and faithlessness (Pss 78; 95:7–11; Heb 3:7–4:13). Even so, Israel's sacrificial system was given to enable fellowship with God (see, e.g., Morales, *Who Shall Ascend*, 23–38). Several passages teach that the Israelites were given to sin and idolatry in Egypt (Josh 24:14;

Second, the exodus demonstrates the singular power of God to save his people. The people were powerless to redeem themselves; only God could do this. This is one of the key emphases of the exodus: divine omnipotence in the face of human weakness.[32]

Third, the exodus displays the love of God and his unmerited favor, and confirms God's faithfulness to his covenant promises. Israel was not better than other people, but God freely chose to deliver them, multiply them, and subsequently to provide them the promised land of Canaan (e.g., Deut 4:32–40; 7:7–11). This also underscores the second point (above): God's grace is necessary because of the people's inability to liberate themselves.

Fourth, the ultimate outcome of the exodus is not simply the liberation of the people from bondage but the glory of the covenant Lord, who redeemed his people. This is consistent with the goal of the exodus being the proper worship of God. It also points to the fellowship with God that ensued after the exodus: God's people were redeemed in order to live in covenant fellowship with him in the promised land.[33] Later the people were threatened with exile for disobedience, which entailed removal from the land and enslavement to foreign powers. Even so, on the other side of exile lay the hope of a new exodus and renewed covenant fellowship with the Lord (e.g., Deut 30:1–10).

Fifth, the exodus highlights God's provision to take away sin. Central to the exodus was the Passover, in which the angel of the Lord passed over the houses that had applied blood to their doorframes by means of hyssop (Exod 12:21–27). Hyssop was later used for sacrifices, and the sacrificial system that came later further elaborated on the need for blood to effect cleansing for God's people (e.g., Lev 17:11). The Passover, in other words, was a type of substitutionary, sacrificial atonement (see Exod 12:27)

Ezek 20:8–9; 23:8, 19–21). Yet in Deuteronomy Moses reminds the Israelites that the Lord had delivered them from bondage (Deut 6:21; 7:18; 15:15; 16:3, 12; 24:18, 22). See, e.g., Iain M. Duguid, *Ezekiel*, NIVAC (Grand Rapids: Zondervan, 1999), 304 and n. 8. Some of these texts are noted by Vos, *Biblical Theology*, 112. In short, Israel's deliverance in the exodus must have, *to some extent*, entailed subjective deliverance from sin for at least some Israelites (see also Irenaeus, *Epid.* 46; *Haer.* 4.16.3).

32. See, e.g., Exod 6:6; Deut 4:34; 5:15; 7:19; 9:29; 11:2; 26:8; 2 Kgs 17:36; Ps 66:1–7; 77:10–20; 78:11–16; 81:10; 105:26–45; 106:6–12; 135:8–12; 136:10–16; Isa 43:16–27; Jer 32:21.

33. See Morales, *Who Shall Ascend*, 78–79.

pointing forward to the final sacrifice of Christ.[34] The exodus shows us that redemption requires a blood ransom for deliverance; this provides important background for the term "redemption" in Scripture.[35]

Sixth, the exodus highlights the structure of redemption: first deliverance, then the giving of the law. God's people were saved by his sovereign grace and power, and then were given the law.[36] Consistent with the emphasis on God's sovereign power and grace, God's people did not earn redemption by means of sufficient obedience; deliverance was granted by divine grace. The pattern of the exodus highlights the indicative-imperative dynamic of biblical religion after the fall. The indicative refers to God's actions to save his people. The imperative refers to the people's call to obedience. The order cannot be reversed, but neither can the two be divided. This structuring feature is highlighted by the order of events in the exodus: first God redeemed his people, then he gave them his law. Fathers are thus instructed to teach this pattern to their children: deliverance yields obedience (Deut 6:20–25). The exodus shows God's people that their obedience is not salvific, but neither is it optional.

Seventh, the exodus highlights the central role of sonship in deliverance. As noted earlier, the logic of the exodus redemption centers on sonship (Exod 4:22b–23). The tenth and climactic plague against Egypt was the death of the firstborn, whereas the benefit for God's covenant people was their liberation as firstborn. Indeed, Israel's deliverance was corporately like the resurrection of God's son—anticipating the greater resurrection in the New Testament.[37] Israel's sonship entails both the tender love of God and the correlating call for Israel to obey as God's son (e.g., Deut 1:31; 8:5–6; 14:1–2; 32:4–6, 18–20).[38] This emphasis on Israel's sonship provides much of the context for understanding Jesus's obedient sonship in the New Testament.

---

34. Vos, *Biblical Theology*, 120. On substitution, see Morales, *Who Shall Ascend*, 80.

35. See also Morales, *Who Shall Ascend*, 80.

36. This is not to deny that they already had some sort of law, as the Pentateuch makes clear before Sinai. Already God's moral law was known to Adam and to others in the patriarchal age. Even so, by saving his people first and then giving the law, the exodus reveals the structure of indicative, then imperative.

37. L. Michael Morales, *Exodus Old and New: A Biblical Theology of Redemption*, ESBT (Downers Grove, IL: IVP Academic, 2020), 49–50.

38. See further Crowe, *Obedient Son*.

Eighth, the exodus is integral to final redemption. We should not merely think of the exodus as a preview of "true" redemption in the New Testament. Instead, the exodus is real deliverance that is of a piece with God's final redemption in Christ. As part of the one covenant of grace, the exodus makes true progress toward the consummation. The conflict between Moses and the covenant Lord and Pharaoh and the gods of Egypt highlights the spiritual conflict in the exodus (Exod 4:1–5; 7:8–13).[39] We can even correlate Pharaoh with the seed of the serpent—the one who seeks to keep the Abrahamic promise from flourishing and who, as the representative for the nation enslaving God's people, seeks to stop their liberation and worship.[40] This is all the more likely in light of the prevalence of serpentine and supernatural themes in the exodus, and the identification elsewhere in Scripture of Pharaoh (though not the same Pharaoh) or Egypt as a sea monster or sea dragon (Ps 74:13; Isa 30:7; 51:9–10; Ezek 29:3; 32:2; cf. Isa 27:1; Rev 12:3, 9).[41] Though the exodus was not the final deliverance, it anticipates the eschatological new exodus accomplished by Christ.

Sacrificial System The exodus is central in Old Testament redemption, and a key aspect of the exodus is the expiation of sin by means of the Passover sacrifice. The role of Moses in the exodus, and ensuing events, is also significant. Moses was the mediator for God's people, who represented God to the people (Exod 19) and the people before God (Exod 24).[42] Moses anticipates the priestly, mediatorial work of Christ—the one who shares in our humanity, even as he remains the eternal Son of God. Compared to Christ, the mediatorial role of Moses was limited. In response to the people's idolatry in the golden calf episode (Exod 32), Moses sought to make atonement for the people and even asked that God might blot him out in order to spare the people (32:30–33). Though Moses interceded for the people (33:12–16) and the Lord showed mercy (33:17; cf. 33:19; 34:6–7), Moses was a sinner who was not able to give his own life for the sins of the people.

---

39. See, e.g., John Currid, *Against the Gods: The Polemical Theology of the Old Testament* (Wheaton, IL: Crossway, 2013), 97–129.

40. See Morales, *Exodus Old and New*, 62–63.

41. See Richard Bauckham, *The Climax of Prophecy: Studies on the Book of Revelation* (Edinburgh: T&T Clark, 1993), 191–98.

42. Morales, *Who Shall Ascend*, 89–93.

The intercession of Moses highlights the need for Israel's forgiveness. In the center of the Pentateuch stands Leviticus, the book that expounds the sacrificial system in detail. This is not the place to deal at length with the numerous issues related to the sacrificial system, but in brief the sacrificial system provided means for sinful Israelites to have fellowship with a holy God.[43] The daily sacrifices, along with the holiness laws, highlighted the unchanging holiness of God, and the inescapable problem of sin.[44] Leviticus 19:2b captures the issue succinctly: "You shall be holy, for I the Lord your God am holy." Yet the Israelites were inherently and perpetually unholy. Thus the sacrificial system provided means of atonement for sin, enabling access to and fellowship with God.[45]

The sacrificial system given to the ancient Israelites was a means of true grace and enabled real fellowship with God. Even so, the Levitical sacrifices were not ultimate. Hebrews teaches that the old covenant sacrifices had no true efficacy in themselves, for they were only shadows of the true sacrifice that takes away sin. The blood of bulls and goats is ultimately ineffectual; only the final sacrifice of the perfect God-man, Jesus Christ, is able truly to take away sin. This means that the one sacrifice of Christ stands behind and provides efficacy to the sacrifices made in the old covenant, which anticipated the coming work of Christ.[46] The access to God enabled in the Day of Atonement was real—Morales even argues it was closer here than it was anywhere post-Eden.[47] Yet Israel still awaited the ultimate presence of God with his people. The New Testament speaks of the Son of God coming to tabernacle among his people, revealing his glory (John 1:14). He is Immanuel—God with us (Matt 1:23)—in a way that surpasses even the access granted on the Day of Atonement. He himself would be exiled and slaughtered for our sin and would then enter the heavenly holy of holies. Yet the details of how these things are must await our consideration of the New Testament.

---

43. Morales, *Who Shall Ascend*, 23–38.

44. See, e.g., L. Michael Morales, "Atonement in Ancient Israel: The Whole Burnt Offering as Central to Israel's Cult," in *So Great a Salvation: A Dialogue on the Atonement in Hebrews*, ed. Jon C. Laansma, George H. Guthrie, and Cynthia Long Westfall, LNTS 516 (London: T&T Clark, 2019), 28–39.

45. See Jay Sklar, *Leviticus: An Introduction and Commentary*, TOTC 3 (Downers Grove, IL: IVP Academic, 2013), 50–55.

46. See WCF 7.5.

47. Morales, *Who Shall Ascend*, 167.

Leviticus 16

If Leviticus is found at the heart of the Pentateuch, the heart of Leviticus is the Day of Atonement (Lev 16).[a] The Day of Atonement was a yearly "sacrifice of sacrifices" (or perhaps better, set of sacrifices) that provided thoroughgoing expiation and cleansing of sin. On this day, the high priest would enter into and cleanse the holy of holies—the most holy place (16:2–3, 11–19). This involved making atonement for his own sins and his household by offering a bull (16:6, 11), and then atoning for the sins of all Israelites (16:15–16). This he did by taking two goats. The first he sacrificed as a sin offering (16:15–16), taking its blood into the holy of holies. The second goat would then be presented alive, in order that the high priest could place all the sins of the Israelites on the live goat (16:20–22). The live goat (i.e., the scapegoat) would then be exiled east into the wilderness, carrying the sins of the people away from the tabernacle and the presence of the Lord.[b]

The Day of Atonement was a solemn affair and was to be remembered in perpetuity as the day when the people would be cleansed from all their sins (16:30). At the same time, it did not provide permanent cleansing, as its yearly repetition would have reminded the people. The concepts of substitution and representation were apparent throughout the sacrificial system: the death of an animal standing in place of the death of the offerer. This arguably would have been doubly clear on the Day of Atonement, as two goats were presented to the people, one slaughtered and one set free to bear their sins.

The slaughtering of the animals is explained in more detail in the following chapter: "For the life of the flesh is in the blood, and I have given it for you on the altar to make atonement for your souls, for it is the blood that makes atonement by the life" (Lev 17:11). At least two questions arise from this text: First, does the blood refer to the life or the death of the victim? The best answer here may be some combination of the two, though the emphasis falls on the death of the sacrifice. Second, how do we understand atonement (Heb. כפר; Gk. ἐξιλάσκομαι)? Here the best answer is again probably a combination, in this case of cleansing and ransom from death.[c] Some of these concepts will be important for our discussions in the New Testament, where we will see debate has persisted about terms such as ἱλάσκομαι and ἱλαστήριον and the nature of expiation or propitiation in view.

---

a. Here I glean from Morales, *Who Shall Ascend*, esp. 23–38.

b. On exile, see Morales, *Who Shall Ascend*, 243, 248.

c. Sklar, *Leviticus*, 50–55; Morales, *Who Shall Ascend*, 130–32.

Prophet, Priest, and King

As we conclude this chapter on the Pentateuch, we return to the themes of prophet, priest, and king. I have introduced these throughout this chapter, but more remains to be said. The threefold office of Christ (*munus triplex*) refers to his roles as prophet, priest, and king, and the foundations for these offices come in the Pentateuch. Adam, Israel, Moses, and others serve as precedents for Christ's threefold office.[48] In what follows I consider each office and institution in a bit more detail.

Prophet. Prophets are entrusted with and make known the word of God. This applies to Adam in the beginning, on whose heart was written the law, and later to Israel. Being entrusted with the word of God also assumes obedience to the word of God, though both Adam and Israel failed to exhibit the filial obedience expected of those entrusted with the word of God. Moses is also a prophet, as the anticipation of a future prophet like Moses makes clear (see Deut 18:15–18). The future, eschatological prophet would be patterned after Moses. Though later prophets such as Jeremiah fit into the Mosaic mold,[49] ultimately the New Testament teaches that Jesus is the prophet like Moses: he is entrusted with the word of God, proclaims the word of God, and obeys the word of God.

Priest. Priests mediate between God and humanity, serving in the house of God. Again Adam was a priest, as was Israel, who collectively is identified as a kingdom of priests (Exod 19:6). Likewise, Moses (from the tribe of Levi) was a priest, for he ordained Aaron, the high priest (Exod 29; Lev 8), and instructed the Israelites in the proper mode of worship throughout the Pentateuch. Though Moses was a sinner unable to offer his life as a perfect substitute, his mediation for the people in wake of the golden calf episode also points to his priestly role. It is even possible that Moses' death, outside and before Israel entered the promised land, highlights the principle of substitution and provided a pattern for the high priest's death, which provided a new start for the people. (For example, those guilty of manslaughter are released from the cities of refuge; see Num 35:25–34.)[50]

48. Thanks to Iain Duguid and Jonny Gibson for their feedback on this point.

49. E.g., Jeremiah's *new covenant* echoes the covenant mediated by Moses (see, e.g., Crowe, *Obedient Son*, 124–28).

50. Morales, *Who Shall Ascend*, 223–24.

Beyond this, other priestly precedents from the Pentateuch help us understand the priestly work of Christ. Aaron the high priest serves as the initial precedent for the high priesthood of Christ, though Christ's service in the inner sanctuary excels that of Aaron and his descendants (Heb 7–10).[51] Phinehas was a priest who was zealous for the Lord's holiness (Num 25:1–13), anticipating the zeal of Christ for the things of God (John 2:13–17), even to the point of sacrificing his own life (John 2:18–22).[52]

We also meet another priest in the Pentateuch, one who is not from the house of Levi (for indeed, he comes before Levi was ever born). In Genesis 14:17–24 Abram met Melchizedek, the king of Salem, to whom Abram paid a tithe. Melchizedek was a priest of God Most High. Melchizedek provides another angle to the priesthood of Christ in the New Testament, for Christ did not come from the tribe of Levi but of Judah (see Heb 6:20–7:22). Further, with Melchizedek's priesthood we have an example of pre-Levitical priesthood, which shows that the Levitical priesthood was not ultimate priesthood. Hebrews will have more to say about this.

In the Levitical system, it is crucial that the priest come from the house of Levi. But in addition to the Levitical priesthood, the Pentateuch provides a more polyvalent view of priesthood, one that includes Adam, the progenitor of all humanity, and Melchizedek, the priest-king. These, together with the Levitical priesthood, provide ample precedents for understanding the priestly work of Christ.

King. Adam was created in the image of the Great King and called to rule over God's creation, reflecting the Creator he served (Gen 1:26–28). Likewise, Israel is identified as a kingdom of priests (Exod 19:6) and called to reflect their covenant LORD's glory in the promised land.

Yet the Pentateuch also foresees a coming king who will rule over God's people. This is evident in Judah's blessing (Gen 49:8–12; see also Num 24:17), and Moses also spoke in Deuteronomy 17:14–17 of a coming day when an individual king would rule over God's people (see also Gen 17:16). This passage provides warrant for Israel's later kingship—for the Lord himself would choose the king the people desired to set over them (Deut 17:15).

51. Morales argues that Aaron is also portrayed as a new Adam (*Who Shall Ascend*, 118).

52. See also Gordon J. Wenham, *Numbers: An Introduction and Commentary*, TOTC 4 (Downers Grove, IL: IVP Academic, 1981), 211–12.

Thus, though there may be questions about the people's later desire for a king to be set over them in the days of Samuel, Deuteronomy 17 shows us that it was not inherently wrong for Israel to desire a king.[53] It was possible both for God to be king and for him to rule via an anointed representative. Deuteronomy 17 is thus important for understanding the rise of David as king and later for understanding Christ's kingship.

Additionally, Moses himself provides precedent for a king, for he spoke of the qualifications of kings and ruled over Israel by judging them (Exod 18:13). He also opposed the king of Egypt (Pharaoh) as the LORD's chosen emissary and the leader of the nation. God's king is to walk in his ways, rule over his people, and indeed like Adam rule over all his creation. These royal aspects anticipate the work of Christ. Melchizedek also anticipates the royal work of Christ, for he was not only a priest but a king. Hebrews will tease out these implications in more detail. Indeed, in the New Testament we will find that the offices of prophet, priest, and king all cohere in Christ.

THE PRESENCE OF THE SON IN THE OLD TESTAMENT

THE OLD TESTAMENT IS FULL of anticipations and types of Christ who will come in the fullness of time in the New Testament. However, we can say even more than this. The Son of God is the eternal Son who was active already in the world in the Old Testament. It is therefore appropriate to speak of Christ himself—that is, as personally present—in the Old Testament. Thus, even though it was not until the fullness of time that the Son took to himself a human nature into a personal union,[54] it is possible that we meet the Son himself appearing in various forms—including human forms—in mysterious ways in various Old Testament texts. Among many memorable examples are Abraham's encounter with three mysterious men, which is described as the LORD appearing to him (Gen 18:1–33); Jacob wrestling with an angel (after which he calls the place "Face of God"; Gen 32:22–32; see also Hos 12:4); and the commander of the LORD's army, who requires Joshua to remove his sandals (Josh 5:13–15).[55] To this we could add many other texts, including appearances

53. See Waltke, *Old Testament Theology*, 690.

54. Compare Owen, *Works* 1:349.

55. Compare also Irenaeus, *Epid.* 44–47; Bavinck, *RD* 1:329; Graham A. Cole, *The God Who Became Human: A Biblical Theology of Incarnation*, NSBT 30 (Downers Grove, IL: InterVarsity,

of the angel of the LORD, in whom the word of God was especially present.[56] At times the angel of the LORD is distinguished from the LORD, while at other times he seems to be identified with the LORD (e.g., Exod 3:2–6; Hos 12:4).

Though we cannot answer definitively all questions we may have about such encounters (and though we cannot isolate the Son's actions from the other Trinitarian persons), it is possible to conclude that (at least some of) these are preincarnate appearances of the Son of God, the Logos and Mediator between God and humanity.[57]

CONCLUSION

THE FIRST FIVE BOOKS OF the Old Testament provide a wealth of background information for understanding the person and work of Christ. In this chapter, I have only begun to scratch the surface. Even so, we have seen that the Son of God is eternal and preexistent, and has been active in the world long before his incarnation. This sonship is reflected in the emphasis on sonship with Adam, Israel, and later the king of Israel. These biblical-theological themes of sonship highlight both the privileged relationship between God and his people and the call to obedience. The Pentateuch also shows us clearly the problem of sin, the power of God to save (especially in the exodus), and the means by which a holy God can have fellowship with a sinful people. Key in the administration of God's people, and crucial for understanding the work of Christ, are the offices and institutions of prophet, priest, and king. All these receive further clarification in the biblical prophets.

FURTHER READING

Beale, G. K. *The Temple and the Church's Mission: A Biblical Theology of the Dwelling Place of God*. NSBT 17. Downers Grove, IL: InterVarsity Press, 2004. Beale shows the importance of God's

2013), 51–69.

56. For this and for the rest of this paragraph, see Bavinck, *RD* 1:328–30; 2:262–63; see also Turretin, *Inst.* 3.4.7–18 (1:185–87); 3.26.9 (1:275–76); Owen, *Works* 1:349–50.

57. See Bavinck, *RD* 1:344; 3:280; Poythress, *Theophany*, 417–24; see also the cautions of Cole, *God Who Became Human*, 116–20; Fred Sanders, *The Triune God*, New Studies in Dogmatics (Grand Rapids: Zondervan, 2016), 224–26.

dwelling place in Scripture and how that is fulfilled in Christ and the church.

Belcher, Richard P., Jr. *Prophet, Priest, and King: The Roles of Christ in the Bible and Our Roles Today*. Phillipsburg, NJ: P&R, 2016. Belcher discusses the three anointed offices in the Old Testament with an eye to how they are fulfilled in Christ.

Estelle, Bryan D. *Echoes of Exodus: Tracing a Biblical Motif*. Downers Grove, IL: IVP Academic, 2018. Considers the role of intertextuality in Scripture and applies this specifically to the exodus. A semitechnical monograph that covers the biblical-theological theme of exodus throughout the Scriptures, with a focus on its fulfillment in Christ.

Morales, L. Michael. *Exodus Old and New: A Biblical Theology of Redemption*. ESBT. Downers Grove, IL: IVP Academic, 2020. Highlights the centrality of the exodus in the outworking of redemption and the movement toward new creation, relates it to the sacrificial system, and shows how Jesus fulfills the exodus in the New Testament.

Vos, Geerhardus. *Biblical Theology: Old and New Testaments*. Repr., Edinburgh: Banner of Truth, 1975. A standard, foundational work on the contents and structure of biblical theology. Vos gives extended attention to the opening chapters of Genesis.

II

THE SON OF GOD PROMISED IN THE PROPHETS

DAVID'S SON AND LORD

In this chapter I consider how the themes introduced in chapter 1 develop in the remainder of the Old Testament in ways that illuminate the person and work of Christ.[1] First is the centrality of sonship: Israel's corporate sonship provides a ballast for understanding redemptive history in the Prophets while also anticipating the fuller revelation of Christ in the New Testament. Additionally, the Prophets focus on the rise of David, Israel's royal son, and his kingdom. Second is the Davidic kingdom's relation to the Son of Man in Daniel 7. Third is the servant of Isaiah, which provides important scriptural backdrop for the work of Christ. Fourth are texts that speak of the coming end-time (i.e., eschatological) salvation, which is ultimately accomplished by Christ.

The Old Testament Prophets develop organically themes encountered in the Pentateuch, but they do so often with heightened eschatological expectations. They speak of the future hope of restoration and cosmic peace that

1. By "Prophets" I include the broader category of prophets from the Hebrew OT (i.e., the Former and Latter Prophets, covering Joshua through Malachi), but by extension will also look to all other portions of the OT as well—the so-called Writings (especially the Psalms and Daniel).

is already anticipated in the Pentateuch, but they do so in more detail. The later books of the Old Testament are crucial for connecting the opening books of Scripture to the eschatological realization in the New Testament.

SON OF GOD AND MESSIAH

Israel as Son of God

As God's beloved, covenantal son, Israel was called to obey. This pentateuchal foundation, covered in the previous chapter, provides much of the context for the Prophets' critiques of Israel's covenantal waywardness. Yet it also casts a vision for future restoration and obedience. Hosea speaks tenderly of the Lord's love for his children; yet in spite of this love, Israel had continually gone astray (Hos 11:1–4). Isaiah begins in a similar way, lamenting the wayward sons that the Lord had reared (Isa 1:2–4). Other prophets speak of the fatherly love of the Lord for his people (e.g., Jer 31:3, 9, 20; Mal 1:2). The depths of divine love and privilege bestowed on Israel also place their persistent rebellion in sharp relief—though the Lord had loved his people, yet they continually went astray (e.g., Isa 1:2–4; Jer 3:14; 4:22; Hos 11:1–4; Mal 1:6).

Even so, the Lord promised to restore his covenant children (e.g., Mal 3:17). Significantly, this future restoration will also answer the people's perpetual disobedience—it will be a day when the Lord's people will truly walk in his ways and thus truly be his sons (Hos 1:10 [2:1 MT]; 11:10; see Jer 31:31–34; Ezek 36:25–27). This will occur in the "latter days" (e.g., Gen 49:1; Deut 4:30; Isa 2:2; Dan 2:28; Hos 3:5; Joel 2:28; Mic 4:1), but those days never fully arrive in the Old Testament era.[2]

Davidic King as Son of God

Davidic Covenant

In the exodus the Lord showed himself to be a great, covenantal king who rescued and guided his people. Yet in the exodus the Lord already anticipated that Israel would be led by a specific king ruling on the Lord's behalf (Deut 17:14–20). The two are closely related, for the king, as son of God, would come from and rule the nation, who corporately was son of God. In one sense, the king was the nation—the

2. On latter days see Beale, *New Testament Biblical Theology*, 92–116.

"Epitome of the People."[3] The king would be God's chosen leader, who would obey God's law and lead God's people in righteousness.[4]

David the son of Jesse emerges as the paradigm for kingship, reflecting Deuteronomy 17. David was chosen by God and anointed by Samuel to lead Israel. During David's forty-year rule, the kingdom was more fully established (2 Sam 5:1–5). David established Jerusalem as the center of the kingdom (2 Sam 5:6–16), defeated the Philistines (2 Sam 5:17–25; 8:1), and expelled the giants from the land (2 Sam 21:16–22; see also 1 Chr 20:4–8).

David later purposed to build a house for the Lord, but instead the Lord promised to build David a house—that is, a dynasty (see 2 Sam 7:11–16; 1 Chr 17:10–15; see also Ps 89:3–4; 132:11–12). In this Davidic covenant, the promise to David is that one of his sons will rule over an everlasting dynasty. This promise is certain, though the warning is also real: for the kingdom to succeed, the king must obey the Lord (e.g., 2 Sam 7:14–15; 1 Kgs 3:14; 8:25; 9:4–9). Beginning already with Solomon, no natural offspring of David ever obeyed sufficiently to realize the full covenant blessings. This helps us understand why the perfect obedience of Jesus Christ, the son of David according to the flesh (Rom 1:3), was necessary for the establishment of God's kingdom.

David was God's anointed (= messiah), though a greater messiah was coming. David himself was a sinner, yet he was also a man after God's own heart (1 Sam 13:14; Acts 13:22) who repented and sought truly to love and obey the Lord (see Ps 51). Even so, David's sin often led to struggles in his own life (see Ps 40:12; 69:5), and when David died he rested in the grave (Acts 2:29). Yet David was also a prophet (Acts 2:30) and spoke in confidence that the Lord would not abandon him to the grave (Ps 16:10). If then David remained in the grave in the days of the apostles, he must have been speaking ultimately about the greater Son of David—the future Messiah—as Peter explicitly states in his Pentecost sermon (Acts 2:30–31).

3. John A. Davies, *A Royal Priesthood: Literary and Intertextual Perspectives on an Image of Israel in Exodus 19:6*, Journal for the Study of the Old Testament Supplement Series 395 (London: T&T Clark, 2004), 180–81; see also G. B. Caird, "Jesus and Israel: The Starting Point for New Testament Christology," in *Christological Perspectives: Essays in Honor of Harvey K. MacArthur*, ed. R. Berkey and S. Edwards (New York: Pilgrim, 1982), 58–68; Joachim Bieneck, *Sohn Gottes als Christusbezeichnung der Synoptiker*, Abhandlungen zur Theologie des Alten und Neuen Testaments 21 (Zürich: Zwingli, 1951), 22, 26.

4. For more on the Davidic covenant, see Brandon D. Crowe, *The Path of Faith: A Biblical Theology of Covenant and Law*, ESBT (Downers Grove, IL: IVP Academic, 2021), 59–77.

Davidic King in the Psalter

Thus the Psalms speak of promises that will be accomplished by the greater Son of David. Though the entire Psalter is eschatologically oriented toward ultimate redemption,[5] some psalms highlight this in a pronounced way—some psalms have a heightened sense of messianic expectation. Psalms 1–2 serve as a royal, Davidic introduction to the entire Psalter.[6] Kingship in the Psalter is idealized: it draws on, even as it transcends, David's historical experiences.[7] Further, the kingship of the Lord is often fused together with his Messiah.[8] It is therefore consistent with the Psalter itself to look for an idealized, royal Messiah who will rule on behalf of the Lord—someone greater than David. Thus, many psalms deal explicitly with kingship (see, e.g., Pss 2; 8; 16; 21–22; 45; 72; 89; 110; 118; 132), and such texts are often applied to Jesus in the New Testament.

In short the Davidic covenant focuses the sonship of Israel in a representative, royal figure, and this covenant underlies the hope of a coming, fuller redemption than was realized in the Old Testament. More aspects of this future redemption are seen in the Prophets.

Psalm 2

The sonship of Psalm 2 has been much discussed. According to the New Testament, Jesus is the Son of Psalm 2:7: "You are my Son; today I have begotten you" (Matt 3:17; Mark 1:11; Luke 3:22; Acts 13:33; Heb 1:5; 5:5). But this raises a host of questions. When is the "today" of Psalm 2? Was it already realized in the Old Testament? Does it perhaps refer, as Augustine taught, to an eternal "today" in God's sight, supporting the doctrine of eternal generation?[a] This is related to a second question: What does it mean for the Davidic king

5. See Geerhardus Vos, "The Eschatology of the Psalter," *Princeton Theological Review* 18 (1920): 1–43. Vos avers, "A redemptive religion without eschatological outlook would be a contradiction in terms" (3). See also Benjamin Breckinridge Warfield, "Christless Christianity," in *The Person and Work of Christ*, ed. Samuel G. Craig (Philadelphia: Presbyterian and Reformed, 1950), 309.

6. See Waltke, *Old Testament Theology*, 870–74; O. Palmer Robertson, *The Flow of the Psalms: Discovering Their Structure and Theology* (Phillipsburg, NJ: P&R, 2015), 13–15, 54–61. Acts 4:25 identifies David as the author of Ps 2.

7. The language of "idealized" comes from Mark D. Futato, *Interpreting the Psalms: An Exegetical Handbook* (Grand Rapids: Kregel, 2007), 76–77.

8. Robertson, *Flow of the Psalms*, 59, 60–61, 168–70.

to be begotten? Is this a way to speak of a king's coronation? Does it refer to Jesus's baptism? His resurrection?

On one hand, the Davidic king is sometimes referred to as "son of God" in the Old Testament, and Psalm 2 can be understood as an idealized portrait of God's chosen king to rule over the nations. Yet because this is an idealized portrait, the realities of Psalm 2 were never realized by any son of David in the Old Testament monarchy. This encourages us to read beyond the horizon of David and Solomon and to look forward to the final Son of David.[b] Thus, even if the borders of David's kingdom extended far and wide (especially under Solomon; see 1 Kgs 4:21), it is far from clear that the Davidic king ever ruled over the ends of the earth and inherited the nations (Ps 2:8–9). These are eschatological hopes that are only fulfilled in Jesus Christ (Rev 12:5; 19:15).

Thus, the Son begotten "today" (Ps 2:7) can be understood as a reference to the ascension of the Davidic king to the throne.[c] Yet Psalm 2 also points ahead to a greater Son of David and a greater reign than was ever realized by any natural son of David. The son of Psalm 2 is ultimately Jesus Christ himself, who is elsewhere identified as God's beloved Son using language from Psalm 2:7 (esp. Mark 1:11; Luke 3:22). Indeed, "the Bible's own handling of the words [Psalm 2:7] is always in regard to Jesus."[d] Psalm 2:7 points to Christ in a variety of ways in the New Testament, especially with respect to his baptism and resurrection (Acts 13:33).[e] The apostle Peter explains that David, as a prophet, spoke in Psalm 16 about the resurrection of the Messiah (Acts 2:30–21; see also Ps 16:8–11). It is by means of Christ's resurrection that he rules over a worldwide kingdom (see Acts 17:30–31), fulfilling the vision of Psalm 2. This is consistent with what Jesus says in Luke about the Psalms testifying to him (Luke 24:44–47). In brief, Psalm 2 is used in the New Testament to speak of the eternal Son of God who accomplishes redemption and rules over the whole world.

---

a. Augustine, *Enarrat. Ps.* 2:6. "Eternal generation" is a way to speak of the eternal sonship of the Second Person of the Trinity. I discuss this important doctrine more fully in ch. 8.

b. See also D. A. Carson, *The Son of God: A Christological Title Often Overlooked, Sometimes Misunderstood, and Currently Disputed* (Wheaton, IL: Crossway, 2012), 47–48.

c. Bruce K. Waltke and James M. Houston with Erika Moore, *The Psalms as Christian Worship: A Historical Commentary* (Grand Rapids: Eerdmans, 2010), 171.

d. James Montgomery Boice, *Psalms 1–41: An Expositional Commentary* (Grand Rapids: Baker Books, 2005), 25.

e. John Calvin, *Commentary upon the Acts of the Apostles*, ed. Henry Beveridge (repr., Grand Rapids: Baker, 2003), 1:535–36; see also Calvin, *Commentaries on the Epistle of Paul the Apostle to the Hebrews*, trans. John Owen (repr., Grand Rapids: Baker, 2003), 42; Brandon D. Crowe, *The Hope of Israel: The Resurrection of Christ in the Acts of the Apostles* (Grand Rapids: Baker Academic, 2020), 58–61.

Psalm 110

Another royal psalm that is fulfilled in the future Son of David is Psalm 110:1:[a] "The Lord says to my Lord: 'Sit at my right hand, until I make your enemies your footstool.'" Later in this psalm the Lord is said to be "a priest forever after the order of Melchizedek" (v. 4). Psalm 110 looks ahead to a royal priest who sits at the Lord's right hand. Two persons are in view in verse 1: "the Lord" (יהוה) and "my Lord" (אֲדֹנִי). Jesus used this psalm to challenge the religious leaders: Is the Messiah David's Son or David's Lord? The answer is both. Psalm 110 looks ahead to a royal-priestly son of David who is more than son of David, for he sits at the right hand of the Lord and is closely associated with the Lord himself.[b] This mysterious figure, though he appears later than David, is David's master (Ps 110:1).[c] The New Testament shows that Jesus fulfills this psalm: he is the preexistent Son of God who is both David's Lord and David's Son, and he fulfills the anticipations of the coming priestly Messiah who reigns over the world (see, e.g., Matt 22:41–46; Rom 1:3–4; Heb 5:6).[d] Bruce Waltke and James Houston put the matter starkly: "Christianity hangs or falls on this testimony of Jesus [Mark 14:61–64] in which he quotes Psalm 110:1."[e]

It therefore makes sense that Jesus and the apostles often used Psalm 110 to highlight the distinctiveness of Christ and his exaltation to God's right hand. Further, the priestly order of Melchizedek points to a priesthood that transcends the Aaronic-Levitical priesthood. Psalm 110 envisions a heavenly high priesthood of the Davidic king. David anticipates this future priest-king,[f] but only Christ finally fulfills it. Christ is a priest in the highest sense, serving as a priest both during his state of humiliation (that is, in his obedience on earth) and in his state of exaltation (that is, in his glorious, present, heavenly ministry).

---

a. E.g., Matt 22:44; Mark 12:36; Luke 20:42; Acts 2:34; 1 Cor 15:25; Heb 1:13; cf. Matt 26:64; Mark 14:62; Luke 22:69; Rom 8:34; Eph 1:20; Heb 1:3; 8:1; 10:12.

b. See Ian J. Vaillancourt, *The Multifaceted Saviour of Palms 110 and 118*, Hebrew Bible Monographs 86 (Sheffield: Sheffield Phoenix, 2019), 85–129.

c. Waltke and Houston, *Psalms as Christian Worship*, 502–3; Vaillancourt, *Multifaceted Saviour*, 96–97 and n. 27.

d. Compare Waltke and Houston, *Psalms as Christian Worship*, 516–17. Additionally, does the enemy's "head" (ראשׁ) that is smashed in Ps 110:6 allude to the crushing of the head of the serpent (Gen 3:15)? See Waltke and Houston, *Psalms as Christian Worship*, 511.

e. Waltke and Houston, *Psalms as Christian Worship*, 485.

f. See, for example, David's wearing the priestly ephod (2 Sam 6:14).

The Davidic King in the Prophets

THE PROPHETS ALSO SPEAK ABOUT the renewal of God's kingdom and the abundance of blessings in the latter days. The coming new order of things, the day of full blessing that the Prophets often anticipate, is closely tied to the coming of a righteous Son of David. The obedience of the coming king will bring blessing for the people.

Similar to Jeremiah 23, Isaiah 11:1 also speaks of a righteous branch, which will come from the stump of Jesse,[9] using two different Hebrew

Jeremiah 23

JEREMIAH FORESAW A RIGHTEOUS BRANCH or "sprout" (צמח) that would be raised up as king from the family tree of David. This royal branch would establish righteousness and justice in the land, leading to lasting security and blessing (Jer 23:5–6; also 33:15–16).[a] Indeed, the branch would be called "the Lord is our righteousness," highlighting God's faithfulness to save his people. The righteous branch would thus execute righteousness and justice in the land, bringing salvation and security for God's people. What Jeremiah envisioned here is something more wonderful and lasting than was true for any natural son of David, for this kingdom would last forever.[b] It is therefore not surprising that many have seen here a reference to the future Messiah's humanity (from the line of David) and his divinity (he is the "Lord our righteousness" who reigns forever),[c] for this passage correlates closely to the New Testament witness to Christ, who is the eternal Son of God, descended from David according to the flesh, who rules over an everlasting kingdom.

a. This paragraph is adapted from Crowe, *Last Adam*, 150.

b. See K&D, 8:217.

c. E.g., John Calvin, *Commentaries on the Prophet Jeremiah and the Lamentations*, trans. and ed. John Owen (repr., Grand Rapids: Baker, 2003), 3:144–45; Amandus Polanus von Polansdorf, *Syntagma Theologiae Christianae* (Hanover: Wechel, 1615), 6.12.F (p. 362); Turretin, *Inst.* 3.28.5 (1:283); Wilhelmus à Brakel, *The Christian's Reasonable Service*, ed. Joel R. Beeke, trans. Bartel Elshout (Grand Rapids: Reformation Heritage, 1992), 1:494–95.

9. See, e.g., R. K. Harrison, *Jeremiah and Lamentations: An Introduction and Commentary*, TOTC 21 (Downers Grove, IL: IVP Academic, 1973), 122–23.

terms (חטר and נצר). Here the "stump" of the Davidic dynasty refers to the need for the dynasty to be reestablished after being cut down. He will be anointed by the Spirit of the Lord (11:2). This Spirit yields (1) wisdom and understanding—he will be a king who rules wisely, like Solomon; (2) counsel and strength—this branch who brings peace will also be equipped as a warrior; and (3) knowledge and the fear of the Lord—the branch will demonstrate true love and obedience to God.[10] This righteous branch will not only benefit the rich and the powerful, but will look after the needs of the poor and weak (11:4–5). He combines strength with wisdom and compassion as the one endowed with the Spirit of the Lord. The result will be an Eden-like peacefulness and harmony of the created order, reflecting the absence of sin's dominion (11:6–9). Instead, his rule shall be expansive and restorative (11:10–16). New Testament writers find in this passage fecund anticipation of Jesus Christ and those who are united to him.[11]

The language of "stump" also anticipates that the Davidic kingdom will be almost wiped out, but new life will spring from the ruined kingdom. The Davidic dynasty—and the people—will be restored. This is apparent in Ezekiel 36–37: whereas the nation experienced the death of exile, eventually the kingdom would be restored and the people united under one king. The people would be like a valley of dry bones come back to life. Though Ezekiel's vision of dry bones speaks largely of the resurrection of God's people collectively, it also assumes the Lord's power to raise the dead.[12] Indeed, the ultimate answer to the people's death will be seen in the New Testament to hinge on the Davidic king's own resurrection from the dead. This will be the means by which the Davidic dynasty will be restored (Amos 9:11–15; see also Acts 15:16–18).

Anticipations of a Divine Son

The coming Davidic king—the Messiah and Son of God—will rule over an everlasting dynasty and bring peace for God's people. This peace is thus more than only the absence of war, but is the shalom of wholeness and flourishing. Indeed, the prophets also speak of the coming of the Messiah in close

10. Here I largely follow Brevard S. Childs, *Isaiah: A Commentary*, OTL (Louisville: Westminster John Knox, 2001), 103.

11. The editors of NA^{28} list 22 references to this passage in the NT.

12. See Calvin, *Inst.* 2.10.21.

relation to the coming of God. For example, Isaiah 7:14 speaks of the promised child who is Immanuel, God with us. The identity of this child has been tirelessly debated: Is it Isaiah's child? King Ahaz's? Does the text make it clear?[13] It is at least quite suggestive that "God with us"—recalling the covenantal formula of God dwelling among his people—is predicated on a coming child. No wonder so many in the history of interpretation have seen this passage referring properly to Christ himself (compare Matt 1:23): the one who is uniquely God and man.[14]

Isaiah 7 is followed in Isaiah 9 by a discussion of a ruler on whose shoulders the government will be set. This child's name will be Wonderful Counselor, Mighty God, Everlasting Father, and Prince of Peace (9:6). These terms are all royal categories to speak of a coming child in whom the people should trust (much like Isa 11).

Two of these four predications merit further discussion.[15] First, "Mighty God" might be a way to refer to the king as the representative for God—he is the earthly implementation of the heavenly rule. Even so, the language is exalted to the point that one may ask whether something more is in view here. Put starkly, should one properly call the Davidic king "Mighty God"? If not, then this text appears to point beyond any natural offspring of David.[16] This suggestive, mysterious statement points ahead to a greater fulfillment and a divine Davidide. This might be similar to the way Psalm 45:6 ("Your throne, O God, is forever and ever"), addressed to the king, is employed in Hebrews 1:8 to refer to the divine sonship of Christ.[17] This is also consistent with the Gospel of John, where we read that Isaiah saw and spoke of the glory of the Son (John

---

13. Childs: "One of the most significant features of this verse is the mysterious, even vague and indeterminate, tone that pervades the entire passage" (*Isaiah*, 66).

14. E.g., Polanus, *Syntagma* 6.12.G (p. 362), 6.13.D (p. 365); Turretin, *Inst.* 3.28.5 (1:283); Maastricht, *Theoretical-Practical Theology* 2:548.

15. For a discussion of interpretive options, see Andrew T. Abernethy, *The Book of Isaiah and God's Kingdom: A Thematic-Theological Approach*, NSBT 40 (Downers Grove, IL: InterVarsity Press, 2016), 125–28.

16. See also Alec Motyer, *The Prophecy of Isaiah: An Introduction and Commentary* (Downers Grove, IL: IVP Academic, 1993), 102–5; John Calvin, *Commentary on the Prophet Isaiah*, trans. William Pringle (repr., Grand Rapids: Baker, 2003), 1:310–11; Turretin, *Inst.* 3.28.5 (1:283); Owen, *Works* 1:311.

17. "[Ps 45:6] is an example of Old Testament language bursting its banks, to demand a more than human fulfillment (as did Ps 110:1, according to our Lord)." Quoted from Derek Kidner, *Psalms 1–72: An Introduction and Commentary*, TOTC 15 (Downers Grove, IL: InterVarsity Press, 1973), 189.

12:41).[18] Second, "Everlasting Father" is another way to speak about kingship (father = king).[19] Everlasting Father likely refers to one who reigns over a lasting dynasty. Yet for such a dynasty truly to be everlasting, death itself would have to be overcome. The New Testament will explain how Jesus, the divine Son, rules over an everlasting kingdom by means of his resurrection.

Likewise, Micah 5:2 (5:1 MT) speaks about a ruler whose coming forth is "from of old, from ancient of days." This is a difficult verse, and several aspects of it are a bit vague. What is meant by "from you … for me" (ממך לי)? To what distant point do "from of old" (מקדם) and "from ancient of days" (מימי עולם) refer? What sort of "going forth" (מוצא) is in view? For example, מוצא is used eschatologically for God's promise of the Davidic covenant in Psalm 89:35.[20] It is clear that Micah 5:2 refers to a coming king from David's line, and Matthew explicitly applies this to Jesus (Matt 2:5–6). Thus, Micah 5:2 has often been taken to refer to the eternal sonship (or eternal generation) of the Son.[21] Many modern commentators demur at this notion, but the suggestive nature of this passage remains, and other commentators are more positively inclined to the tradition that finds eternal generation here.[22] This seems to be the best approach: even if Micah 5:2 refers at some level to a natural son of David, it is best to see that son's ancient, Davidic origins foreshadow a greater Son's more ancient (that is, eternal) origins.

Texts such as these are weighty and mysterious. They point the reader to something more transcendent and lasting than what was true for any natural son of David. The Davidic kingdom anticipates Christ's greater sonship and kingship.[23] He is "God with us" in the strictest sense—the one

---

18. Owen, *Works* 1:315; Mark Jones, *Knowing Christ* (Edinburgh: Banner of Truth, 2015), 36.

19. See also Childs, *Isaiah*, 8; Motyer, *Isaiah*, 102; John N. Oswalt, *The Book of Isaiah: Chapters 1–39*, NICOT (Grand Rapids: Eerdmans, 1986), 247–48.

20. Francis I. Andersen and David Noel Freedman, *Micah: A New Translation with Introduction and Commentary*, AB 24E (New York: Doubleday, 2000), 467.

21. E.g., Bavinck, *RD* 2:275; Turretin, *Inst.* 3.28.13 (1:285); 3.29.13 (1:297); 13.3.22 (2:303–4); Mastricht, *Theoretical-Practical Theology* 2:542–47; Maresius, *Theologiae elenchticae nova synopsis*, 3.1 (1:76, 81); BC 10; Muller, *PRRD* 4:305.

22. Examples of the former include Bruce K. Waltke, *A Commentary on Micah* (Grand Rapids: Eerdmans, 2007), 265–77; Johannes C. de Moor, *Micah*, Historical Commentary on the Old Testament (Leuven: Peeters, 2020), 249. Examples of the latter include Mark S. Gignilliat, *Micah: An International Theological Commentary*, International Theological Commentary (London: T&T Clark, 2019), 173–81; Andersen and Freedman, *Micah*, 468. See also Richard Bauckham, *The Testimony of the Beloved Disciple: Narrative, History, and Theology in the Gospel of John* (Grand Rapids: Baker Academic, 2007), 233–34.

23. Bavinck, *RD* 3:366.

who has existed from all eternity and who has come in the flesh and established an everlasting, righteous kingdom as the one who conquered death.

Daniel 7

CLOSELY RELATED TO THE KINGSHIP of Christ is the coming kingdom of the son of man (Aramaic: בר אנש). The phrase "son of man," which is Jesus's most common way of referring to himself in the Gospels, has been widely debated. The most likely source for this phrase comes from Daniel 7:13–14. This passage recounts night visions of terrifying beasts, representing kingdoms, that arose in succession from the sea. These all passed away, and instead there arose the kingdom of the son of man:

> I saw in the night visions,
> and behold, with the clouds of heaven
> there came one like a son of man,
> and he came to the Ancient of Days
> and was presented before him.
> And to him was given dominion
> and glory and a kingdom,
> that all peoples, nations, and languages
> should serve him;
> his dominion is an everlasting dominion,
> which shall not pass away,
> and his kingdom one
> that shall not be destroyed.

In this vision the kingdom of the son of man outlasts the beastly, ungodly kingdoms that preceded. This kingdom also recalls Daniel's interpretation of Nebuchadnezzar's dream that spoke of a massive stone cut without hands—representing a kingdom that will crush all other kingdoms (Dan 2:34–35, 44–45). It is this kingdom that the son of man appears to rule over in Daniel 7.[a]

The contrast between the son of man's kingdom and the beastly kingdoms recalls the original dominion of Adam over creation.[b] Sin has corrupted Adam's rule over creation, but in the future the son of man will fulfill the mandate given to Adam to rule over the fauna. Daniel 7 thus builds on the Adamic imagery of Psalm 8, in which humankind is crowned with glory and honor and rules over God's creation (Ps 8:4–8). This is more than just a reference to the role of humanity in general, but is interpreted christologically in the New Testament (perhaps via Dan 7) to speak of Christ's representative, human role over all creation (e.g., 1 Cor 15:27). Since humanity is made in God's image, it is fitting for the Son of God to come as the Son of Man to fulfill the task originally given to Adam.

Further highlighting the royal dimensions of the son of man in Daniel 7 is the interplay between the individual and the corporate. Whereas the son of man is a particular figure in 7:13–14, later in the chapter the dominion of the son of man seems to be given to the saints of the Most High (7:18, 22, 27). This most likely refers to the biblical concept, which we have already noted, that God's king represents God's people.[c] The dominion of the son of man is, in some sense, the dominion of the people of God.

Another aspect of "son of man" makes it fitting as a self-referential term for Jesus. Not only is the son of man portrayed as a royal and Adamic figure, but the son of man also appears to be divine. The son of man approaches the throne of the Most High with the clouds of heaven (7:13). These clouds indicate an appearance of God (i.e., theophany),[d] and on them the son of man approaches the throne of the Most High. This is highly suggestive. Does the son of man share the throne with the Most High? Is he divine? Further clarity will come in the New Testament, which identifies Jesus as Son of Man, with the characteristics of the Ancient of Days (Rev 1:14; see also Dan 7:9). All told, what is perhaps suggestive in Daniel is clarified in the New Testament: the Son of Man is divine and does indeed share the throne with the Father (e.g., Matt 19:28; 25:31; Rev 5:11–14; 7:10; 19:10; 22:8).[e]

Jesus is the last Adam and a divine figure who reigns over an everlasting kingdom; both of these are communicated by the son of man language from Daniel 7.

---

a. See, e.g., Beale, *New Testament Biblical Theology*, 111.

b. In the following two paragraphs I glean from Crowe, *Last Adam*, 37–40.

c. Joyce G. Baldwin, *Daniel: An Introduction and Commentary*, TOTC 23 (Downers Grove, IL: IVP Academic, 1978), 151; see also Alfons Deissler, "Der 'Menschensohn' und 'das Volk der Heiligen des Höchsten' in Dan 7," in *Jesus und der Menschensohn: Für Anton Vögtle*, ed. Rudolf Pesch and Rudolf Schnackenburg (Freiburg: Herder, 1975), 81–91.

d. E.g., Exod 14:19–20; 19:9, 16; 24:15–18; 34:5–7; 40:34–38; Lev 16:2; Num 9:15–22; 11:25; 12:5; Deut 5:22; 31:15; 1 Kgs 8:10–11; Ps 99:7; Matt 17:5; 24:30; 26:64; Mark 9:7; 13:26; 14:62; Luke 9:34–35; 21:27; Acts 1:9; Rev 1:7.

e. See Benjamin L. Gladd, "An Apocalyptic Trinitarian Model: The Book of Daniel's Influence on Revelation's Conception of the Trinity," in *The Essential Trinity: New Testament Foundations and Practical Relevance*, ed. Brandon D. Crowe and Carl R. Trueman (London: Apollos, 2016), 169 and 170–71n27; see also Markus Zehnder, "Why the Danielic 'Son of Man' Is a Divine Being," *BBR* 24 (2014): 331–47.

SERVANT OF THE LORD

The servant of the Lord also illuminates the person and work of Christ. Moses is the first person in Scripture to be identified as the servant of the Lord (Deut 34:5), and this terminology is only used rarely in the Old Testament (Joshua: Josh 24:29; David: Ps 18 [superscription]; 36 [superscription]). Yet four passages in Isaiah speak of a figure(s) identified as the servant of the Lord (Isa 42:1–9; 49:1–6; 50:4–9; 52:13–53:12). It is not entirely clear who this figure is, but the servant plays a key role in the coming of eschatological salvation. It should be admitted that the concept of a singular servant figure is highly debated in biblical scholarship, and studies of Isaiah debate whether these were original or later to the book.[24] For sake of the present argument I assume the unity of the book of Isaiah and the viability of speaking of a unified servant figure. The most famous of these passages today is probably the suffering servant of Isaiah 52–53, but the servant's task is multifaceted, and the New Testament will make it clear that Jesus fulfills various aspects of the servant's task.[25]

Isaiah 42

The Servant Songs begin in Isaiah 42 in a passage that requires an appreciation of the interrelationship between the personal and the corporate dimensions of the servant. Some see the servant here to be the nation of Israel; others see it as an individual figure. Regardless of one's decision on that issue, a close relationship exists between the servant and the nation. I am particularly interested in focusing on the servant's task, especially in light of Christology. The first verse sets the stage: "Behold my servant, whom I uphold, my chosen, in whom my soul delights; I have put my Spirit upon him; he will bring forth justice to the nations" (42:1). Anointed with the divine Spirit, the chosen servant is pleasing to the Lord and will establish justice (מִשְׁפָּט) for the nations (42:1, 4). The role of the servant is thus bigger than Israel, but also involves blessings for the nations. The far reaches of the earth, even the coastlands, await his message (42:4). The servant will be a light to the nations, bringing freedom and light to the whole earth (42:5–7).

---

24. See, e.g., Childs, *Isaiah*, 323.

25. For a helpful overview of the Servant, see Abernethy, *Isaiah and God's Kingdom*, 137–60, from which I have benefited in the following discussion.

Isaiah 49 THE CLOSE RELATIONSHIP BETWEEN THE servant and Israel is also apparent in the second Servant Song (49:1–6; see also 49:3, 5). The servant has a key role in the renewal and regathering of Israel (49:5). Yet again the servant also serves as a light to the nations (49:1, 6). The servant is strengthened by the LORD for this task, for it is a struggle (49:4–5).

Isaiah 50 IN ISAIAH 50:4–9 THE SUFFERING of the servant comes into view even more acutely. The servant is weary (50:4). He is beaten and spit on (50:6), but upheld by the LORD (50:7). Those familiar with the passion narratives may identify adumbrations of Christ's suffering. Yet he will in the end be vindicated (50:8).

In summary, the servant's task is multifaceted. Though it is probably not best to identify the servant directly with the Davidic king, the task of the servant overlaps with that of the king.[26] As Bavinck argues, "In the Old Testament this promise of the Suffering Servant and that of the anointed king still in part run parallel. Both promises are rooted in the firmness of God's covenant."[27] In the New Testament these tasks coalesce in Jesus himself. Indeed, one might even find in the servant echoes of the prophetic, priestly, and kingly ministries of Israel. Like a king, the servant establishes justice and righteousness (Isa 42:1, 4; see also 53:11).[28] Like a prophet, the word of the LORD is in the mouth of the servant (50:4). Like a priest, the servant will sprinkle many nations (52:15), and he is himself identified as a guilt offering (53:10).

Isaiah anticipates a day of salvation in which covenant curses will be overcome through the righteous king and the work of the servant.[29] Though some details of the servant and his task remain a bit fuzzy in Isaiah, in the New Testament it is clear that Jesus fulfills the various roles of the servant.

---

26. See also Abernethy, *Isaiah and God's Kingdom*, 139–40.

27. Bavinck, *RD* 3:335.

28. On 53:11, see Alec Motyer, "'Stricken for the Transgression of My People': The Atoning Work of Isaiah's Suffering Servant," in *From Heaven He Came and Sought Her: Definite Atonement in Historical, Biblical, Theological, and Pastoral Perspective*, ed. David Gibson and Jonathan Gibson (Wheaton, IL: Crossway, 2013), 258, who notes the hiphil form יצדיק followed by an indirect object marked by ל communicates "provide righteousness for" and is found only here in the OT. This supports the imputation of Christ's righteousness.

29. See also Crowe, *Last Adam*, 149; H. G. M. Williamson, *Variations on a Theme: King, Messiah and Servant in the Book of Isaiah* (Carlisle, UK: Paternoster, 1998).

He is a greater servant of the Lord than Moses, for Moses remains a servant, whereas Christ is the Son of God (Heb 3:5–6).

Isaiah 52–53

The fourth and perhaps most famous Servant Song (Isa 52:13–53:12) speaks of the surprising effectiveness of the work of the servant, who will ultimately be exalted (52:13).[a] Key is the servant's vicarious suffering.[b] Again the interplay of corporate and personal is important, and in this passage the servant (singular) in some sense bears the sin for the people corporately (53:4–6, 8–9, 11–12). It is possible that the song exhibits a chiastic structure, which would further highlight the centrality of vicarious suffering in 53:4–6:[c]

> Surely he has borne our griefs
> and carried our sorrows;
> yet we esteemed him stricken,
> smitten by God, and afflicted.
> But he was pierced for our transgressions;
> he was crushed for our iniquities;
> upon him was the chastisement that brought us peace,
> and with his wounds we are healed.
> All we like sheep have gone astray;
> we have turned—every one—to his own way;
> and the Lord has laid on him
> the iniquity of us all.

The sheep in 53:6 (and 53:7) may recall Levitical atonement rituals, in which lambs were regularly sacrificed for sins. Indeed, later the servant is described in language used for a guilt offering (אשם, 53:10), which often featured lambs as sacrifices (e.g., Lev 5:6; 14:12–14, 21–25, Num 6:12).[d] Similarly, the sprinkling (נזה) of many nations (52:15) is language used elsewhere of priestly activity denoting atonement and cleansing from sin, including the Day of Atonement (e.g., Lev 16:14–15, 19).[e] If ritual language is used here for the servant—and if it recalls the Levitical cult—then it is striking that this language is applied to a figure who is not explicitly Levitical or perhaps not engaging the Levitical cult as set forth in the law of Moses.[f] For indeed, the servant offers not a sheep but himself as the sacrifice who bears iniquity—an option not set forth in the law of Moses.[g] Further, whereas the servant in Isaiah 53 sounds priestly, earlier the servant figure is portrayed in kingly terms (e.g., Isa 42:1–4).[h] This is similar to other Old Testament passages that combine king and priest, preparing us for Christ's work as Melchizedekian priest-king—the Son of Man who will give his life as a ransom for many (Matt 20:28; Mark 10:45).[i]

In the end, this servant will be exalted (Isa 52:13; 53:10–12), many will be astonished (52:14–15), and his work will be known beyond Israel (52:15). Suffering is not the final word.[j]

---

a. The language of exaltation is used elsewhere for God himself in Isaiah (6:1; 33:10; 57:1), which is one way the distinctive work of the servant is brought into sharp focus. See J. Alan Groves, "Atonement in Isaiah 53: 'He Bore the Sins of Many,'" in *The Glory of the Atonement: Biblical, Historical and Practical Perspectives*, ed. Charles E. Hill and Frank A. James III (Downers Grove, IL: InterVarsity Press, 2004), 80–81.

b. For defenses, see Abernethy, *Isaiah and God's Kingdom*, 151–55; Groves, "Atonement in Isaiah 53," 61–89.

c. See John Goldingay and David Payne, *A Critical and Exegetical Commentary on Isaiah 40–55*, ICC (London: T&T Clark, 2006), 2:277. They present their structure as follows (quoted verbatim):

52:13–15 My servant will triumph despite his suffering
53:1 Who could have recognized Yhwh's arm?
53:2–3 He was treated with contempt
53:4–6 The reason was his suffering for us
53:7–9 He did not deserve his treatment
53:10–11aα By his hand Yhwh's purpose will succeed
53:11aβ–12 My servant will triumph because of his suffering.

d. Abernethy, *Isaiah and God's Kingdom*, 153; See also Motyer, *Isaiah*, 439; R. B. Jamieson, *Jesus' Death and Heavenly Offering in Hebrews*, SNTSMS 172 (Cambridge: Cambridge University Press, 2019), 171–74.

e. Abernethy, *Isaiah and God's Kingdom*, 152.

f. Similar points have been made by Turretin, *Inst.* 13.14.11 (2:355); Bavinck, *RD* 3:335; Groves, "Atonement in Isaiah 53."

g. Groves, "Atonement in Isaiah 53."

h. Thanks to Stephen Coleman for insights on this point.

i. J. Alec Motyer argues that the servant is divine and human, especially in light of Isa 51:9–10 and 53:10. See Motyer, "'Stricken for the Transgression of My People,'" 251, 256.

j. "In Is. 53, the twofold state of the Messiah is so graphically painted that Isaiah seems rather an evangelist relating events rather than a prophet predicting the future" (Turretin, *Inst.* 13.9.2 [2:333]).

ESCHATOLOGICAL REDEMPTION IN THE PROPHETS

THE PROPHETS SAY MUCH ABOUT the coming day of blessings "in the latter days." In what follows I mention a few aspects of the multifaceted vision of the future age of fulfillment that the Prophets address, which are all fulfilled through Christ.

Blessings of a New Exodus

THE EXODUS SERVES AS A paradigm of salvation in the Old Testament, and the Prophets use exodus imagery to speak of a coming, greater salvation. In short, the Prophets anticipated a new exodus, which will be a grander work of God with more copious blessings. God's people (his "son") will be redeemed and brought through the wilderness to a lasting place of blessing (see Isa 40:1–11; 42:15–16; 43:14–21; 51:10; 52:12; Jer 16:14–15; Hos 11:1–11). The new exodus will include a greater cleansing and deliverance from sin: in coming days the LORD will sprinkle water on his people, and they will truly be clean (Ezek 36:25–29). Indeed, Jesus likely alludes to this passage to underscore the new work that had arrived in Nicodemus' own day (John 3:5).

The new exodus will also entail a better covenant than the one made with Moses (Jer 31:31–34).[30] This new covenant will never be broken, and in this covenant the law will be written on the hearts of God's people. In the new covenant, all of God's people will know him—there will be no dichotomy between believer and unbeliever in the covenant community. Though we await the final fulfillment of these promises, Jesus has inaugurated this covenant and sealed it in his blood (Matt 26:28; Luke 22:20).

Other benefits of this new covenant include his reestablishment of David's dynasty (Amos 9:11–12), the Davidic king's rule over a reunited people (Ezek 34:23–24; 37:24; Hos 1:10–11; Zech 11:7), and permanent security in the promised land (e.g., Isa 2:2–3; 30:19; Jer 23:5–6; Mic 4:1–2, 8; Zech 8:7–8).[31] Indeed, the people's restoration will be like a resurrection for God's people (Ezek 37:1–14). Yet national restoration is not the only hope of Israel, but there will also come a day of physical resurrection, in which death itself will be overcome (Isa 25:8; 26:19; Dan 12:2). These blessings are secured by

30. Exodus imagery is apparent earlier in Jer 31 (v. 20), and is also assumed in 16:14. Further, Jeremiah emphasizes the father-son relationship in close connection to the covenant, which is also emphasized in the exodus. See Crowe, *Obedient Son*, 124–28.

31. See further Crowe, *Path of Faith*, 88–94.

the resurrection Christ. Even so, this new covenant is not entirely new, for it is part of the one covenant of grace extending from the days of Adam to present day. God's people have always been saved by grace through faith, yet the new covenant marks the era of fulfillment and greater blessings.[32]

This new exodus will also be greater than the first exodus because the nations will be included to an even greater degree. The word will sound forth from Jerusalem (Isa 2:2–3; 45:22–23; Mic 4:1–2), and the nations will benefit (Isa 42:1–4, 6; 52:15; 55:1–4; 56:1–8); they will come to see the glory of Israel's God (Isa 24:15–16; 42:10–12; 49:6–7, 22–23; 60:1–22; 66:18; Jer 16:19–20; Hab 2:14).

This new exodus will be accomplished by the God of all the earth. No one is like him; he alone is the Redeemer (Isa 35:4; 40:9–11; 41:14; 43:1, 14; 44:6, 22–24; 47:4; 48:17, 20; 49:7, 26; 52:9; 54:5, 8; 63:16). He is the only Savior; there is no other (Isa 43:3, 11; 45:15, 21; 49:26; 60:16; 63:8). The coming day of salvation will be a day of liberation, freedom, restoration, and good news for the poor (Isa 61:1–4). It will be a day of abundance, when the wine will flow like water (Amos 9:13–14), and the Lord will pour out his Spirit abundantly on all people (Joel 2:28–32).

In bringing redemption, the Lord employs agents.[33] In many cases, it is clear that the agent is distinct from the Lord (e.g., the servant). Yet in other cases, including in the coming of the king, the Lord's coming is more difficult to distinguish from coming of his earthly agent. For example, we saw that Isaiah 9 celebrates the coming of a Davidic king who will be called "mighty God" (9:6 [9:5 MT]). Isaiah also looks forward to a redeemer—a title used often for the Lord in Isaiah—who will come forth from Zion (Isa 59:20). Paul explains that this redeemer is the Lord Jesus (Rom 11:26–27).[34] In Ezekiel the Davidic king is the shepherd (Ezek 34:23–24), but so is the Lord himself (Ezek 34:11–16). And earlier I argued that the glorious son of man in Daniel 7:13–14, who comes to the throne with the ancient of days, is divine.

32. See also Scott R. Swain, "New Covenant Theologies," in *Covenant Theology: Biblical, Theological, and Historical Perspectives*, ed. Guy Prentiss Waters, J. Nicholas Reid, and John R. Muether (Wheaton, IL: Crossway, 2020), 551–69.

33. Following the language of Abernethy, *Book of Isaiah*, 119–70, though his focus is on Isaiah.

34. E.g., Thomas R. Schreiner, *Romans*, 2nd ed., BECNT (Grand Rapids: Baker Academic 2018), 603.

Malachi anticipates the day when the Lord will come quickly to his temple (Mal 3:1). He speaks cryptically about two or three figures: the Lord's messenger, the Lord (אדון) whom they were seeking, and the messenger of the covenant (3:1). In the New Testament John the Baptist fulfills the role of the Lord's messenger (Mark 1:2–4). But what about the other two figures: the Lord and the messenger of the covenant? Are these the same or different figures? These most likely refer to the same person.[35] In the New Testament John the Baptist prepares the way for Jesus, who comes quickly to his temple (see Mark 1:2–3; 11:11–25), thus closely identifying Jesus with the Lord of Malachi.[36] This is remarkably high Christology.[37]

In short, the Prophets anticipate the coming day of redemption. Though contours of how this will play out are not fully revealed in the Prophets, the New Testament will clarify how Jesus, the God-man, brings divine deliverance.

Prophet, Priest, and King

Both Adam and Israel are identified as prophet, priest, and king, and in this chapter we have seen that kingship receives more attention in the Old Testament. We have seen, for example, that King David also engages in priestly and prophetic tasks. We have also seen how the servant of Isaiah may fulfill prophetic, priestly, and kingly tasks. I mention here few more words about prophet, priest, and king.

Prophet. Deuteronomy 18:15–18 promises that a prophet like Moses will arise in the future, but this is never fully fulfilled in the Prophets. Though in one sense Moses is the paradigm for all later prophets, and though Jeremiah is particularly viewed as a new Moses, the coming of the ultimate prophet like Moses remains unfulfilled at the dawning of the New Testament era.

Priest. The Levitical priesthood dominates the Old Testament, and an everlasting priest is predicted (1 Sam 2:35). An eschatological portrait of

35. See Poythress, *Theophany*, 339–40; Jonathan Gibson, *Covenant Continuity and Fidelity: A Study of Inner-Biblical Allusion and Exegesis in Malachi*, The Library of Hebrew Bible/Old Testament Studies 625 (London: Bloomsbury T&T Clark, 2016), 165–69.

36. See, e.g., Rikki E. Watts, "Mark," in *Commentary on the New Testament Use of the Old Testament*, ed. G. K. Beale and D. A. Carson (Grand Rapids: Baker Academic, 2007), 119–20; Joel Marcus, *Mark 1–8: A New Translation with Introduction and Commentary*, AB 27 (New York: Doubleday, 2000), 148.

37. Compare Muller, *PRRD* 4:305.

the high priest Joshua (Gk. Ἰησοῦς) is given in Zechariah 3 and 6. Joshua stands arrayed—shockingly—in filthy garments; he is in need of cleansing himself, which he receives (3:1–5). Then in the following verses (3:6–10) the angel of the Lord proclaims to Joshua that he will rule if he walks in the ways of the Lord. This is, intriguingly, connected to the Lord's royal branch (צמח) who will arise (3:8). This is clarified later, when Joshua himself (the priest!) receives the crown, and both king and priest feature prominently in the hope for the future (6:9–15). Thus the Old Testament includes adumbrations of non-Levitical priestly expectations, such as when David speaks in Psalm 110 of the Melchizedekian priesthood.[38] The Old Testament emphasis on the temple is also a priestly theme. Given the priestly emphases of Ezekiel (see Ezek 1:3; 40–48), the application of passages from Ezekiel to Jesus in the New Testament will highlight priestly aspects of Christ's work.

King. The messianic-Davidic hopes of Israel loomed perhaps largest of all. After the split of the Northern and Southern Kingdoms, the exile of the people, and even after the restoration and rebuilding of the temple, the people were looking for the full rehabilitation of the Davidic dynasty. The promise to David was an everlasting kingdom. When and how would this come to pass? Solomon did not turn out to be the final son of David, and his failure in later life is clearly recorded in Scripture (1 Kgs 11). Neither did King Zerubbabel prove to be the final son of David after the exile (see Hag 2:23), for he fades from the pages of Israel's history. The Old Testament concludes without a satisfactory answer to the question of when and how the Lord will fulfill his promise to David and secure his scattered people in the promised land.

In light of this, it is perhaps not surprising that Jewish writings from this era display an eager expectation of a deliverer who will throw off foreign oppression and restore the kingdom (see, e.g., Pss. Sol. 17–18). We can also see expectations of a coming prophet, especially in light of traditions about Moses as well (see John 6:14). Priestly expectations were also in vogue, not least with respect to the shadowy figure of Melchizedek, who was the focus of some attention of the community behind the Dead Sea Scrolls (11Q13). The Dead Sea Scrolls also include, for example, the

38. See similarly Vaillancourt, *Multifaceted Saviour*, 106–7.

extensive Temple Scroll (11Q19–21; 4Q524; 4Q365a),[39] which not only speaks of a new temple, but presents itself as direct revelation from God—the author presented himself as a new Moses who wrote a new, eschatological Deuteronomy.[40] Sometimes, indeed, these three categories were combined, as with Josephus's famous reference to John Hyrcanus as prophet, priest, and king (Ant. 13.10.7).[41] Richard Bauckham even argues that the expectations for a coming, ideal prophet, priest, and king in the reconstitution of Israel not only were present in a first-century Jewish milieu (1QS IX, 11 and 4QTest 5–20; see also John 1:19–21), but should also be evident from the Old Testament itself.[42]

This survey of the importance of prophet, priest, and king provides helpful context, and indeed a historically plausible context, for the threefold office of Christ as prophet, priest, and king. This *munus triplex* is not something first discovered by later theologians, but grows organically from the Jewish eschatological soil that proved fruitful ground for the flourishing of messianic expectations.

CONCLUSION

The Prophets speak of the day when the Lord will fulfill his covenant promises. These promises are focused on the coming of an individual(s) who will lead the people in righteousness and deliver them from the curse of sin. These blessings will also belong to other nations, who will benefit from the kingdom of God's people. The royal hopes emerge particularly clearly, but prophetic and priestly strands also form part of the Prophets' eschatological vision. In the New Testament the multifaceted anticipations of deliverance find their fulfilment in Jesus of Nazareth, descended from David according to the flesh. The Son is proclaimed more obscurely in the Old Testament, but explanation of his person and work finds fuller flower in the New Testament.

---

39. See also Michael O. Wise, Martin G. Abegg Jr., and Edward M. Cook, *The Dead Sea Scrolls: A New Translation*, rev. ed. (San Francisco: HarperOne, 2005), 593–94.

40. Michael Owen Wise, *A Critical Study of the Temple Scroll from Cave 11*, Studies in Ancient Oriental Civilizations 49 (Chicago: University of Chicago Press, 1990), 200.

41. See, e.g., Everett Ferguson, *Backgrounds of Early Christianity*, 3rd ed. (Grand Rapids: Eerdmans, 2003), 410.

42. Bauckham, *Testimony of the Beloved Disciple*, 207–38, esp. 209–12.

FURTHER READING

Behr, John, ed. and trans. *Irenaeus of Lyons: On the Apostolic Preaching*. PPS 17. Crestwood, NY: St. Vladimir's Seminary Press, 1997. An example of biblical theology from the second century, arguing for the pervasive presence of the Son of God in the Old Testament.

Harmon, Matthew S. *The Servant of the Lord and His Servant People: Tracing a Biblical Theme through the Canon*. NSBT 54. Downers Grove, IL: IVP Academic, 2020. Highlights the theme of servant not only in Isaiah but throughout Scripture and shows how it is fulfilled in Christ and in Christ's followers.

Waltke, Bruce K., and James M. Houston with Erika Moore. *The Psalms as Christian Worship: A Historical Commentary*. Grand Rapids: Eerdmans, 2010. Marries interest in the church's theological heritage with detailed exegesis of select psalms, which are used frequently in messianic ways in the New Testament. This commentary covers Psalms 1–4; 8; 15–16; 19; 22–23; 51; 110; 139.

Wright, Christopher J. H. *Knowing Jesus through the Old Testament*. Downers Grove, IL: InterVarsity, 1992. Sheds light on the person and work of Christ by placing Jesus in the context of Old Testament history and institutions, addressing covenants, promises, fulfillment, typology, ethics, and so forth. Gives particular attention to the Gospel of Matthew and Jesus as Son of God. Serves as a useful summary of both Jesus in light of the Old Testament and the Old Testament in light of Jesus—though Wright does less with Adamic themes.

III

THE SON OF GOD IN THE GOSPELS

THE INCARNATION IN THE FULLNESS OF TIME

We turn now to the presentations of Christ in the four Gospels, which are ultimately one gospel; they speak with a unified voice of the same Son of God. As I noted in the introduction, to appreciate the Gospels' christological portraits, it is imperative to give sustained attention to their narrative contours. Though more extensive explanations of the person and work of Christ are found in New Testament epistles, the Gospels are themselves rich resources for Christology. Appreciating the narrative presentations of Christ's person and work in the Gospels requires careful reading of their plots, structures, characterization, and thematic developments. Even so, christological titles are also important and will be useful as an organizing features for the discussion that follows.

SON OF GOD AND MESSIAH

Son of God is arguably the most dominant christological motif in the Gospels. To understand what the Gospels mean by Son of God (or simply Son) requires considering several biblical precedents, some of which were covered in prior chapters. As Son of God, Jesus is portrayed as a new David, a new Israel, a new Adam—and indeed as the supernatural, eternal Son of God.

Son of God like Israel

The Gospels present Jesus as Son of God like Israel. At Jesus's baptism the heavenly voice affirms Jesus's sonship in terms that recall not only the king and servant (Ps 2:7; Isa 42:1) but also Israel's sonship (see Exod 4:22; Deut 32:5, 19–20; Jer 31:20).

Jesus's embodiment of Israel is especially clear in the temptation episodes of Matthew and Luke (Matt 4; Luke 4). Jesus obeyed in the face of three temptations, and in each case he responded to the devil from Deuteronomy (Deut 6:13, 16; 8:3). These quotations all recall the test of Israel as son of God in the wilderness, and Jesus's sonship was likewise tested in the wilderness. The first quotation (Deut 8:3) is particularly clear that Israel was tested *as son*, so that the Lord could know what was in their heart (8:2) and whether they would obey their Father (8:5–6). The temptations thus show that Jesus's obedience is one of the emphases of the comparison to Israel. The temptation of Christ shows us that Son of God has "to do in part with Jesus as the personification or embodiment of true, obedient Israel."[1]

Jesus's identification with corporate Israel is often invoked through the lens of sonship. As a public and representative figure, Jesus sums up the people in himself. Matthew's ten fulfillment quotations, for example, speak of the way that Jesus's obedience overcomes Israel's disobedience.[2] Thus Hosea 11:1 ("Out of Egypt I called my son"), which speaks corporately of Israel as son of God, is fulfilled in Jesus's flight to and return from Egypt (Matt 2:15).

Royal Son of God

Jesus is both the true son of Abraham and the true son of David (Matt 1:1). The Son of God is thus the Messiah, the heir to the Davidic throne. Even before his birth, Gabriel told Mary that her son would be given the throne of David and reign over the house of Jacob forever (Luke 1:31–33). He was then born in the city of David (Bethlehem, 2:4) as the Savior, Messiah, and Lord (2:11). This fulfilled the prophecy of a ruler whose coming out would be from ancient of days (Mic 5:2 in Matt 2:5–6). In a surprising twist, the magi (i.e., pagan astrologers)

---

1. W. D. Davies and Dale C. Allison Jr., *A Critical and Exegetical Commentary on the Gospel according to St. Matthew*, 3 vols., ICC (Edinburgh: T&T Clark, 1988–97), 1:263–64.

2. See Brandon D. Crowe, "Fulfillment in Matthew as Eschatological Reversal," *WTJ* 75 (2013): 111–27.

were more interested in Jesus's royal birth than they were in King Herod. They were led by the star to Jesus, providing an initial fulfillment of the coming of the nations to the glory of Israel (Isa 60:1–3). Further, the genealogies of Matthew 1:2–17 and Luke 3:23–38 show that Jesus is the heir to David's throne (Matt 1:1, 6, 17; Luke 2:31). It is also highly likely that Matthew's three sets of fourteen generations correlate to the numeric value of David's name in Hebrew (three letters equaling fourteen).[3]

It was as royal Son of God that Jesus brought and announced the kingdom of God (Matt 4:17; Mark 1:14–15). This marks a new era in the history of redemption in which God's kingdom breaks into this age, focused on Jesus himself. In response to the Pharisees who asked when the kingdom of God would come, Jesus responded that it was already in their midst (ἐντὸς ὑμῶν ἐστιν, Luke 17:21)—that is, the kingdom was present in the person of Jesus himself. Jesus's special anointing with the Holy Spirit led to a powerful word and deed ministry that should have made it clear that Jesus was God's chosen one to bring the kingdom. Yet, though the powerful miracles were undeniable, too often those who saw them did not understand rightly, sometimes even attributing his mighty acts to the devil. The miracles were signs that the kingdom had come, and by casting out demons Jesus showed that Satan's kingdom was under attack (see Matt 12:22–30; Mark 3:22–30; Luke 11:14–23). Jesus, as the royal Son of God anointed by the Spirit, fulfilled the prophecy of the stump of Jesse endowed with the Spirit (Isa 11:1–5).

This inbreaking of the kingdom was thus apparent in various ways in Jesus's ministry, and these point to the messianic status of Jesus himself. A helpful episode is recorded in Matthew 11:2–19; Luke 7:18–28. In response to the many miracles that Jesus had done, John the Baptist sent messengers to Jesus to ask whether he was the one who was to come (ὁ ἐρχόμενος), or whether they should wait for another. In other words, the messengers asked whether Jesus was the promised Messiah. Presumably one reason for this question was that the Messiah was expected to announce freedom for the captives (Isa 61:1–2; Luke 4:16–21), and John was languishing in prison. If Jesus was the Messiah, shouldn't John be freed? In response Jesus pointed the messengers to the miracles he had done: the blind saw, the lame walked, lepers were cleansed, the deaf heard, the dead were raised,

3. E.g., Davies and Allison, *Matthew* 1:163–65.

and good news was preached to the poor. This answer should ring loud and clear that yes, Jesus is the Messiah. The works that Jesus did fit the expectations of the coming messianic age (Isa 25:8; 26:19; 35:5–6; 61:1; see also 29:18; 42:18; 4Q521).[4] Matthew further correlates Jesus's healing ministry to his title as Son of David (Matt 9:27; 12:23; 15:22; 20:30–31), which also points to his role as Messiah.

Thus Jesus is clearly portrayed as the Messiah in the Gospels, even where the term "messiah" (χριστός) is not used. This point bears emphasis, for many scholars point to the relative scarcity of the term "messiah" in the Gospels to argue (quite dubiously) that Jesus himself never claimed to be the Messiah. Instead, on those sparse occasions where Jesus does seem to say he is the Messiah (e.g., Matt 16:16), they argue we have the theology of the early church rather than the words of the "historical Jesus."

I offer a few brief points in response. First, such conclusions may be built on source-critical reconstructions that assume multiple layers of material in the Gospels that reveal various stages of the early church's beliefs. Often such approaches assume that the words of the "historical Jesus" (a problematic term in itself, typically assuming critical methodologies' ability to reconstruct the "real Jesus") have been embellished by the biblical authors, and only with careful consideration can we distinguish what Jesus actually said from what the early church attributed to him. Such approaches are invariably too subjective and speculative. Instead, it is better to understand that everything included in the Gospels is evidence of the biblical writers' conviction that Jesus is the Messiah, and it is not prudent to attribute inconsistencies to them in ways that presume contradictions in their writings (i.e., that Jesus himself denied he was the Messiah, but the biblical authors anachronistically claimed he was).

Second, the word-concept distinction reminds us that the absence of a particular word (in this case, the rarity of the term "messiah" in the Gospels) is not evidence that the concept is absent.

Third, narrative approaches to the Gospels rightly recognize that important theological truths are communicated by the ways that the narratives are constructed. Put starkly, determining whether Jesus is the

---

4. See, e.g., R. T. France, *The Gospel of Matthew*, NICNT (Grand Rapids: Eerdmans, 2007), 424.

messiah takes more than only counting the number of uses of the term in a book, for the narratives communicate sufficiently that he is the Messiah.

Fourth, it seems eminently likely that Jesus intentionally avoided referring to himself as "messiah" in order not to short-circuit his ministry.[5] In other words, use of the term would have brought increased scrutiny given that the Messiah was often understood in a revolutionary or militaristic sense that did not accurately portray Jesus's understanding of his own mission. This likely explains one reason why Jesus preferred to speak of himself as Son of Man, which had less interpretive and cultural baggage.

Thus, the messianic actions of Jesus in the Gospels reveal his messianic status. Appreciating this opens many avenues for fruitful investigation. For example, the feeding of the five thousand in the wilderness (Matt 14:13–21; Mark 6:32–44; Luke 9:10–17; John 6:1–15)[6] appears to be a messianic action, since after this event in John the people tried to make Jesus king by force (John 6:14–15). Some have also argued that here Jesus stepped into an expectation that in the future the Lord would provide a feast for his people in the wilderness (Isa 25:6).[7] If Jesus's provision of bread in the wilderness does indeed echo the provision of manna in the wilderness for the exodus generation, we may have more than just messianic actions—these may be divine actions, for it was God who fed the Israelites (see John 6:31–32; also Neh 9:15). Similarly, Jesus's raising of the dead during his ministry (e.g., Luke 7:11–17) was a sign that the end-time age of blessing had arrived (Isa 25:8), which was closely associated with the coming of the Messiah (see 4Q521).[8] At the same time, giving life to the dead is a work that only God can do (Deut 32:39).[9] Even the preaching of the gospel, as in Matthew 11:5; Luke 4:18; 7:22, is evidence that the kingdom had come and that Jesus was indeed the Messiah. Indeed, it is striking that the preaching of the good

5. Here I am following Crowe, *Last Adam*, 41–42; further documentation can be found there.

6. This miracle occurs in all four Gospels and serves as a turning point for the public ministry of Jesus—after this point "Jesus sifts the disciples he had gathered." See Benjamin Breckinridge Warfield, "The Historical Christ," in *Person and Work of Christ*, 30.

7. See discussions in, e.g., William L. Lane, *The Gospel according to Mark*, NICNT (Grand Rapids: Eerdmans, 1974), 232; Davies and Allison, *Matthew* 2:481–85.

8. On 4Q521, see France, *Gospel of Matthew*, 424 nn. 19–20.

9. A text noted by Bauckham, *Testimony of the Beloved Disciple*, 246–48.

news was the final and climactic evidence given to the disciples of John the Baptist that demonstrated the kingdom's arrival.

The messianic actions of Jesus, especially the miracles early in Jesus's ministry, provide the background for Jesus's question to his disciples at Caesarea Philippi: "Who do you say that I am?" I covered this already in the introduction, but more can be said here. In light of the eschatological blessings that attended the inbreaking of the kingdom, Peter correctly answered that Jesus was the Christ (Matt 16:16; Mark 8:29; Luke 9:20). Peter recognized that Jesus's powerful kingdom actions were evidence that Jesus truly was the Messiah, and Jesus confirmed Peter's assessment (Matt 16:17–20; see also John 4:26). Even so, the nature of Jesus's messiahship would be surprising, for immediately after Peter's confession Jesus offered the first of three predictions that he would be rejected and killed, and after three days would rise from the dead (Matt 16:20–23; Mark 8:31–33; Luke 9:22).[10] What sort of messianic reign was this?

Soon after Peter's confession, Jesus "set his face toward Jerusalem (Luke 9:51; 13:33)." When the final week of his life came, Jesus entered Jerusalem as a king (Matt 21:1–11; Mark 11:1–11; Luke 19:28–40), fulfilling Zechariah 9:9 and showing the humble nature of his messiahship.[11] It was therefore appropriate for the crowds to shout "Hosanna to the Son of David," quoting Psalm 118:25–26, for Jesus truly was the son of David and he had indeed come to save his people (Matt 1:21). The messianic actions of Jesus continued to be on stark display throughout the week leading to his death. Even the cleansing (or perhaps better cursing) of the temple must be understood as messianic, for it was the king who had the authority over the temple.[12] Jesus's discussion of the temple being torn down and rebuilt after three days (John 2:19–21) was thus a statement from someone claiming to be the king—the Son of God (1:49). It was also in this final week of his life that Jesus posed the challenge: How could the Messiah be both David's son and

---

10. See, e.g., Lane, *Mark*, 292–93.

11. Others argue, especially in light of parallels with Zeph 3:14–15 and Zech 2:10, that the king in Zech 9:9 is the Lord, not the Davidic king. See, e.g., David L. Petersen, *Zechariah 9–14 and Malachi*, OTL (Louisville: Westminster John Knox, 1995), 57–58; Gregory Goswell, "A Theocratic Reading of Zechariah 9:9," *BBR* 26 (2016): 7–19. Perhaps it is not necessary to bifurcate sharply between the two.

12. See N. T. Wright, *Jesus and the Victory of God*, COQG 2 (Minneapolis: Fortress, 1996), 483.

David's Lord (Ps 110:1)? The answer is that only Jesus is both David's son (i.e., Israel's true king) and David's Lord (i.e., the one who is superior to David).

Finally, Jesus was crucified by the Romans as a messianic claimant. The high priest Caiaphas asked Jesus whether he was the Messiah, the Son of God (Matt 26:63; Mark 14:61; see also Luke 22:70). While "Messiah" and "Son of God" are closely related (compare John 1:49), "Son of God" is more than a messianic title. "Son of God" is a divine title, which is evident in the charge of blasphemy leveled at Jesus, the high priest's rending his robes, Jesus's invoking of Daniel 7, and the capital punishment levied against Jesus (Matt 26:64–66; Mark 14:62–63; Luke 22:69–71).[13] Even so, the charge before Pilate was that Jesus was a rival king to Caesar (Matt 27:11, 17; Mark 15:2, 9, 12; Luke 23:2–5; John 18:33–38), though, in fact, it was Caesar who was the rival to Jesus (see Acts 10:36)![14] Though ironic in the context of the narratives, the royal robe, crown, scepter, and homage received by Jesus at this moment also point us to Jesus's kingship (Matt 27:27–30; Mark 15:16–20; Luke 23:11; John 19:1–5), as does the *titulus* above Jesus on the cross (Matt 27:37; Mark 15:26; Luke 23:38; John 19:19–22), and those who passed by mocking Jesus pointed to his purported royal sonship as a point of ridicule (Matt 27:39–43). Yet, again ironically, it was in being lifted up on the cross that Jesus reigned as Messiah, for in his death he sealed the new covenant in his blood and drew all people to himself (John 12:32).

In short, Jesus is presented in the Gospels as Messiah, the Son of David, but the suffering messiahship of Jesus was different than many expected. Yet he was raised as the one with all authority in heaven and on earth (Matt 28:18). Indeed, Jesus made it clear after his resurrection that it was necessary for the Messiah to suffer, die, and rise again (Luke 24:25–27, 44–47). Though surprising, these events were all in accord with Scripture. This will be teased out further in Acts.

13. See James R. Edwards, *The Gospel according to Mark*, PNTC (Grand Rapids: Eerdmans, 2002), 448–49.

14. See C. Kavin Rowe, *World Upside Down: Reading Acts in the Graeco-Roman Age* (New York: Oxford University Press, 2009), 112.

Son of God like Adam

Jesus is also portrayed in the Gospels as Son of God like Adam.[15] That is, he is portrayed as a new Adam, the embodiment of true humanity, and the truly obedient man. This category of Adamic sonship is especially important for understanding the work of Christ to save us from our sins, for fundamentally Jesus does this by overcoming the sin of Adam.

Luke's genealogy, which traces Jesus all the way back to Adam (3:38), helps us see the contours of this Adam Christology.[16] This genealogy comes immediately after Jesus's baptism and just before his temptation in the wilderness. This most likely means that Jesus's obedience in the wilderness, while clearly echoing Israel's sojourn in the wilderness, is also the obedience of the new Adam. Similarly, in Mark's temptation account (Mark 1:12–13), Jesus's (peaceful) presence with the wild animals likely recalls the original created state of humanity, with Jesus's obedience beginning to reestablish the original, paradisal state on the basis of his own obedience.

Further, the baptism of Jesus may also communicate new creational and Adamic imagery, particularly with respect to the descent of the Spirit on Jesus as a dove. This dovelike hovering recalls the Spirit's hovering at creation (Gen 1:2), which is later echoed in the Spirit's hovering in the exodus (Deut 32:11). The dove may also recall the dove of Noah's ark who went forth into a new creation after the flood.[17] The Spirit's descent was understood by Cyril of Alexandria to be the restoration of the Spirit to humanity, and the baptism of Jesus was like the re-creation of the human race in Christ.[18] Cyril goes even further, arguing that Jesus's baptism was the vicarious obedience of the last Adam, who washed away the sin of the first Adam.[19]

---

15. For themes covered in this section, see further Crowe, *Last Adam*; Beale, *New Testament Biblical Theology*, 381–437.

16. Richard Bauckham argues that the seventy-seven names in Luke's genealogy point to "Jesus as the furthest the generations of world history will go, both in number and in significance." See Bauckham, *Jude and the Relatives of Jesus in the Early Church* (London: T&T Clark, 1990), 319.

17. E.g., France, *Gospel of Matthew*, 122; Davies and Allison, *Matthew* 1:331–34.

18. Cyril of Alexandria, *Commentary on John* §184, in *Commentary on John*, trans. David R. Maxwell, ed. Joel C. Elowsky, Ancient Christian Texts (Downers Grove, IL: IVP Academic, 2013–2015), 1:82; Daniel Keating, "The Baptism of Jesus in Cyril of Alexandria: The Re-creation of the Human Race," *ProEccl* 8 (1999): 201–22.

19. Cyril, *John*, §184 (1:82); Keating, "Baptism of Jesus," 208–11. See also Robert Louis Wilken, "St. Cyril of Alexandria: The Mystery of Christ in the Bible," *ProEccl* 4 (1995): 470–72.

The Gospels underscore the true humanity of Jesus as the Son of God like Adam. He is not only the true king of Israel; he is the true human being, and his work applies much more broadly than only to Israel. He was born of Mary in the line of David and Adam. He hungered and thirsted (Matt 4:2; Luke 4:2; 19:28). He got tired (Mark 4:38; Luke 8:23), suffered (Luke 12:50), bled (Matt 26:28; 27:24–26, 29; Mark 15:15, 17; Luke 2:21; 22:20; 22:44(?);[20] John 19:1–2, 5, 34; cf. 6:53–56), and died (Matt 27:50; 28:7; Mark 15:37, 44–45; 16:6; Luke 23:46; 24:7, 20, 46; John 2:19–22; 12:24, 33; 18:32; 19:33–37; 20:9). Jesus was crucified as the last Adam. Indeed, Jesus in his royal attire was mocked by Pilate as a pretend king in words that recall the LORD's words concerning Adam in Genesis 3:22, "Behold the man!"[21]

Yet it was also as the new Adam that Jesus rose from the dead, overcoming the curse of sin as the perfectly obedient, divine Son of God. Just as Adam fell in a garden, so it was fitting for Christ to emerge victorious over sin in a garden (John 20:15).[22] Whereas Adam received the breath of life passively (Gen 2:7), Jesus the new Adam breathed out and commanded his disciples to receive the Holy Spirit (John 20:22). He has all authority in heaven and on earth (Matt 28:18–20), which recalls even as it surpasses Adam's original dominion in the beginning. These elements—Jesus's Adamic suffering and rising to new life in the resurrection—are also communicated by the Son of Man title, which I will consider below.

Divine Son of God THE GOSPELS ALSO PRESENT JESUS as the preexistent, divine Son of God. Not every Gospel explores this aspect of Jesus's sonship in detail (it is most extensive in John), but all four Gospels agree that Jesus is the supernatural Son of God. Too often the Son of God in the Gospels is understood in biblical-theological terms rather

20. Luke 22:44 presents a significant textual question; it is absent from many quality manuscripts. However, this text is not necessary to affirm that Christ truly bled.

21. M. David Litwa, "Behold Adam: A Reading of John 19:5," *Horizons in Biblical Theology* 32 (2010): 142; Edward W. Klink III, *John*, ZECNT (Grand Rapids: Zondervan, 2016), 777–79. Litwa (followed by Klink) points particularly to Gen 3:22 and LAE 13.3. Notice too that Jesus wears a crown of thorns, recalling the curse of Adam. See also Crowe, *Last Adam*, 136–37.

22. See Crowe, *Last Adam*, 137, 195. See also Francis J. Moloney, SDB, *Love in the Gospel of John: An Exegetical, Theological, and Literary Study* (Grand Rapids: Baker Academic, 2013), 141n19; Alistair Begg and Sinclair B. Ferguson, *Name above All Names* (Wheaton, IL: Crossway, 2013), 34–35; Mary L. Coloe, PBVM, "The Garden as a New Creation in John," *The Bible Today* 53 (2015): 158–64.

than in ontological terms. But the Gospels present Jesus as both the fulfillment of the biblical concept of sonship and as the second person of the Trinity. In other words, Jesus as eternal Son of God also fulfills the biblical-theological categories of sonship embodied in Adam, Israel, and David.

Synoptic Gospels

Because the Gospels are narratives, we must allow the cumulative force of the narratives to be appreciated, and we understand more about the Son of God the further we read. Even so, already the infancy narratives of Matthew and Luke adumbrate fuller discussions of Jesus's divine sonship. Matthew and Luke both portray Jesus as being born of Mary, not of Joseph. One reason for Jesus's virginal conception seems to be that it would have been theologically problematic for the eternal Son of God to have had a natural human father. In Luke, Zechariah describes Jesus as the sunrise from on high (Luke 1:78), which most likely assumes Jesus's preexistence as Son of God.[23] Interestingly, the term "sunrise" (ἀνατολή) in the OG translates the Hebrew term צמח ("branch") in Jer 23:5; Zech 3:8; 6:12—messianic passages I covered in the previous chapter.[24]

While Jesus was born in obscurity in Bethlehem, the angelic announcements to Joseph and Mary, the glory of the heavenly army of angels announcing Jesus's birth (Luke 2:13),[25] and the supernatural star that guided the magi attest to the supernatural sonship of Jesus. Further, some argue that Luke's Gospel intentionally alternates (especially in the opening chapters) between identifying God the Father as Lord (e.g., 1:32; 2:26) and identifying Christ as Lord (e.g., 2:11).[26] This communicates an exalted Christology already in the Gospel, though it is in Luke's second volume

---

23. See, e.g., Simon J. Gathercole, *The Preexistent Son: Recovering the Christologies of Matthew, Mark, and Luke* (Grand Rapids: Eerdmans, 2006), 238–42.

24. Richard B. Hays, *Echoes of Scripture in the Gospels* (Waco, TX: Baylor University Press, 2016), 230–31.

25. J. A. Bengel, *Gnomon of the New Testament*, trans. Andrew R. Fausset, 3rd ed. (Edinburgh: T&T Clark, 1860), 2:30; followed by Marvin R. Vincent, *The Synoptic Gospels, Acts of the Apostles, Epistles of Peter, James, and Jude*, vol. 1 of *Word Studies in the New Testament* (New York: Scribner's Sons, 1887), 270.

26. C. Kavin Rowe, *Early Narrative Christology: The Lord in the Gospel of Luke*, BZNW 139 (repr., Grand Rapids: Baker Academic, 2009).

that Jesus's exalted status as Lord is exposited, which comes after Jesus has accomplished his earthly work (Acts 2:36).

The Gospel of Mark also speaks of Jesus's sonship in supernatural terms. Though readers know Jesus is the Son of God (Mark 1:1), and supernatural voices affirm this (1:11; 3:11; 5:7; 9:7 see also 1:24), no nonpossessed, human character in Mark confesses Jesus as the Son of God until the end of the Gospel (Mark 15:39). Here is a case where a careful narrative reading of Mark delivers what simply counting titles cannot: the Gospel progressively reveals who Jesus is, and only when his work is completed does someone confess that Jesus is the Son of God. This is the most profound christological confession in Mark.[27]

Jesus's divine sonship is emphasized by the heavenly voice at two key moments: at his baptism (Matt 3:17; Mark 1:11; Luke 3:22) and his transfiguration (Matt 17:5; Mark 9:7; Luke 9:35). In the transfiguration the glory of Jesus is manifested in an unusually clear way. Whereas Moses reflected the divine glory, Jesus himself shone with theophanic, divine glory (Matt 17:2; Mark 9:3; Luke 9:32). The transfiguration also anticipates Jesus's coming glory in redemptive history but not to the exclusion of Jesus's inherent glory as divine Son of God.

Elsewhere Jesus's divine sonship is seen in Jesus's unique, unfettered relationship to his Father, as we see in Jesus's own prayer (Matt 11:25–27; Luke 10:21–22). This prayer speaks of the full knowledge and power of the Son in a way that distinguishes him from all created beings. The Gospels also present Jesus as receiving worship as Son of God. When Jesus walked on the water and calmed the storm in Matthew 14, the disciples responded with a confession of Jesus's sonship, and their response is described as προσκυνέω, which is best understood, in the context of the Gospel, as worship. It is striking that earlier in Matthew, Jesus stated that worship must only be given to the Lord God (Matt 4:10, see Deut 6:13), but when the same actions were directed toward Jesus, he did not rebuke them (Matt 14:33; 28:9, 16).[28] And where the magi prostrate themselves before Jesus (2:11),

27. C. E. B. Cranfield suggests that "Son of God" in Mark 1:1 assumes preexistence in *The Gospel according to St. Mark*, 2nd ed., Cambridge Greek Text Commentary (Cambridge: Cambridge University Press, 1963), 19; see also R. T. France, *The Gospel of Mark: A Commentary on the Greek Text*, NIGTC (Grand Rapids: Eerdmans, 2002), 50.

28. See also Richard Bauckham, "Worship of Jesus," *ABD* 3:813.

they are portrayed positively in the narrative, in contrast to Herod, who sought to kill Jesus.

The actions of the disciples in the boat in Matthew 14 receive further clarification when Peter confesses Jesus as Christ in Matthew 16:16. Here Peter's confession, "Son of the living God," in light of the worship rendered to Jesus earlier, assumes the ontological claim that Jesus is divine, sharing the quality of living that characterizes the true God.[29] This is the proper response to Jesus's divine actions, such as raising the dead, forgiving sins, calming the chaos of storm and sea, and knowing others' thoughts. If Jesus's actions are divine, then Jesus must be divine. Later theologians spoke of the same names, attributes, works, and worship ascribed to the Son (and Spirit) as proper only to God.[30] In more recent years this accords with what Richard Bauckham calls divine identity Christology: Jesus's actions demonstrate that he is included in the identity of the one God of Israel.[31]

Jesus's unique relationship to the Father is the focus of Mark 12:28–37.[32] In Mark 12:28–34 Jesus answered that the most important commandment is to love the Lord your God with all your being, quoting Deuteronomy 6:4–5. Immediately after this (Mark 12:35–37) Jesus challenged the teachers in the temple, asking how the Christ could be both David's Lord and David's son, quoting Psalm 110:1. The apposition of these Old Testament texts encourages us to see that the oneness of God in Deuteronomy 6:4 must take into account the one who is identified in Psalm 110:1 as David's son and David's Lord.

Matthew's presentation of Jesus as Immanuel provides a fitting conclusion to this section. Immanuel means "God with us" (Matt 1:23–25), which echoes the highest covenant blessing of the Lord's presence with his people.

---

29. See Athanasius, *C. Ar.* 2.18; John P. Meier, *The Vision of Matthew: Christ, Church, and Morality in the First Gospel* (repr., Eugene, OR: Wipf & Stock, 2004), 109; Geerhardus Vos, *The Self-Disclosure of Jesus: The Modern Debate about the Messianic Consciousness*, 2nd ed., ed. Johannes G. Vos (repr., Phillipsburg, NJ: P&R, 2002), 180.

30. E.g., WLC 11; Turretin, *Inst.* 3.28 (1:282–92); Muller, *PRRD* 4:245–46, 302; à Brakel, *Christian's Reasonable Service* 1:494.

31. Richard Bauckham, *God Crucified: Monotheism and Christology in the New Testament* (Grand Rapids: Eerdmans, 1999).

32. Here I follow Daniel Johansson, "*Kyrios* in the Gospel of Mark," *Journal for the Study of the New Testament* 33 (2010): 101–24; see also John J. R. Lee, *Christological Rereading of the Shema (Deut 6.4) in Mark's Gospel*, WUNT 2/533 (Tübingen: Mohr Siebeck, 2020), 84–148.

It may be unclear at the outset whether this means that Jesus is divine, but this suggestive phrase at the beginning of the Gospel is teased out throughout Matthew. By the end of the Gospel it is clear that Jesus is with his disciples where two or three are gathered in his name (18:20), and is indeed with them forever (28:20). Jesus is indeed the divine Son of God.[33] Jesus will save his people from their sins (1:21). This too is a divine task, for only God is the Savior of his people (e.g., Isa 45:21).

Gospel of John THE SYNOPTIC GOSPELS HAVE MUCH to say about the divine sonship of Jesus, but the Gospel of John adds even more clarity. A key text is the prologue of John's Gospel (1:1–18), which Martin Hengel considers "the most influential christological text in the New Testament."[34] Whereas Matthew and Luke start with the incarnation and Mark starts with the public ministry of Jesus, John begins with the Son's existence and activity before creation. I noted in chapter 1 that John 1:1 echoes the language of Genesis 1:1 and makes it clear that the divine Son (who is the Word) is the Creator.

Identifying Jesus as the Word (Gk. λόγος) is distinctively Johannine and points to the mediatorial role of the Son even before the incarnation, for the Word was active in enlightening all people (1:4–5).[35] The background for this term has been widely debated, but the clear allusion to Genesis means that we ought to look first to the Old Testament as the most prominent background. As I noted in chapter 1 and will discuss also in chapter 6, many church fathers seized on this concept of the Logos to discuss the preexistent work of the Son, particularly with respect to mediation (including theophanies) and the spoken word of God (including speaking in the Old Testament Scriptures), even before the incarnation. By speaking of life in the Logos, John speaks of the quality of life-in-himself that characterizes the true God. Later in the prologue we are said to receive from the fullness of the Son grace upon grace, and this in contrast to Moses, by whom the law

---

33. Matthew 28:19 includes the singular "name" (ὄνομα) and the threefold repetition of the Greek article. This shows both the unity of God and the distinction between persons. See Bavinck, *RD* 2:270, 305–6.

34. Martin Hengel, "The Prologue of the Gospel of John as the Gateway to Christological Truth," in *The Gospel of John and Christian Theology*, ed. Richard Bauckham and Carl Mosser (Grand Rapids: Eerdmans, 2008), 289.

35. See Vos, "Range of the Logos."

was mediated (1:16–17). There is a qualitative difference between the Son as Mediator and merely human mediators. Strikingly, this eternal Word became man, and in his incarnate state—including in his being lifted up on the cross—we have beheld his glory (1:18). John 1:1–18 is an important passage for the development of orthodox Christology.

The exalted Christology of John 1 does not, however, threaten the unity of God. Some have tried to argue that the Greek construction of John 1:1 speaks of Jesus as a god based in large measure on the absence of the Greek article before "God" in the final phrase θεὸς ἦν ὁ λόγος ("God was the Word"). However, this approach is extremely forced and uncompelling: it misunderstands the nature of the Greek grammatical construction and the import of other texts in the near and far context, and asks us to consider that John was a polytheist. In terms of Greek construction, the inclusion of the Greek article before θεός would not strengthen the theology of the sentence, but would be inconsistent with Trinitarian doctrine. Put simply, if the article were included before θεός, John would sound like a modalist. If John would have written ὁ θεὸς ἦν ὁ λόγος ("the God was the Word"), it would have too strictly identified the persons of the Godhead and would have communicated that only the Word is God.[36] But that is not the case, since the Father is also God. As it is, John has written with nuance to speak of two divine persons without undermining the one essence of God. Put simply, the anarthrous (i.e., without the article) use of "God" describes the divine nature of the Word.[37]

Elsewhere in John's prologue this same Word is identified as God (1:18),[38] which further supports understanding the Word as fully divine (see also 20:28). John was written from a monotheistic worldview, in which it is clear that Israel's God is the only true God, and this God is one (Deut 6:4). John's Gospel does not undermine this oneness of God, but assumes it even as it relates Jesus closely to the one God by placing him on the Creator side of the Creator/creature distinction. A key passage in this regard, which becomes a key text for many church fathers, is John 10:30, where Jesus said,

---

36. See C. K. Barrett, *The Gospel according to St. John: An Introduction with Commentary and Notes on the Greek Text*, 2nd ed. (London: SPCK, 1978), 156.

37. See also Daniel B. Wallace, *Greek Grammar Beyond the Basics: An Exegetical Syntax of the Greek New Testament* (Grand Rapids: Zondervan, 1996), 262–69.

38. Following the readings that include [ὁ] μονογενὴς θεός, attested in 𝔓66, 𝔓75, א, B, et al.

"I and the Father are one" (ἐγὼ καὶ ὁ πατὴρ ἕν ἐσμεν).[39] This verse has often been taken to refer to the unity of the power of the Father and Son; there should be no argument with that.[40]

But John seems to be saying even more here. He is most likely echoing the language of oneness of God from the Shema (Deut 6:4) to speak of the oneness of God to include both Father and Son.[41] The point in John 10 is that the sheep are safe in Jesus's care because he has the same power as the Father, who is greater than all (10:29).[42] The response to Jesus is telling, as the Jewish leaders perceive him to be claiming equality with God (10:33). This also comes after Jesus states he is the Good Shepherd (10:11, 14) in language recalling the description of God from Psalm 23. All this provides context for Jesus's claim in 10:30. In light of this context, John's emphasis is on the divine essence of the Son as well as on the divine power of the Son. This is a claim to divinity.[43] A similar point is made in John 14:10, where Jesus says, ἐγὼ ἐν τῷ πατρὶ καὶ ὁ πατὴρ ἐν ἐμοί ἐστιν ("I am in the Father and the Father is in me"), which also denotes that the Father and the Son share the same essence.[44]

John's prologue also introduces us to the distinctively Johannine term μονογενής (John 1:14, 18; 3:16, 18; 1 John 4:9), traditionally translated as "only begotten." In recent years translators and commentators have gravitated toward the translation "one and only," partly due to the doubtfulness that some sort of begetting is in view. However it is far from clear that "one

39. See, e.g., Athanasius, *C. Ar.* 4.16–17.

40. See Herman Ridderbos, *The Gospel according to John: A Theological Commentary*, trans. John Vriend (Grand Rapids: Eerdmans, 1997), 371 (following Calvin), who denies this is about the shared essence of the Father and Son.

41. See Bauckham, *Testimony of the Beloved Disciple*, 250–51. Bauckham observes, in line with writers we will consider in later chapters, that the neuter for "one" (ἕν) is used rather than the masculine "one" (εἷς) found in Deut 6:4, because Father and Son are one *God*, not one *person*.

42. John 10:29 contains one of the most difficult textual questions in John. My reading assumes the masculine relative pronoun (ὅς) and the neuter comparative adjective (μεῖζον).

43. In contrast, Jesus's statement in John 14:28 that the Father is greater is more about redemptive history. I address this text in relation to Paul's teaching in chapter 4.

44. See, e.g., Owen, *Works* 1:71; Maresius, *Theologiae elenchticae nova synopsis* 3.1 (1:84). Turretin sees here emperichoresis, or "that union by which the divine persons embrace each other and permeate (if it is right to say so) each other" (*Inst.* 3.23.13 [1:257]). On emperichoresis and John 1:18, see Maresius, *Theologiae elenchticae* 3.2 (1:89).

and only" is a better translation.[45] Instead, in each context where John uses "only begotten" it is tethered to a discussion, in some way, of birth.[46] On balance, it seems best to translate μονογενής as "only begotten."[47] This also leads us to discussions surrounding the eternal generation of the Son—a concept I will take up in chapter 8.

John 5

ANOTHER KEY TEXT FOR UNDERSTANDING the divine sonship of Jesus in John is the speech occasioned by the controversy over healing in Jerusalem in John 5:1–16. In this instance Jesus sought out the man to be healed and used it as an opportunity to manifest his authority. That the healing occurred on the Sabbath (5:16) was central to the controversy. In response to challenges about his actions on the Sabbath, Jesus boldly stated, "My Father is working until now, and I am working" (5:17). This elicited another negative response, for not only was Jesus healing on the Sabbath, but he was apparently making himself equal to God by claiming God as his Father (5:18).

In response, Jesus explains that he was not making himself God, nor was he inappropriately usurping divine authority in what he was doing and saying. Instead, Jesus has divine authority in a way that is proper to the Son of God. In other words, he spoke both of his authority as *divine* Son and in his role as divine *Son*. On the one hand, the Son can do only what the Father does (5:19a; see also 5:30); yet that which the Father does—in this case, giving life on the Sabbath—the Son also does (5:19b). The Sabbath was God's day; only God was to work on the Sabbath.[a] Here Jesus said, in effect, that the Sabbath was also his day and he rightly gives life on the Sabbath.[b] For, just as (ὥσπερ) the Father raises the dead and gives life, so also (οὕτως) the Son grants life to whomever he wills (5:21). The Old Testament makes clear that it is only God who kills and makes alive (Deut 32:39).[c] In John this life is specifically resurrection life, as the double "amen, amen" statements emphasize in 5:24–25, along with the final statements in this section (5:29–30).[d]

---

45. See Charles Lee Irons, "A Lexical Defense of the Johannine 'Only Begotten,'" in *Retrieving Eternal Generation*, ed. Fred Sanders and Scott R. Swain (Grand Rapids: Zondervan, 2017), 98–116.

46. Letham, *Systematic Theology*, 114–21.

47. See Barrett, *John*, 166.

An important and debated verse with respect to Christology in this section is 5:26: "For as the Father has life in himself, so he has granted the Son also to have life in himself" (ὥσπερ γὰρ ὁ πατὴρ ἔχει ζωὴν ἐν ἑαυτῷ, οὕτως καὶ τῷ υἱῷ ἔδωκεν ζωὴν ἔχειν ἐν ἑαυτῷ). Many see the close parallel in this text between the Father, who has life in himself (eternally), and the Son, who has been granted to have life in himself to reflect an eternal granting of life to the Son.[e] This would support the doctrine of eternal generation, whereby the Father begets the Son eternally, and both Father and Son possess the same divine essence.[f] Others see in John 5:26 a reference specifically to the Son's role in the economy of redemption,[g] which fits well with the focus on Jesus's role as Son of Man (5:27)—an incarnate reality.

This is a difficult exegetical question. At the very least, the role of the Son in giving resurrection life in the economy of redemption must in some way reflect and assume the eternal Father-Son relationship: what the Son can do as Son of Man in executing judgment and raising the dead is different from any created being. But we can likely go further: speaking of the Father granting the Son to have life in himself seems to reflect both (1) what is true uniquely of God himself ("life in himself") and (2) the life that is granted (ἔδωκεν) to the Son as Son, which does not differ from the "life in himself" that is true of the Father.[h] In other words, the quality of "life-in-himself" is not something that can be fully explained by means of the economy of redemption; it most likely alludes to the eternal begetting of the Son. John 5:26 is a text that brings us to the edge of what we can glean about the eternal Father-Son relationship; we may never be able to answer all our questions exhaustively.

The sort of life that will be granted to those with faith in the Son is resurrection life, which depends on the Son's resurrection as the firstfruits of new creation. This is the Son who has the authority both to lay down his life and to take it up again (10:17–18). The Gospel of John recounts the time of fulfillment, the eschatological hour that has come, when the eternal Son of God comes in flesh (1:14) to redeem us by granting new life on the basis of his perfect obedience.

Jesus also spoke of the goal that all might honor the Son just as (καθώς) they honor the Father. Jesus was not seeking to usurp the authority of the Father, but showed that the Son is to be honored in the same way the Father is to be honored (compare Exod 20:2–3; Deut 5:6–7; 6:4–5). No creature should speak this way. Jesus's discussion of God as "my Father" was likewise unexpected.[i] Though we have seen that God was amply known as Father in the Old Testament, Jesus spoke of his Father with unprecedented intimacy. Jesus spoke and acted with divine authority, yet his authority was also that of the Son. At the end of Jesus's life came another important insight into the Father-Son relationship, which we find in the opening verses of the farewell prayer of Jesus (John 17:1–5). The Father granted the Son authority over all flesh, and eternal life entails not only knowing the Father but also Jesus Christ, the sent one (17:2–3). This Son was entrusted with a work, which is the accomplishment of salvation (17:4). As he approached the consummation of his earthly work in his coming glorification (i.e., crucifixion-resurrection-ascension), he looked forward to returning to the Father and the glory he had before the creation of the world (17:5). In these verses the veil is pulled back, and we see glimpses of the unsearchable depths of the intra-Trinitarian personal relations.

---

a. See D. A. Carson, *The Gospel according to John*, PNTC (Grand Rapids: Eerdmans, 1991), 247–49.

b. Elsewhere Jesus speaks of the Son of Man as Lord of the Sabbath (Matt 12:8; Mark 2:28; Luke 6:5).

c. See also Bauckham, *Testimony of the Beloved Disciple*, 246–48.

d. If we take 5:19–30 as a unit, then 5:24–25 appears to be the center of a chiastic structure. My view of this passage has been informed by Charles H. Talbert, *Reading John: A Literary and Theological Commentary on the Fourth Gospel and the Johannine Epistles* (New York: Crossroad, 1992), 124.

e. Owen, *Works* 1:71–72; Mastricht, *Theoretical-Practical Theology* 2:229–31; Turretin, *Inst.* 3.28.20 (1:287), 3.28.28 (1:289); *SPT* 8.14 (1:210–11); Muller, *PRRD* 4:251; Bavinck, *RD* 2:275, 309, 342; Barrett, *John*, 262; D. A. Carson, "John 5:26: *Crux Interpretum* for Eternal Generation," in Sanders and Swain, *Retrieving Eternal Generation*, 82–85; Stephen J. Wellum, *God the Son Incarnate: The Doctrine of Christ*, FET (Wheaton, IL: Crossway, 2016), 162; Matthew Barrett, *Canon, Covenant, and Christology: Rethinking Jesus and the Scriptures of Israel*, NSBT 51 (Downers Grove, IL: IVP Academic, 2020), 256–60; Barrett, *Simply Trinity: The Unmanipulated Father, Son, and Spirit* (Grand Rapids: Baker, 2021), 179–85; Richard D. Phillips, *John*, Reformed Expository Commentary (Phillipsburg, NJ: P&R, 2014), 1:323.

f. I discuss eternal generation more fully in ch. 8.

g. See, e.g., John Calvin, *Commentary on the Gospel according to John*, trans. William Pringle (repr., Grand Rapids: Baker, 2003), 1:207; Calvin, *Inst.* 4.17.9; Hodge, *Systematic Theology* 1:470–71; Geerhardus Vos, *Reformed Dogmatics*, ed. and trans. Richard B. Gaffin Jr. (Bellingham, WA: Lexham, 2012–2016), 1:55.

h. See similarly Carson, "John 5:26," 82–87; Keith E. Johnson, "Eternal Generation in the Trinitarian Theology of Augustine," in Sanders and Swain, *Retrieving Eternal Generation*, 170–71. For a brief discussion of Augustine's view of John 5, see the post by Fred Sanders: https://fredfredfred.com/2022/10/reduction-back-to-eternal-generation.

i. Compare also Richard Bauckham, "The Sonship of the Historical Jesus in Christology," *SJT* 31 (1978): 245–60.

SON OF MAN AND SERVANT

No title is more characteristic of Jesus's own usage in the Gospels, and perhaps no title is as widely debated, as Son of Man.[48] Some see this as an exalted title; others see it simply as a way to refer to "a man like myself." Often this debate centers on the prehistory of the term from Aramaic.[49] In this section I consider primarily the way that "Son of Man" is used in the Gospels. In the Gospels, "Son of Man" is most likely a title, and the most prominent background appears to be the glorious, kingdom-ruling son of man in Daniel 7:13–14. In the previous chapter I argued that the son of man would rule over a kingdom as the one who fulfilled the calling of Adam in contrast to the beastly, ungodly kingdoms. Daniel 7 also suggests the divinity of the son of man. This passage is most likely the key background for Jesus's use of Son of Man in the Gospels.

Daniel 7's influence becomes increasingly clear the further we progress in the Gospel narratives. What may be less clear when Jesus uses "Son of Man" early in the Gospels becomes increasingly clear the closer Jesus gets to his death and resurrection, climaxing with the affirmation before Caiaphas of the Son of Man's future, glorious coming with the clouds (Matt 26:63–64; Mark 14:61–62; see also Luke 21:27). In this climactic scene, Jesus's explanation of the Son of Man's glory appears to be taken directly from Daniel 7:13–14. Similarly, after his resurrection, in the Great Commission (Matt 28:18–20) all authority in heaven and on earth has been given to Jesus in a way that reflects Daniel's authoritative son of nan. This son of man will one day return in the full glory, a preview of which is glimpsed by the disciples on the Mount of Transfiguration (e.g., Mark 8:38–9:1; 13:26; 14:62).

Jesus used this term even though it was not a common messianic title in the first century. Because it was not widely used, it apparently did not have as much interpretive baggage associated with it in the way that terms such

48. For further discussion and more extensive bibliography on Son of Man, see Crowe, *Last Adam*, 37–51.

49. Often the debate centers on reconstructing the Aramaic phrasing, and whether the Aramaic phrase "Son of Man" would have been definite or indefinite and whether there was any difference between the two. The continuing distinction between definite and indefinite has been made by William Fullilove, "The Representation of Definiteness in Qumran Aramaic: Unsolving the Son of Man Problem" (paper presented at the Annual Meeting of the Society of Biblical Literature, Atlanta, 23 November 2015).

as "messiah" did.[50] Jesus therefore used it to refer to his earthly work and to evoke his Adamic vocation of ruling as God's vice-regent. But the term also communicated his divine authority. "Son of Man" further appears to have been a term that was fitting to use for oneself, which perhaps explains its relative lack of use by other New Testament authors to describe Jesus (see Acts 7:56).[51] It also makes sense historically for Jesus to have used a term that would not immediately have raised suspicions of the Roman (and Jewish) authorities in the way that "messiah" would. This reticence to use the latter term seems to have been necessary to avoid a premature end to his public ministry.

Jesus thus used Son of Man as his primary self-reference to speak of his earthly work, his suffering, and his coming again in glory. In terms of his earthly work, Jesus spoke of the sweeping authority of the Son of Man to forgive sins (Matt 9:6; Mark 2:10; Luke 5:24) and as Lord of the Sabbath (Matt 12:8; Mark 2:27; Luke 6:5). Yet this same Son of Man, surprisingly, had not even a place to lay his head (Matt 8:20; Luke 9:58). This is indicative of the larger irony of the Son of Man's suffering in the Gospels. If Jesus is indeed the authoritative, glorious Son of Man of Daniel 7 (as the Gospels increasingly make clear), then how can he suffer?

One of the most important texts in this regard is Matthew 20:28; Mark 10:45: "For even the Son of Man came not to be served but to serve, and to give his life as a ransom for many." This statement, which one Markan commentator considers to be "by far the most remarkable ... saying in Mark,"[52] speaks not only of the suffering of the Son of Man but of his vicarious suffering. Three points stand out in this regard. First, the language of "ransom" (λύτρον) communicates something (or here, someone) given in place of someone else (see Ps 49:7–9). Second, the prepositional phrase "for many" (ἀντὶ πολλῶν) most naturally speaks of substitution, especially

50. To be sure, many point to 1 Enoch as a place where we may find a glorious son of man precedent. Even so, this does not make the usage of the title *common*. For more on 1 Enoch, see Loren T. Stuckenbruck, "The *Book of Enoch:* Its Reception in Second Temple Jewish and in Christian Tradition," *Early Christianity* 4 (2013): 7–40.

51. See I. Howard Marshall, "Son of Man," in *Dictionary of Jesus and the Gospels*, ed. Joel B. Green, Scot McKnight, and I. Howard Marshall (Downers Grove, IL: InterVarsity Press, 1992), 776.

52. Craig A. Evans, *Mark 8:27–16:20*, WBC 34B (Grand Rapids: Zondervan, 1988), 119.

in conjunction with λύτρον.[53] Third, the likely allusion to Isaiah's Servant Songs, especially the suffering servant, is to one who is also given for many (Isa 53:10–12).[54] Even so, this one who gives his life as a ransom will be vindicated in the end, just as we saw of the servant in Isaiah 53.

It is thus as the Son of Man that Jesus predicted his death and resurrection three times (Matt 16:21–23; 17:22–23; 20:17–19, and pars).[55] Significantly, Jesus's first death and resurrection prediction came just after Peter's confession of Jesus as the Messiah; Jesus's natural pivot to speak of the Son of Man's suffering was thus a way for him to speak of the Messiah's suffering, as unexpected as that may have been. The one who suffers was, at the same time, the one who would be vindicated when he rose from the dead. "Son of Man" communicates both suffering and vindication.

Jesus's ransom statement portrays Jesus as the fulfillment of the servant of the Lord, especially (but not limited to) the suffering servant. Whether the Gospels present Jesus as the servant is a debated issue, but thematic and verbal parallels to the Servant Songs of Isaiah 42; 49; 50; 52–53 are evident in the Gospels and throughout the New Testament. Allusions to these chapters of Isaiah are particularly prevalent in the passion narratives and in the death of Christ,[56] though Jesus fulfills the role of servant throughout his ministry.[57] Indeed, we should not sharply dichotomize between the earlier and latter stages of Jesus's ministry as if he were doing something different at the end; Christ's work is an integrated whole. Matthew quotes explicitly from two Servant Songs during the ministry of Jesus (Isa 53:7 in Matt 8:17; Isa 42:1–4 in Matt 12:17–21), and the divine good pleasure in the servant from Isaiah 42:1 is pronounced on Jesus at his baptism and transfiguration (Matt 3:17; 17:5 and pars.).

---

53. See also Murray J. Harris, *Prepositions and Theology in the Greek New Testament: An Essential Reference Resource for Exegesis* (Grand Rapids: Zondervan, 2012), 52–54.

54. See Joel Marcus, *The Way of the Lord: Christological Exegesis of the Old Testament in the Gospel of Mark*, Studies of the New Testament and Its World (Edinburgh: T&T Clark, 1993), 187.

55. See, e.g., Joel Marcus, *Mark 8–16: A New Translation with Introduction and Commentary*, AB 27A (New Haven: Yale University Press, 2009), 604.

56. On allusions to the Servant Songs in the passion narratives, see Marcus, *Way of the Lord*, 187–90. Some examples he notes include (1) Isa 53:12 in Mark 10:45; 14:24; (2) Isa 53:7 in Mark 14:61; 15:5; (3) Isa 50:6 in Mark 14:65.

57. A point emphasized by Wright, *Jesus and the Victory of God*, 588–611.

"Servant" thus also describes the work of Christ in bringing the kingdom. Though in Isaiah it is unclear whether the king and the servant are the same, in the Gospels both king and servant are united in Christ.[58] Both the king as Son of God and the servant are anointed with the Spirit (Isa 11:2; 42:1; 52:15; see also 61:1), and both bring justice to the nations (Isa 9:6[7]; 11:4–5, 9–10; 16:5; 32:1, 16; 42:1). Matthew combines the servant and the Spirit-empowered work of the royal Son of Man who brings the kingdom (see Matt 12:15–32). The quotation of Isaiah 42 also makes it clear that this servant's work will succeed.

That Jesus is the suffering servant is also apparent at the end of his public ministry in John. After completing the signs of the public ministry, he departed, and the sad reality was that many who saw the signs did not truly believe (12:37). This fulfilled Isaiah 53:1, "Lord, who believed our report? And to whom has the arm of the Lord been revealed?" John then explains their lack of belief (indeed, their inability to believe) from Isaiah 6:9–10. Isaiah saw Jesus's glory (John 12:41), and the glory of the only begotten Son was seen preeminently when he was lifted up (12:27–28). This was not the world's glory (12:43) but the glory of the crucified and risen Servant. It may even be that John's combination of quotations from Isaiah 6 and 52–53, the latter of which also sees the servant as high and lifted up, is a way to highlight that the divine glory was seen when Jesus was lifted up—in the cross and resurrection.[59] That is, the glory of God in Isaiah was made known through the work of the suffering servant, and this was realized in the work of Jesus incarnate.[60] This transitions to the final words, death, and resurrection of Jesus (John 13–20), which scholars often refer to as John's book of glory.[61]

As Son of Man, Jesus is also the Savior. Though the title is not often used in the Gospels, the theme of salvation in Jesus is especially prominent

58. See further Crowe, *Last Adam*, 140–50.

59. So, e.g., Craig S. Keener, *The Gospel of John: A Commentary*, 2 vols. (Peabody, MA: Hendrickson, 2003), 885; Carson, *John*, 450; see also Bauckham, *God Crucified*, 49–51.

60. Andreas J. Köstenberger, "John," in Beale and Carson, *Commentary on the New Testament Use*, 483.

61. See, e.g., Raymond E. Brown, *The Gospel according to John: Introduction, Translation, and Notes*, AB 29–29A (New York: Doubleday, 1966–1974), 1:cxxxviii–cxxxix.

in Luke (e.g., 1:69; 2:11, 30; 19:9–10; see also Acts 2:21).[62] Jesus was already Savior at his birth (Luke 2:11), but it becomes clearer in Luke how he saved as he moved toward Jerusalem. As Jesus approached Jerusalem he encountered Zacchaeus (Luke 19:1–10), and Jesus told him that the Son of Man had come to seek and to save the lost (19:10). Jesus was headed to Jerusalem when he encountered Zacchaeus (19:11), and the way that Jesus saved the lost was particularly by his death and resurrection. Jesus would soon die and rise again, as he had predicted and as Scripture itself prophesied (see 24:25–27, 44–47).

The Son of Man saves by suffering but also by rising from the dead. The glory of Christ that was anticipated in the transfiguration and manifested after his resurrection was the divine glory of the Son of Man who conquered death in redemptive history. As the Son of Man Jesus rules over an everlasting, glorious kingdom.

PROPHET, PRIEST, AND KING

THE THREEFOLD OFFICE OF JESUS (prophet, priest, and king) is amply attested in the Gospels. This correlates to his role as the last Adam, and even as the new Israel and true David. We have seen manifold ways that Jesus is the royal Son of David who ushers in the kingdom. More remains to be said about the ways that the Gospels present Jesus as prophet and priest—though we should remember that prophet, priest, and king are inseparably intertwined in Christ.

King

Prophet

JESUS IS A PROPHET WHO taught the word of God with authority. His use of parables was a prophetic mode of speech (משלים), which fulfilled prophecy (Ps 78:2; Matt 13:34–35).[63] In the Sermon on the Mount Jesus ascended a mountain and spoke in a way that recalled Moses' reception and giving of the law at Sinai, even as Jesus

62. I. Howard Marshall, *Luke: Historian and Theologian* (Grand Rapids: Zondervan, 1970), 92–93.

63. Compare Klyne R. Snodgrass, *Stories with Intent: A Comprehensive Guide to the Parables of Jesus* (Grand Rapids: Eerdmans, 2008), 37–42.

introduced a new era of redemptive history that was greater than Moses'.[64] Like the Old Testament prophets, Jesus showed the true intention of the law of God. Jesus's prophetic teaching fulfilled the expectation of a coming prophet like Moses to whom the people would listen (see Deut 18:15, 18; Luke 9:35)—and Moses himself listened to Jesus on the Mount of Transfiguration. As a prophet Jesus also predicted the future (e.g., Matt 24:29–31), and Jesus knew that he would be unjustly murdered, as were many prophets before him (see Matt 16:21; 23:29–36).

Further, Jesus's miracles function as signs (see especially John), like enacted parables utilized by Old Testament prophets. It is no wonder that many thought Jesus was Jeremiah, Elijah, or one of the prophets (Matt 16:14; Mark 8:28; Luke 9:19). Jesus was recognized by the people as a prophet mighty in word and deed (Luke 7:16; 24:19; see also John 6:14), who came (perhaps surprisingly) from Galilee (Matt 21:11; John 7:52). The people rightly recognized Jesus was a prophet (Matt 13:57; Luke 13:33), but were mistaken if they thought he was only a prophet. For Jesus outranks even the greatest prophet; he preexisted (and spoke) before any of them (John 1:15, 30).

Priest AS PRIEST, JESUS BORE OUR sins during his ministry as the suffering servant (Matt 8:17; Isa 53:4).[65] And already during his ministry Jesus forgave sins, which recalls the priestly work of making atonement, even as it also points to his divinity. Jesus was thus high priest not only in his sacrificial death but even during his ministry. His miracles were redemptive and restorative, which also corresponds to his priestly office.[66] When he healed a leper, the language used is priestly language for cleansing (Mark 1:40–42). Irenaeus speaks of the public ministry of Jesus in high priestly terms: "For He did not make void, but fulfilled the law, by performing the offices of the high priest, propitiating God for men, and cleansing the lepers, healing the sick, and Himself suffering death" (*Haer.*

64. See also Dale C. Allison Jr., *The New Moses: A Matthean Typology* (Minneapolis: Fortress, 1993), 172–80.

65. See Crowe, *Last Adam*, 145, citing Meier, *Vision of Matthew*, 69; Beale, *New Testament Biblical Theology*, 906.

66. See Herman Bavinck, *The Wonderful Works of God: Instruction in the Christian Religion according to the Reformed Confession*, trans. Henry Zylstra (repr., Philadelphia: Westminster Seminary Press, 2019), 325–27; see also Bavinck, *RD* 3:366

4.8.2).[67] Jesus's sacrificial, substitutionary death was also priestly, which is evoked by allusions to Isaiah 53 (see, e.g., Matt 20:28; Mark 10:45). Jesus is the sacrificial lamb of God who takes away the sin of the world (John 1:29). This may explain part of Jesus's rationale for clearing the temple of sacrificial animals in the Gospels (e.g., Mark 11:15–17)—he was showing that the final sacrifice had come, and the need for repetitive sacrifices was coming to an end.[68]

Jesus's high priesthood was also on display when he was led before the high priest Caiaphas when he was tried before the crucifixion. Caiaphas, who was but a shadow of what a true high priest should be, was brought face to face with the true high priest. This may remind readers of the magi's question to King Herod; the magi were most interested in where they could find the true king (Matt 2:2).

Another priestly theme—the temple—is the focus of Jesus's trial in the Gospels. Mark's Gospel makes it clear that Jesus's speech against the temple formed part of the basis for the accusations against him (Mark 14:58). Though this misconstrued what Jesus said, Jesus is indeed the true temple[69]—the means by which and in whom heaven and earth are brought together.[70] He is the substance of Jacob's ladder (John 1:51), for he is the way to the Father (John 14:6). In Christ is greater glory than the tabernacle or temple (John 1:14); indeed, this glory is seen—surprisingly—in the flesh, including in his work as the suffering servant. Jesus is the true temple from whom flow life-giving waters (John 7:37–38; see also 4:10, 14), as envisioned in Ezekiel's new temple (Ezek 47:1–12).[71] Jesus expressly identified his body as the temple that would be raised after three days (John 2:19–23).

---

67. Trans. *ANF* 1:471.

68. See David E. Garland, *A Theology of Mark's Gospel: Good News about Jesus the Messiah, the Son of God*, Biblical Theology of the New Testament (Grand Rapids: Zondervan, 2015), 491–93.

69. See Edmund P. Clowney, "The Final Temple," *WTJ* 35 (1973): 156–89; Beale, *Temple and the Church's Mission*.

70. See, e.g., Wright, *Jesus and the Victory of God*, 205.

71. See Bauckham, *Testimony of the Beloved Disciple*, 271–84. The one from whom the waters come in John 7:37–38 is most likely Jesus himself.

John 17

Commentators regularly note that historically, dating back at least to David Chytraeus (1530–1600) and perhaps to Cyril of Alexandria, many have seen the final prayer of Jesus in John 17 to be a high priestly prayer.[a] There are certainly echoes of priestly prayers in John 17:1–26, including language of sanctification (e.g., 17:17, 19), reference to his glorification (which includes his final sacrifice, 17:1), and the way that Jesus prayed concentrically for those nearer to him and those who were further off, which some have argued echoes the high priest's order of intercession on the Day of Atonement (Lev 16).[b] Even so, we need not oversimplify Jesus's final prayer and view it only through one lens; there is more here than only what a high priest would do.[c]

---

a. E.g., Edwyn Clement Hoskyns, *The Fourth Gospel*, ed. Francis Noel Davey (London: Faber and Faber, 1947), 494; Carson, *John*, 552–53; Ridderbos, *John*, 546; Keener, *John*, 1051; Barrett, *John*, 500; Oscar Cullmann, *The Christology of the New Testament*, rev. ed., trans. Shirley C. Guthrie and Charles A. M. Hall (Philadelphia: Westminster, 1963), 105–6.

b. See Sinclair B. Ferguson, *Lessons from the Upper Room: The Heart of the Savior* (Sanford, FL: Ligonier, 2021), 179–82.

c. This is noted even by many who suggest this is a high priestly prayer, such as Barrett, *John*, 500; see also Bavinck, *RD* 3:366.

Finally, Jesus's priesthood is seen in the way he pronounced blessings (Mark 10:16; Luke 18:15; compare Num 6:4–27). Luke ends with the risen Christ delivering a priestly blessing to his disciples as he ascends into heaven (Luke 24:50–53), which shows us that Christ's priestly work relates not only to his state of humiliation but also to his state of exaltation.

Jesus did not merely relive the three major offices of the Old Testament, prophet, priest, and king—he fulfilled them and united them in himself. The unity of the three offices in Jesus is helpfully seen in his miracles, which were kingly manifestations of the powerful inbreaking of the kingdom, prophetic signs that show the nature of that kingdom, and priestly in the way that they were restorative. Put differently, Jesus is greater than Jonah (prophet), the temple (priest), and Solomon (king; Matt 12:6, 41–42).[72]

---

72. Thanks to Josh Leim, who first pointed me to this.

This threefold office (*munus triplex*) became standard fare for theological discourse in explaining the work of Christ early in the Christian tradition, evident already from the days of Eusebius (*Hist. eccl.* 1.3).[73] For example, Turretin finds in John 14:6 the *munus triplex* in short scope:

> Thus in the New Testament these three offices are often joined together as in Jn. 14:6 when Christ is said to be "the way, the truth, and the life"—the Way leading, the Truth teaching, the Life saving. The Way in his priesthood, when by his own blood he opened a way for us to heaven (Heb. 10:20); the Truth in his prophetic office because he reveals to us the word of the gospel, the only saving truth; the Life in his kingly office by which he quickens and protects us through his efficacy; the Way in death, the Truth in the word, Life in the spirit.[74]

NEW EXODUS

The Gospels narrate the coming of the expected new exodus in a variety of ways. Jesus saved his people from their sins by leading them to the lasting deliverance from spiritual bondage that was anticipated in the original exodus. He delivered not only from political entities but from the oppression of sin and death, and he established a new covenant on the basis of his own obedience, sealed with his blood. It will never be broken.

The new exodus motif is evident in Matthew's genealogy (Matt 1:2–17). This list of royal figures, organized as three sets of fourteen (1:17), is a selective and theologically organized summary of Israel's history that focuses on the kingship, exile, and restoration in Jesus.[75] Matthew opens by showing readers how Christ's birth marked the end of Israel's spiritual exile and the beginning of a new era of the kingdom. The exile is again recalled in the lament over the children murdered at Bethlehem (Matt 2:18; see Jer 31:15). The weeping of Rachel for her children at Ramah refers to the nation's entering exile.[76] Jesus's providential deliverance from this pogrom enabled him to save his people from their sins (Matt 1:21) and lead them

73. See, e.g., Bavinck, *RD* 3:341, Vos, *Reformed Dogmatics* 3:87.
74. Turretin, *Inst.* 14.5.7 (2:393).
75. See Hays, *Echoes of Scripture in the Gospels*, 109–14.
76. See France, *Matthew*, 87.

on a new exodus. This is further reflected in his baptism in the Jordan and his temptation in the wilderness.[77] For as the first exodus God's Son was led through the waters into the wilderness before entering the promised land, in the new exodus the pioneer of salvation was proclaimed as Son in his baptism, passed through the waters, and entered the wilderness, on the way to establishing final salvation.[78]

Mark also begins with a new exodus, combining three Old Testament texts in 1:2–3 (Exod 23:20; Isa 40:3; Mal 3:1):[79] "As it is written in Isaiah the prophet, 'Behold, I send my messenger before your face, who will prepare your way, the voice of one crying in the wilderness: "Prepare the way of the Lord, make his paths straight."'" That Mark identifies this compound citation as coming simply from Isaiah highlights the Isaianic context for the new exodus.[80] Mark thus opens with a word of both warning and hope: warning that the Lord is coming to his temple like a refiner's fire, and so repentance is necessary (Mal 3:1); hope that the Lord's coming will coincide with the long-anticipated new exodus. Isaiah 40:3, used for John the Baptist's ministry in all four Gospels, speaks of the promise of the lasting salvation that will come when God comforts his people, delivering them from their bondage. A highway will be opened for the people to return to the promised land. Thus, John the Baptist is "the forerunner of a new entry into the land of promise,"[81] and Jesus is the Lord who comes to his temple. John prepares the way for the Lord (Isa 40:3) by preparing the way for Jesus. In this way, Mark's new exodus attests to the divinity of Christ. As Craig Keener argues, Mark is similar to John in this respect: "Mark also believes Jesus is deity: his reapplication of the 'Lord' of Isa 40:3 to Jesus (Mark 1:3) can be understood in no other way."[82]

---

77. See also Sinclair B. Ferguson, *The Holy Spirit*, CCT (Downers Grove, IL: InterVarsity, 1996), 40.

78. Compare, e.g., Davies and Allison, *Matthew* 1:328; Wright, *Jesus and the Victory of God*, 168, 437, 577, *et passim.*

79. See esp. Rikki E. Watts, *Isaiah's New Exodus and Mark*, WUNT 2/88 (Tübingen: Mohr Siebeck, 1997), 53–90.

80. Watts, *Isaiah's New Exodus*, 88–90; Marcus, *Way of the Lord*, 18–20; Hays, *Echoes of Scripture in the Gospels*, 21.

81. Hays, *Echoes of Scripture in the Gospels*, 23.

82. Keener, *John*, 305.

In Luke Jesus quotes Isaiah 61:1–2 at the outset of his ministry (Luke 4:17–19), which likewise anticipates the eschatological new exodus. Jesus came to announce good news, which includes liberty for the captives. This language echoes the original exodus and also the freedom for slaves in the Year of Jubilee (Lev 25). But the freedom is more than only physical freedom from servitude; it is holistic freedom that includes freedom from sin. This freedom is also a freedom from the effects of sin, including the recovering of sight for the blind. This was fulfilled through the literal restoration of sight throughout Jesus's ministry, which served a sign of the need for spiritual sight. This is especially clear in Mark 8:22–26, where the two-staged healing of the blind man serves as an enacted parable illustrating the need even for Jesus's disciples to have greater spiritual understanding.[83] Yet these miracles were also ways that the dominion of sin was overcome and the reign of God established.

Jesus's role in bringing the eschatological new exodus, especially through his mighty works in his ministry, is seen especially in the feeding of five thousand in the wilderness. When Jesus explained the significance of what he had done in John 6, he pointed specifically to the role of the bread in pointing to himself—the bread of life, the true manna come down from heaven (John 6:30–40, 48–50, 53–58). This recalls the provision of bread given to the exodus generation and shows that a greater work of God was accomplished through and focused on Christ himself. The new exodus inaugurated by Jesus was also evident when the messengers of John the Baptist came to Jesus to ask whether he was the Messiah (Matt 11:3; Luke 7:19), as discussed earlier. Here I note that Jesus alludes to the vision of eschatological restoration from Isaiah 35, which is new exodus language. For where the blind, deaf, and lame are healed, there will be a way of holiness opened up—a path for the redeemed who are marching to Zion (Isa 35:8–10). The Lord will come to save his people (35:4), which is realized through the mighty coming of Jesus of Nazareth. He brought restoration and salvation in his earthly ministry, in anticipation of and in continuity with the full, final restoration that will occur when the kingdom is consummated.

83. See Marcus, *Mark 8–16*, 599–600.

If much of Jesus's ministry can be viewed in terms of leading a new exodus, this is particularly true of his death and resurrection. On the Mount of Transfiguration in Luke, Jesus spoke with Elijah and Moses specifically about his exodus (ἔξοδος), which he was about to accomplish in Jerusalem (Luke 9:31). This language could refer simply to one's death or departure (2 Pet 1:15),[84] but coupled with mention of Moses and Elijah, Jesus's exodus surely elicits memory of the first exodus, invokes the eschatological hopes of the future salvation, and portrays the climactic actions of Jesus in Jerusalem as a new exodus.[85] This term also entails Jesus's resurrection and ascension. For later in Luke Jesus explains that it was necessary to be raised from the dead to accomplish salvation, and at the end of Luke Jesus's departure comes by means of his ascension.[86]

As we saw in chapter 1, the exodus also highlights God's provision to take away sin. Jesus willingly and intentionally laid down his life as the final sacrifice for sin. Jesus's actions and words of institution at the Last Supper, itself a Passover meal, recalled the words celebrated at the time of Passover and the divine deliverance in the exodus. On a likely reconstruction, the four cups of wine at the dinner recalled the exodus (see Exod 6:6–7), and Jesus related his own death to the third cup, which symbolized deliverance.[87] Regardless, Jesus identified the wine at the supper with his blood, which was poured out for many for the forgiveness of sins (Matt 26:28; Mark 14:24; Luke 22:20). Jesus spoke of his own blood in covenantal terms, recalling also the cleansing blood sprinkled in Exodus 24:6–8 at Mount Sinai. The blood poured out for "many" in Matthew and Mark recalls Jesus's earlier statements about his life serving as a ransom for many (Matt 20:28; Mark 10:45), thus relating Jesus's death to the suffering servant of Isaiah 53.

After dinner, in John, Jesus portrays himself as a Servant, and the water he uses when he washes his disciples' feet most likely denotes the

84. See BDAG, "ἔξοδος," 350–51.

85. See also Heb 11:22, where ἔξοδος refers to the event of the exodus.

86. See, e.g., David E. Garland, *Luke*, ZECNT (Grand Rapids: Zondervan, 2011), 393–94.

87. See, e.g., Joachim Jeremias, *The Eucharistic Words of Jesus*, trans. Arnold Ehrhardt (Oxford: Basil Blackwell, 1955), 34–35; Lane, *Mark*, 506–9.

cleansing that he brings.[88] Jesus spoke of himself as the way, the truth, and the life. Much as we saw from Isaiah 35; 40, the language of "way" most likely denotes the way of the eschatological new exodus that Jesus accomplished in his glorification, which in John includes Jesus's death/resurrection/ascension.[89] Especially clear in John are the exodus contours of Jesus's death as a Passover sacrifice. The timing of the Passover in John is an area of perpetual debate, but John's timing likely highlights Jesus himself as the Passover lamb (see, e.g., John 19:14, 36).[90] John writes that Jesus's bones were not broken on the cross, which fulfills the symbolism of the Passover lamb, whose bones were not broken (Exod 12:46; John 19:36). John may even include an exodus inclusio, identifying Jesus as the Passover lamb in both 1:29 and 19:36 in a way that brackets the narrative.[91]

The blood of Jesus sealed the new covenant in his blood; yet this final salvation was not complete apart from his entrance into the state of glory, commencing with his resurrection from the dead. This too—as we have seen—was his exodus. For it is not just one or two aspects of Jesus's work that save us; it is his entire, unified work that brings eschatological salvation.

CONCLUSION

As christological narratives, the Gospels provide distinctive windows into the person and work of Christ. Though many christological points are explained in more detail by other biblical writers, we dare not downplay the theological voice of the Gospels themselves. In the Gospels we come face to face with Christ himself but also with our call to commitment. As with Christology more broadly, the Gospels are not given for esoteric theology but for practical discipleship.

88. See, e.g., Carson, *John*, 458–59. On Jesus portraying himself as a servant, I am especially indebted to Ferguson, *Lessons from the Upper Room*, 3–19.

89. See also Keener, *John*, 940–41.

90. See Carson, *John*, 603–5, 627; Keener, *John*, 1130–31, 1156; Brown, *John* 2:883.

91. So Morales, *Exodus Old and New*, 162–64.

FURTHER READING

Bauckham, Richard. *God Crucified: Monotheism and Christology in the New Testament*. Grand Rapids: Eerdmans, 1999. This short but significantly influential work argues that Jesus shares the unique identity of the one God of Israel. Bauckham seeks to move beyond the misleading distinction between "functional" and "ontic" christological discussions that has too often plagued New Testament scholarship (see page 41).

Cullmann, Oscar. *The Christology of the New Testament*. Rev. ed. Translated by Shirley C. Guthrie and Charles A. M. Hall. Philadelphia: Westminster, 1963. A classic study of Christology by titles from the mid-twentieth century; despite some limitations, it remains valuable. Cullmann argues for the centrality of the suffering servant, and vicarious suffering, for New Testament Christology.

Grindheim, Sigurd. *Christology in the Synoptic Gospels: God or God's Servant?* London: T&T Clark, 2012. In this student-friendly resource, Grindheim argues that the presentation of Jesus in the Synoptic Gospels ultimately agrees with the theology expressed in the Nicene Creed.

Ratzinger, Joseph [Pope Benedict XVI]. *Jesus of Nazareth: From the Baptism in the Jordan to the Transfiguration*. Translated by Adrian J. Walker. London: Bloomsbury, 2007. The first of three volumes on Jesus written by the former pope, who did not consider this to be a work of the magisterium but his own "personal search 'for the face of the Lord'" (xxiii), this book wrestles with the limits of historical-critical scholarship when speaking of Jesus. It is a valuable study of the opening stages of Jesus's ministry, written from a Roman Catholic perspective. Another Roman Catholic approach that questions the value of historical-critical research is Thomas G. Weinandy, *Jesus Becoming Jesus: A Theological Interpretation of the Synoptic Gospels* (Washington, DC: Catholic University of America Press, 2018).

Warfield, Benjamin Breckinridge. "The Emotional Life of Our Lord." Pages 91–145 in *The Person and Work of Christ*. Edited by Samuel G. Craig. Philadelphia: Presbyterian and Reformed, 1950. Warfield's classic study on the presentation of Christ in the Gospels particularly focuses on Christ's emotions.

IV

THE SON OF GOD IN ACTS AND PAUL'S LETTERS

BOTH LORD AND CHRIST

ACTS AND THE THIRTEEN PAULINE epistles provide distinctive emphases that help us construct a fuller picture of the person and work of Christ. Acts focuses on the continuing work of Christ in his state of exaltation—Jesus is both Lord and Christ (Acts 2:36). Paul's Christology is likewise multifaceted and is central to his letters. Both Paul and Acts speak of Jesus as the Messiah promised in the Old Testament and also as the divine Son of God. Jesus is the God-man whose work alone is sufficient for salvation.

THE PERSON AND WORK OF CHRIST IN ACTS

THE ACTS OF THE APOSTLES, Luke's second volume, speaks of all that Jesus continued to do and teach (see Acts 1:1). Though Jesus ascends into heaven in the first few verses, he continues to guide his church in Acts, and the apostolic preaching focuses preeminently on Christ himself. In what follows we will look at what Acts contributes to Christology, which is quite significant.

"Both Lord and Christ"

DISTINCTIVE TO ACTS'S CHRISTOLOGY IS the discussion of Jesus's ongoing work in the state of glory.[1] That is, Acts gives much attention to the resurrection, ascension, heavenly session at the right hand of God, and future return. The resurrection and its scriptural logic are narrated with much less prolixity in the Gospels; they are expounded to a greater degree in Acts. Acts opens with the resurrected Jesus meeting with his disciples, showing himself with many (resurrection) proofs, and speaking about the kingdom of God (1:3). Throughout Acts one finds a close relationship between the resurrection of Jesus and the firm, permanent establishment of the kingdom of God.

In Peter's Pentecost sermon (2:14–36), he explains the outpouring of the Holy Spirit in christological fashion: the Spirit has been poured out because Jesus of Nazareth, who was crucified, has been raised and exalted to God's right hand. Jesus is the Messiah predicted by David (see 2:30), who reigns from heaven and pours out the Holy Spirit. Jesus is the greater Son of David, who, unlike David, was not left in the grave, nor did his body see corruption. Indeed, by means of his resurrection and exaltation the greater Son of David rules over an everlasting kingdom, fulfilling the Davidic covenant promise of 2 Samuel 7:12–13. As the true Son of David, Jesus of Nazareth is both Lord and Christ (Acts 2:36). Elsewhere Peter emphasizes that the same Jesus who was known for his Spirit-empowered miracle working is actually Lord of all (10:36–38). As Christ (that is, Messiah), Jesus is the true Son of David. As Lord, Jesus has completed his work of humiliation and entered into his state of glory. The title "Lord" thus highlights Jesus's exaltation, and this is discussed with particular clarity in Acts.

Likewise, Paul speaks of the real death of Jesus and his exaltation to the right hand of God (esp. 13:30–37). Key for Paul was his encounter with the risen Jesus (recounted three times in Acts), which demonstrated that Jesus was not irreversibly cursed (see Deut 21:23), but is the blessed one of God, evident in his resurrection to glorious life. Through Jesus's resurrection the fallen kingdom of David is restored (15:15–18; see also Amos 9:11–12) and the people are reunited under one king, fulfilling Ezekiel 37. By means of his exaltation Jesus rules over a kingdom that will last forever, consummating in the restoration of all things (Acts 3:20–21; see also 1:6). In these ways we see again that Jesus is both Lord and Christ.

---

1. For fuller discussion and bibliography, see Crowe, *Hope of Israel*.

Acts also speaks of Jesus as the supernatural Son of God. This is assumed in many ways throughout Acts, but receives attention in Paul's sermon at Pisidian Antioch in Acts 13. In 13:33 Paul applies Psalm 2:7 ("You are my Son; today I have begotten you") primarily to the resurrection of Jesus and thus to the accomplishment of salvation. Even so, the sonship in view here is more than only messianic sonship; it is preexistent, divine sonship on which the particularities of messianic sonship are predicated.[2] This is consistent with Luke's preexistent, divine sonship mentioned elsewhere (Luke 1:78; 3:22; 9:35; 10:21–22; 20:41–44) and with the other New Testament texts (see, e.g., Heb 1:5). In sum, the "today" of Acts 13:33 speaks to the accomplishment of salvation—to the day in which the divine Son of God is enthroned as resurrected, victorious king of glory.[3]

Acts 20:28

Historically, many have taken Acts 20:28 as a prominent prooftext for the divinity of Jesus. This is quite possible, but involves a complex text-critical question that is not easily resolved. The key portion of the Nestle-Aland Greek text reads: ποιμαίνειν τὴν ἐκκλησίαν τοῦ θεοῦ, ἣν περιεποιήσατο διὰ τοῦ αἵματος τοῦ ἰδίου ("to care for the church of God, which he obtained with his own blood"). Two key issues must be addressed. First, should the underlined portion of the text read τοῦ θεοῦ ("of God")? Or is another reading correct, such as τοῦ κυρίου ("of the Lord") or (less likely) τοῦ κυρίου καὶ θεοῦ ("of the Lord and God")? Second, does this debated phrase attach primarily to "church" or "blood"? That is, does Paul speak first of the *church* of God/Lord? Or does Paul speak first of the *blood* of God/Lord?

The most likely textual reading is reflected in the Nestle-Aland text (τοῦ θεοῦ="of God"). However, this may not be a reference to Jesus as θεός. It depends on whose blood is intended in the next phrase. The traditional interpretation understands "his own blood" to refer back to God, and therefore to Jesus as God, since God the Father was not incarnate and did not shed blood. Yet on balance it is more likely that a different divine person is in view in the latter phrase of this verse. A key issue must be addressed here: What does Paul mean by the phrase διὰ τοῦ αἵματος τοῦ ἰδίου? Does τοῦ ἰδίου refer to

2. Crowe, *Hope of Israel*, 60.
3. Crowe, *Hope of Israel*, 61.

God's *own* blood (thereby referring to Jesus as God)? Or is τοῦ ἰδίου a christological title for Jesus? (i.e., "the blood of God's Own [Son]")? This latter option, which understands ὁ ἴδιος as a christological title, maintains a distinction in the text between God (the Father) and Jesus (God's Own [Son]). A decision is difficult, though the latter option is more likely. This yields the translation "the church of God, which he bought with the blood of his Own [Son]."[a] If so, then Acts 20:28 would turn out to be an explicitly Trinitarian text: God, the Son, and the Spirit would all be mentioned.[b] However, we must admit this is a difficult exegetical question. Thankfully, establishing the divinity of Jesus does not rest on this text.

a. In favor of "his Own" as a christological title, see Rom 8:3; Diogn. 9.2; Rouven Genz, *Jesaja 53 als theologische Mitte der Apostelgeschichte: Studien zur ihrer Christologie und Ekklesiologie im Anschluss an Apg 8,26–40*, WUNT 2/398 (Tübingen: Mohr Siebeck, 2015), 296; Murray J. Harris, *Jesus as God: The New Testament Use of Theos in Reference to Jesus* (Grand Rapids: Baker, 1992), 139–41; Larry W. Hurtado, "Christology in Acts: Jesus in Early Christian Belief and Practice," in *Issues in Luke-Acts: Selected Essays*, ed. Sean A. Adams and Michael W. Pahl, Gorgias Handbooks 26 (Piscataway, NJ: Gorgias, 2013), 223n17. Also favorable to this option are Ben Witherington III, *The Acts of the Apostles: A Socio-Rhetorical Commentary* (Grand Rapids: Eerdmans, 1998), 623; Raymond E. Brown, *An Introduction to New Testament Christology* (New York: Paulist, 1994), 178. Alternatively, see Heb 9:12.

b. Alan J. Thompson, "The Trinity and Luke-Acts," in Crowe and Trueman, *Essential Trinity*, 80–81.

Further, divine sonship is seen in Acts where Jesus is identified as the Lord of the Old Testament who grants salvation. Peter quotes from Joel 2:28–32 in his Pentecost sermon, invoking the theological truth that everyone who calls on the name of the Lord shall be saved (Acts 2:21). In the context of Acts, the Lord of Joel 2 is Jesus of Nazareth, on whom we call for salvation. Jesus is also the Savior (Acts 5:31; 13:23; see also Luke 19:10), a title reserved for God alone in Isaiah (e.g., Isa 43:11; 45:21). Indeed, there is no other name under heaven by which we must be saved (Acts 4:12). This is a remarkable statement of exclusivity; there is no other means of salvation apart from Christ for any person who has ever lived. At the Jerusalem Council Peter attributes our salvation to the grace of the Lord Jesus Christ (15:11)—probably focusing on Old Testament believers.[4] Elsewhere Peter

4. See Calvin, *Commentary upon the Acts* 2:58–60; Calvin, *Inst.* 3.5.4; cf. 2.10.23; Turretin, *Inst.* 12.5.11 (2:195–96); cf. 11.23.10 (2:144); 11.24.14 (2:150); 12.5.9 (2:195); 12.7.36 (2:228–29); 17.2.16 (2:699); Bavinck, *RD* 3:223; 4:105; Mastricht, *Theoretical-Practical Theology*

speaks of Christ as the focus of the Old Testament prophets, the one in whose name forgiveness of sins is offered (10:43). The divinity of Christ is probably also in view in the account of the Philippian jailer, who was saved by believing in Jesus (16:31), and later it is stated that he had believed in God (16:34).

Other Christological Contributions of Acts

THE CHRISTOLOGY OF ACTS EMPHASIZES the messianic sonship and lordship of Jesus; but the christological portrait of Acts is richer yet. When explaining the healing of the lame man in Jerusalem, Peter spoke of Jesus as the exalted servant of the Lord (3:13, 26), recalling the exaltation of the Servant in Isaiah 52:13.[5] This Jesus, who has been glorified, will come again (Acts 3:19–21; see 1:11). Similarly, Philip the evangelist explained to the Ethiopian eunuch that Jesus was the suffering servant of Isaiah 53:7–8 (Acts 8:30–35).[6]

Acts also speaks twice of Jesus as the ἀρχηγός, both times in relation to his resurrection (3:15; 5:31). This Greek term is notoriously difficult to translate. Some examples include Author (so ESV in 3:15), Leader (so ESV in 5:20), Pioneer, Founder, Forerunner, Prince, Ruler, Originator, and Champion.[7] Whatever English term one chooses, ἀρχηγός communicates that Jesus is the one who goes before, as one with authority, and stands in

---

1:158. See further discussions in C. K. Barrett, *A Critical and Exegetical Commentary on the Acts of the Apostles*, ICC (Edinburgh: T&T Clark, 1994–98), 2:720; Guy Prentiss Waters, *A Study Commentary on the Acts of the Apostles*, EP Study Commentary (Pistyll, Holywell, UK: Evangelical Press, 2015), 357

5. So, e.g., David G. Peterson, The *Acts of the Apostles*, PNTC (Grand Rapids: Eerdmans, 2009), 174; Eckhard J. Schnabel, *Acts*, ZECNT (Grand Rapids: Zondervan, 2012), 208; André Wénin, "Enracinement vétérotestamentaire du discours sur la résurrection de Jésus dans le Nouveau Testament," in *Resurrection of the Dead: Biblical Traditions in Dialogue*, ed. Geert Van Yen and Tom Shepherd, Bibliotheca Ephemeridum Theologicarum Lovaniensium 249 (Leuven: Peeters, 2012), 9–11. This speech is marked by a παῖς ("servant") inclusio in 3:13, 26.

6. See Genz, *Jesaja* 53, e.g., 123.

7. For discussions, see Paul-Gerhard Müller, ΧΡΙΣΤΟΣ ΑΡΧΗΓΟΣ: *Die religionsgeschichtliche und theologische Hintergrund einer neutestamentlichen Christusprädikation*, Europäische Hochschulschriften: Reihe 23, Theologie 28 (Bern: Lang; Frankfurt: Lang, 1973); Craig S. Keener, *Acts: An Exegetical Commentary*, 4 vols. (Grand Rapids: Baker Academic, 2012–2015), 2:1097–99; Paul Ellingworth, *The Epistle to the Hebrews*, NIGTC (Grand Rapids: Eerdmans, 1993), 159; William L. Lane, *Hebrews 1–8*, WBC 47A (Nashville: Thomas Nelson, 1991), 56–57.

solidarity with his people.[8] This concept may also allude to the new exodus that Jesus brings: as our ἀρχηγός, Jesus goes before us, through death and resurrection, to prepare the way (John 14:6) and accomplish final redemption.[9] He is the Savior (Acts 5:31). Jesus as ἀρχηγός is thus closely tethered to the authority he has over life (3:15). His resurrection also proves him to be the Holy and Righteous One (3:14; see also Luke 23:47; Acts 7:52; 22:14).[10] Indeed, "this Life" (τῆς ζωῆς ταύτης) might even be used as a christological title in Acts 5:20 (see John 11:25; 1 John 1:1–2).[11]

Building on the Adam Christology of Luke, Acts also presents Jesus as the glorious, resurrected, last Adam who has authority over all humanity. This comes into view before the Areopagus in Athens. In Acts 17:26 Paul introduces a likely allusion to Adam, and his argument assumes the fundamental unity of humanity: just as all people have a common source, so all people have a common judge, who is Jesus of Nazareth, the one resurrected with all authority in heaven and on earth (17:30–31; see also 10:42). Paul proclaimed this in the midst of a trial; it was thus a remarkable turning of the tables to tell his judges that they would themselves be judged by Jesus, the Lord over all (10:36; see also 17:7).

Prophet, Priest, King

ACTS ALSO ATTESTS THE THREEFOLD office of Christ as prophet, priest, and king. Much of the attention in Acts is on kingship. Jesus is the true Son of David—the Christ—who reigns over an everlasting kingdom and over all nations. This correlates also to the strong emphasis on the kingdom throughout Acts, including a kingdom *inclusio* (1:3, 6; 28:30–31).[12]

---

8. On this point, see Geerhardus Vos, "The Priesthood of Christ in the Epistle to the Hebrews," in Gaffin, *Redemptive History and Biblical Interpretation*, 133.

9. The early disciples' being described as followers of "the Way" (ὁ ὁδός; e.g., Acts 9:2) raises the possibility that a new exodus theme was part of the self-awareness of early Christians. See also the discussion of Keener, *Acts* 2:1626–27.

10. See Crowe, *Hope of Israel*, 31–32.

11. Cf. Joseph A. Fitzmyer, *The Acts of the Apostles: A New Translation with Introduction and Commentary*, AB 31 (New York: Doubleday, 1998), 9, 335; R. B. Rackham, *The Acts of the Apostles: An Exposition*, 11th ed., Westminster Commentaries (London: Methuen, 1930), 72. But see Acts 13:26.

12. See Alan J. Thompson, *The Acts of the Risen Lord Jesus: Luke's Account of God's Unfolding Plan*, NSBT 27 (Downers Grove, IL: InterVarsity Press, 2011), 44–48.

Acts also speaks to the prophethood of Christ. In Acts David is explicitly said to be a prophet (Acts 2:30), and as the greater Son of David we can be sure that the words he speaks are true and powerful. Not only are the words he spoke in Luke proven to be true (see Luke 24:44–47), but his speech in his state of exaltation is true, and by this speech he guides his church (Acts 9:4–5, 10–16; 22:17–18, 21; see also 1:24–26). Jesus is the fulfillment of the prophet like Moses from Deuteronomy 18:15, 18 (Acts 3:22–23; see also Luke 9:35).

As priest, Jesus is the substitutionary, suffering servant given for the sins of his people (Isa 53:7–8; Acts 8:32–33). Jesus is also the goal of the temple. This is one of the main emphases of Stephen's speech in Acts 7: the people were wrong to cling to the physical temple as though it were the final work of God. God had never been limited to one place, but the temple pointed forward to the coming of Christ, the true, mediating presence of God with his people. All that the temple was designed to communicate is fulfilled in Christ. To cling to the old ways, now that Christ has come, would be idolatry (note "made with hands" in 7:48, which denotes idolatry). Similar logic about the church as the temple is apparent at Pentecost, where the Spirit was poured out on all of God's people to empower them for service.[13] This itself was a christological reality (since it correlates to the exaltation of Christ in the heavenly temple) and corresponds to the move away from the earthly temple in Jerusalem (see also Acts 15:16–18). No longer is the physical temple central to worship; Jesus himself is the locus of worship.[14]

Conclusion to Acts

Acts presents Jesus of Nazareth as the preexistent, divine Son of God who has conquered sin and death and brings salvation. He is the risen and exalted prophet, priest, and king with authority over all people.

It would be mistaken, therefore, to conclude that "there is in Acts no profound christological thought."[15] Instead, Acts provides us crucial information for understanding Christ's person, earthly work, and his state of glory.

---

13. See especially G. K. Beale, "The Descent of the Eschatological Temple in the Form of the Spirit at Pentecost, Part 1: The Clearest Evidence," *TynBul* 56 (2005): 73–102.

14. See also Beale, *Temple and the Church's Mission*, 233–36.

15. Barrett, *Acts*, 2:lxxxvii.

THE PERSON AND WORK OF CHRIST IN PAUL'S LETTERS

Few biblical authors are as important for understanding the person and work of Christ as Paul. More than any other author Paul explains the gospel, the nature of salvation history, and the person and work of Christ. Paul understood Jesus Christ to be the eternal Son of God who accomplished eschatological salvation in his incarnate state, inaugurating the resurrection era dominated by the Spirit. He now reigns at God's right hand and will return in judgment and to consummate the kingdom of God.

1 Corinthians 15

Paul sets out the contours of the gospel he preached in 1 Corinthians 15:1–5:

> Now I would remind you, brothers, of the gospel I preached to you, which you received, in which you stand, and by which you are being saved, if you hold fast to the word I preached to you—unless you believed in vain. For I delivered to you as of first importance what I also received: that Christ died for our sins in accordance with the Scriptures, that he was buried, that he was raised on the third day in accordance with the Scriptures, and that he appeared to Cephas, then to the twelve.

The gospel centers on the person and work of Jesus Christ. It is a message about objective, historical events (see also HC 22–23). This summary reminds us of Jesus's own words that the Messiah must suffer, die, and rise, and this message would go forth in his name (Luke 24:44–47). We benefit from this message by faith, as the similar discussion in 2 Thessalonians 2:13–15 also makes clear. By faith in this message—faith in the Christ and his work for us—we stand and are saved. Faith looks away from ourselves and our own works to the One whose work alone is sufficient to save us. Even so, 1 Corinthians 15:1–4 provides only a summary of the gospel message; other texts fill out the contours of this gospel with more detail, such as Paul's sermon at Pisidian Antioch (Acts 13:16–41) and his fuller expositions of the gospel in his letters, such as in Romans (Rom 1:16; 2:16), Galatians (see Gal 1:6–9), Ephesians (Eph 3:7), 1–2 Timothy, and Titus.

The Gospel and Redemptive History

Paul's gospel summary in 1 Corinthians 15, in combination with what he says elsewhere (including later in 1 Cor 15:21–28, 45–49), highlights various aspects of the person and work of Christ. The gospel deals with the death of Christ (1 Cor 1:17–25) and the acceptance of that message by faith, resulting in righteousness (Rom 1:16–17). Paul's gospel also includes the conviction that Christ, who has been resurrected (2 Tim 2:8), is coming again as judge (Rom 2:16; 2 Thess 1:5–10).

Paul's summary statements provide orientations for his fuller expositions of the gospel; the concept of the gospel is quite often present even where the term "gospel" (εὐαγγέλιον) is not used explicitly. Paul speaks of the true incarnation and humanity of the Son (Rom 1:3; 8:3; Gal 4:4; Eph 4:9–10; 1 Tim 3:16), his life of obedience under the law (Rom 5:18–19; Gal 4:4–5), his inauguration of the eschatological kingdom of God (Rom 14:17; 1 Cor 4:20; 6:9–10; 15:24; Col 1:13),[16] his death (e.g., Rom 5:6–10; 2 Cor 5:17–21; Gal 2:20; 3:13; Phil 2:6–8; Col 2:13; 1 Tim 6:13), his resurrection (Rom 1:4; 1 Cor 15:42–49; Eph 1:20; Phil 2:9; Col 1:18; 1 Tim 3:16), his ascension and present reign (Eph 1:20–23; 4:7–10; Phil 2:9–11; 1 Tim 3:16), and his future return in glory (Rom 13:11; 14:9; 2 Cor 5:10; Phil 1:6; 3:20; Col 3:4; 1 Thess 1:10; 4:13–18; 2 Thess 2:1; 2 Tim 4:1, 18). These events form the backbone of Paul's gospel and call for the response of faith, as we are also called to live in a way worthy of the gospel (Phil 1:27)—a way that accords with the mystery of godliness (1 Tim 6:3; Titus 1:1; see also 1 Tim 3:16).

Another key passage in which Paul speaks about the gospel is Romans 1:1–4:

> Paul, a servant of Christ Jesus, called to be an apostle, set apart for the gospel of God, which he promised beforehand through his prophets in the holy Scriptures, concerning his Son, who was descended from David according to the flesh and was declared to be the Son of God in power according to the Spirit of holiness by his resurrection from the dead, Jesus Christ our Lord.

---

16. On kingdom in Paul, see Douglas J. Moo, *The Letters to the Colossians and Philemon*, PNTC (Grand Rapids: Eerdmans, 2008), 104–5; cf. Herman N. Ridderbos, *When the Time Had Fully Come: Studies in New Testament Theology* (repr., Jordan Station, ON: Paideia, 1982), 48–49: "Paul does nothing but explain the eschatological reality which in Christ's teachings is called the Kingdom."

The gospel was promised beforehand by the prophets and fully accords with the Old Testament. Paul also assumes the preexistent, divine sonship of Jesus Christ: the Son of God, existing prior to the incarnation, was descended from David according to the flesh. Clearly in view as well is the true humanity of Jesus Christ.

Historically, many have seen further reference to the divinity of Christ in the phrase "Son of God in power according to the Spirit of holiness."[17] While this is possible, it is better to understand Paul as referring to two ages here, which hinge on Christ himself.[18] The first age is one of anticipation and humiliation: the age "according to the flesh." The term "flesh" in Paul often refers to the old era.[19] In contrast, "declared to be the Son of God in power according to the Spirit of holiness by his resurrection from the dead" refers to age defined by the resurrection of Christ, which is also the age of the Holy Spirit.[20] Paul often refers to these two ages: this present age, which continues to be characterized by sin (1 Cor 2:6, 8; Gal 1:4; Eph 1:21; 2:1–2; 1 Tim 6:17; 2 Tim 4:10; Titus 2:12), and the new age of fulfillment, glory, and revelation (1 Cor 2:7; 2 Cor 3:7–18; Eph 3:1–13; Col 1:26–27; 2 Tim 4:18; Titus 2:13). Christ's resurrection marks his transition from the state of humiliation to the state of glory, resulting in the dawning of this new age.

---

17. See Turretin, *Inst.* 13.6.16 (2:315); see also 13.15.12 (2:360); 13.17.4 (2:365).

18. See, e.g., Geerhardus Vos, "Paul's Eschatological Concept of the Spirit," in Gaffin, *Redemptive History and Biblical Interpretation*, 104–5; Richard B. Gaffin Jr., *The Centrality of the Resurrection: A Study in Paul's Soteriology*, Baker Biblical Monograph (Grand Rapids: Baker 1978), 98–113; Ferguson, *Holy Spirit*, 105; see also Bavinck, *RD* 3:293, 300.

19. Herman Ridderbos, *Paul: An Outline of His Theology*, trans. John Richard De Witt (Grand Rapids: Eerdmans, 1975), 66–67.

20. Vos, "Eschatological Aspect," 100–125.

The Person of Christ in Paul's Letters

Son of God and Messiah

Two emphases that stand out in Paul's multifaceted Christology are Jesus as Son and Lord. "Son (of God)" is a multifaceted term for Paul. It includes Jesus's role as the Messiah, the Son of David. Yet Paul also understands Jesus to be the divine, preexistent Son of God. We can label these two lenses as (1) redemptive-historical sonship ("Christ") and (2) divine sonship. I will begin with divine sonship, since it is foundational to understanding redemptive-historical sonship.

1. Divine sonship. Jesus is the preexistent, divine Son of God. Preexistence undergirds many of Paul's arguments. For example, in addition to Romans 1:3–4, in Philippians 2:6–8 Christ, who emptied himself in the incarnation, is said to have existed already in the form of God (ἐν μορφῇ θεοῦ ὑπάρχων). This potentially ambiguous phrase "in the form of God" is clarified as "being equal to God" (τὸ εἶναι ἴσα θεῷ) in 2:6.[21] Similarly, preexistence is foundational for 2 Corinthians 8:9: Jesus is the one who, though rich, became poor for our sake that we might become rich in him. Christ, the Son of God, was already active in the old covenant, as Paul explains in 1 Corinthians 10:4: Christ was the Rock that followed the wilderness generation of the Israelites.[22]

Further discussion of preexistent, divine sonship is found in Colossians 1:15–20—certainly one of Paul's most important christological statements:

> He is the image of the invisible God, the firstborn of all creation. For by him all things were created, in heaven and on earth, visible and invisible, whether thrones or dominions or rulers or authorities—all things were created through him and for him. And he is before all things, and in him all things hold together. And he is the head of the body, the church. He is the beginning, the firstborn from the dead, that in everything he might be preeminent. For in him all the fullness of God was pleased to dwell, and through him to reconcile to himself all things, whether on earth or in heaven, making peace by the blood of his cross.

---

21. So Moisés Silva, *Philippians*, 2nd ed., BECNT (Grand Rapids: Baker Academic, 2005), 101; Gordon D. Fee, *Paul's Letter to the Philippians*, NICNT (Grand Rapids: Eerdmans, 1995), 207–8.

22. For discussions see Anthony C. Thiselton, *The First Epistle to the Corinthians: A Commentary on the Greek Text*, NIGTC (Grand Rapids: Eerdmans, 2000), 728–30; Turretin, *Inst.* 19.26.11, 13 (3:472–73).

Here Paul explains in greater detail the Son whom the Father loves (1:13), and combines divine and Davidic sonship. The Son is the image of the invisible God, the one by whom all things were created. More than that, he is the goal of creation (τὰ πάντα δι᾽ αὐτοῦ καὶ εἰς αὐτὸν ἔκτισται). He thus precedes creation and is placed on the Creator side of the Creator-creature distinction. This is not contradicted by the Son's identification as the firstborn of all creation (1:15) for a few reasons. First, Paul speaks in this same passage of Jesus as the Creator (1:16), and thus in the broader scope of biblical theology it is clear that the Creator is God alone; no created being assists in creation. Second, the term for "firstborn" (πρωτότοκος) is most likely an honorific title, probably echoing the discussion of the Davidic king in Psalm 89:27 (88:28 LXX).[23] The phrase does not mean that Jesus is created but that Christ is the true king over all creation.[24] Third, if Paul would have wanted to argue that Jesus was the first created being (which would contradict 1:16), then a different Greek term would have been more explicit (πρωτόκτικτος).[25] In sum, by speaking of Christ as firstborn, Paul affirms the preexistent sonship of Christ and his authority over all creation—he is the eternal Son of God.[26]

The Son is also the image of the invisible God (Col 1:15), a statement that has been widely discussed. In Scripture "image of God" recalls the creation of humanity in the beginning (Gen 1:26–28), and some relation to Adam is likely in view as well. However, the focus here is not on the incarnate

23. This option is commonly noted by commentators. See, e.g., N. T. Wright, *Colossians and Philemon: An Introduction and Commentary*, TNTC (Downers Grove, IL: InterVarsity Press, 1986), 75; G. K. Beale, *Colossians and Philemon*, BECNT (Grand Rapids: Baker Academic, 2019), 87.

24. Further, κτίσεως may be a genitive of subordination ("firstborn *over* all creation"). This option is also preferred by Beale, *Colossians*, 90–91; Wallace, *Greek Grammar*, 103–4. Compare also à Brakel, *Christian's Reasonable Service* 1:499.

25. See John Chrysostom, as noted in John Piper, *The Pleasures of God: Meditations on God's Delight in Being God*, rev. ed. (Sisters, OR: Multnomah, 2000), 39, following Henry Alford. A similar point is made by Thomas Kingsmill Abbott, *A Critical and Exegetical Commentary on the Epistles to the Ephesians and to the Colossians*, ICC (New York: Scribner's Sons, 1909), 212: "πρωτόκτιστος or πρωτόπλαστος would have implied that Christ was created like πᾶσα κτίσις."

26. See, e.g., Mastricht, *Theoretical-Practical Theology* 2:547; Lane G. Tipton, "Christology in Colossians 1:15–20 and Hebrews 1:1–4: An Exercise in Biblio-Systematic Theology," in *Resurrection and Eschatology: Theology in Service of the Church; Essays in Honor of Richard B. Gaffin Jr.*, ed. Lane G. Tipton and Jeffrey C. Waddington (Phillipsburg, NJ: P&R, 2008), 185–88.

state of the Son but on his glorious preexistence.[27] Thus, the Son is (ἐστιν) the image of the invisible God eternally; this is not limited to his incarnate state.[28] Here Paul's "image of God language clarifies the Son's consubstantial relation to the Father."[29] "Image of God" entails glory, and the Son as image of God serves as archetype for humanity. Humanity's call to reflect the image of God (Col 3:10), along with Adam's created state of holiness, further suggests that image of God entails moral holiness as well. That Jesus Christ is the image of the invisible God, and that to see him is to see the glory of the Father also is, according to John Owen, "the principal fundamental mystery and truth of the Gospel."[30]

2. Redemptive-historical sonship. As Son of God, Jesus is also the Christ, the promised Son of David. Romans 1:3–4 speaks of Jesus descended from David according to the flesh, and the reference to Christ as firstborn from the dead (again alluding to Ps 89:27) in Colossians 1:18 adds a redemptive-historical angle to the divine sonship already established in this passage: "Jesus's unique dignity as firstborn from among the dead manifests his prior uniqueness as firstborn over all creation."[31]

More broadly, where "Christ" is used in Paul, it refers to his coming in redemptive history from the line of David to rule over the Davidic kingdom. Though Paul sometimes invokes other sonship emphases from the Old Testament (such as Adam or Israel as son), his main biblical-historical emphasis with respect to sonship is Jesus as the Son of David. Kingship is thus in view when Paul speaks of Jesus as Christ.

Divine Lord of Glory THE SECOND MAJOR EMPHASIS OF Paul's Christology is the lordship of Christ. Paul often speaks of the Lord (κύριος), and he almost always applies this title to Jesus.[32] Though this

27. In this discussion I have benefited from Beale, *Colossians*, 80–86. See also Richard Bauckham, "Confessing the Cosmic Christ (1 Corinthians 8:6 and Colossians 1:15–20)," in *Monotheism and Christology in Greco-Roman Antiquity*, ed. Matthew V. Novenson, NovTSup 180 (Leiden: Brill, 2020), 139–71.

28. See Beale, *Colossians*, 81–83.

29. Tipton, "Christology in Colossians 1:15–20," 188, emphasis original.

30. Owen, *Works* 1:305.

31. Tipton, "Christology in Colossians 1:15–20," 189.

32. See Gordon D. Fee, *Pauline Christology: An Exegetical-Theological Study* (Peabody, MA: Hendrickson, 2007), e.g., 558–59.

aspect of Paul's writing is frequent and familiar, we should not miss its significance. To say that Jesus is Lord is to say that he is the risen, ascended, divine Lord of glory (1 Cor 2:8). In 1 Corinthians 8:5–6 Paul lays out how he understands Christ's lordship: "For although there may be so-called gods in heaven or on earth—as indeed there are many 'gods' and many 'lords'—yet for us there is one God, the Father, from whom are all things and for whom we exist, and one Lord, Jesus Christ, through whom are all things and through whom we exist." Here Paul downplays the presence of many "gods" in the ancient world by affirming the central Old Testament confession that God is one from Deuteronomy 6:4. Similar to Mark 12 and John 10, in 1 Corinthians 8 Paul echoes the language of God and Lord from the Shema and explains that God is the Father, and the Lord is Jesus Christ. So, while not denying the oneness of God, Paul speaks of two divine persons.[33] Thus, the one God of Deuteronomy 6 includes Jesus Christ the Lord.

"Lord" thus means at least two things for Paul. First, "Lord" is the fitting title for the victorious, heavenly Jesus—he is Lord of glory. Second, as Lord of glory Jesus is divine. The glory that was reserved for the Lord in the Old Testament can be applied to the Father and the Son in the New Testament (see also 1 Thess 2:12 with 2 Thess 2:14).[34]

Paul clarifies the divinity of Christ in other ways. For example, in his letter greetings, Paul often speaks of the grace and peace (and sometimes mercy) that come from God the Father and the Lord Jesus (Rom 1:7; 1 Cor 1:3; 2 Cor 1:2; Gal 1:3; Eph 1:2; 2 Thess 1:1–2; 1 Tim 1:2; 2 Tim 1:2; Titus 1:4; Phlm 3; see also 1 Thess 1:1). Not only does Paul speak of the Father and Son in the same breath, but the benefits that he speaks of are divine grace, mercy, and peace. Jesus himself is full of grace (1 Tim 1:14). Indeed, in Christ all the fullness of the deity dwells bodily (Col 2:9; see 1:19).[35] Paul emphasizes that we should not think of Christ in terms of partial deity or part of the deity dwelling in Christ (as if that were even possible!), but all the fullness of the deity

33. See Larry W. Hurtado, *Lord Jesus Christ: Devotion to Jesus in Earliest Christianity* (Grand Rapids: Eerdmans, 2003), 114; Bauckham, *God Crucified*, 37–39; Fee, *Pauline Christology*, 88–94.

34. Fee, *Pauline Christology*, 70–71. See also Benjamin Breckinridge Warfield, "The 'Two Natures' and Recent Christological Speculation," in Craig, *Person and Work of Christ*, 224: "For κύριος is not with Paul of lower connotation than θεός."

35. Col 1:19 does not include "God"; instead, it more elliptically reads "all the fullness" (πᾶν τὸ πλήρωμα). Based on a comparison with Col 2:9 (τῆς θεότητος), it is appropriate to assume "of God."

dwelling in Christ bodily and perpetually. Thus, "all the fullness of deity" (πᾶν τὸ πλήρωμα τῆς θεότητος) refers to all the fullness that characterizes the deity.[36] This language likely invokes temple imagery: as the divine fullness dwelled in the temple, so now the divine glory is most fully apprehended in the incarnate Christ.[37] There is no need to "supplement" Christ, for in him dwells all the treasures of wisdom and knowledge (2:3), and he has authority over all created beings (1:16–18; 2:10). Whereas Moses reflected the glory of God, in Christ we come face to face with the glory of God (2 Cor 4:6).

Occasionally Paul even applies the term "God" (θεός) to Jesus. In Romans 9:5 Paul speaks of Christ, who is identified as God over all and blessed forever (ὁ ὢν ἐπὶ πάντων θεὸς εὐλογητὸς εἰς τοὺς αἰῶνας).[38] Many have objected that the starkness of this phrase renders it unlikely that Paul has Jesus Christ in view, and instead Paul switches to speak of God the Father.[39] It also seems to be a break with Paul's normal usage, where θεός consistently refers to the Father.[40] To be sure, this is a rather surprising statement for Paul to make in the context of the Jewish lineage of Jesus Christ, but Paul's point seems to be not so different from Romans 1:3–4: Jesus is the Christ descended from David according to the flesh, but is also (as the Son) God over all.

This rare statement from Paul in Romans 9 is corroborated in the Pastoral Epistles. In Titus 2:13 Paul speaks of "our great God and Savior Jesus Christ" (τοῦ μεγάλου θεοῦ καὶ σωτῆρος ἡμῶν Ἰησοῦ Χριστοῦ). This Greek construction is an example of the Granville Sharp rule, which states that when two singular, personal nouns are joined by καί ("and"), and the Greek article is only used before the first noun, then the two nouns refer to the same person.[41] Thus, in Titus 2:13 the "great God" is identical to the "Savior," who is identified as Jesus Christ. Even so, the divinity of Christ in Paul is not

36. Thus, attributive genitive (so Beale, *Colossians*, 177) or possibly genitive of content (so Wallace, *Greek Grammar*, 94).

37. See especially Beale, *Colossians*, 176; also Moo, *Colossians*, 193–94.

38. One author who argues for this view is George Carraway, *Christ is God Over All: Romans 9:5 in the Context of Romans 9–11*, LNTS 489 (London: Bloomsbury, 2013).

39. E.g., James D. G. Dunn, *Romans 9–16*, WBC 38B (Dallas: Word, 1988), 535–36.

40. See Fee, *Pauline Christology*, 16–17. Fee holds to a high, preexistence Christology in Paul, but opts for different translations of Rom 9:5 and Titus 2:13 (*Pauline Christology*, 272–78, 440–46).

41. See Wallace, *Greek Grammar*, 270–77.

contingent on one or two texts where Paul may (or may not) use θεός for Jesus. Elsewhere in Titus Paul can move seamlessly between God as Savior (Titus 1:3; 3:4) and Jesus as Savior (1:4; 2:13; 3:6). Traditionally 1 Timothy 3:16 has been read as a reference to Jesus as "God manifested in the flesh," but this relies on a textual variant and the text more likely reads "who was manifested in the flesh."[42]

Titus 3:4–6 is also one of several Pauline Trinitarian statements, where he speaks fluently of the Father, Son, and Spirit. Other examples include the benediction of 2 Corinthians 13:14, the discussion of unity and diversity in 1 Corinthians 12:4–6, and the extended blessing of Ephesians 1:3–14, which includes three statements of "to the praise of the glory of his grace" correlating to the work of Father (1:6), Son (1:12), and Spirit (1:14).

Yet it is not only such statements that reveal Christ's divine sonship; Paul's use of κύριος ("Lord") for Jesus is typically sufficient to communicate the divinity of Christ, especially in light of the way that Paul speaks of Jesus as Lord.[43] We see this in Philippians 2:9–11, where Paul states that every knee in creation will bow and confess that Jesus Christ is Lord.[44] This is a remarkable statement in itself, but it is brought into greater focus by attending to the likely allusion to Isaiah 45:23, which speaks of every knee bowing to the true God of the world—the one who has no rivals. Paul applies this to Jesus as the exalted Lord in Philippians 2, which means that Jesus must be fully divine.

Likewise, the coming of the Lord from Zechariah 14:5 is understood by Paul to be the coming of the Lord Jesus (1 Thess 3:13),[45] and Jesus's name is the name of the Lord by which we are saved, echoing Joel 2:32 (Rom 10:9–13). This high Christology is consistent with what we saw in the previous chapter—that the divinity of Jesus is demonstrated where the names, attributes, works, and worship attributed to him are proper only to God (e.g., WLC 11). Once we take this tack, then other texts that assume the divinity of Christ open up. For example, in contrast to Adam, who passively was

---

42. Thus, notice the slight difference between the relative pronoun OC ("who") and ΘC as an abbreviation for θεός ("God") in the manuscript tradition.

43. See David B. Capes, *Old Testament Yahweh Texts in Paul's Christology*, WUNT 2/47 (Tübingen: Mohr Siebeck, 1992).

44. See Bauckham, *God Crucified*, 56–60; Fee, *Pauline Christology*, 396–400.

45. See Fee, *Pauline Christology*, 43–44.

brought to life, Jesus is the one who grants life (1 Cor 15:45). Jesus, the last Adam, is life-giving Spirit, in a way that echoes the prerogative of God to give life (see Gen 2:7; Deut 32:39). This observation leads us into other categories for understanding the person of Christ.

Romans 5:12–21

Paul portrays Jesus as the second man and last Adam. This is especially important where Paul speaks of the representative obedience of Jesus and the resurrection life of Jesus as a true man. The two most explicit texts in this respect are Romans 5:12–21 and 1 Corinthians 15:21–26, 44–49, but other texts invoke Adamic imagery as well (e.g., Eph 1:20–23; Phil 2:5–11; Col 1:15–20; 1 Tim 2:5; 3:16).[a] In Romans 5:12–21 Paul organizes all of world history around two covenant heads, Adam and Christ. Whereas Adam's disobedience led to condemnation and death, Christ's obedience leads to justification and life (Rom 5:18–19).[b] In Romans 5:18 Paul speaks summarily of Christ's perfect obedience as "the righteous act of one man" (my trans.), which leads to justification and life for all people (5:18–19).[c] Paul speaks here of the unified obedience of Jesus, which is the foundation of our justification, leading to eternal life (5:21). Not only did Jesus obey and suffer for us, but he was raised for our justification (Rom 4:25). The resurrection is thus the vindication of Christ's perfect obedience in its entirety.[d]

Similarly, in Paul's exposition of the resurrection in 1 Corinthians 15:20–28, 44–49 he relates the superior work of Christ to Adam. Christ is the last Adam (ὁ ἔσχατος Ἀδάμ, 15:45) and the second man (ὁ δεύτερος ἄνθρωπος, 15:47). As the second and last Adam, Jesus is fully human (15:21), and he realizes the vocation of humanity to represent God in glorious, immaculate dominion over creation (15:22, 25–27; see also Ps 8:7; 110:1). Adam is the man of dust, denoting original creation; Jesus is the man of heaven, denoting eschatological, new creation (1 Cor 15:45–49).[e]

---

a. See, e.g., Owen, *Works* 1:207; Gaffin, *Resurrection*, 124.

b. For further discussion, see Brandon D. Crowe, *Why Did Jesus Live a Perfect Life? The Necessity of Christ's Obedience for Our Salvation* (Grand Rapids: Baker Academic, 2021), 40–57.

c. For a defense of this translation of ἑνός δικαιώματος as "righteous act of one man," see Crowe, *Why Did Jesus Live a Perfect Life?*, 45–46.

d. I will address Christ's obedience further in ch. 10 in relation to Christ's humiliation and representative obedience.

e. Compare Gaffin, *Resurrection*, 34–36.

Prophet, Priest, and King

Bavinck notes the close relationship between Christ's humanity and his threefold office: "To be a mediator, to be a complete savior, he had to be appointed by the Father to all three and equipped by the Spirit for all three offices. The truth is that the idea of humanness already encompasses within itself this threefold dignity and activity."[46] Adam in the beginning was prophet, priest, and king, and Christ is a new Adam. It thus makes sense that Paul likewise speaks of Christ's person and work in a way that accords with the threefold office.

Jesus is the Son of David and Son of Adam: he is the true human king, who will hand over the kingdom to his Father (1 Cor 15:24; see also 2 Tim 4:1, 18). As prophet Jesus is the Word of God, whose teaching is authoritative in the churches (1 Cor 7:10; 2 Cor 13:3). He is God's final revelation, the mystery hidden in ages past, now revealed (Eph 3:1–5; Col 2:2).[47] Christ's priestly role is seen in his identification as the true temple. Christ is the cornerstone of the new creational temple, which is the church (Eph 2:20–22). He is also the head of his body, the church (1:22–23; 4:15; 5:23). He is the propitiation (ἱλαστήριον) for our sins by his blood (Rom 3:25),[48] which means he is the means by which our sins are taken away and God's wrath appeased. His death is a sacrifice (Eph 5:2),[49] by which he has made peace (2:15) and canceled our debts (Col 2:14).

Other Christological Emphases

Paul utilizes numerous other categories to speak of the work of Christ, many of which assume preexistence. Wisdom is personified in early Judaism (Wis 6:12–21). Wisdom cries out in the streets (Prov 1:20–33; see Sir 4:11). Wisdom was there in the beginning at creation; by wisdom were all things made (Prov 3:19; 8:22–36; see Wis 7:22; 9:2, 9; 10:1; Sir 1:4;

46. Bavinck, *RD* 3:367.

47. For Christ as the content of the mystery in Eph 3:4, see Andrew T. Lincoln, *Ephesians*, WBC 42 (Nashville: Thomas Nelson, 1990), 176; Markus Barth, *Ephesians 1–3: A New Translation with Introduction and Commentary*, AB 34 (Garden City, NY: Doubleday, 1974), 331.

48. Leon Morris, *The Apostolic Preaching of the Cross* (Grand Rapids: Eerdmans, 1955), 167–74. Further, Schreiner (*Romans*, 200) recognizes that ἱλαστήριον is a sacrificial term that draws on Leviticus (and the Day of Atonement in particular) and Isa 53, along with other texts.

49. So Bavinck, *RD* 3:366.

24:9). Wisdom is thus closely related to the Word of God.[50] This provides background for Paul's letters, where he speaks of the preexistent Jesus as the agent of creation (Col 1:15). Wisdom is sometimes associated with God's firstborn (Prov 8:22–27).[51] Even so, wisdom is not one of Paul's major christological categories; Beale suggests wisdom is in the background of Colossians 1, rather than the foreground, though the conceptual and verbal echoes are sufficient to establish some measure of resonance.[52] Elsewhere Paul counters worldly wisdom by speaking of Christ as the wisdom of God (1 Cor 1:23, 30). Similarly, Paul speaks of Christ as the Rock who followed the Israelites in the wilderness (10:4). Paul's argument necessitates the preexistence of Christ and underscores the sacramental unity of the Old Testament and New Testament. This emphasis on preexistence may also be closely related to Wisdom, which also was understood to guide and nourish Israel in the wilderness—which is squarely in view in 1 Corinthians 10.[53] Additionally, by calling Christ "the Rock," Paul applies an Old Testament name for God (e.g., Deut 32:4, 15, 18) to Christ.[54] The preexistent Christ is the divine Christ.

Preexistence Christology is also evident in Galatians. In Galatians 3:16 Paul identifies Christ as the seed, or offspring, of Abraham (see Gen 12:1–3). Christ is the one in whom the covenant promises to Abraham are ultimately realized. This concept of "seed" (Gk. σπέρμα; Heb. זרע) in Genesis 12 already echoes the promise given to Adam and Eve in the beginning, that the seed of the woman would overcome the serpent (Gen 3:15). Yet in Galatians 3:16 Paul states that the covenantal promises were spoken to Abraham and to his seed. This singular seed, or offspring, is Christ. To be sure, Christ here is the culmination and realization of the promises that were given to Abraham and his immediate children. But when and in what sense were the promises spoken to Christ? Paul seems to have more than only redemptive history in view; he seems to understand that at some point

50. See Bauckham, *God Crucified*, 20–22.

51. See, e.g., Beale, *Colossians*, 121.

52. Beale, *Colossians*, 121–24.

53. See Thiselton, *First Epistle to the Corinthians*, 728–30.

54. See, e.g., Roy E. Ciampa and Brian Rosner, *1 Corinthians*, PNTC (Grand Rapids: Eerdmans, 2010), 451, who also cite David E. Garland, *1 Corinthians*, BECNT (Grand Rapids: Baker Academic, 2003), 457.

"prior" to the incarnation, the promises to Abraham were also promised to Christ. Galatians 3:16 has thus often been taken in Reformed theology as a reference to the covenant of grace made with Christ (WLC 31).[55] Christ, the head of the covenant of grace, fulfills not only the Abrahamic covenant but also the promise to destroy the serpent.[56] Paul also speaks of Christ as the Passover Lamb (5:7), manifesting his theology that the substance to which the Passover looked is Christ himself.

To sum up, Paul himself identifies Christ as the one in whom all things are summed up (ἀνακεφαλαιώσασθαι τὰ πάντα ἐν τῷ Χριστῷ, Eph 1:10).[57] Christ is the focal point of the universe, the one in whom all things subsist and in whom all things find their unity; he provides order in a chaotic universe by overcoming sin. This statement provides a transition point for us to discuss in more detail the work of Christ in Paul.

The Work of Christ in Paul's Letters

Salvation Accomplished

Paul speaks of the work of Christ effecting many benefits: justification, sanctification, adoption, glorification, and so forth. These and similar benefits are often linked together under the heading of *ordo salutis* ("order of salvation"), which refers to the experience or application of the work of Christ. In this section I am going to focus instead on the foundation of the *ordo salutis* in the work of Christ. This can be labeled *historia salutis* ("history of salvation") and draws attention to the work that Christ has accomplished in history.[58] Put simply, the work of Christ in the context of *historia salutis* secures *ordo salutis* realities for those who trust in Christ.

---

55. See David Gibson, "'Fathers of Faith, My Fathers Now!' On Abraham, Covenant, and the Theology of Paedobaptism," *Them* 40.1 (2015): 17–19; see also Turretin, *Inst.* 12.2.12 (2:177); Bavinck, *RD* 3:228; Owen, *Works* 1:215.

56. I return to this in ch. 8.

57. See Max Turner, "Mission and Meaning in Terms of 'Unity' in Ephesians," in *Mission and Meaning: Essays Presented to Peter Cotterell*, ed. Anthony Billington, Tony Lane, and Max Turner (Carlisle, UK: Paternoster, 1995), 138–66; Lincoln, *Ephesians*, 31–32; see also Owen, *Works* 1:372: "There is no contemplation of the glory of Christ that ought more to affect the hearts of them that do believe with delight and joy, than this, of the recapitulation of all things in him."

58. The term *historia salutis* appears to have originated with Herman Ridderbos, "The Redemptive-Historical Character of Paul's Preaching," in *When the Time*, 48–49, noted by Richard B. Gaffin Jr., *"By Faith, Not by Sight": Paul and the Order of Salvation* (Waynesboro, GA: Paternoster, 2006), 18–19n2.

For Paul, the coming of Christ marks the turning point of redemptive history. Christ is the focus of our faith, and what he has done in the incarnation secures our salvation. This is why Paul speaks so starkly about the time before "faith" coming (Gal 3:23). By this Paul emphatically does not mean that the Old Testament period was devoid of faith, nor that salvation was by works before the coming of Christ. For the Bible speaks of one covenant of grace administered both in the Old Testament and the New Testament. Instead, "before faith came" (πρὸ τοῦ δὲ ἐλθεῖν τὴν πίστιν, Gal 3:23) refers specifically to the new era of redemptive history marked by faith specifically in Christ (see 3:22), which is more fully revealed in the New Testament.[59] This is clarified in the following verses, where Paul speaks of the coming of faith and the coming of Christ in similar terms (3:24–26). In this context in Galatians, Paul speaks of Christ and his work as the key juncture in world history, which can be divided into the era prior to the coming of Christ and the era after.

Incarnation and Life under the Law

Paul's focus on the role of Christ in redemptive history finds a concise summary later in Galatians: "But when the fullness of time had come, God sent forth his Son, born of a woman, born under the law, to redeem those who were under the law, so that we might receive adoption as sons" (Gal 4:4–5). This passage refers to Christ, the eternal Son of God, being born of a woman and subject to the law as a man. As such, it assumes both his divinity and humanity and his humiliation to obey the law of God for our benefit. Paul has already spoken of the universal curse of the law on all people (3:10) and of Christ redeeming us from the curse of the law (3:13). Paul's mention of Christ redeeming us from the law recalls that universal curse, even while it assumes Christ himself was free from it.[60] This

59. Compare, e. g., Ridderbos, *Paul*, 174, 233, 237; F. F. Bruce, *The Epistle to the Galatians: A Commentary on the Greek Text*, NIGTC (Grand Rapids: Eerdmans, 1982), 194; Richard B. Gaffin Jr., *In the Fullness of Time: An Introduction to the Biblical Theology of Acts and Paul* (Wheaton: Crossway, 2022), 274–75; Douglas J. Moo, *Galatians*, BECNT (Grand Rapids, Baker Academic, 2013), 241, 244; Thomas R. Schreiner, *Galatians*, ZECNT (Grand Rapids: Zondervan, 2010) 245–46; Turretin, *Inst.* 12.5.37 (2:203–4); 12.12.21 (2:267–68). The article τήν in 3:23 is anaphoric, and refers back to the same faith mentioned in 3:22. See, e.g., Richard N. Longenecker, *Galatians*, WBC 41 (Nashville: Thomas Nelson, 2006), 145.

60. Following Bruce, *Galatians*, 196.

redemption from the law assumes Christ's full obedience to the law[61] and thus is not far from what Paul says elsewhere about Christ's full obedience in contrast to Adam's disobedience (Rom 5:18–21).

Redemption and New Exodus

REDEMPTION REQUIRES MORE COMMENT. PAUL'S language of "redemption" (ἀπολύτρωσις, λύτρωσις) and "redeem" (ἀπολυτρόω, ἐξαγοράζω; especially λυτρόω) recalls the exodus, in which God's people were redeemed from Egypt.[62] God alone is sufficient to save, demonstrating his power over opposition and his care for his people. The exodus was the paradigm of redemption in the Old Testament and the blueprint for God's future deliverance (see Isa 35:8–10; 43:14). Sometimes this redemption is more corporate; sometimes it is more personal;[63] often it is focused on the king as the leader of the nation (2 Sam 4:9; 1 Kgs 1:29; Pss 31:5, 7; 55:18; 69:18; 144:10).

It is therefore not surprising that Paul employs the exodus to explain the work of Christ. The first exodus, though true deliverance, anticipated the greater deliverance that comes through Christ. Christ redeems us even more fully from sin and the dominion of darkness. The Old Testament speaks of the impossibility of one man redeeming another (Ps 49:7); only God can redeem (49:15). Paul makes it clear that Christ has redeemed us by his blood (see Gal 3:13; 4:5; Eph 1:7; see also Col 1:14). The blood of the Passover lamb in the exodus anticipated the coming of the true Passover Lamb (1 Cor 5:7)—Christ himself—who fully delivers us from sin. As Israel was freed from the rule of ungodly Pharaoh, so in a greater way Christ has freed us from the dominion of darkness and brought us into the kingdom of the Son (Col 1:12–14; see also Gal 1:4; Eph 5:8; 6:12). He has defeated the devil (Eph 6:10–11) and will soon crush him under our feet (Rom 16:20). In God's beloved Son we are redeemed and have received an inheritance (Col 1:13–14; see also Eph 1:13–14), manifesting the centrality of sonship in the Bible's plan of redemption.

---

61. See again Bruce, *Galatians*, 196.

62. E.g., Beale, *New Testament Biblical Theology*, 474; Morris, *Apostolic Preaching*, 10–15.

63. Corporate: e.g., Exod 6:6; 15:13; Deut 7:8; 9:26; 13:5; 15:15; 21:8; 24:18; 2 Sam 7:23; 1 Chr 17:21; Neh 1:10; Pss 25:22; 44:26; 74:2; 77:15; 130:8; 136:24; Isa 41:14; 43:1; 44:22–24; 51:11; 52:3; 62:12; Jer 15:21; 31:11; 50:34; Hos 13:14; Mic 4:10; 6:4; Zeph 3:15 LXX; Zech 10:8. Personal: Pss 31:5; 34:22; 49:7, 15; 71:23; 72:14; 78:42; 103:4; 106:10; 107:2; 119:134, 154; Lam 3:58; Dan 3:88 LXX; 6:28 LXX.

Christ has redeemed us, but Paul says even more than this. It is not just that Jesus grants us abstract benefits; instead, he gives us himself. Christ himself is our redemption (1 Cor 1:30; see also Acts 7:35).[64] Our redemption is found in Christ (Rom 3:24). This is the fullest manifestation of the grace of God: "He who did not spare his own Son but gave him up for us all, how will he not also with him graciously give us all things?" (Rom 8:32). In the exodus the firstborn of those who disbelieved were struck down, and the firstborn of the Israelites were saved if they applied the blood of the lamb to their doorposts. In the gospel, God does not spare his own Son, that by his blood we might be finally redeemed from bondage. We look forward to sharing in Christ's resurrection, when our bodies themselves will be redeemed (τὴν ἀπολύτρωσιν τοῦ σώματος ἡμῶν) and we will enjoy the full benefits of adoption (υἱοθεσία, Rom 8:23).

To know redemption is, preeminently, to know Christ, who loved us and gave himself up for us (Gal 2:20; Titus 2:13–14). All this flows back in praise to God, to whom be all glory (Rom 11:36; 16:27; 2 Cor 4:15; Gal 1:5; Eph 1:12, 14, 17; 3:21; 1 Tim 1:17; 2 Tim 4:18). The glory seen by Moses at the conclusion of the first exodus—on Sinai and in the tabernacle—is surpassed by the glory of God in the face of Jesus Christ (2 Cor 3:18; 4:6). For, as Paul makes clear (e.g., Rom 9:5; Titus 2:13), our Savior not only is a perfect man, but is God incarnate. Both these are necessary for our full redemption.

The Cross and Reconciliation

REDEMPTION ACCOMPLISHED BY CHRIST THUS includes Christ's full obedience as well as his death, which facilitated the reconciliation of God and humanity. Reconciliation (καταλλάσσω, καταλλαγή) is a key Pauline concept for understanding Christ's work. This terminology is especially prominent in Romans 5 and 2 Corinthians 5. God's love for us is seen in Christ's death for us—even while we were still sinners (Rom 5:8; see also Gal 2:20). Jesus has saved us from the wrath of God by his blood; his death reconciles us to God. Though we were by nature enemies due to sin, Christ reconciles us and brings peace between us and God by means of his sacrifice (Rom 5:10–11; see also Eph 2:13, 16).

64. See Bavinck, *Wonderful Works of God*, 442, 447.

2 Corinthians 5

Paul further expounds the nature of reconciliation in 2 Corinthians 5:17–21. If we are reconciled to God, then he does not count our sins against us (2 Cor 5:19).[a] Further, all those who are reconciled in Christ are participants in new creation (5:17–18). Christ himself became sin for us (5:21). By this Paul might mean that Christ became a sin offering for us, since sin offerings are often referred to simply as "sin" by metonymy in the OG (e.g., Exod 29:14; Lev 4:8, 20–21, 24, 29, 34, et al.).[b] However, while this is possible, "sin" is not used to refer to a sin offering earlier in the verse.[c] Thus perhaps a better view is that Christ became sin by means of imputation, by being a sin-bearing substitute for his people.[d] In the end, there may be only slight difference between these two views.[e] Either way, the cross of Christ is squarely in view—Christ was the sinless substitute who died to reconcile us to God (see Col 1:22). Similarly, elsewhere Christ is identified as the one who was cursed so that we might receive the blessing (Gal 3:13–14). The purpose of this death in 2 Corinthians 5 is so that in Christ "we might become" (γενώμεθα) "the righteousness of God." The "we" in 5:21 refers to all of God's people who are counted righteous in Christ.[f] In short, "becoming the righteousness of God" means that when we are reconciled we are considered righteous in God's sight in the context of our union with Christ.[g]

---

a. My discussion of 2 Cor 5 builds on (and updates) Brandon D. Crowe, "'By Grace You Have Been Saved through Faith': Justification in the Pauline Epistles," in *The Doctrine on Which the Church Stands or Falls: Justification in Biblical, Theological, Historical, and Pastoral Perspective*, ed. Matthew Barrett (Wheaton, IL: Crossway, 2019), 259–60.

b. So, e.g., Beale, *New Testament Biblical Theology*, 472n8; Richard L. Pratt Jr., *1 & 2 Corinthians*, Holman New Testament Commentary (Nashville: Holman Reference, 2000), 360.

c. Compare Murray J. Harris, *The Second Epistle to the Corinthians: A Commentary on the Greek Text*, NIGTC (Grand Rapids: Eerdmans, 2005), 452–54; David E. Garland, *2 Corinthians*, NAC 29 (Nashville: Broadman, 1999), 300; Hugh Martin, *The Atonement: In Its Relations to the Covenant, the Priesthood, the Intercession of Our Lord* (repr., Edinburgh: Banner of Truth, 2013), 143.

d. Martin, *Atonement*, 143–65; à Brakel, *Christian's Reasonable Service* 1:588; Robert Letham, *The Work of Christ*, CCT (Downers Grove, IL: InterVarsity, 1993), 134, 262–63n3.

e. See, e.g., Turretin, *Inst.* 14.10.29 (2:426); 14.11.12 (2:430).

f. See Thomas R. Schreiner, *Faith Alone—The Doctrine of Justification: What the Reformers Taught ... and Why It Still Matters*, Five Sola Series (Grand Rapids: Zondervan, 2015), 187; Harris, *Second Epistle to the Corinthians*, 455–56n207.

g. See also Garland, *2 Corinthians*, 302.

Reconciliation has not only a personal dimension (i.e., salvation of sinners) but a cosmic dimension as well. Indeed, since those who are in Christ are participants in new creation (2 Cor 5:17), personal reconciliation should be understood in tandem with cosmic reconciliation. The one to whom we are united by faith is the one who has conquered every rule and authority by his incarnate work (Col 1:20; see also Eph 1:10). Since our Redeemer is also our Creator, the work of redemption extends to the whole realm of creation[65]—visible and invisible. All that has been disrupted and alienated by sin will eventually be made right, and that has already begun now. Beale refers to this as "a 'pacification' of *all* hostile and friendly forces (human and angelic)."[66] Thus, not only does Christ's work affect all spiritual authorities, but he has also reconciled sinners by his sacrificial work, bringing them near by the work of the cross (Col 1:22; Eph 2:16).

Victorious, Resurrected King

Christ provides full redemption because he has conquered every enemy. He was shamefully nailed to the cross as a curse (Gal 3:13), but was vindicated by means of the resurrection and taken up into glory (1 Tim 3:16). His resurrection demonstrates the effectual nature of sacrifice and is crucial to our own justification (Rom 4:25). As the resurrected Lord, all things are under his feet (1 Cor 15:20–28; Eph 1:20–23). This includes the whole created realm, whether things visible or invisible (Col 1:15–20). His resurrection is the inbreaking and inauguration of new creation (Col 1:18), the new Adam who reigns over an everlasting kingdom. His resurrection not only results in new life for himself, but it marks the coming of the age of consummation—the age of the resurrection characterized by the Spirit.[67]

Christ's victory is thus seen in the outpouring of the Holy Spirit on the church, equipping the saints for ministry (Eph 4:7–16; see also Ps 68:18). The Holy Spirit's effusive outpouring represents the victory spoils of the conquering, risen, resurrected, ascended Christ who sits at God's right hand. The diverse array of spiritual gifts is for the upbuilding of his people, who are united as his body, with Christ himself as the exalted head. The

65. This is a major theme throughout Bavinck's *RD*.

66. Beale, *Colossians*, 111, emphasis original.

67. Vos, "Eschatological Aspect," 91–125.

outpouring of the Spirit is the manifestation that Christ reigns over all from heaven.

Paul summarizes the work of Christ in Philippians 2:5–11. In 2:6–8 Jesus's work as suffering servant is described—he became obedient even unto death. The results are summarized in 2:9–11: "therefore (διό) God highly exalted him and has given him the name above all names." The victory of Christ in his resurrected state is thus the result of his perfect obedience throughout his life. Even so, Christ's own life of obedient suffering provides the paradigm for what believers should expect in this age. Christ, the victorious one, leads us in triumph (2 Cor 2:14). But this is an ironic statement, for Paul most likely has in view here his own position as a slave, being led as a captive in a victory parade.[68] Though Paul is a slave for Christ, he knows that his suffering will eventually yield glory, for he follows in the footsteps of his master, who has been raised and is victorious over all (see Phil 3:7–11).

Paul's suffering as an apostle is therefore temporary, just as Christ's suffering was temporary, and he can glory in his sufferings (see 2 Cor 11:16–33) because he is seated with Christ in heavenly places (Col 3:1). The already/not-yet structure of Paul's theology tells us that this present age is one of continued suffering, even as the resurrection era has dawned. But just as surely as Christ has risen from the dead, he will eventually hand the kingdom over to his Father (1 Cor 15:24). Christ's glory will one day be manifested for all to see, for he lives and is coming again (Romans; 1 Cor 1:7–8; 4:5; Phil 3:20–21; Col 3:4; 1 Thess 1:10; 2:19; 3:13; 4:15–16; 5:23; 2 Thess 1:7, 10; 2:1–9; 1 Tim 6:14–15; 2 Tim 4:1; Titus 2:13).[69]

Salvation Secured It is a sure and trustworthy statement: Christ Jesus came into the world to save sinners (1 Tim 1:15). This is good news, for all have sinned and fall short of the glory of God (Rom 3:23). We benefit from the work of Christ by faith (see Rom 1:16;

---

68. See Garland, *2 Corinthians*, 140–48; Scott J. Hafemann, "Roman Triumph," in *Dictionary of New Testament Background*, ed. Craig A. Evans and Stanley E. Porter (Downers Grove, IL: InterVarsity, 2000), 1004–8.

69. A helpful listing of texts can be found in Berkhof, *Systematic Theology*, 353–54; see also James P. Ware, ed., *Synopsis of the Pauline Letters in Greek and English* (Grand Rapids: Baker Academic, 2010), §88.

10:10; Eph 1:13; 2 Thess 2:13; 2 Tim 3:15). The one Mediator between God and humanity, Jesus Christ, gave his own life as a ransom for us (1 Tim 2:5–6). We are saved not because of our own works but because of his purpose and grace in Christ (2 Tim 1:9–10; also Titus 3:4–6). Jesus is our great God and Savior who gave himself for us, in order to redeem us (Titus 2:13–14). Because of his work, those who trust in him are not destined for wrath but for salvation (1 Thess 5:9–10). For Paul salvation is deliverance from sin and participation in the hope of the glory of eternal life (Rom 5:18, 21; 6:22–23; 1 Tim 1:16; 6:12; 2 Tim 1:9–10; Titus 3:4–7). Christ has been crucified and was raised, triumphing over every power, so that those who trust in him are united with him in the heavenly places (Eph 1:20–23; 3:9–11; Col 3:1–3).

Salvation is broader than justification by faith (it also includes, e.g., adoption, sanctification, glorification), but justification by faith alone is certainly a crucially important aspect of salvation. Justifying faith is specifically faith in Jesus Christ (Gal 2:16).[70] Our works—whether preconversion or postconversion—are insufficient to meet the demand of God's justice for eternal life. Only the perfect obedience of Christ suffices for justification (Rom 5:18–19). This is why the gospel calls us to faith (Rom 1:16–17): the gospel is good news because sinners can be saved by faith alone, trusting that Christ did for us what we could not do for ourselves.

---

70. I take the phrase διὰ πίστεως Ἰησοῦ Χριστοῦ in Gal 2:16 as an objective genitive that is emphatic: through faith *in* Jesus Christ. However, if one opts for the subjective genitive here ("through the faithfulness of Jesus Christ") Paul still speaks of faith in Christ in this verse (καὶ ἡμεῖς εἰς Χριστὸν Ἰησοῦν ἐπιστεύσαμεν). Even so, reading Paul's letters in light of other NT witnesses that speak of faith *in* Christ provides strong corroboration for the objective genitive reading. See, e.g., John 2:11; 6:29; 9:35–38; 12:44; 17:20; Acts 9:42; 11:17; 16:31; 20:21; 24:24; see also Acts 13:38–39; Gal 2:16; Eph 1:15; Col 1:4; 2:5; Phlm 5; 1 John 3:23. Though sometimes proponents of the subjective genitive reading argue that the subjective reading best accounts for Christ's work on our behalf, this is not necessarily the case. For the objective genitive reading emphasizes our need to trust in Christ, with faith understood instrumentally as that which adds nothing to the work of Christ. Thus, our faith is not a work, properly speaking. Instead, our faith rests on Christ's work alone for justification. This point has sometimes been misunderstood; see, e.g., Richard B. Hays, *The Faithfulness of Jesus Christ: The Narrative Substructure of Galatians 3:1–4:11*, 2nd ed., Biblical Resource Series (Grand Rapids: Eerdmans; Dearborn, MI: Dove, 2002), xxix–xxxi. For further discussion, see Crowe, *Why Did Jesus Live a Perfect Life?*, 158–64; R. Barry Matlock, "Detheologizing the ΠΙΣΤΙΣ ΧΡΙΣΤΟΥ Debate: Cautionary Remarks from a Lexical Semantic Perspective," *Novum Testamentum* 42 (2000): 21–23. See also Rom 4:1–12, where Abraham and David are models of justification by faith.

CONCLUSION

Acts and the Pauline Letters speak of Christ as the long-awaited Son of David, who is also the divine Son of God. He has completed his earthly work and now reigns in heaven. His resurrection shows that he has conquered sin and death, and his work alone is sufficient for salvation. His work is cosmically significant, and by his death and resurrection he has inaugurated the new creational age of the Spirit. Christ lives and reigns over all, and he will return in glory. In the end, every tongue will confess that Jesus Christ is Lord to the glory of God the Father.

FURTHER READING

Beale, G. K. *A New Testament Biblical Theology: The Unfolding of the Old Testament in the New*. Grand Rapids: Baker Academic, 2011. This thorough volume deals extensively with Paul's theology of already/not-yet new creation. It is an exegetical treasure trove that illuminates christological issues.

Capes, David B. *Old Testament Yahweh Texts in Paul's Christology*. WUNT 2/47. Tübingen: Mohr Siebeck, 1992. Capes looks at the use of key Old Testament passages in Paul where "Lord" (κύριος) is applied to Jesus and concludes that for Paul, Jesus is both distinguished from and "fully identified" with Yahweh (p. 185).

Fee, Gordon D. *Pauline Christology: An Exegetical-Theological Study*. Peabody, MA: Hendrickson, 2007. Fee covers all thirteen Pauline epistles and key passages, organized in both canonical order and topical order. He includes extensive, detailed exegetical discussions. For a condensed version, see *Jesus the Lord according to Paul the Apostle: A Concise Introduction* (Grand Rapids: Baker Academic, 2018).

Hengel, Martin. *The Son of God: The Origin of Christology and the History of Jewish-Hellenistic Religion*. Translated by John Bowden. London: SCM, 1976. Hengel argues for a Jewish background to the Son of God title in the New Testament, with particular attention given to Paul's theology and the *early* rise of high Christology.

Though a bit dated now, the voluminous footnotes in this short book continue to be a wealth of impressive information.

Ridderbos, Herman. *Paul: An Outline of His Theology*. Translated by John Richard De Witt. Grand Rapids: Eerdmans, 1975. A classic work on Paul's theology from a Reformed perspective, situating Paul's theology in light of the history of redemption accomplished in Christ; Ridderbos brings eschatology to the forefront.

V

THE SON OF GOD IN HEBREWS TO REVELATION

THE EXALTED AND RETURNING KING

WE TURN NOW TO THE remaining nine books of the New Testament: Hebrews through Revelation all speak to the challenges of life in a fallen world and how a proper understanding of Christ is key to living faithfully. These books provide additional teaching on the atoning sacrifice of Christ, his heavenly high priesthood, his preexistence and activity in the Old Testament, his resurrection authority, and his future reign. Collectively these letters show us that we need to think of Christ not only in his incarnate state of suffering and humiliation but also in his present state of glory and his future return.

HEBREWS

Identity of Christ

The Eternal Son of God

HEBREWS TEACHES THAT CHRIST IS the eternal Son of God who has become incarnate for our salvation and fulfills the role of great high priest.[1] Hebrews 1:1–4 can be arranged in chiastic fashion, centering on the ontology of the divine Son in 1:3a–b: the Son is the radiance of God the

1. For further exploration of the person and work of Christ in Hebrews (which expands on this discussion), see Brandon D. Crowe, "Son and Priest, Then and Now: Christology and Redemptive History in Hebrews in Light of the History of Interpretation," *WTJ* 84 (2022): 19–38. Used with permission.

Father's glory. He created (1:2) and upholds the world (1:3). Further, the eternal Son became incarnate as a true man and has accomplished salvation, thus inheriting a better name than the angels (1:4). To summarize the Christology of Hebrews, Christ is both Son and high priest. More extensively, Hebrews speaks of Christ as prophet (e.g., 1:1–2; 2:12–13), priest (e.g., 3:1; 4:14; 5:1–10; 7:26), and king (e.g., 1:3–5; 5:5–6).

This interplay of eternal and redemptive-historical sonship is also apparent in the Old Testament quotations in Hebrews 1:5–13. These are bracketed by Psalm 2:7 and 110:1, which highlight the accomplishment of salvation by the eternal Son in the economy of redemption. The "today" on which the Son was begotten is most likely a reference to the resurrection of Jesus (see also 5:5), though this is the resurrection of the eternal Son of God. Psalm 110:1 is frequently used in the New Testament to speak of the victorious Christ in his glorified state (see Heb 10:12–14), and the same psalm (Ps 110:4) elsewhere in Hebrews speaks of the Melchizedekian high priesthood of Christ (Heb 5:6; 7:17, 20; see also 5:10).

Psalm 45:6–7 (44:7–8 LXX) in Hebrews 1:8–9 has in view the Messiah who sits on the throne of David (see also 2 Sam 7:14 [cf. 1 Chr 17:13] in 1:5), also attesting the divinity of Christ. Here God addresses God who sits on the throne.[2] The quotation of Psalm 102:25–27 (101:26–28 LXX) in Hebrews 1:10–12 further attests the divinity of the Son: he is the Lord who laid the foundations of the earth and who will remain forever. Similarly, the author speaks of "Jesus Christ as the same yesterday and today and forever" (13:8). The sameness (indeed, immutability) of Christ in perpetuity assumes his divinity,[3] even as it assumes the perpetuity of his high priesthood.[4] Hebrews 13:8 may also reflect the threefold affirmation of eternity common in the context of the first century, which (along with correlations to Ps 102) does indeed highlight the eternity of the Son.[5]

---

2. See F. F. Bruce, *The Epistle to the Hebrews*, NICNT (Grand Rapids: Eerdmans, 1964), 20; Nick Brennan, *Divine Christology in the Epistle to the Hebrews: The Son as God*, LNTS 656 (London: T&T Clark, 2021), 61–62.

3. Compare Owen, *Hebrews* 7:426–28; Brennan, *Divine Christology*, 66–70; Muller, *PRRD* 4:319.

4. Ellingworth, *Epistle to the Hebrews*, 705; Bruce, *Hebrews*, 396.

5. See, e.g., Richard Bauckham, "The Divinity of Jesus in the Letter of the Hebrews," in *Jesus and the God of Israel: God Crucified and Other Studies on the New Testament's Christology of*

Hebrews 2

The work of Christ as Messiah and high priest assumes his incarnation, which receives extended attention in Hebrews 2:5–18. The eternal Son has defeated death and salvation in the flesh, thus fulfilling God's design for humanity. To this end in 2:5–8 the author cites Psalm 8:4–6 (8:5–7 LXX), which reflects on the role of humanity to rule over God's creation (see Gen 1:26–28). There is, however, a disconnect: If all of creation is to be subject to humanity, why is this not our experience (Heb 2:8)? Though we do not see this reality yet, we do see Jesus, who has been crowned with glory and honor.

Hebrews 2:5–18 thus extols the logic and wonders of the true humanity of the Son in the incarnation. Psalm 8 helps readers understand why it was fitting for the Son to suffer and die (Heb 2:10). For humanity to realize the dominion envisioned in the beginning, and thus to receive an inheritance of salvation, sin and death had to be defeated. This had to be done by a man. Yet no natural, sinful person could do this—nor could any angel. It was therefore fitting for the eternal Son of God to become a man that he might defeat the devil who holds the power of death and slavery (2:14–15). By assuming human nature, suffering, dying, and rising again, Jesus has conquered Satan and delivers us from sin, realizing the vision for humanity of ruling over God's creation. The Son's suffering qualified him to be a merciful and faithful high priest (2:17).

The Son as Truly Human

As a true man who has defeated death, Jesus is the ἀρχηγός of salvation (2:10; see also 12:2). As we saw in Acts, ἀρχηγός communicates the solidarity of Jesus with his people: Jesus leads the way and identifies with us.[6] Moreover, it is striking that this term is always used in the New Testament to refer to the resurrection of Jesus,[7] since there is true solidarity between Jesus, the firstfruits of the resurrection, and the resurrection of believers (see 1 Cor 15:20).[8] The term is also used in the Old Testament to refer to Israel's

Divine Identity (Milton Keynes, UK: Paternoster, 2008), 252–53; Brennan, *Divine Christology*, 134.

6. Vos, "Priesthood of Christ," 133.
7. So Ellingworth, *Hebrews*, 160.
8. See Gaffin, *Centrality of the Resurrection*, 34–36.

leaders in the wilderness (Num 10:4; 13:2–3; see also Exod 6:14; Num 14:4)[9]—as ἀρχηγός Jesus leads his redeemed people to the promised land by his resurrection from the dead.

Because Jesus accomplishes salvation by rising to new life, it is fitting for the one who is the radiance of God's glory to suffer, and only through him does world history realize its goal through humanity.

Human High Priest

Jesus is not only the divine Son of God, but he is also one of us and is not ashamed to call us brothers and sisters (2:11). Hebrews teaches that Jesus is truly human, and this is closely related to his role as high priest. However, an important caveat is necessary here: it would not be appropriate to say that Jesus is only a priest inasmuch as he is a man.[10] That would be to deny the pre-incarnate realities of prophet, priest, and king that are true of the Son as Mediator already in the days of the Old Testament.[11] This is important, for as we will see below, it is common in Hebrews studies today to deny that Christ was a priest in his state of humiliation. However, such an approach fails to recognize the importance of the priestly ministry of the Son prior to the incarnation and thus too strongly disassociates the person of the mediator from his mediatorial work.[12]

Even so, the incarnation is important for the priestly work of Christ in Hebrews. Hebrews teaches that Jesus is uniquely qualified to serve as a high priest because he is not only divine, but also truly human. The climactic work of the divine Mediator as priest comes when he assumes a human nature in organic continuity with those he came to save. He made purification for sin and sat down at the right hand of God (1:3), in the heavenly sanctuary, behind the inner curtain (6:19–20). He has entered the heavenly world (1:6;[13] 2:5; 4:14) as a high priest forever after the order

9. Craig R. Koester, *Hebrews: A New Translation with Introduction and Commentary*, AB 36 (New York: Doubleday, 2001), 228–29, 236.

10. See the important contribution of Brennan, *Divine Christology*, 115–46.

11. See Bavinck, *RD*, 3:364–65; Brennan, *Divine Christology*, 117–18.

12. I will discuss concept this in more detail in chs. 7–9.

13. On οἰκουμένην as the "heavenly world" in 1:6, see Koester, *Hebrews*, 193; Ellingworth, *Hebrews*, 117–18; David M. Moffitt, *Atonement and the Logic of Resurrection in the Epistle to the Hebrews*, NovTSup 141 (Leiden: Brill, 2011), 53–118.

of Melchizedek (5:5–6, 10; 6:20; 7:1–28). Like Melchizedek, Jesus is not only a king but a priest.

The royal and priestly also come together in Psalm 110, which speaks of the Lord seated at the right hand of the LORD (110:1). This "Lord" is a priest forever (110:4). Melchizedek's priesthood is not according to the genealogical descent of the later Levitical priesthood. In this sense, he is without father or mother (7:3). Melchizedek was a real man who anticipated the divine priest-king, whose everlasting kingship is likewise not according to the law of Levitical descent. Indeed, Melchizedek resembles the Son of God, not vice versa (7:3); Jesus is preeminent to Melchizedek.[14] Jesus has conquered death and serves as a priest forever by the power of an indestructible life (7:16)—likely referring to the resurrection (which also assumes his divinity).[15] It is thus as a glorified man that the Son of God in heaven intercedes for his people. He lifts our shared humanity to the innermost sanctum of heaven.[16]

Before ascending in indestructible glory, the Son suffered in human weakness and was made perfect as a high priest (2:9–10, 18; 5:8–10). He has been tempted in every way, just as we are, yet he remained without sin (4:15); he can therefore sympathize with us and help us when we are tempted (2:18).[17] Further, since he never gave in to temptation, he has in one sense been tempted even more than we have, for at some point we have all caved to the pressure of temptation.[18] As it has often been observed, "Sinlessness heightens, not lessens, temptations."[19]

Christ understands our struggles and can help us. Even so, there are limitations to how far we can push the similarities between our temptations and Christ's temptations. I will return to this topic in chapter 9, where I address the question of whether Christ could or could not sin (that is, whether Christ in his state of humiliation was peccable or impeccable). There I will argue

14. Vos, "Priesthood of Christ," 152; Koester, *Hebrews*, 343 (following Bengel); Karen H. Jobes, *Letters to the Church: A Survey of Hebrews and the General Epistles* (Grand Rapids: Zondervan, 2011), 106.

15. See Brennan, *Divine Christology*, 122, 142–44.

16. Morales, *Who Shall Ascend*, 258.

17. See Vos, "Priesthood of Christ," 145–46.

18. E.g., Jones, *Knowing Christ*, 114–15.

19. Jones, *Knowing Christ*, 114.

more extensively for Christ's impeccability. Hebrews presents Jesus as the perfectly holy Son of God; unlike us, he had no internal pull toward sin.[20] His temptations toward evil were purely external, not internal. Moreover, the emphasis in Hebrews on Christ's temptation was not to evil in particular, but seems specifically to have been temptation to avoid suffering—whether he would persevere in his calling as messianic priest (see 2:18).[21] Suffering can lead us to sin; we therefore need a high priest who can keep us from apostasy.[22] The perfection in view in Hebrews (e.g., 5:8–10) is not ontological perfection, for the divine Son of God lacks no perfection. This is instead perfection in a redemptive-historical sense: he is made perfect as the high priest, come in the fullness of time, to bring redemptive history to a climax.[23]

This focus on the Son's knowledge of our weakness and the way he has shared in the weakness of our humanity help us see that not only is Christ a heavenly high priest now, but he was already a priest during his earthly ministry (e.g., 5:7; 10:1–10). To be sure, there is a unique focus in Hebrews on the heavenly high priesthood of Christ, but his priestly ministry also includes his work in the state of humiliation, including his lifelong obedience and his sacrifice on the cross.

Achievement of Christ

New Covenant

As HIGH PRIEST JESUS HAS inaugurated the new covenant, which is better than the Mosaic covenant (see Heb 8:6–7). Central to this new covenant is the blood of the Mediator. It was not possible ultimately for the blood of bulls and goats to take away sins; only through the mediation of the unique God-man (θεάνθρωπος), whose blood is truly effectual, can our sins be taken away. This new covenant has a better foundation, since its priestly mediator is established not by Levitical law but by an oath (7:15–22; see also 5:5). In light of this new covenant, the Mosaic covenant is no longer a viable option for governing life today; it is obsolete (8:13). To be sure, it was a real administration of the one covenant of grace, and the efficacy of Christ's sacrifice applied to true believers even in the Old Testament (WCF 7.5). But now that Christ has come, the Mosaic covenant has served its

20. Bavinck, *RD* 3:315; see also 3:252–53; 3:408; Calvin, *Inst.* 2.16.12 (1:518–19).
21. See Vos, "Priesthood of Christ," 149; Bavinck, *RD* 3:315n233.
22. Compare Vos, "Priesthood of Christ," 146.
23. See similarly Moisés Silva, "Perfection and Eschatology in Hebrews," *WTJ* 39 (1976): 60–71.

purpose as a governing covenant administration. In contrast, the new covenant is the eternal covenant that will never be broken, for it is founded on the work of the resurrected Christ (Heb 13:20). Its Mediator is Christ himself (9:15). The new covenant is better because it is the perfect covenant—that is, it is the final covenant, which will not be surpassed and will not grow obsolete. It is the substance to which the Mosaic covenant pointed.

Hebrews 9–10

One of the reasons the new covenant is better is the final, perfect sacrifice of Christ. Whereas the old covenant required repeated sacrifices to cleanse earthly copies of heavenly realities (9:23), Christ by one sacrifice has perfected for all time those who are being sanctified (10:10, 14). His bodily sacrifice is the final, perfect sacrifice (10:10; see also 10:1). It is perfect both in its finality (10:2–3) and efficacy (10:4). It is once for all, and by means of this sacrifice he now serves not in an earthly tent but in heaven itself (9:24). He does not simply enter the sanctuary once a year, but always dwells and intercedes for us at God's right hand (1:13; 8:1; 10:12; 12:2) as the one who has secured forgiveness.[a] Jesus's one sacrifice provides true forgiveness, obviating the need for any future sacrifice (10:18).

The priesthood of Christ includes his perfect obedience, which is evidenced in the quotation of Psalm 40:6–8 (39:7–9 LXX) in Hebrews 10:5–7.[b] Though David sought the Lord and obeyed the Torah (40:8), David experienced trouble for his own sins (Ps 40:12), and David did not rise from the dead (Acts 13:37–38). David anticipated a greater Son who would more fully obey, yielding lasting deliverance. Jesus's lifelong, bodily obedience enabled him to serve as the final sacrifice. The finality of his sacrifice is seen in his resurrection (which vindicated his perfect obedience), in his ascension, and in the true forgiveness effected by his one offering. In contrast to previous priests, Jesus had no sin for which atonement was needed (Heb 7:27), and there was no dichotomy between sacrifice and obedience in Christ himself.[c] Jesus rose from the dead in accord with his perfect obedience, enabling him to serve in his body as the final, effectual sacrifice (Heb 10:8–10).

a. See also Owen, *Works* 1:254.

b. See e.g., Owen, *Works* 1:207, 323, 335–36, 339; Turretin, *Inst.* 14.8 (2:403–8); 14.12.6, 8 (2:439–40); 14.13 (2:445–55); Bavinck, *RD* 3:394.

c. See also Lane, *Hebrews 1–8*, cxxxiv; William L. Lane, *Hebrews 9–13*, WBC 47B (Nashville: Thomas Nelson, 2000), 266.

Priest on Earth and in Heaven

THE SACRIFICE OF CHRIST IS thus the culmination of his entire life of obedience. Christ was a priest already on earth (and indeed, already in the Old Testament), even though he now serves as a high priest in heaven as the exalted God-man. Yet Hebrews says that if Jesus were on earth, he would not be a priest at all (8:4). This certainly sounds like Jesus was not a priest while on earth, and many affirm this interpretation today.[24] But what the author of Hebrews has in view the type of priesthood Jesus fulfills—8:4 refers to Levitical priesthood. Jesus is not a Levitical priest based on bodily descent (see 7:14), but is instead a priest after the order of Melchizedek, which requires a heavenly ministry. Jesus occupies a different realm of priesthood. So while we can affirm the importance of Christ's heavenly priestly ministry, that is not the same thing as denying altogether the earthly ministry of Jesus.

I make a few brief points here about the importance of affirming Christ's earthly priestly work.[25]

1. First, the death of Christ is indeed central to the atonement theology of Hebrews.[26] On the Day of Atonement, which Hebrews invokes, the bull and the goat did not simply have some of their blood let, but were actually slaughtered (Lev 16:11, 15).[27] Additionally, Jamieson has argued helpfully that Leviticus 17:11 is best understood as a "life-for-life exchange" and thus has in view the death of the victim.[28]

Further, ἱλάσκομαι in Hebrews 2:17 points to the wrath-bearing nature of his death.[29] The bodily appearance of Jesus in heaven does not entirely capture the means by which propitiation was made. Propitiation requires

---

24. E.g., Moffitt, *Atonement*, 198–208; David M. Moffitt, "It Is Not Finished: Jesus's Perpetual Atoning Work as the Heavenly High Priest in Hebrews," in Laansma, Guthrie, and Westfall, *So Great a Salvation*, 161, 162n14; Jamieson, *Jesus' Death and Heavenly Offering*, 24, 34–35, 70.

25. A fuller discussion is found in Crowe, "Both Son and Priest."

26. So rightly Jamieson, *Jesus' Death*, 97–179.

27. Hebrew: שׁחט; Greek: σφάζω.

28. Jamieson, *Jesus' Death*, 135; see also 135–41.

29. Compare Morris, *Apostolic Preaching*, 108–24. He argues persuasively that the blood typically refers to the *death* rather than the *life*. He further argues that ἱλάσκομαι in Heb 2:17 is best translated "propitiate" (*Apostolic Preaching*, 125, 174–77).

the death of the sacrificial victim, even if the point in 2:17 is on the propitiatory aspects of his ongoing, heavenly ministry.[30]

Christ's death is probably also in view in Hebrews 1:3, where the aorist participle ποιησάμενος ("having made") modifying the aorist verb ἐκάθισεν ("he sat") most likely refers to antecedent time. Thus, Christ sat down after making purification. To be sure, this does not solve the question of precisely when and where purification took place, for Christ may have appeared in the sanctuary to present himself as the offering and then sat down.[31] But this is more probably a reference to Christ's death, which then culminates in his heavenly priestly activity. The same is true for 9:12, where the aorist participle εὑράμενος ("having obtained") speaks of redemption accomplished, after which Christ entered (εἰσῆλθεν) into the heavenly holy of holies.[32]

This perspective may find support in 10:12, 14, which speaks of the one offering of Christ. Though this one offering is commonly taken today to refer to Christ's heavenly offering,[33] given the focus on the earthly obedience of Jesus and the sacrifice of his body in 10:5–10, it is more likely that in 10:10 Jesus's offering is his death on the cross, rather than the presentation of himself in heaven. To be clear, this is not to deny that Christ's heavenly priesthood is emphasized in Hebrews. It is instead to affirm that Christ is a priest both on earth and in heaven, and we cannot sharply divide between these aspects of his priesthood.[34] It is also artificial to bracket off the resurrection or ascension from the death of Christ (or, for that matter, from his lifelong obedience). The work of Christ is a unified whole.[35]

---

30. See, e.g., Vos, "Priesthood of Christ," 145; Richard B. Gaffin Jr., "The Priesthood of Christ: A Servant in the Sanctuary," in *The Perfect Saviour: Key Themes in Hebrews*, ed. Jonathan Griffiths (Nottingham, UK: Inter-Varsity, 2012), 52–56. Both understand this verse to refer to the heavenly high priestly ministry of Christ but not to the exclusion of his propitiatory death.

31. Thus, e.g., Ribbens says that the ambiguity here is clarified later in the epistle, and it refers to the *heavenly* offering of Christ. See Benjamin J. Ribbens, *Levitical Sacrifice and Heavenly Cult in Hebrews*, BZNW 222 (Berlin: de Gruyter, 2016) 99; see also Jamieson, *Jesus' Death*, 83–84.

32. See BDAG, "εὑρίσκω," 412 (#3); Robert J. Cara, *Hebrews: A Mentor Commentary* (Fearn, UK: Mentor, forthcoming).

33. E.g., Ribbens, *Levitical Sacrifice*, 127–29; Jamieson, *Jesus' Death*, 74–78.

34. See Vos, "Priesthood of Christ," 157; see also WLC 42; WSC 23.

35. E.g., Bavinck, *RD*, 394–95; see also Jamieson, *Jesus' Death*, 155; similarly, Ribbens, *Levitical Sacrifice*, 132–34.

In sum, we must not deemphasize the role of Christ's death in Hebrews and transfer the efficacy entirely to the heavenly priesthood of Christ.

2. Second, Hebrews does indeed teach that Christ was priest on earth. Hebrews 8:4 should thus not be taken in an ultimate sense but in a comparative or specific sense.[36] That is, Christ could not serve in the earthly sanctuary according to the Levitical law, for he was from the tribe of Judah. In this specific sense Jesus is properly a priest only in heaven.[37] Even so, this does not mean that Christ did not occupy the office of a priest, more broadly speaking, while on earth.

We are thus not faced with an either-or scenario for the timing of and location of Christ's priesthood. Yes, Christ serves as a priest in heaven in a consummate sense, but he also served as a priest on earth, during his days of humiliation. This is also highlighted in Hebrews 5:7, where Jesus's prayers, which were accepted, are portrayed as priestly service.[38] Simply put, the death of Christ was a priestly act, and this priestly act occurred on earth.[39]

3. Christ's priesthood is not a Levitical priesthood but a Melchizedekian priesthood. Therefore, it is no problem to say that Christ served as a priest even though he was not from the tribe of Levi. For the Melchizedekian priesthood preceded and has priority over the Levitical priesthood. The Melchizedekian priesthood was in effect prior to the law of Moses and persists beyond the fulfillment of the law of Moses.[40]

4. The word/concept distinction is important. Sometimes a theological term can describe a concept in a text, even where that theological term is not used in the text. We have seen throughout this study that Christ's priesthood (as part of his threefold office) is amply attested throughout Scripture, even though the term "priest" is rarely used explicitly for Jesus. Likewise in Hebrews, even though the terminology of "priest" (Gk.

---

36. See also Turretin, *Inst.* 14.8.8 (2:405–6); Vos, "Priesthood of Christ," 154–59; à Brakel, *Christian's Reasonable Service* 1:543. Contrast Ribbens, *Levitical Sacrifice*, 108; Jamieson, *Jesus' Death*, 24, 34–35 (though also see 191–93).

37. See Vos, "Priesthood of Christ," 133: "the only place where [the Savior and true high priest] can properly dwell and effectually minister is the heavenly sanctuary" (see also 142).

38. See, e.g., Lane, *Hebrews 1–8*, 119–20; Luke Timothy Johnson, *Hebrews: A Commentary*, New Testament Library (Louisville: Westminster John Knox, 2006), 146. See also Martin, *Atonement*, 61–62; à Brakel, *Christian's Reasonable Service* 1:542.

39. So, e.g., Turretin, *Inst.* 14.8.6 (2:404–5).

40. See Letham, *Work of Christ*, 109; compare Turretin, *Inst.* 14.9.2 (2:406).

ἀρχιερεύς, ἱερεύς) is reserved for Christ's heavenly ministry, his earthly ministry is described in priestly ways.

5. 3 distinctive testimony about the priesthood of Christ does not conflict with other New Testament witnesses. Elsewhere in the New Testament the death of Christ is central,[41] and if we end up with an interpretation of Hebrews that is one-sided against the view that Christ's death is important, then we need to reassess our interpretation. It may be that the distinctive teaching of Hebrews about Jesus in his heavenly state is not so different from the Pauline teaching on the glorified and ascended Christ who pours out his Spirit on his church (see Eph 4),[42] or the Lukan discussion of the ongoing work of Christ in his state of exaltation. Indeed, in Paul's letters both the death of Christ and his exaltation are important (e.g., Rom 4:25; 5:6–8; 10; Phil 2:6–11; 1 Tim 3:16).

The Work of Christ and the History of Redemption

Hebrews speaks of the priestly work of Christ as that which provides perfection. This teaching can be understood in two major ways. First, Christ brings objectively the perfection of the final, eschatological age. This refers to *historia salutis*, or the history of salvation, as noted in the previous chapter. Christ inaugurates the new covenant age of fulfillment.[43] He accomplishes a more lasting redemption even than the exodus (see Heb 9:15). His blood is truly effectual (10:4) and speaks a better word than Abel's (12:24). The Mosaic covenant was provisional, which has now yielded to the perfect, new covenant (13:20), including the final sacrifice, which fulfills the Levitical sacrificial system.[44] Christ's death has provided the true ransom for sin (9:15).

Second, the perfection that Christ brings in the history of redemption also affects the experience of salvation, that is, the *ordo salutis*. Hebrews does not teach that those who lived under the Levitical sacrificial system

41. A point also made by Benjamin J. Ribbens, "Ascension and Atonement: The Significance of Post-Reformation, Reformed Responses to Socinians for Contemporary Atonement Debates in Hebrews," *WTJ* 80 (2018): 22–23; Jamieson, *Jesus' Death*, 99, 116.

42. See also Vos, who argues that the teaching of Hebrews mirrors that of Paul's focus on the application of salvation by the glorified Christ ("Priesthood," 158).

43. See Silva, "Perfection and Eschatology," 64–68.

44. Morales, "Atonement in Ancient Israel," 37. See also Heb 2:10; 5:9; 7:11; 8:5; 10:1; 12:2.

did not have true forgiveness of sins (see 9:15).[45] But the Levitical sacrifices were not ultimate or final; they anticipated the coming of the perfect sacrifice in Christ. His sacrifice is the truly effectual sacrifice and is applied not only prospectively to those who come after him but retrospectively to those who came prior to him in redemptive history.[46] They had true forgiveness of sins, though there are some differences in the "perfect" age: especially greater cleansing of conscience (Heb 9:9, 14), greater confidence (4:14–16), and greater intimacy with God (6:19–20; 7:19, 25).[47]

Leader of a New Exodus

HEBREWS SPEAKS OF GOD'S PEOPLE on a journey through the wilderness of this age as we anticipate entrance into the heavenly rest of the eternal Sabbath (see Heb 3:7–4:13). The exodus is central to the way that the author communicates this already/not-yet reality. Already we have been delivered and participate in the new covenant; but we have not yet entered the eschatological promised land of the heavenly Jerusalem (see 4:1, 11; 13:14). But things are better in the new covenant. For our leader is not Joshua, who provided entrance into the provisional promised land (4:8), but our leader is Jesus himself, the forerunner (ἀρχηγός) who has gone through suffering and death, has risen to new life, and is ascended in heaven (2:10; 12:2).

Jesus is thus the forerunner and apostle (ὁ ἀπόστολος) of our confession (3:1), who leads us on a greater exodus than Moses (Exod 3:10–15).[48] Likewise, the covenant he inaugurates is greater than the Mosaic covenant, for Christ's blood seals the eternal (i.e., new) covenant (13:20). Thus, while the Mosaic covenant and the new covenant are both part of the one covenant of grace, the shadows of the Mosaic administration have met their goal in the realities of the new covenant. Jesus, the resurrected high priest, is the great shepherd of the sheep (Heb 13:20; see also John 10:10–11). He is coming again for the salvation of those who are eagerly awaiting him (Heb 9:27–28).

---

45. So Cara, *Hebrews*.

46. A helpful contemporary discussion is Ribbens, *Levitical Sacrifice*. For a classic discussion, see Turretin, *Inst.* 12.12.15 (2:266).

47. See also Turretin, *Inst.* 12.8.19–25 (2:238–40); WCF 20.1.

48. See Koester, *Hebrews*, 228–29, 236, 243, 249; see also Ellingworth, *Hebrews*, 200.

We therefore congregate at a better mountain than Mount Sinai. Instead, we come to the heavenly Jerusalem (12:18–24), gathered in the new covenant by the blood of our Mediator. We worship not in the provisional ceremonies of the Mosaic covenant but in the permanent substance of the new covenant. Christ's kingdom cannot be shaken (12:28); it lasts forever.

CATHOLIC EPISTLES

James

The Epistle of James focuses mostly on how we ought to live in light of the coming of Christ; the person and work of Christ are largely assumed.[49] Even so, James speaks of the Lord Jesus Christ (Jas 1:1) and of Jesus Christ, the Lord of glory (2:1).[50] As we have already seen, to identify Jesus as Lord of glory is to identify him with the glory that is characteristic of the one true God. Additionally, the title "Lord" (κύριος) in James can be used for both the Father (1:7; 3:9; 4:10; 5:4, 10–11) and the Son (1:1; 2:1; 5:7), further attesting the divinity of Jesus. Sometimes it is even difficult to know whether the Father or Son is in view (e.g., 5:14–15). Likewise, both Father (4:12) and Son (5:9) appear to be identified as judge in James.[51]

James also assumes that Christ has fulfilled the law of God. James speaks of the perfect law (1:25), the royal law (2:8), and the law of liberty (1:25; 2:12). These refer to the Old Testament law in relationship to Jesus himself. Though David could say that the law was perfect in the Old Testament (Ps 19:7 [19:8 MT; 18:8 LXX]; Heb. תמים; Gk. ἄμωμος), the terminology used in James for "perfect" (τέλειος) seems to denote realization of an eschatological goal that comes through Christ (1:4; see also Matt 5:48; 19:21; Eph 4:13; Col 1:28; Heb 9:11). In this sense, it is similar to the verb τελειόω (see Jas 2:22) and the concept of fulfillment (πληρόω) in the Gospels. Christ is the goal to which the law of Moses points (see Rom 10:4). The law is the

49. See Benjamin Breckinridge Warfield, "The Person of Christ according to the New Testament," in Craig, *Person and Work of Christ*, 38, 50–51. More recently, see Karl-Wilhelm Niebuhr, "One God, One Lord in the Epistle of James," in Novenson, *Monotheism and Christology*, 172–88.

50. On the Greek construction (τοῦ κυρίου ἡμῶν Ἰησοῦ Χριστοῦ της δόξης), see Ralph P. Martin, *James*, WBC 48 (Waco, TX: Word, 1988), 59–60. *Pace* Dale C. Allison Jr., *A Critical and Exegetical Commentary on the Epistle of James*, ICC (New York: Bloomsbury T&T Clark, 2013), 382–84, who argues for omitting ἡμῶν Ἰησοῦ Χριστοῦ.

51. See also Brandon D. Crowe, "The Trinity and the General Epistles," in Crowe and Trueman, *Essential Trinity*, 139–55.

perfect law of liberty preeminently because Christ has fulfilled it.[52] James emphasizes the moral aspects of God's law, summarized by Jesus's two great commands (see 2:8, 19). This royal law is the law of the kingdom—the law of Christ (see also 1 Cor 9:21). This glorious Lord Jesus Christ lives today, and he will return as judge of the world (Jas 5:7, 9).

1 Peter

Person of Christ in 1 Peter

First Peter speaks even more extensively of the person and work of Christ. The opening verses speak of salvation in Trinitarian terms: the elect are chosen according to God the Father's foreknowledge, sanctified by the Holy Spirit, and sprinkled with the blood of Jesus, whom we are to obey (1:1–2). The ease with which Peter speaks of salvation in these terms points us to the divinity of Christ. Further, Christ was foreknown before the foundation of the world (1:20), which most likely speaks as his being foreknown as the mediator of the covenant of grace.[53] The identification of the Holy Spirit as the Spirit of Christ who was active in the Old Testament (1:10–11) also attests the preexistence of Christ: "Not only does prophecy bear witness to Jesus, but Jesus bears witness through prophecy."[54]

This is a striking apposition of ideas: the Son who preexisted is also the Son who became incarnate for us and for our salvation, suffering for us. He is our prophet, priest, and king. As prophet, it was the Spirit of Christ who predicted his coming through the prophets; they all anticipated the coming of the greater prophet. Yet this prophet spoke nothing deceitful, and he remained silent before his accusers (2:22–23; see also Isa 53:9).

---

52. Similar observations are made by Dan G. McCartney, *James*, BECNT (Grand Rapids: Baker Academic, 2009), 123–24; Douglas J. Moo, *The Letter of James*, PNTC (Grand Rapids: Eerdmans, 2000), 94.

53. See, e.g., Turretin, *Inst.* 4.10.5–6 (1:352); 12.2.15 (2:178); 14.5.2 (2:391); Owen, *Works* 1:56; Bavinck, *RD* 3:214, see also 3:387; Berkhof, *Systematic Theology*, 113; Edmund Clowney, *The Message of 1 Peter: The Way of the Cross*, The Bible Speaks Today (Downers Grove, IL: InterVarsity Press, 1988), 72.

54. Clowney, *1 Peter*, 58.

As priest, he was led like a lamb, silent to the slaughter (see Isa 53:7), and by his wounds we have been healed (1 Pet 2:24; see also Isa 53:4–5, 12).[55] His blood provides true redemption (1 Pet 1:18–19). Likewise, he is the (temple) stone rejected by people, but raised by God (2:4). The Old Testament cultic system finds its goal in Christ, the lamb of God. Not only is Christ the sacrificial Lamb, but he is also the Shepherd (2:25; 5:4).

And to speak of Christ as Shepherd is to speak of him as king. David was both a shepherd and a king. God himself is both Shepherd and King (Ps 23:1–6; Ezek 34:11–16).[56] If 1 Peter 2:13 is a reference to Jesus as Lord,[57] then it may be significant that this comes in a context exhorting the audience to subject themselves to every human institution. Given the context of the Roman Empire, Peter seems to say: be subject to the "lordship" even of the emperor in light of the more universal lordship of Christ (2:13–17). As Lord, Jesus Christ is King of kings.

Work of Christ in 1 Peter UNDERSTANDING JESUS AS PROPHET, PRIEST, and king leads us to consider his work in more detail. We are redeemed by his sacrificial, substitutionary death (1:18–19) and, like God's people at Mount Sinai, set apart as God's covenant people by the sprinkling of his blood (1:2; see also Exod 24:6–8; 1 Pet 2:9–10). Central to his mission is his suffering and subsequent glories. This was predicted in the Old Testament (1 Pet 1:10–11) and fulfilled in his earthly life, death, and resurrection. Just as Christ's earthly lot was suffering that yielded glory (1:3, 21; 2:4, 23), so also his disciples, who follow in his steps, should keep the impending glory in mind as we face suffering (1:14–21; 2:4–5, 21–25; 4:13; 5:1).

---

55. The application of Isa 53 to Jesus in 1 Pet 2 further confirms the legitimacy of speaking of Christ as the suffering servant.

56. See also Clowney, *1 Peter*, 199–201.

57. So Thomas R. Schreiner, *1 & 2 Peter and Jude*, Christian Standard Commentary, 2nd ed. (Nashville: Holman Reference, 2020), 139. Alternatively see Paul J. Achtemeier, *1 Peter: A Commentary on First Peter*, Hermeneia (Minneapolis: Fortress, 1996), 182.

1 Peter 3

Christ's suffering and subsequent glories help us understand 1 Peter 3:18–22, which is one of the most difficult passages in the New Testament. The basic thrust of this passage is found in verse 18, with the details of verses 19–22 providing supporting and supplemental discussion. Particularly important for the main point is verse 18b, which contains a purpose or result clause in Greek, introduced by ἵνα ("in order to"). In this passage Christ was "put to death in the body but made alive by the Spirit" (NIV 1984). The phrase ζῳοποιηθεὶς δὲ πνεύματι ("but made alive by the Spirit") is probably best understood as a dative of means with reference to the Holy Spirit. This differs from the previous dative phrase (θανατωθεὶς μὲν σαρκί, "put to death in the body"), where σαρκί ("in/by the flesh") is best taken as a dative of sphere. Thus, the two datives are not entirely parallel.[a] The dative "in/by the flesh" (σαρκί) refers to the sphere of Christ's death, and the dative "in/by the Spirit" (πνεύματι) refers to the agency of the Holy Spirit in the resurrection of Jesus.[b]

In light of these observations, 1 Peter 3:18 makes several points.[c] Jesus Christ is the righteous one who died as a substitute for the unrighteous. The purpose of this suffering was to provide access—or reconcile us—to God. The means of this reconciliation was his death in the flesh and his rising again to new life in his bodily resurrection by the power of the Holy Spirit.

But we still have to deal with 3:19–21b.[d] Who are the spirits in prison? When and how did Christ preach to them? The best two options are that the spirits in prison refer either to departed souls of the unrighteous who lived in the days of Noah (see also Heb 12:23) or to fallen angels—which are mentioned in 2 Peter 2:4–5; Jude 6. Either of these might be said to be imprisoned. In the former case, Jesus spoke to the souls of those who formerly disobeyed during the days of Noah by the Spirit through Noah (see 1 Pet 1:10–11).[e] In the latter case Jesus (most likely) proclaimed openly his victory over evil spirits in conjunction with his resurrection (see also Eph 1:15–23). In neither case is the best option that Jesus descended himself to the realm of the dead and preached to the souls of believers in prison. The Bible does not teach the so-called *limbus patrum*, which states that after Jesus's death he liberated the souls of believers who were waiting to be freed. Nor does this text teach a postmortem opportunity for repentance (see Heb 9:27). I will return to these issues in chapter 10, where I discuss the resurgent conversations centering on the phrase "he descended to hell" from the Apostles' Creed. To anticipate that discussion, there is nothing in 1 Peter 3:18–22 that requires us to affirm a "geographical" or "local" descent (*descensus*) of Jesus to the realm of the dead between his death and resurrection.

We ought not to get tangled in the exegetical weeds of 1 Peter 3:18–22. The main point is clear: Jesus, the righteous one, died to reconcile us to God. Further, he has risen from the dead to glorious resurrection life. He lives today and is coming again (1:7, 13; 5:4).

a. So also Schreiner, *1 & 2 Peter and Jude*, 208–9; see also Owen, *Works* 3:182.

b. It is also possible that the two datives refer to two different ages or realms: the realm of the flesh and the realm of the Spirit (compare Rom 1:3–4). The first would refer to the subeschatological age and the second to the eschatological age. In this case, Spirit would still be a reference to the Holy Spirit, but the emphasis is more on realized eschatology.

c. Here I am loosely following Brandon D. Crowe, *The Message of the General Epistles in the History of Redemption: Wisdom from James, Peter, John, and Jude* (Phillipsburg, NJ: P&R, 2015), 25–26.

d. See Crowe, *Message of the General Epistles*, 181–84.

e. See Turretin, *Inst.* 13.15.12 (2:360–61); see also 14.7.12 (2:400).

2 Peter, Jude

Person of Christ in 2 Peter, Jude

SECOND PETER 1:1 CONTAINS ONE of the clearest affirmations of the divinity of Christ: he is our God and Savior (τοῦ θεοῦ ἡμῶν καὶ σωτῆρος Ἰησοῦ Χριστοῦ).[58] His divine (θεῖος) power has granted us all we need for life and godliness (1:3). To participate in the divine (θεῖος) nature (1:4) means to become more like Christ in practice. Elsewhere Jesus is our Lord and Savior (1:11; 2:20; 3:2, 18).[59] The divinity of Christ is also assumed in Peter's recounting of the transfiguration, as I argued in chapter 3. Jesus is the bright morning star (1:19; see also Rev 22:16), the fulfillment of the messianic star to arise from Judah (Num 24:17; see also Mal 4:2). He is the glorious Lord whose return is certain.

Jude speaks of Jesus Christ as our only Master and Lord (1:4), and of Christ's preexistence in verse 5: "Now I want to remind you, although you once fully knew it, that Jesus, who saved a people out of the land of Egypt, afterward destroyed those who did not believe." The ESV identifies the one who delivered the Israelites to be Jesus (Ἰησοῦς), though this is a difficult

58. This is another example of the Granville Sharp rule, which states that when two singular personal nouns are joined by καί ("and") and the article appears only before the first noun, then the two nouns refer to the same person. See Wallace, *Greek Grammar*, 270–77. It is also possible that 3:12 refers to Jesus's return as the coming of God.

59. These are also examples of the Granville Sharp rule.

text-critical question. The ESV rendering agrees with the printed reading of the Nestle-Aland twenty-eighth edition, which is most likely correct.[60] Yet even if the best reading is κύριος, the referent would still be Jesus.[61] This verse, and what precedes in verse 4 (where Jesus is identified as "our only master and Lord" [τὸν μόνον δεσπότην καὶ κύριον ἡμῶν]; see also 2 Pet 2:1), communicates an extremely high Christology.[62] Interestingly, if the best reading of verse 5 is 'Ιησοῦς, this could be translated as either "Joshua" or "Jesus." But since Joshua himself did not destroy those who did not believe, then 'Ιησοῦς must refer to Jesus the Lord. This again is exodus language and correlates the experience of the Israelites in the first exodus with the experience of the church in the new covenant (see 1 Cor 10:4). In both cases unbelief will be punished. Holding these together is the same person, whom Jude identifies as Jesus the Lord.

Jude's doxological conclusion speaks of the glory due to the only God through Jesus Christ our Lord (Jude 24–25). The glory of God is understood in relation to Jesus Christ—a remarkable statement that attests the divinity of Christ, since God shares his glory with no other (Isa 48:11).

Work of Christ in 2 Peter, Jude

SECOND PETER AND JUDE ALLUDE to the work of Christ in accomplishing salvation. Jude 3 speaks of the faith once delivered, which refers to the objective content of the gospel accomplished by Christ in which we believe.[63] Likewise, 2 Peter 1:1 speaks of those "who have obtained a faith of equal standing with ours by the righteousness of our God and Savior Jesus Christ." The faith that has been obtained (λαχοῦσιν) might better be translated as the faith "we have received," and like Jude 3 here "faith" (πίστις) refers to the

60. The Nestle-Aland 27th edition printed κύριος ("Lord"); so also NIV 2011. The THGNT and the SBLGNT also both prefer 'Ιησοῦς.

61. See Gathercole, *Preexistent Son*, 36–40; Richard Bauckham, *Jude, 2 Peter*, WBC 50 (Nashville: Thomas Nelson, 1996), 49; Tommy Wasserman, *The Epistle of Jude: Its Text and Transmission*, Coniectanea Neotestamentica 43 (Stockholm: Almqvist & Wiksell, 2006), 264–65; Schreiner, *1 & 2 Peter and Jude*, 534–36. Alternatively, see Bauckham, *Jude and the Relatives*, 307–12.

62. So Jörg Frey, *The Letter of Jude and the Second Letter of Peter: A Theological Commentary*, trans. Kathleen Ess (Waco, TX: Baylor University Press, 2018), 85; see also 76–77, though he argues that v. 5 should read κύριος instead of 'Ιησοῦς (pp. 79–82).

63. That is, *fides quae creditur* ("the faith that is believed"), not *fides qua creditur* ("the faith by which it is believed"). See Richard A. Muller, *Dictionary of Latin and Greek Theological Terms: Drawn Principally from Protestant Scholastic Theology*, 2nd ed. (Grand Rapids: Baker Academic, 2017), 123.

objective contents of the Christian faith. The righteousness of Jesus Christ in 2 Peter 1:1 is probably a reference to the saving righteousness of Jesus Christ.[64] Jesus Christ is our Savior (see also 2 Pet 1:11; 2:20; 3:2, 18).

Jude 9, which refers to the archangel Michael contending with the devil for the body of Moses, may indirectly speak to the authority of Jesus as well.[65] Whereas Michael did not presume to rebuke (ἐπιτιμάω) the devil, Jesus consistently and successfully rebuked the devil and the demonic in his ministry, and this he did without invoking anyone else's name and without any sort of magical incantation.[66] He simply rebuked, perhaps reflecting the authoritative, unique action of God in the Old Testament when he rebukes (גער) Satan, the Red Sea, and the nations (see esp. Zech 3:2). Thus, if not even the highest archangel has the authority to rebuke the devil, then Jesus does not belong to the realm of angels, but must be understood as himself divine.[67]

Both Jude and 2 Peter speak of the return of Christ, which assumes his resurrection. In fact, 2 Peter is largely about the return of Christ (see esp. 2 Pet 3), which was anticipated in his transfiguration (1:16–19). The coming of the Lord with his holy ones in Jude 14 speaks of the return of Christ, as does Jude 21. He is the glorious Lord who reigns over an everlasting kingdom (2 Pet 3:11, 18).

1–3 John MUCH LIKE THE GOSPEL OF John, 1 John identifies Jesus as the divine, preexistent Son and as the source of eternal life (1:1–2; cf. 2:24–25). The final phrase of 1 John 5:20 is particularly succinct: οὗτός ἐστιν ὁ ἀληθινὸς θεὸς καὶ ζωὴ αἰώνιος ("He is the true God and eternal life"). The near demonstrative pronoun οὗτος ("this one/he") most likely refers to Jesus Christ, the nearest antecedent. Though it is remarkable for the clarity with which it identifies Jesus as God, such a statement is not unique in John's literature (John 1:1, 18), nor is it unique among the General Epistles (2 Pet 1:1). Jesus is the only begotten Son (1 John 4:9), who was in the beginning with God (1:1–3). The language of "that which" in 1 John 1:1 may sound abstract, but

64. See, e.g., Douglas J. Moo, *2 Peter and Jude*, NIVAC (Grand Rapids: Zondervan, 1996), 35; John Calvin, *Commentaries on the Catholic Epistles*, trans. and ed. John Owen (repr., Grand Rapids: Baker, 2003), 366–67; Schreiner, *1 & 2 Peter and Jude*, 337–38.

65. For this paragraph I am indebted to Richard Bauckham, "Mark's Christology of Divine Identity" (lecture delivered at the Tyndale House Colloquium on Divine Identity Christology, Cambridge, 11 December 2008). See also Bauckham, *Jude, 2 Peter*, 61–62.

66. See also Hurtado, *Lord Jesus Christ*, 203–5, 287.

67. See also Frey, *Letter of Jude*, 101.

the language is personal—in view is the Son of God, the Word of life (1:1–3). This recalls John 11:25, where Jesus pronounces himself the resurrection and the life, along with John 14:6, and may also support reading "this life" Acts 5:20 as a christological title. Further, the reference to "the one born of God" (ὁ γεννηθεὶς ἐκ τοῦ θεοῦ) in 1 John 5:18 is most likely also a reference to Jesus.[68]

1 John

Jesus is also identified as the Paraclete or Advocate (παράκλητος) in 1 John 2:1. In the Farewell Discourse of the Gospel of John, Jesus identified the coming Spirit as another Advocate (ἄλλον παράκλητον), which also assumes that Christ is himself an Advocate and highlights the continuity between the Spirit's work and Christ's work (John 14:26; 15:26).[a] The good news is that Jesus is the fully righteous one (1 John 2:2), whose intercession for us is effectual. He is also our propitiation (ἱλασμός, 2:2; 4:10)—a term I covered briefly earlier in this chapter, but deserves more attention here. In the twentieth century a lively debated centered on the translation of this word, featuring New Testament scholar C. H. Dodd on the one hand, and responses by scholars such as Leon Morris on the other. Dodd argued that ἱλασμός in the New Testament did not refer to propitiation, which entails wrath bearing (he thought this was a pagan idea) but rather intended only expiation—taking sins away.[b] In response, it has been shown that wrath bearing is indeed entailed in the term ἱλασμός and in its Old Testament background, so propitiation (which does include expiation, but says more than that) is a more appropriate English translation.[c] God is indeed angry at sin, and his wrath is poured out against it. This is why it is necessary for Christ to be our wrath-bearing substitute. I will return to this in a later chapter where I discuss the atonement (ch. 10), but Leon Morris's summary of propitiation in 1 John 4:10 captures the matter well: "It is the combination of the deep love for the sinner and the reaction against sin which brings about the situation in which the Bible refers to propitiation."[d]

a. Both the Gospel of John and 1 John are richly Trinitarian (see 1 John 4:13–16; 5:6–8).

b. See C. H. Dodd, "ΙΛΑΣΚΕΣΘΑΙ, Its Cognates, Derivatives, and Synonyms, in the Septuagint," *Journal of Theological Studies* 32 (1931): 352–50.

c. E.g., Morris, *Apostolic Preaching*, 125–85.

d. Morris, *Apostolic Preaching*, 183.

68. For discussions of the translational options, see Raymond E. Brown, *The Epistles of John: Translated with Introduction, Notes, and Commentary*, AB 30 (New Haven: Yale University Press, 2008), 620–22; Stephen S. Smalley, *1, 2, and 3 John*, rev. ed., WBC 51 (Grand Rapids: Zondervan, 2008), 302–3; Colin J. Kruse, *The Letters of John*, PNTC (Grand Rapids: Eerdmans, 2000), 195.

First John's focus on Christ as propitiation coheres with the letter's overall emphasis on the true incarnation of the Son of God—his suffering and death, in the flesh, really matter. Jesus, resurrected in the flesh, could be seen and touched (1:1–3). Apparently some of the false teachers to whom John responded posited some sort of a dichotomy between Jesus and the Christ (see 2:22; 5:1). Some may have even denied that Jesus Christ had truly come in the flesh, or at least may have denied the reality or efficacy of the bodily suffering of Jesus (4:2; 2 John 7).[69] Yet John insists that Jesus's blood cleanses us from sin (1 John 1:7) and that Jesus Christ truly came by both water and the blood (5:6–7).[70] The incarnation of Jesus Christ, the Son of God (see 4:15; 5:5; 2 John 3), is necessary for our salvation. This anticipates what became a point of contention in the early church: the true incarnation of the Son of God. For in his flesh he obeyed, suffered, died, and rose again; thereby destroying the works of the devil (1 John 3:8; see also John 12:31). Just as surely as he died, he rose again in the flesh. The risen Christ is likely what John had seen, heard, and touched (1 John 1:1–3; see also John 20:26–28).[71] It is also possible that "Jesus Christ having come in the flesh" (Ἰησοῦν Χριστὸν ἐν σαρκὶ ἐληλυθότα) in 1 John 4:2 is a reference to the resurrection appearances of Jesus.[72] And consistent with the rest of the New Testament, this risen Christ is going to return (1 John 2:28; 3:2; 4:17).

THE BOOK OF REVELATION

Divinity of Christ

Christ is the both the revealer of heavenly mysteries (Rev 5:5–10—along with the Father and Spirit) and the source of revelation.[73] His words are the word of God—sharp, like a two-edged sword (2:12, 16; 19:15; see also Heb 4:12). In fact, he is the Word of God (Rev 19:13). Further, he is the judge (2:5, 23; 14:14–16; 19:11; 22:12), who knows all things (see 2:1). We must believe in him (14:12). He is not limited to one place,

69. See Kruse, *Letters of John*, 2–4.

70. This most likely means that it is the same Jesus who was baptized and crucified; there is no dichotomy, no docetism here. See D. A. Carson, "The Three Witnesses and the Eschatology of 1 John," in *To Tell the Mystery: Essays on New Testament Eschatology. Festschrift for Robert H. Gundry*, ed. Thomas E. Schmidt and Moisés Silva, Journal for the Study of the New Testament Supplement Series 100 (Sheffield: JSOT, 1994), 216–32.

71. See further Crowe, *Hope of Israel*, 186–87.

72. See Matthew D. Jensen, *The Resurrection of the Incarnate Christ: A Reading of 1 John*, SNTSMS 153 (Cambridge: Cambridge University Press, 2012), 146–70.

73. Gladd, "Apocalyptic Trinitarian Model," 160–62, also citing (162n15) Bauckham, *Climax of Prophecy*, 135.

but walks among the churches (2:1; see also Matt 28:20). He is not dependent on us to open the door—he is the master who will return and demand entrance (3:20; see also Luke 17:7–8).[74] He has authority over life and death (Rev 2:5, 10–11; 3:5; 21:27; 22:17; see also 22:14), for indeed as the Bread of Life (John 6:35) he is the goal to which the sacramental images of life point (Rev 2:5, 17; see also 19:7–9). He is King of kings and Lord of lords (19:16). He is the bright morning star (2:27–28; 22:16; see also 2 Pet 1:19)—the messianic child prophesied to rule over the nations (Num 24:17; Ps 2:8–9).[75]

Revelation 1

Revelation speaks clearly of the divinity of Christ. In Revelation 1:12–16 Jesus is described in theophanic language that echoes the visions of God appearing in human form in texts such as Ezekiel 1:26–28 and Daniel 7:9–14; 10:5–6.[a] In these texts the divine appearance resembles that of a glorious man, and some include this man seated on the heavenly throne (Ezek 1:26; Dan 7:9, see also 7:13). Christ's white, wool-like hair (1:14) speaks of his divine wisdom (see Dan 7:9, where this is predicated of the Ancient of Days). The shining bronze of his feet (1:15; 2:18) and piercing fire of his eyes (1:14; 2:18; 19:12; see also Dan 10:6) both attest his divinity.[b] He comes with a cloud, like the Son of Man—another sign of theophany (14:14; see also Dan 7:13).

a. See Poythress, *Theophany*, 59–72, 328–30.

b. Compare G. K. Beale, *The Book of Revelation: A Commentary on the Greek Text*, NIGTC (Grand Rapids: Eerdmans, 1999), 208–9, 259, 951–52.

Further attesting Christ's divinity in Revelation is his identification as the first and the last, the Alpha and Omega, the beginning and the end (1:17; 2:8; 22:13). This language echoes the aseity (i.e., self-existence) of God the Father elsewhere in Revelation—the one who is also the first and the last, the Alpha and Omega (1:8; 21:6). This echoes God's uniqueness from Isaiah

74. See Bauckham, *Climax of Prophecy*, 108.

75. See also Beale, *Revelation*, 268–69.

(41:4; 44:6; 48:12).[76] Similarly, the Father is the "one who is, who was, and who is to come" (Rev 1:4, 8; 4:8; see also 11:17; 16:5)—he lives forever (4:9–10; 7:2; 10:6; 15:7)—and throughout Revelation Jesus is the one who lives (1:18) and who is going to return (19:11–16).[77] Indeed, it is striking that Jesus is the one who is coming (ἔρχεται) in (1:7)—with the clouds (!)—and in the next verse it is the Father who comes (ὁ ἐρχόμενος, 1:8).[78] Both Father and Son are described as both living and coming.[79]

Further, both the Father and the Son are recipients of worship. The Father sits on the throne and is worshiped (4:9–11). But as Revelation progresses, not only does the Father sit on the throne, but the Lamb is there as well. The four living creatures surround the throne of God (4:6–8), but between the throne and the living creatures is the Lion of Judah (5:5). Yet—surprisingly—this Lion is actually the Lamb (5:6). He has been crucified but is risen, with all authority and knowledge, full of the Holy Spirit (see 3:1).[80] As the Lamb takes the scroll to unseal it, the four living creatures then bow down and worship the Lamb (5:9–14). Thus, not only is God the Father worshiped, but so is the Lamb (5:13)! This is extraordinary, since only God is to be worshiped—as Revelation attests explicitly (19:10; 22:8–9). Thus the throne is the throne of God and the Lamb (3:21; 22:1, 3; compare also Rev 22:4).[81]

The pattern is also seen in Revelation 7, where the great multitude of God's people stand before the throne and the Lamb (7:9). Though the worship is explicitly said to be given to God on the throne (7:11–12), the people cry out that salvation belongs to God and to the Lamb (7:10)—which, as we have seen, is a prerogative of God alone in Scripture (see Jonah 2:9). Further, the Lamb is in the midst of the throne (7:17), so the Lamb is associated with

76. See also Bruce, *Hebrews*, 395–96.

77. See also Bruce, *Hebrews*, 395–96n15, who relates Rev 1:17; 2:8; 22:13 to Heb 13:8.

78. Elsewhere in the NT ὁ ἐρχόμενος is used as a christological title (Matt 11:3; 21:9; 23:39; Mark 11:9; Luke 7:19–20; 13:35; John 12:13; Heb 10:37; see also John 6:14).

79. Bauckham observes that Jesus declares seven (!) times in Revelation that he is coming (*Climax of Prophecy*, 435).

80. Thus, seven horns and seven eyes = seven spirits of God (which refers to the Holy Spirit; cf. 1:4). See further Beale, *Revelation*, 355.

81. See also Bauckham, *Climax of Prophecy*, 139. In 22:3 God's servants will worship/serve (λατρεύω) "him" (αὐτῷ), which may refer *both* to God and to the Lamb. Beale argues, "The two are conceived so much as a unity that the singular pronoun can refer to both" (*Revelation*, 1113).

God and his worship. This is no place for a created being. The Song of Moses, celebrating God's work of salvation, is also the song of the Lamb (15:3–4). This also points to the work of the Lamb as the work of a new exodus: as Beale writes, "The saints pride the Lamb's victory as the typological fulfillment of that to which the Red Sea victory pointed."[82]

If the exodus was central to the old covenant, so was the temple. This also finds fulfillment in Christ. In the consummate state there will be no separate temple, for the Lord God Almighty and the Lamb will be the temple (21:22). The temple was the place of worship (see 11:1), the place of forgiveness, the place of God's covenant presence. The temple and its functions are fulfilled in Christ, whom we worship as God with us, who is our mediator and opens to us the way of heaven (see also John 1:51).

The worship of Jesus in Revelation requires that he is divine. Yet Revelation does not attest multiple gods but one God in three persons.[83] This is central to Revelation: Whom will we worship? Worship can be given properly to God (cf. Rev 4:10; 5:14; 7:11; 11:16; 14:7; 15:4; 19:4; 20:4), or we can be deceived to worship the devil and his minions (9:20; 13:4, 8, 12, 15; 14:9, 11; 16:2; 19:20). The beast from the sea (13:1–10) serves as the false messiah of the unholy, counterfeit trinity in Revelation 12–14.[84] This beast serves the dragon with his authority (13:2; cf. 12:9), and he is a feeble reflection of Christ. Whereas Christ died and rose again, the beast from the sea only appears to have recovered from a mortal wound (13:3, 14).[85] All those who dwell on earth worshiped the dragon and the beast, whom no one could oppose (13:4, 8, 12, 15; 14:9, 11; 16:2; 19:20). Yet the beast from the sea is, as Richard Bauckham observes, a "christological parody."[86] He mirrors the work of Christ, but in a deceitful, ineffectual way. This beast does not have all authority on heaven and earth; he does not live forever; he will

82. Beale, *Revelation*, 792.

83. See further Gladd, "Apocalyptic Trinitarian Model," 156–74; Murray J. Smith, "The Book of Revelation: A Call to Worship, Witness, and Wait in the Midst of Violence," in *Into All the World: Emergent Christianity in Its Jewish and Greco-Roman Context*, ed. Mark Harding and Alana Nobbs (Grand Rapids: Eerdmans, 2017), 355–62.

84. See esp. Vern S. Poythress, "Counterfeiting in the Book of Revelation as a Perspective on Non-Christian Culture," *JETS* 40 (1997): 411–18.

85. See also Beale, *Revelation*, 688.

86. Bauckham, *Climax of Prophecy*, 431–50.

not return to reign over an everlasting kingdom (see 17:8, 11).[87] He is a counterfeit of Christ himself, who will rule forever. The beast and those who worship him will be destroyed (19:20–21). Thus, Revelation is largely concerned with whom we worship—will we worship the beast, or will we worship the Lamb?

Work of Christ Incarnate

THE DIVINE SON OF MAN in Revelation is also the human Son of Man.[88] He is not only the bright morning star, but is also the root (ῥίζα) and offspring of David (22:16; see also 5:5), which recalls the messianic vision of Isaiah 11:1, 10.[89] In Revelation 5:5 he is not only the root of David, but is also the Lion of Judah (see Gen 49:9), which further highlights his kingship. In this context Jesus is not only the Lion but also the Lamb who was slain (5:6; see also 11:8; 12:11; 13:8).[90] His everlasting rule comes by means of his death and resurrection—the Lion is the Lamb, who conquers by laying down and taking up his life.[91] He is holy, faithful, and true (3:7, 14). By his death he has ransomed his people in a greater redemption than the exodus (5:9–10). And just as the Israelites were liberated from Egypt to be a kingdom of priests and a holy nation (Exod 19:5–6), so now Christ's greater work of redemption makes his people from every tribe and nation to be a kingdom and priests (Rev 1:6; 5:9–10; see also 1:6). Christ's blood liberates us from sin (1:5).[92]

87. See Bauckham, *Climax of Prophecy*, 431–41.

88. See Poythress, *Theophany*, 328–29.

89. "Root" could refer to the root from which David came, or it could refer to Christ as the offspring of David. Some see both, perhaps echoing Jesus as David's Son and David's Lord from Ps 110:1. For this latter view, see Dennis E. Johnson, *The Triumph of the Lamb: A Commentary on Revelation* (Phillipsburg, NJ: P&R, 2001), 328; Vern S. Poythress, *The Returning King: A Guide to the Book of Revelation* (Phillipsburg, NJ: P&R, 2000), 109; William Hendriksen, *More than Conquerors: An Interpretation of the Book of Revelation* (Grand Rapids: Baker, 1998), 209. However, Beale argues this phrasing does not refer to preexistence (*Revelation*, 1146–48).

90. Revelation 13:8 could refer either to the Lamb, whose death was decreed before the foundation of the world (see WCF 8.6), or to those whose names were not written in the book of life from the foundation of the world. Both are true. For a balanced discussion, see Beale, *Revelation*, 702–3.

91. See also Bauckham, *Climax of Prophecy*, 179–85.

92. Rev 1:5 contains a textual question: Has Christ freed (λύσαντι) us or washed (λούσαντι) us by his blood? Both are true, but "freed" is more likely. For Christ's blood as "cleansing," see 1 John 1:7; see also Rev 7:14; 22:14.

The earthly ministry of Christ is referenced in various ways in Revelation, notably in Revelation 12; 20. Revelation 12 speaks of a spiritual conflict of cosmic proportions, as the devil wages war against the messianic Son and his people. Jesus conquered the devil during his earthly work and especially in his death, resurrection, and ascension (see 12:5, 7–9).[93] He is the male child who will rule the nations (12:5), and by his obedience he has defeated the devil and inaugurated the kingdom of God. This latter reality is emphasized in the millennial passage in Revelation 20:1–3. Christ inaugurated the kingdom of God during his ministry; thus the thousand-year reign of Christ is already a present reality. Christ's binding of the strong man, and the spread of the gospel to the nations, appears to be reflected in the devil's being bound from deceiving the nations in Revelation 20:2–3.[94]

As the resurrected one, Jesus, the descendant of David, is the ruler of the kings of the earth (1:5; cf. Ps 2:10; Rev 2:26). He died but now lives forevermore, and he has the keys of death and Hades (1:18; see also 3:7)—he has authority over the realm of the dead (see Isa 22:22).[95] He is the firstborn of the dead (Rev 1:5), the beginning of God's creation (3:14), which highlight Jesus's role as the beginning of God's new creation (see Col 1:18).[96] These verses (Rev 1:5; 3:14) also speak of Christ as the faithful witness, which refers both to his faithfulness during his earthly life and to his role as the "firstborn" Davidic king who rules over the everlasting kingdom, especially given the echoes in 1:5 to the Davidic covenant from Psalm 89 (esp. 89:27, 37).[97] His resurrection is also in view in Revelation 1:10, which mentions "the Lord's day." In the New Testament and early Christianity the Lord's day is the day of the resurrection of Jesus.[98] Revelation 1:10 thus not only marks his resurrection, but attests the remarkable fact that the Sabbath moved from Saturday to Sunday based on Jesus's resurrection (WCF 21.7).

93. See also Beale, *Revelation*, 639, 650–56.

94. See Crowe, *Last Adam*, 165, 197.

95. See Beale, *Revelation*, 214–15.

96. See similarly Beale, *Revelation*, 297–98.

97. Beale, *Revelation*, 190–91, 296.

98. See Crowe, *Hope of Israel*, 120–21.

Jesus is the resurrected Lord, and though the Lamb and his people are attacked in this age, the Lamb will conquer, for he is King of kings and Lord of lords (17:14; 19:16).[99]

In light of what we have seen about Christ in Revelation, it is apparent that here, too, Jesus is presented as a prophet, priest, and king. As prophet, Jesus's name is the Word of God, and his words are a sharp, two-edged sword. His words are, like Jesus himself, faithful and true. As the Lamb of God who has laid down his life as a sacrifice, Jesus is a priest. He provides forgiveness of sins; he is the fulfillment of the temple and the goal of God's presence with his people. As king, Jesus is the resurrected Son of David who rules over the kings of the earth and is the head of an everlasting kingdom (see 2 Sam 7:12–16). He is the Lion of Judah, who will reign forever.

Christ's everlasting reign is also seen in the promise of his return to consummate the kingdom (see Rev 11:15). His role as conquering, consummating king is portrayed in 19:11–16: Christ has a crown, seated on a white warhorse. He sits arrayed in a blood-soaked robe (probably the blood of his enemies; see Isa 63:1–6)[100] at the head of the armies of heaven. He will rule over the nations and execute the wrath of God against the beasts and those who follow them (19:20–21). On his robe and thigh are written "King of kings and Lord of Lords."[101]

In contrast to the wrath of the Lamb (see 19:17) is the marriage supper of the Lamb (19:9). This is the consummation to which the Lord's Supper points, with Christ himself—the Bread of Life—present. He is the groom who has prepared a bride (21:9; 22:17; cf. 21:2). The Lamb is coming again to deliver his people and consummate his kingdom. Indeed, he is coming soon (22:7, 12, 20)

---

99. Hendriksen sees this verse as a summary of the whole book (*More than Conquerors*, 9).

100. See Johnson, *Triumph*, 270–71; Beale, *Revelation*, 957.

101. James R. Edwards suggests that the thigh inscription has particular reference to the cult of Apollo: Jesus is portrayed as the true light who triumphs over the evil serpent. See Edwards, "The Rider on the White Horse, the Thigh Inscription, and Apollo: Revelation 19:16," *Journal of Biblical Literature* 137 (2018): 519–36. However, though this may explain why the *thigh* is inscribed, the writing on the thigh is quite different—Rev 19:16 echoes the wording of Dan 4:37. Thanks to Greg Beale for this observation. See also G. K. Beale, "The Origin of the Title 'King of Kings and Lord of Lords' in Revelation 17.14," *NTS* 31 (1985): 618–20. Another suggestion is that of Michael P. Theophilos, who argues that "King of kings" likely refers to the threat of the Parthians—Rome's historic enemy. See Theophilos, "ΒΑΣΙΛΕΥΣ ΒΑΣΙΛΕΩΝ [Rev 17.14; 19.16] in Light of the Numismatic Record," *NTS* 65 (2019): 526–51.

The end of the Scriptures clarifies that Jesus Christ is both the beginning and the end, the Alpha and the Omega (22:13). He is the preexistent Son of God who has come as David's Son to accomplish salvation for us, by his suffering, death, and resurrection, and he will reign forever as the exalted King of kings.

CONCLUSION

Jesus is the great high priest who lives and serves in the heavenly sanctuary and who will soon return. He truly suffered as a man, but is also truly God—the eternal Son who was active already in the Old Testament. He has saved us by his righteous acts, and he will rule over an everlasting kingdom. He is coming soon. As we await his return, let us look to the final words of Scripture, which speak to the greatness of Christ and our greatest need—may the grace of the Lord Jesus be with us all (Rev 22:21). Amen.

FURTHER READING

Bauckham, Richard. *The Climax of Prophecy: Studies on the Book of Revelation*. London: T&T Clark, 1993. Bauckham's collection of studies covers various themes of Revelation, many of which touch on Christology. These include chapter 4 ("The Worship of Jesus") and chapter 6 ("The Lion, the Lamb and the Dragon").

———. *Jude and the Relatives of Jesus in the Early Church*. London: T&T Clark, 1990. See especially chapter 6 on Jude's Christology.

Brennan, Nick. *Divine Christology in the Epistle to the Hebrews: The Son as God*. LNTS 656. London: T&T Clark, 2021. Brennan's is an important work arguing for the prevalence and relevance of the divinity of the Son throughout Hebrews, interacting with both contemporary scholarship and historical theology.

Jensen, Matthew D. *Affirming the Resurrection of the Incarnate Christ: A Reading of 1 John*. SNTSMS 153. Cambridge: Cambridge University Press, 2012. Jensen argues for the centrality of the resurrection in the theology of 1 John and helpfully situates the teaching of the letter with respect to the Old Testament and argues that the audience is to be viewed as the heir to "true Israel."

Vos, Geerhardus. "The Priesthood of Christ in the Epistle to the Hebrews." Pages 126–60 in *Redemptive History and Biblical Interpretation: The Shorter Writings of Geerhardus Vos.* Edited by Richard B. Gaffin Jr. Phillipsburg, NJ: P&R, 1980. Vos's discussion of the high priesthood of Christ is lengthy and sometimes difficult to read, but is still relevant. He argues that while the focus of Hebrews is on Jesus's heavenly high priesthood, he was nevertheless a priest already on earth. A more accessible compendium of his teaching on Hebrews is *The Teaching of the Epistle to the Hebrews*, ed. Johannes G. Vos (Grand Rapids: Eerdmans, 1956).

PART 2

DOGMATIC DEVELOPMENT

VI

PRE-NICENE CHRISTOLOGY

AFFIRMING DIVINITY AND HUMANITY

In part 2 we turn to a consideration of Christology in dogmatic or systematic perspective. Here we consider how the church wrestled with the biblical texts, arriving at precise and careful formulations about Christ. In part 2 we will encounter technical terminology that does not come from the Bible, but does indeed reflect the Bible's teaching. Though it has often been said that Christian theologians began to move away from biblical teaching when they began to use nonbiblical terms and concepts for theological formations, this is an unnecessary conclusion. It is legitimate and often useful to employ nonbiblical terms to explain with precision and clarity the teaching of Scripture.

The next two chapters focus on key christological developments in church history. In this chapter I focus on the pre-Nicene period (pre-AD 325, before the Council of Nicaea). In the next chapter I consider Christology in the remainder of church history: from the era of the first great creeds of the church, beginning with the council of Nicaea, all the way to the modern age. The material I include will necessarily be selective, but I aim to sketch the broad sweep of the development of Christology, while also giving attention to the contributions of particular figures.

In the remainder of this chapter, I will therefore consider how the biblical teaching on the person and work of Christ was received and appropriated by early, orthodox Christian writers. It should be emphasized that Scripture was important for the early church's development of Christology. For indeed, as J. N. D. Kelly notes, "almost the entire theological effort of the fathers, whether their aims were polemical or constructive, was expended upon what amounted to the exposition of the Bible. Further, it was everywhere taken for granted that, for any doctrine to win acceptance, it had first to establish its Scriptural basis."[1] Thus, the church fathers looked to Scripture—both Old Testament and New Testament—to understand and articulate the person and work of Christ.

This chapter is important because too many studies—whether scholarly or popular level—have argued that high Christology was a late development in the church, or perhaps that orthodox beliefs were simply one strand of many possible options in the early church that just happened, eventually, to win the day. But this canard needs to be identified as such, called out as anachronistic, and put to rest as an insufficient handling of the extant historical and biblical evidence.

In addition to the teaching of Scripture already considered, the earliest recoverable, orthodox Christian sources from the Christian era attest a widespread belief in the preexistence and divinity of the Son, along with his full humanity in the incarnation. Often Christology is assumed in these writings (rather than argued for), which most likely indicates commonly accepted christological beliefs among the orthodox Christians in the early church. As we would expect, some sources are more explicit than others, but high Christology is shared among many of our sources. There were also challenges to these views from the heterodox, which were consistently and variously countered by the orthodox. I will not discuss the erroneous views themselves (e.g., Ebionitism, Gnosticism, docetism, et al.), which are often difficult to reconstruct.[2] Instead, my aim is to lay out the views of orthodox Christology positively, though these views were often responding to erroneous views.

---

1. J. N. D. Kelly, *Early Christian Doctrines*, 5th rev. ed. (Peabody, MA: Prince, 2007), 46.

2. For an introduction to second-century theological debates, see Michael J. Kruger, *Christianity at the Crossroads: How the Second Century Shaped the Future of the Church* (Downers Grove, IL: IVP Academic, 2018), 108–34; see also James L. Papandrea, *The Earliest Christologies: Five Images of Christ in the Postapostolic Age* (Downers Grove, IL: IVP Academic, 2016); David E. Wilhite, *The Gospel according to Heretics: Discovering Orthodoxy through Early Christological Conflicts* (Grand Rapids: Baker Academic, 2015), 21–104.

APOSTOLIC FATHERS

The variegated, modern collection of early Christian writings known as the Apostolic Fathers (which, in fact, are postapostolic fathers) includes several texts that are important for understanding the Christology of the early church.[3]

Ignatius of Antioch

Particularly engaging on christological issues are the (seven) letters of Ignatius of Antioch.[4] Written probably sometime in the first three decades of the second century, these seven letters manifest a robust and high Christology.[5] Ignatius wrote with the authority of an early church leader of a major city. It is therefore reasonable to conclude that his views most likely represent much of mainstream Christian thought at this early stage.

Ignatius explicitly identifies Jesus as God (ϑεός) on multiple occasions (e.g., Ign. *Eph.* inscr.; 1.1; 7.2; 15.3(?); 18.2; 19.3; Ign. *Rom.* inscr. (2x); 3.3; 6.3; Ign. *Smyrn.* 1.1; Ign. *Pol.* 8.3). Additionally, Ignatius's letters exhibit a striking number of passages in which the roles for God and Jesus are conflated or interchanged.[6] For example, both God (Ign. *Magn.* 3.1) and Jesus (Ign. *Rom.* 9.1) can be described as bishop of the church; prayers are to be made to both God (Ign. *Eph.* 10.1; Ign. *Rom.* 1.1; Ign. *Phld.* 5.1) and Jesus (Ign. *Eph.* 20.1; Ign. *Rom.* 4.2); Ignatius desires to reach both God (Ign. *Rom.* 4.1) and Jesus (Ign. *Rom.* 5.3). Additionally, Ignatius can use the same title for different persons in the same context. For example, in *To the Ephesians* 1.1 Ignatius speaks of God, apparently as distinct from Christ Jesus, then in the next phrase mentions the blood of God, which must refer to the blood of Jesus. It is clear that Ignatius is quite eager to identify Jesus as ϑεός.

---

3. For the Apostolic Fathers I follow the texts and translations of Michael W. Holmes, ed., *The Apostolic Fathers: Greek Texts and English Translations*, 3rd ed. (Grand Rapids: Baker Academic, 2007), though I sometimes modify Holmes's translations.

4. Debates have circled around which letters claiming to be from Ignatius are authentic. I follow Holmes and the common sentiment today, that seven are authentic—the so-called middle recension.

5. For the argument that Ignatius has a highly developed Christology, see Thomas G. Weinandy, "The Apostolic Christology of Ignatius of Antioch: The Road to Chalcedon," in *Trajectories through the New Testament and the Apostolic Fathers*, ed. Andrew F. Gregory and Christopher M. Tuckett (Oxford: Oxford University Press, 2005), 71–84.

6. The remainder of this paragraph is adapted from Brandon D. Crowe, "Like Father, Like Son: Unraveling the Proto-Trinitarian Approach of *2 Clement*," *WTJ* 77 (2015): 255.

Echoing John, Ignatius identifies Jesus as the Word (λόγος, Ign. Magn. 8.2; see also Ign. *Rom.* 8.2). He is the preexistent Son of God who spoke in the Old Testament (see Ign. *Eph.* 7.2; Ign. *Magn.* 6.1; Ign. *Smyrn.* 1.1; Ign. *Phld.* 8.2).[7] As such, Jesus is the key to understanding the Old Testament (see Ign. *Phld.* 9.2).[8] He is the door to the Father—even for Old Testament believers (Ign. *Phld.* 9.1). Jesus is present wherever his people are gathered, perhaps echoing the Immanuel theme of Matthew 18 (Ign. *Smyrn.* 8.2). Jesus is our life (Ign. *Eph.* 3.2; 11.1; Ign. *Smyrn.* 4.1; see also Ign. *Eph.* 20.2), which, as in the New Testament, assumes Christ's divinity. He is the gracious Savior (Ign. *Eph.* 1.1; Ign. *Magn.* inscr.; Ign. *Phld.* 8.1; 9.2; 11.1; Ign. *Smyrn.* 6.2; 7.1) who loved the church (Ign. *Trall.* 6.1; 8.1; Ign. *Pol.* 5.1). We place our faith in him (Ign. *Eph.* 1.1; see also Ign. *Magn.* 1.1). He is our hope (Ign. *Phld.* 11.2; Ign. *Smyrn.* 10.2) and refreshment (Ign. *Smyrn.* 9.2).

Yet Ignatius also stridently emphasizes the true humanity of Jesus. Jesus is the new man (Ign. *Eph.* 20.1), the Christ descended from David according to the flesh, much like Romans 1:3–4 (Ign. *Eph.* 18.2;[9] Ign. *Rom.* 7.3; Ign. *Smyrn.* 1.1; Ign. *Trall.* 9.1; see also *Eph.* 7.2). He came in obedience to the one who sent him (Ign. *Magn.* 8.2; see also 13.2). This same Jesus suffered and died that we might escape death (Ign. *Trall.* 2.1). This is why Ignatius can call Jesus the God who suffered (see Ign. Smryn. 1.1–2)—though God cannot suffer (see Ign. *Eph.* 7.2), Jesus is the divine Son who suffered in the flesh (Ign. *Magn.* 11.1; Ign. *Trall.* inscr.; 2.1; 9.1; 10.1; Ign. *Rom.* 7.3; Ign. *Phld.* inscr.; 3.3: 4.1; 5.1; 8.2; 9.2; Ign. *Smyrn.* 2–5; 7.1–2; 12.2). As the Savior who loved the church (Ign. *Pol.* 5.1), Jesus's flesh and blood are powerful, and we should believe in them (Ign. *Smyrn.* 1.1; 6.1; Ign. *Trall.* 8.1). Not only did Christ die, but he also rose again from the dead (Ign. *Trall.* 9.2; Ign. *Magn.* 11.1; Ign. *Rom.* 4.3; Ign. *Smyrn.* 2.1; 3.1–3 [compare Acts 10:41]; 7.2; 12.2; Ign. *Phld.* inscr.; see also Ign. *Trall.* 2.1).

---

7. On the relationship of "the archives" in Ign. *Phld.* 8.2 to the OT, see Bruce M. Metzger, *The Canon of the New Testament: Its Origin, Development, and Significance* (Oxford: Clarendon, 1986), 48–49; Michael J. Kruger, *Canon Revisited: Establishing the Origins and Authority of the New Testament Books* (Wheaton, IL: Crossway, 2012), 215.

8. John J. O'Keefe and R. R. Reno, *Sanctified Vision: An Introduction to Early Christian Interpretation of the Bible* (Baltimore: Johns Hopkins University Press, 2005), 27.

9. It is also possible that the star that appears in Ign. *Eph.* 19.2–3 is a reference to Jesus himself, especially with respect to his divinity. See the argument in Jonathan Lookadoo, "The Role of the Star in *Ephesians* 18–20: Ignatius of Antioch, Polymorphic Christology, and Second Temple Stars," *Journal of Early Christian History* 7 (2017): 62–88, esp. 75–76.

Ignatius's emphasis on the true humanity and true suffering of Jesus contradicts those who downplayed or denied the bodily suffering of Jesus (Ign. *Trall.* 6.1; 10.1; 11.1; Ign. *Phld.* 3.1–3; 6.1–3; Ign. *Smyrn.* 2.1; 4.1). Jesus's suffering and death really matter; by the suffering of the divine Son of God, we are saved. Further, Ignatius's desire to die a martyr's death is embraced in imitation of the Lord who suffered for him (e.g., Ign. *Magn.* 9.1). Ignatius is eager to show not only that Jesus is divine but that he is truly human.

One of Ignatius's driving interests in his letters is Christian unity (e.g., Ign. *Trall.* 9.1–2; Ign. *Phld.* 3.3; 4.1; Ign. *Smyrn.* 6.2; 7.2), which is predicated on shared theological convictions, including those about Jesus Christ. Anticipating later formulations of the *regula fidei* ("rule of faith"),[10] Ignatius speaks of Jesus as the preexistent Son of God and also as the offspring of David who came as a true man and suffered for our salvation (e.g., Ign. *Eph.* 7.2; Ign. *Trall.* 9.1–2; Ign. *Smyrn.* 1.1–2). He also speaks of the Father, Son, and Spirit in ways that anticipate later Trinitarian formulations (e.g., Ign. *Magn.* 13.1; Ign. *Phld.* inscr.). As we will see, Ignatius is not unique among early Christian writers in these ways.

Clement of Rome First Clement derives from Clement of Rome in the last decade of the first century. Like Ignatius, Clement was also a church leader in a major city, and we can assume his views are representative of those he represented. He was not the first to speak of these truths, but speaks about the known canon (κανών) of their shared tradition (7.2; see also 1.3; 41.1)—likely an early reference to the *regula fidei*. Like Ignatius, 1 Clement speaks of Jesus as divine. Echoing Hebrews, the Son is the radiance of God's glory and is superior to the angels (36.2–5; see also Heb 1:3–5, 7, 13). Glory is ascribed to God through Jesus Christ (1 Clem. 61.3), and elsewhere glory and majesty are ascribed to Jesus

10. The rule of faith is a summary of the apostolic gospel dating back at least to the second century that, though varied in its ancient instantiations, typically looks similar to what we know as the Apostles' Creed today. It bears a Trinitarian character, affirming one God who created heaven and earth, Jesus as the divine Son of God who became incarnate to accomplish salvation (highlighting his death, resurrection, and ascension), and affirms the Holy Spirit. For discussions see Everett Ferguson, *The Rule of Faith: A Guide*, Cascade Companions (Eugene, OR: Cascade, 2015); Kruger, *Christianity at the Crossroads*, 136–45; see also the discussion of Irenaeus below.

himself (20.12).[11] Clement speaks of our faith in Christ (22.1), in whom is our salvation (see inscr.; 36.1), through whom we are chosen (64.1). Grace and peace come not only from God but also from Jesus Christ (inscr.; 65.2). Clement speaks of Father, Son, and Spirit in close relationship (46.6; 58.2).

The divine Son is also our heavenly high priest of salvation (36.1; 61.3; 64.2), again echoing Hebrews. He was sent by God (42.1–2) and descended from the family of Jacob according to the flesh, and thus he shares a common ancestor with the Levites (32.2). He suffered for us in the flesh (21.6; 49.6), and his blood is our salvation (7.4). He is the servant (παῖς, 59.2–4; see also Acts 3:13, 26; 4:27) who fulfills Isaiah 53 (1 Clem. 16.3–14), even though he is "the scepter of God's majesty" (16.2). He was also raised bodily (1 Clem. 24–26); he is the firstfruits of the resurrection (24.1; see also 1 Cor 15:23). We are saved not by our works but by faith in him (1 Clem. 32.4; see also 22.1). For he gave his life for us (49.6).

2 Clement Written probably sometime in the first half of the second century, the early Christian homily known as 2 Clement (not written by Clement of Rome) is also an early witness to high Christology.[12] This begins in the first verse, which is programmatic for the entire homily: "Brothers and sisters, we ought to think of Jesus Christ as [ὡς] we do of God, as judge of the living and the dead. And we ought not to belittle the one who is our salvation." The author's point seems to be that whatever we think of God, we ought to think of Jesus in the same way. The author sees an overlapping associative relationship between the Father and the Son that drives his exhortation—sometimes blurring the lines between Father and Son, while not collapsing the two persons. Thus the divinity of Jesus—and thus also his preexistence (9.5)—is assumed as programmatic for the entire letter.

In 1.4 Jesus is likened to a father, and our salvation is attributed to his mercy and compassion, for he has called us into being from nothing (1.7–8). Just as the Father is Judge, so is the Son (1.1), and the author speaks alternatively of the will of the Father (8.4; 9.11; 10.1; 14.1a) and the will of the Son (5.1; 6.7; 14.1b). Both the Father (10.1; 16.1) and the Son (1.8; 2.4–7; 5.1; see also

11. The most likely antecedent to 20.12 is Jesus Christ in 20.11.

12. This discussion of 2 Clement builds on Crowe, "Like Father, Like Son," 251–64.

1.4) call disciples to salvation. Elsewhere the return of Christ is described as the appearance of God (12.1), and the words of Jesus are the words of God (13.3–4).[13] Yet only Jesus is said to save (σῴζω, 1.4; 2.7; 4.1–2; 9.5; probably 1.7; 3.3; 8.2), and to think of salvation is to think specifically of Jesus (1.1–2). And it is through Jesus that we know the Father (3.2). The greatness of the Son in 2 Clement thus underscores the greatness of our salvation.[14]

The Son is also the Savior and Founder (τὸν σωτῆρα καὶ ἀρχηγόν) of immortality (20.5), likely echoing Acts 5:31 (ἀρχηγὸν καὶ σωτῆρα), and thus probably brings into view the resurrection. Second Clement thus also emphasizes the human suffering of Jesus (1.2). The emphasis on exhortation in 2 Clement is, as is consistent with many early Christian writings, tightly tethered to the work of Christ in history and in the hope of resurrection (1.1–8; 9.1–11).

Epistle of Barnabas

THE EPISTLE OF BARNABAS ALSO reveals a high, preexistent Christology. Jesus is the Son of God (Barn. 5.9; 6.12; 12.10), the Lord of the whole world, and to him was spoken the words of Genesis 1:26, 28 (Barn. 5.5; 6.12). He himself gave grace to the Old Testament prophets, who in turn prophesied of him (5.6). Moreover, all things are in and for Jesus (ἐν αὐτῷ πάντα καὶ εἰς αὐτόν, 12.7; see also Rom 11:36; 1 Cor 8:6; Eph 4:15; Col 1:15–20), and "the Lord of glory and all grace" (21.9) might refer to Jesus, since this section apparently distinguishes between God and the Lord Jesus (21.2–6).

Yet this divine Son is also truly human. He suffered in the flesh that we might be cleansed from sin, channeling Isaiah 53 (Barn. 5.1–2). By coming in the flesh and dying on the cross, he is able to provide forgiveness of sins and renewal (5.10–14; 6.11; see also 6.7; 7.1–8.7) and fulfills the promises to the fathers (5.7). By his death he has destroyed death and inaugurates the resurrection of the dead (5.6–7; see also 1 Cor 15:26; Heb 2:14). He rose and ascended on the eighth day, which marks the day of the week that his people meet together in his name (Barn. 15.9). One day he will return (15.5;

13. 2 Clem. 4.4 is another possible reference to Jesus as God.

14. Here I am closely reflecting the language of Klaus Wengst, *Schriften des Urchristentums: Didache (Apostellehre), Barnabasbrief, Zweiter Klemensbrief, Schrift an Diognet: Eingeleitet, herausgegeben, übertragen und erläutert* (Munich: Kösel, 1984), 228. Wengst writes, "Die Größe Christi unterstreicht die Größe des von ihm gewirkten Heils."

21.3, 6). He is the only source of salvation, in whom we hope (12.3). Though Barnabas makes its own contributions to early Christian theology, it also manifests numerous strong resonances with New Testament Christology.

Polycarp of Smyrna POLYCARP OF SMYRNA, SAID TO have been the disciple of the apostle John,[15] provides a bridge from the apostolic era to the postapostolic era. Written in the first half of the second century, his letter *To the Philippians* is suffused with New Testament Christology. Polycarp opens with mercy and peace from both the Father and our Savior, Jesus Christ (inscr.; see also 14.1), reflecting the New Testament collocation of the Father and Son (see also 6.2–3). He extols love for both Father and Son (3.3), and deacons are to be servants of God and Christ (5.2). Jesus is the Lord (1.1)—the one who has suffered for our sins and is now raised and ascended (1.2; 2.1; 8.1; 9.2; 12.2; see also Acts 2:24; Phil 2:6–11). We are saved by faith in Christ, not by works that we have done (1.3). Polycarp affirms the true humanity of Jesus: anyone who does not confess Jesus Christ has come in the flesh is antichrist (7.1; see 1 John 4:2–3; 2 John 7). Jesus is our hope and the down payment, or guarantee, of our righteousness (τῇ ἐλπίδι καὶ τῷ ἀρραβῶνι τῆς δικαιοσύνης ἡμῶν), to whom we must hold steadfastly (8.1). Jesus Christ is the eternal high priest, the Son of God himself, who has been raised from the dead (12.2). Jesus is both the divine Son of God and the true man who suffered for our sins and reigns now in heaven.

The writing known as the Martyrdom of Polycarp is also from the second century and evidences high Christology. Perhaps echoing Polycarp's *To the Philippians*, the Martyrdom of Polycarp speaks of Jesus as the eternal and heavenly high priest (14.3), the Son of God (14.1; 17.3). He is the blameless one who suffered for sinners (17.2) and who is worshiped by the Christians (17.2–3). Jesus is the Savior of our souls, the Pilot (κυβερνήτης) of our bodies, and the Shepherd of the whole church (19.2). Martyrdom of Polycarp also records how Polycarp refused to confess that "Caesar is Lord" (8.2; see also Acts 10:36), because Jesus Christ is the king who saved him (Mart. Pol. 9.3; see also 17.3) and who reigns forever; glory is due him (21.1; 22.1; see also 20.2). The author moves with ease between Father, Son, and

15. See, e.g., Irenaeus, *Haer.* 5.33.4; *Letter to Florinus* 2; Eusebius, *Hist. eccl.* 3.39.

Holy Spirit (14.2–3; 22.3 alt.).[16] This latter ending also mentions the "ecclesiastical and catholic rule" (ἐκκλησιαστικὸν κανόνα καὶ καθολικόν, 22.2 alt.), though again this reading is textually uncertain. Even if this ending is secondary, this reading does reveal interest in the orthodox faith of Polycarp and Irenaeus of Lyons (see further below) over against the Marcionite corruption of the faith.

Didache

The Didache does not expound Christology at length, but it does manifest a keen interest in the historical teaching and ministry of Jesus. Jesus is the servant from the family of David who grants eternal life (9.1–10.6). Further, wherever the lordship (κυριότης) of Jesus (i.e., the Lord) is preached, there the Lord is as well (4.1). This may echo the promise of Immanuel in Matt 18:20. Jesus has been raised, which is presumably marked by "the Lord's own day" (Did. 14.1), and Jesus, the Lord, is coming again (10.6; 16.1, 6–8).[17] Didache 7.1–3 provides early—perhaps as early as the first century—evidence for a proto-trinitarianism. Further, Didache 14.3 is probably a reference to Jesus, the Lord, who spoke in Malachi.

APOLOGISTS AND HERESIOLOGISTS

Many writings that we still have from the earliest centuries of the church are from apologists, such as Justin Martyr, who defended Christianity against pagan and Jewish objections.[18] A second category of prominent early Christian writings is heresiology—such as the approach of Irenaeus in *Against Heresies*. Heresiologists catalogued heretical teachings and responded with biblical truth.

Justin Martyr

Justin Martyr (d. c. 165) is perhaps the earliest Christian writer from whom we have extensive works. Particularly pertinent for his views on Christology is *Dialogue with Trypho*,

16. This portion of Martyrdom of Polycarp is less textually certain.

17. See further Murray J. Smith, "The Lord Jesus and His Coming in the Didache," in *The Didache: A Missing Piece of the Puzzle in Early Christianity*, ed. Jonathan A. Draper and Clayton N. Jefford, Early Christianity and Its Literature 14 (Atlanta: SBL Press, 2015), 363–407.

18. See Robert M. Grant, *Greek Apologists of the Second Century* (Philadelphia: Westminster, 1988).

which in large measure addresses the person and work of Christ and his relationship to the Old Testament.[19] Jesus is both Christ and God (*Dial.* 124); he is Lord of all (*1 Apol.* 46). Justin has a rich repository of christological titles he invokes: King, Priest, God, man, Angel, Apostle, Rock, Cornerstone, Commander (ἀρχιστράτηγος), Son, Lord, Word (λόγος), Wisdom, new Israel, new Jacob, Day, East, Sword, Flower, and glory of the Lord (*Dial.* 34, 58–59, 61, 64, 68, 70, 86, 100, 126; cf. *1 Apol.* 4–5, 12, 63). Justin thus explicitly identifies Jesus as God. Jesus is also the new covenant, the eternal law, and the new Israel (*Dial.* 11). He is the preexistent Son of God (*Dial.* 45; 64; 87; see also 48) who spoke and was active in the Old Testament as the Word of God and was addressed at creation (*Dial.* 62; see Gen 1:26). He is the Wisdom of God, the God begotten before all else (*Dial.* 61; see Prov 8:22). He is spoken of in the Psalms (*Dial.* 56), often as God (e.g., Ps 24; 45; 110; see *Dial.* 37–38, 56; *1 Apol.* 45). He appeared to Abraham, wrestled with Jacob, spoke to Moses from the burning bush (*Dial.* 56, 58, 125, 127; *1 Apol.* 62), and was present in the fiery furnace (*Dial.* 76).

Justin further states that Christ is "another God besides the Maker of all things" (θεὸς ἕτερός ἐστι τοῦ τὰ πάντα ποιήσαντος θεοῦ, *Dial.* 56.11; see also *Dial.* 60). Yet by this Justin does not mean that the Son is a rival God (see his critique of Marcion, *1 Apol.* 58). Rather, he is different in number (ἀριθμῷ) but not in mind (γνώμῃ, *Dial.* 56.11; see also 126). His power is indivisible (ἄτμητον) and inseparable (ἀχώριστον) from the Father—as light is inseparable from the sun (*Dial.* 128.3). The Son ("Power") has been begotten (γεγεννῆσθαι), but not as if he were cut off (ἀποτομή) from the Father, for the substance (οὐσία) of the Father is not divided (ἀπομεριζομένης, *Dial.* 128.4).

Justin's language on the relationship of the Father to the Son is not as precise as later theological formulations. It has been argued that by so emphasizing the invisibility of the Father, Justin creates a problem for how Christ could reveal the Father in the incarnation, but that Irenaeus takes

19. For the church fathers that follow (including Justin), I have generally utilized the translations from *ANF* along with other translations noted in the footnotes. For Justin, I have sometimes opted for my own translations based on the critical editions of Miroslav Marcovich, ed., *Iustini Martyris: Apologiae pro christianis*, PTS 38 (Berlin: de Gruyter, 1994); Marcovich, *Iustini Martyris: Dialogus cum Tryphone*, PTS 47 (Berlin: de Gruyter, 1997).

a different view that does not risk subordinationism (*Haer.* 4.6.6.; 4.20.5).[20] Even so, Justin anticipates later formulations: he understands Jesus to be a second God in a way that does not divide the essence of the Father and wherein Jesus is not a rival God. In places his language combines Father, Son, and Spirit (*1 Apol.* 6; 61, 65, 67). Later theologians worked out with more precision how both these things could be true.

Justin also seems seem to reflect a publicly affirmed christological tradition already in the mid-second century, similar to the *regula fidei*: Jesus was from the family of Abraham, descended from David, born of a virgin, suffered and crucified under Pontius Pilate, rose from the dead, and is the judge of all people (e.g., *Dial.* 43, 45, 85, 100, 118, 126, 132; *1 Apol.* 23, 46).

For Justin, the divinity of Christ does not undermine or deny his true humanity and suffering (e.g., *Dial.* 41; *1 Apol.* 53). Justin quite frequently refers to Jesus's supernatural virgin birth (i.e., virginal conception; *Dial.* 23, 43, 45, 48, 50, 54, 57, 63, 66–68, 71, 75, 77, 84–85, 100, 105, 113, 120, 127; *1 Apol.* 22, 31–33, 46, 54, 63; *2 Apol.* 6), which means he was born without sin (*Dial.* 23). Jesus performed many miracles, by the power of the Spirit, fulfilling the restoration prophecies of Isaiah 35 (*Dial.* 69, 86; see also *1 Apol.* 31). Justin speaks often of Christ's suffering and death on a cross (*Dial.* 32, 51; *1 Apol.* 41), frequently invoking Isaiah 53 as a prediction of Jesus's suffering (*Dial.* 13, 17, 63; *1 Apol.* 50). Jesus was truly crucified under Pontius Pilate (*Dial.* 30, 76, 85; *1 Apol.* 61), and he is to be worshiped (*Dial.* 38, 63, 68; *2 Apol.* 13; see also *1 Apol.* 61, 67). Jesus was the only righteous one (*Dial.* 16–17; 102; see also *Dial.* 67), and his blood brings forgiveness of sins and salvation (*Dial.* 13, 24, 44, 54, 63, 74, 94–95), for his blood is the power of God (*Dial.* 54). We are saved by faith in him (*Dial.* 35), and this applies both to Jews and gentiles (*Dial.* 26, 28, 41, 47, 64, 121–122, 134) and also to Old Testament believers (*Dial.* 45). Suffering on a cross is clearly a problem for Trypho, which according to Scripture means a man is cursed (*Dial.* 89–97; see Deut 21:23) but Justin shows how it is a representative/substitutionary cursing (*Dial.* 94–95, 111). Not only did Jesus die, but he rose again (*Dial.* 51, 85; *1 Apol.* 31, 42, 63, 67), ascended into heaven (*Dial.* 32–33, 37; *1 Apol.* 42), and pours out gifts on his church (*Dial.* 39, 87). Justin also speaks frequently of two

20. John Behr, *The Way to Nicaea*, The Formation of Christian Theology 1 (Crestwood, NY: St. Vladimir's Seminary Press, 2001), 104–5, 114. Compare Bavinck, *RD* 2:262.

advents of Jesus: one in obscurity and the other in glory. (*Dial.* 14, 31–32, 40, 49, 51–52, 69, 110–111; *1 Apol.* 52). He will come again (*Dial.* 34, 45) and will raise his people (*Dial.* 69).

I mention three other aspects of Justin's Christology. First, Justin couches the person and work of Christ in Adamic terms. Jesus submitted to baptism for the sake of the human race, which had fallen under the power of sin and the devil (*Dial.* 88). Whereas the serpent led to the transgression of Adam, by his death Jesus has defanged the serpent and defeated death (*Dial.* 45, 94, 124). Jesus's birth of the virgin Mary recalls the virgin Eve (*Dial.* 100), and his obedience is the answer to the disobedience of Adam (*Dial.* 103).

Second, Justin attests, at least implicitly, the *munus triplex* of Jesus: he speaks of Jesus as prophet, priest, and king. As prophet, he spoke in the Old Testament (e.g., *Dial.* 113), and the Old Testament prophets spoke of him (e.g., *Dial.* 35, 42, 113; see also 100), and sometimes the Spirit of prophecy speaks from the person of the Son (*1 Apol.* 38)—thus, Jesus speaks himself in prophecy.[21] Jesus taught during his earthly ministry, summarizing the law of God with the two love commands (*Dial.* 93). He is the true Word of which the philosophers spoke (*2 Apol.* 8, 10, 13). Even more explicitly, Jesus is the priest, whose offering is acceptable to God (*Dial.* 116). Justin combines king and (high) priest (*Dial.* 34, 96, 113, 115,[22] 118), identifying Jesus as both eternal priest (*Dial.* 42, 96, 113) and eternal king (*Dial.* 118). The kingship of Christ is emphasized throughout (e.g., *Dial.* 34, 36, 38, 70, 86, 96, 113, 135).

Third, Justin draws attention to the role of the preexistent Christ in the events surrounding the exodus. This is the context for his speaking to Moses in the burning bush, and Jesus is identified as the angel who led the Israelites out of Egypt in Exodus 23:20 (*Dial.* 75; see also 120; *1 Apol.* 62–63). This is combined with Justin's rich Joshua typology (e.g., *Dial.* 61–62, 75, 89–90, 106, 111–113, 115–116, 128) to highlight the work of Christ in the Old Testament. It also seems to anticipate the greater redemption wrought by the greater Joshua in the new covenant, especially when Christ returns

---

21. Identifying different persons of the Godhead speaking in biblical texts is common in the church fathers and is known as prosopological exegesis. For a discussion and assessment, see Brandon D. Crowe, "Prosopological Exegesis," in *Dictionary of the New Testament Use of the Old Testament*, ed. G. K. Beale et al. (Grand Rapids: Baker Academic, forthcoming).

22. In *Dial.* 115 Justin also identifies the priest as God.

to conquer his enemies (see *Dial.* 111, 120). The Passover blood saved those who were in Egypt, and now the blood of Christ saves those who believe in him (*Dial.* 111).

Irenaeus of Lyons

IRENAEUS OF LYONS (c. AD 130–202) is another major figure of the second century who helps us trace the christological views of the earliest Christians. As with figures like Ignatius and Polycarp,[23] Irenaeus was an early church leader, and his views are those of mainstream orthodox Christianity in the earliest decades. Two works in particular provide Irenaeus's views: *Against Heresies* and *Demonstration of the Apostolic Preaching*.[24]

In *Against Heresies* Irenaeus is particularly interested in disproving heretical views about God and Christ and in positively expounding the truth from the Scriptures. A helpful place to start is on the summary of Christian tradition about Christ in *Against Heresies* 1.10.1 (see also 1.22.1):[25]

> The Church, though dispersed through out the whole world, even to the ends of the earth, has received from the apostles and their disciples this faith: [She believes] *in one God, the Father Almighty,* Maker of heaven, and earth, and the sea, and all things that are in them; and in *one Christ Jesus, the Son of God,* who became incarnate for our salvation; and in the *Holy Spirit,* who proclaimed through the prophets the dispensations of God, and the advents, and the birth from a virgin, and the passion, and the resurrection from the dead, and the ascension into heaven in the flesh of the beloved Christ Jesus, our Lord, and His [future] manifestation from heaven in the glory of the Father "to gather all things in one," and to raise up anew all flesh of the whole human race, in order that to Christ Jesus, our Lord, and God, and Saviour, and King, according to the will of the invisible Father, "every knee should bow, of things in heaven, and things in earth, and things under the earth, and that every tongue should confess" to Him, and that

23. Irenaeus states that he was acquainted with Polycarp personally (e.g., *Haer.* 3.3.4).

24. For the English editions I have utilized Behr, *St. Irenaeus of Lyons*, and *ANF* for *Adversus Haereses*. For critical editions of *Adversus Haereses*, see *Irénée de Lyon: Contre les hérésies*, ed. Adelin Rousseau et al., SC, 10 vols. (Paris: Cerf: 1965–2002).

25. See Ferguson, *Rule of Faith*.

> He should execute just judgment towards all. (*ANF* 1:330, emphasis added; see also *Haer.* 1.22.1)

This early instance of the *regula fidei* manifests a Trinitarian character, focused on Father, Son, and Spirit. The Scriptures properly understood present us with the portrait of a king, who is Christ (*Haer.* 1.8.1). This same emphasis is present in Irenaeus's Demonstration, which defends and expounds the rule of faith from the Scriptures (*Epid.* 1, 3–6). Irenaeus speaks of

> the Word of God, the Son of God, Christ Jesus our Lord, who was revealed by the prophets according to the character of their prophecy and according to the nature of the economies of the Father, by whom all things were made, and who, in the last times, to recapitulate all things, became a man amongst men, visible and palpable, in order to abolish death, to demonstrate life, and to effect communion between God and man.[26]

These statements speak both of the divinity of the Son and of his true humanity—emphases found throughout Irenaeus's writings (e.g., *Haer.* 3.12.4, 9; 3.16.6; 4.6.7; 5.14.4; 5.24.4). The Son is the man Christ Jesus crucified under Pontius Pilate, and the God who gives eternal life (*Haer.* 4.23.2). I will consider Irenaeus's teaching on the divinity and humanity of Christ in order.

First, Irenaeus understands Jesus to be the preexistent Son of God (e.g., *Epid.* 43, 51–52, 71; *Haer.* 4.6.2; 4.14.1; 5.18.3). Both Father and Son are Lord and God (*Epid.* 47; see also *Haer.* 3.6.1; 3.9.2; 3.21.4; 4.5.2)—there is one substance (οὐσία), though a difference in economy (οἰκονομία; *Epid.* 47). He speaks of Father, Son, and Spirit as Trinity, yet there is only one divinity (*Epid.* 100; see also *Epid.* 3; *Haer.* 4.20.1, 3; 4.33.15; 5.18.2); Irenaeus argues stridently against multiple gods (e.g., *Haer.* 3.12.2–4; 4.9.3). The Son is the Word—the Creator of all things (*Epid.* 5; *Haer.* 3.8.2–3; 3.10.5)—and has always been present with humanity (e.g., *Epid.* 12, 45; *Haer.* 4.28.2). He was active and spoke in the Old Testament to Abraham (*Epid.* 24, 44; *Haer.* 3.6.1) and to Moses (*Epid.* 40, 46; *Haer.* 4.2.3; 4.5.2), appeared in Jacob's dream (*Epid.* 45), and was present in the fiery furnace (*Haer.* 4.20.11; 5.5.2). He gave wisdom

26. Behr, *Demonstration*, 43–44.

in the Old Testament (*Haer.* 4.27.1), and he is attested as God in texts such as Psalms 45; 110 (*Epid.* 47–48; *Haer.* 3.6.1). He is also Immanuel—God with us—and Mighty God (*Epid.* 53–55; *Haer.* 3.21.4; see Isa 7:14; 9:6–7). His divinity is further proved from Isaiah 11, for he will not show favoritism, but will give to the poor (*Epid.* 60). We are only saved by believing in the name of the Son of God (see Acts 4:12), who is himself God (*Epid.* 96). For indeed, only God can save us.[27] The Son is also, rarely, spoken of in Irenaeus as one of the two "hands" of God—presumably highlighting creation—since the Word and Spirit were always with the Father (*Haer.* 5.1.3; 5.5.2; 5.6.1).

Second, though Jesus is by nature and always the divine Son of God, in the last times he became incarnate to accomplish redemption (e.g., *Epid.* 22; *Haer.* 1.9.3). Though it was no mere man who died for us (*Haer.* 3.20.4), the Son became true man (*Haer.* 4.33.2, 4; 5.14.1–2; 5.18.3; 5.21.2). Like Justin, Irenaeus speaks often of Jesus's birth of a virgin (e.g., *Epid.* 32–33, 36, 54, 57; *Haer.* 3.21.5). His blood effects redemption (*Haer.* 5.1.1; 5.2.1–2), forgiveness of sins (*Haer.* 5.17.3), and reconciliation with God (*Haer.* 3.16.9). For he is the truly righteous man (*Epid.* 72). In contrast to those who deny the full humanity of Jesus (e.g., *Haer.* 1.9.3; 3.4.2; 5.2.1), the Son in the incarnation truly was made man, died, and was raised from the dead (e.g., *Epid.* 37–41; *Haer.* 3.19.3), and he will return at the time determined by the Father (*Epid.* 85). By his death he has destroyed death (*Haer.* 2.20.3), and he has been raised bodily (*Haer.* 5.7.1). Indeed, Irenaeus closely associates the virgin birth with the resurrection: "if one does not accept His birth from a Virgin, how can he accept His resurrection from the dead?" (*Epid.* 38).[28] As a man he was anointed with the Holy Spirit (*Epid.* 9, 41, 53; *Haer.* 5.1.2–3) so that the Spirit might dwell in humanity (5.20.2). It would therefore be a grave error to conclude by his anointing any sort of disjunction between Jesus and Christ (*Haer.* 3.9.3; 3.16.9; 3.17–18; see 1 John 2:22; 4:2; 5:1). Though he came in the last days, he effects redemption for both Old Testament and New Testament saints, for all are saved the same way (*Haer.* 4.27.2); Old Testament saints too were members of Christ (*Haer.* 4.33.10). He is the Lord of the beginning and the end, and unites them both (*Haer.* 4.34.4).

27. See James L. Papandrea, *Novation of Rome and the Culmination of Pre-Nicene Orthodoxy*, Princeton Theological Monograph Series (Eugene, OR: Pickwick, 2011), 25.

28. Behr, *Demonstration*, 64.

This brings us to Irenaeus's teaching on recapitulation (ἀνακεφαλαίωσις, e.g., *Epid.* 6, 30–33; 3.18; 3.21.10; 3.23; 4.40.3; 5.14.1; 5.19.1; 5.20.2; 5.21.1–3; see Eph 1:10).[29] Recapitulation speaks of the way that the Son of God became man and, by his obedience in the flesh, undid the sin of Adam. He thereby reconciled humankind to God and abolished death, that humanity might become like the Son of God, in whose image we are made (e.g., *Epid.* 86; *Haer.* 3.10.2; 3.18.1, 7; 3.19.1; 3.21.1, 7, 8; 4.28.2; 4.38.7; 5 [preface]; 5.16.2–3; 5.21.2–3). By his obedience, he regained what we lost in Adam's disobedience (*Haer.* 3.18.1–2). Just as Adam's disobedience by a tree brought death to humanity, so Christ's obedience on a tree brought life to humanity (*Epid.* 33–34; *Haer.* 5.16.3; see also *Haer.* 3.22.3–4). By his obedience to the law and his death on the cross, he freed us from the curse of the law (*Haer.* 3.18.1–3; 4.2.7; 4.4.2). "He fought and conquered; for He was man contending for the fathers, and through obedience doing away with disobedience completely" (*Haer.* 3.18.6 [*ANF* 1:447–48]; see also 5.17.1, 3). Jesus is the stronger man who by his obedience bound the strong man (i.e., the devil), thereby liberating his people from captivity (*Haer.* 3.8.2; 3.18.6). Further, by becoming a man, he has sanctified every age of our human experience: from infancy, to childhood, to mature adulthood (*Haer.* 2.22.4; 3.18.7). The invisible became visible; the impassible became passible, summing up all things in himself (*Haer.* 3.16.6). This he did because of his great love toward his creation (*Haer.* 3.4.2); "He is a most holy and merciful Lord, and loves the human race" (*Haer.* 3.18.6; *ANF* 1:448).

Like Justin, Irenaeus speaks of Jesus as prophet, priest, and king. As prophet: not only did the prophets speak of him (e.g., *Epid.* 30; *Haer.* 3.16.2; 4.33.10–15), but the Son is the Word who spoke through the prophets (*Epid.* 34, 40). Jesus is also priest forever, as prophesied in Psalm 110 (*Epid.* 48). Notably, Irenaeus also speaks of Jesus's high priestly work on earth, during the days of his humiliation, when he healed the sick, cleansed lepers, made propitiation for sins, and suffered death (*Haer.* 4.8.2). Irenaeus also speaks often of Jesus as king. He fulfills the promise to David of an everlasting kingship and reigns over an everlasting kingdom (*Epid.* 36; 56–66; *Haer.*

29. See Eric Osborn, *Irenaeus of Lyons* (Cambridge: Cambridge University Press, 2001), 95–140.

3.12.6; 3.16.2–4; see also *Epid.* 52), and he rules over all nations (*Epid.* 49; see Ps 2:7; Isa 45:1).

Additionally, Irenaeus speaks of the Son's role in the first exodus and in the greater new exodus in the new covenant. The first exodus was a true deliverance (*Haer.* 4.16.3) accomplished by the Son (*Epid.* 46; *Haer.* 3.6.2; see Exod 3:8), but it was also "a type and image of the exodus of the Church," and a greater inheritance is granted by Jesus in the new era than Moses in the old (*Haer.* 4.30.4; see also *Epid.* 46). For the Son has descended and ascended for our salvation (*Haer.* 3.6.2).

Melito of Sardis FROM THE SECOND CENTURY, MELITO of Sardis's Homily on the Passover (*Peri Pascha*) reflects the common view that the Old Testament prophesied of the coming of Christ.[30] Jesus suffered and died as a man and rose from the dead as God (*Peri Pascha* 8–9). He is the Logos, grace, Father who begets, Son who is begotten, and sheep (*Peri Pascha* 9). Later theologians (rightly) oppose the notion that the Son begets (rather, it is proper to say he is begotten), but Melito appears to say Jesus is both Father and Son[31] —though his point may be that God is both begetter and begotten. Either way, more clarity came in later years as the orthodox wrestled with the biblical testimony.

In the exodus the angel of the Lord was deterred from striking down the Israelites because of the mystery of the Lord prefigured in the death of the Passover lamb (*Peri Pascha* 33–34). The work of Christ applies trans-testamentally, and salvation was truly granted in the Old Testament. The work of Christ undoes the disobedience of Adam (*Peri Pascha* 48–49, see also 56–59). The Son was born of a virgin, taking a body capable of suffering, and destroyed suffering and death (*Peri Pascha* 66, 69–70). Christ is both God and man. Melito puts it starkly: "He who hung the earth in place is hanged. He who fixed the heavens in place is fixed in place. … God is murdered" (*Peri Pascha* 96).[32] Yet he also rose from the dead and sits at the right

30. Melito also wrote an apology to Marcus Aurelius, but *Peri Pascha* is a homily. See further Grant, *Greek Apologists*, 92–99.

31. See Melito of Sardis, *On Pascha: With the Fragments of Melito and Other Material Related to the Quartodecimans*, trans. Alistair Stewart-Sykes, PPS (Crestwood, NY: St. Vladimir's Seminary Press, 2001), 39n3.

32. Translation from Richard A. Norris, *The Christological Controversy*, Sources of Early Christian Thought (Philadelphia: Fortress, 1980), 46. The Greek text with translation can be

hand of the Father as Alpha and Omega, the beginning and end, Christ, King, Lord, and Leader (στρατηγός; *Peri Pascha* 102–5).

Athenagoras of Athens

Athenagoras in *Legatio pro Christianis* (*Plea for Christians*), written to the second-century Roman emperors Marcus Aurelius and Commodus, speaks of God as Trinity (*Leg.* 6.2; 10; 12.3; 24.2), but is also insistent that there is only one God (*Leg.* 4.2).[33] In God is a power in union and a distinction in order (τάξις; *Leg.* 10.5; 12.3; 24.2). The Father and the Son are one (ἑνὸς ὄντος τοῦ πατρὸς καὶ τοῦ υἱοῦ; *Leg.* 10.2; see also John 10:30).[34] The Son of the Father is his Word and is not a different god, but Father and Son share the same essence and a deep communion (*Leg.* 12.3; 24.2). The Son is the Word of the Father in idea (ἐν ἰδέᾳ) and energizing power (ἐνεργείᾳ; *Leg.* 10.2). These terms may reflect philosophical ideas common in the second century,[35] but Athenagoras's exalted Christology is manifest.

Epistle to Diognetus

The Epistle to Diognetus, perhaps also from the second century, speaks of the distinctive beliefs and lifestyles of Christians in the midst of an ungodly world. It is not that Christians have been entrusted with some human mystery or teaching, but the invisible God of all sent the divine Son of God: the one who is the Craftsman (τεκνίτης) and Creator (δημιουργός) of the universe (Diogn. 7.1–2). He was sent as God (ὡς θεὸν ἔπεμψεν); he was sent as man to men (ὡς ἄνθρωπον πρὸς ἀνθρώπους[36] ἔπεμψεν, 7.4). The Father revealed his plan of salvation to his child (παῖς) alone (8.9), yet the child also planned it with him (9.1). God's own Son became a ransom (λύτρον; see also Matt 20:28; Mark 10:45) for us (Diogn. 9.2). His righteousness covers our sins; only by

---

found in Stuart George Hall, ed. and trans., *Melito of Sardis: On Pascha and Fragments* (Oxford: Clarendon, 1979).

33. For the Greek text, see Miroslav Marcovich, ed., *Athenagoras Legatio pro Christianis*, PTS 31 (Berlin: de Gruyter, 1990). For the Greek text and translation, see William R. Schoedel, ed. and trans., *Athenagoras: Legatio and De Resurrectione* (Oxford: Clarendon, 1972). I have also consulted *ANF*.

34. See Marcovich, *Athenagoras*, 41.

35. See the assessment of Schoedel, *Athenagoras*, 21n2.

36. Here ἀνθρώπους is textually uncertain; it is provided by Holmes, following the emendation of Karl Lachmann.

him can we be justified (δικαιόω, 9.2–4). His life was given for sinners in the "great exchange" (9.5), which probably refers to the totality of the work of the Son in the incarnation given for sinful humanity.[37] He "was from the beginning, who appeared as new yet proved to be old, and is always young as he is born on the hearts of the saints. This is the Eternal One who today is accounted a Son, through whom the church is enriched and grace is unfolded and multiplied among the saints" (11.4–5).[38]

CHRISTOLOGY IN OTHER GREEK-SPEAKING FATHERS

SPACE PRECLUDES A FULLER DISCUSSION of pre-Nicene Christology; a small sample of other important voices will have to suffice.

Early Alexandrians

THE ALEXANDRIANS ARE CRUCIAL FOR understanding orthodox Christology, and some of the key figures date from the pre-Nicene era. Some of the writings we have already covered may derive from Alexandria (e.g., Barnabas). In what follows I want to consider briefly two important Alexandrian figures from the pre-Nicene era: Clement and Origen.

Clement of Alexandria

THE SURVIVING WORKS OF CLEMENT of Alexandria (c. 150–c. 215) cohere with the widespread early Christian belief that Jesus is both God and man (*Protr.* 1; 10; *Paed.* 1.2–3; 2.8). In *Christ the Educator* (= *Paedagogus*), Clement focuses on the Son as teacher, both divine and human: "But our Instructor is the holy God Jesus, the Word, who is the guide of all humanity" (*Paed.* 1.7; also 1.1).[39] He is one with God—the first and only begotten Son (προγεννηθέν, πρωτόγονος υἱός, μονογενής),[40] the Creator, the image of God's glory, who is God's fellow counselor; he is always with the Father (*Strom.* 5.1; 6.7; 7.3). We must believe

37. See further Brandon D. Crowe, "Oh Sweet Exchange! The Soteriological Significance of the Incarnation in the *Epistle to Diognetus*," *Zeitschrift für die neutestamentliche Wissenschaft* 102 (2011): 96–109.

38. Trans. Holmes, *Apostolic Fathers*, 715.

39. Trans. *ANF*.

40. For these Greek terms, see PG 9:280b–c, 421a, 424d.

in him rightly (*Strom.* 5.1). The Son is omnipresent and cannot be contained (*Strom.* 7.2).

Jesus is the Word who was active in the Old Testament, was predicted by the prophets (*Strom.* 7.2), and appeared in the last days (*Protr.* 1). He is the face of God who wrestled with Jacob (*Paed.* 1.7), delivered the people from Egypt, and spoke the Ten Commandments (*Protr.* 1; *Paed.* 1.7, 9). He is merciful, loves humanity, and saves us—for he is the sinless one who has conquered the ancient serpent and death, forgiving our sins (*Protr.* 10–11; *Paed.* 1.2, 9; 2.8). He is the Savior in whom is life (*Strom.* 4.7), the Tree of Life who by the wood of the cross brings us life (*Strom.* 5.11). He brings a greater day of grace than Moses (*Paed.* 2.2, 8). He is our Great High Priest (*Protr.* 12), and he is the king—"the commander-in-chief" (*Strom.* 1.24; *Paed.* 1.8; *Hymn* 1–2). Thus Clement of Alexandria speaks of Jesus as prophet, priest, and king.

Beyond these, Clement's writings attest a wide array of christological titles: Sun of the Resurrection (*Protr.* 9), Good Shepherd (*Protr.* 11), General (στρατηγός, *Paed.* 1.8),[41] Musical Instrument (*Protr.* 1), Rudder (*Paed. Hymn* 1), and the competitor or wrestler (ἀγωνιστής) who overcomes the devil (*Protr.* 1; 10–11).[42]

Origen of Alexandria

Clement's probable student Origen (c. 185–c. 254) is a complex figure with a checkered reception, but he is widely regarded as the premier scholar of the early church.[43] Origen applied his Alexandrian, scholarly training to the biblical corpus, and he is often the first commentator for biblical books.[44] His influence is largely felt in the realm of biblical interpretation, but given his influence it is helpful to consider what he may say about early Christology.

41. For this Greek term in *Paed.* 1.8, see PG 8:329.

42. For the Greek term ἀγωνιστής of *Protr.* 1; 10–11, see Clement of Alexandria, *The Exhortation to the Greeks; The Rich Man's Salvation; To the Newly Baptized*, trans. G. W. Butterworth, Loeb Classical Library 92 (Cambridge: Harvard University Press, 1919), 6, 236.

43. E.g., Bryan M. Litfin, *Getting to Know the Church Fathers: An Evangelical Introduction* (Grand Rapids: Brazos, 2007), 143.

44. See Michael A. G. Haykin, *Rediscovering the Church Fathers: Who They Were and How They Shaped the Church* (Wheaton, IL: Crossway, 2011), 76–77.

Origen's corpus is extensive, yet only some of these survive.[45] Among his most influential works is *On First Principles* (Greek: *Peri Archōn* = Latin: *De Principiis*).[46] Origen begins this wide-ranging work with a preface that discusses the rule of faith. Here Origen places his own views in the Christian mainstream. Origen draws attention to the words of Christ, from both the New Testament and Old Testament—for the Word of God spoke already with Moses. Otherwise, the prophets would not have been able to prophesy of Christ (pref. 1). He then outlines his understanding of the rule of faith in preface 4. Jesus was born before all creatures and became a man, yet without ceasing to be truly God. He was born of a virgin, truly died, rose again, and ascended into heaven.

Origen says more about Christology in book 1 of *First Principles*. There is one deity, and this is shared between Father and Son (*Princ.* 1.1.8; 1.2.6; 1.2.10). The deity of Christ is one thing, and his humanity, which he assumed in the last days, is another (*Princ.* 1.2.1). The eternal Son of God is the Wisdom of God existing substantially (*substantialiter*, *Princ.* 1.2.2). The Father is never without Wisdom; he is therefore never without the Son (*Princ.* 1.2.2; 1.2.10). The Son is eternally begotten (*Princ.* 1.2.2, 4).[47] The Son is the Creator (*Princ.* 2.6.1–3) and the source of life and illumination for all of creation—he is the Life, Truth, and Resurrection (*Princ.* 1.2.4; 1.2.7), the image of the invisible God (*Princ.* 1.2.6). His deity was manifested when he emptied himself of his glory for our salvation (*Princ.* 1.2.8). Indeed, the incarnation of the divine Son of God, in which he became subject even to death, is the most glorious of all of God's mighty acts (*Princ.* 2.6.2). Here Origen states that some things apply to Christ's humanity and some to his deity—a teaching that anticipates later formulations of the *communicatio idiomatum* ("communication of properties").[48]

In *Contra Celsus* Origen defends orthodox Christianity, including Christology, from the challenges of Celsus.[49] Origen appeals again to the

45. Behr, *Way to Nicaea*, 168.

46. See the critical edition of John Behr, ed. and trans., *Origen: On First Principles*, 2 vols., Oxford Early Christian Texts (Oxford: Oxford University Press, 2017).

47. See also Behr, *Way to Nicaea*, 187.

48. Behr, *Way to Nicaea*, 198–99.

49. For a critical edition, see M. Marcovich, ed., *Origenes: Contra Celsum libri VIII*, Supplements to Vigiliae Christianae 54 (Leiden: Brill, 2001).

rule of faith (*Cels.* 1.7; also 3.2): Jesus was born of a virgin, died, and rose again (see also *Cels.* 1.32–37). Jesus is both divine and human (*Cels.* 1.47, 56, 60, 66; 2.8; 3.28; 4.15). He and the Father are one and united in will (*Cels.* 8.12; see John 10:30). His miracles show his divine power (*Cels.* 2.9). Origen, like Clement, speaks of Jesus as a great competitor or wrestler (ἀγωνιστής) who overcame temptation (*Cels.* 1.69). He really suffered for our sins (*Cels.* 2.16; 8.43), fulfilling Isaiah 53 (*Cels.* 1.54–55). Though his first advent was in humiliation, he will return again in glory (*Cels.* 1.56). As with On First Principles, Origen states that Jesus died in his human nature (*Cels.* 3.17, 25). In a statement that sounds different from later formulations, Origen also states that Jesus's body and soul were mixed together with his divinity and changed into God (εἰς θεὸν μεταβεβληκέναι, *Cels.* 3.41). Regardless of what Origen means by this, later theologians clarified that the two natures of Jesus (divine and human) are not mixed.

One lingering question about Origen's Christology is whether it was subordinationist: that is, whether the Son is ontologically inferior to the Father in some sense. This, it is argued, may be evident in the apparent distinction between the wills of the Father and Son (*Martyrdom* 29), and his rejection of prayer to Christ (*On Prayer* 15).[50] As Rowan Greer argues, these difficult passages may stem from Origen's main concern to see Christ as Mediator.[51] Sometimes Origen does mention prayer (and praise) to Jesus, our High Priest, but such prayers often seem to be made to God through Jesus (see, e.g., *Cels.* 3.34; 8.13, 26, 34, 37, 67). Further, Origen does say Christians sing to and praise both the Father and the Son (*Cels.* 8.67).

A fuller discussion of Origen's Christology would require a much longer treatment, but Origen himself affirmed the rule of faith and saw himself defending it.[52] The idea that Origen is subordinationist has been challenged recently with an impressive array of primary sources.[53] If we allow Origen's own voice to be heard sympathetically, he affirms the rule of faith's teaching

50. All these examples come from the introduction of Rowan A. Greer, ed. and trans., *Origen: An Exhortation to Martyrdom, Prayer, First Principles: Book IV, Prologue to the Commentary on the Song of Songs, Homily XXVII on Numbers*, Classics of Western Spirituality (New York: Paulist, 1979), 9–10.

51. Greer, *Origen*, 9; see also Behr, *Way to Nicaea*, 186–88.

52. See Greer, *Origen*, 30.

53. Ilaria L. E. Ramelli, "Origen's Anti-Subordinationism and Its Heritage in the Nicene and Cappadocian Line," *VC* 65 (2011): 21–49.

on the divinity and humanity of Christ. This he believed, whatever lingering questions, ambiguities, inconsistencies, and/or even errors we may find in Origen's corpus. Even so, some today continue to see later subordinationist Christology—such as the teaching of Arius from Alexandria (which I address in the next chapter)—to be heavily indebted to Origen.[54] Others argue that Origen is a predecessor of Nicene orthodoxy and Cappadocian Trinitarianism.[55]

Theophilus of Antioch

WRITTEN IN THE SECOND CENTURY, Theophilus's *Ad Autolycum* is an apologetic work that defends the biblical portrait of God and Christ.[56] To speak of Wisdom is to speak of God's offspring (γέννημα, *Autol.* 1.3). Yet this does not mean that Jesus is created. Theophilus later explains that the Son (i.e., the Word) came forth along with the wisdom of God from the heart of God, echoing Psalm 45:1 (*Autol.* 2.10).[57] For indeed the Word is God's power and wisdom, being eternally the Son and the Creator of all (*Autol.* 2.22). Yet begetting does not mean that the Father sends the Son away, for he is never without his Word (*Autol.* 2.22). He is therefore the preexistent Word who spoke to Adam in the garden (*Autol.* 2.22).

Hippolytus of Rome (and Refutation)

HIPPOLYTUS, WHO PROBABLY WROTE EARLY in the third century, is one of the more mysterious authors of the early church (it is also wondered whether there were two different Hippolytuses).[58] Today it is widely doubted that he is the author of *Refutation of All Heresies*, which has traditionally been attributed to him. More likely from Hippolytus is *Contra*

54. Donald Fairbairn and Ryan M. Reeves, *The Story of Creeds and Confessions: Tracing the Development of the Christian Faith* (Grand Rapids: Baker, 2019), 55, 148; see also Wellum, *God the Son Incarnate*, 277; Frances M. Young, *Biblical Exegesis and the Formation of Christian Culture* (Peabody, MA: Hendrickson, 2002), 297.

55. Ramelli, "Origen's Anti-Subordinationism."

56. A brief introduction to his theology can be found in Papandrea, *Novation of Rome*, 11–15. For the Greek text, see Miroslav Markovich, ed., *Theophili Antiocheni: Ad Autolycum*, PTS 44 (Berlin: de Gruyter, 1995).

57. See the editorial note in *ANF* 2:98.

58. See, e.g., Behr, *Way to Nicaea*, 141–62.

Noetus.[59] This latter, short work is particularly relevant for Christology. Hippolytus maintains a distinction in divine persons: the Son is not the Father, nor is the Father the Son (*Noet.* 1). It was therefore not the Father who suffered but the Son (*Noet.* 1–3). To acknowledge Christ as God (which Hippolytus does) does not therefore mean that he is the same person as the Father (*Noet.* 2). There is one God—one mind and one power, but not one person (*Noet.* 7–8, 11, 14; see John 10:30).

On John 10:30 Hippolytus notes that Jesus uses the plural verb ἐσμεν ("we are") rather than the singular εἰμι ("I am")—this demonstrates that the Father and Son are distinct persons. God was alone in the beginning, but he existed not as a singular monad but "in plurality" (*Noet.* 10; trans. *ANF*). The Word was with God in the beginning and was begotten by him as light of light, as the Son of God, "before the morning star" (*Noet.* 10–11, 16; see also Ps 110:3). He was begotten even before his incarnation, in which he was manifested as Son (*Noet.* 11, 15). It seems, however, that here Hippolytus is weaker on the personal identity of the Son prior to creation.[60] This departs from later Trinitarian formulations. Yet Hippolytus is clear that this begetting does not threaten the unity of God, for the Word is not another god, but is like the ray of the sun or water from a fountain (*Noet.* 11). He spoke of himself already through the prophets and is indeed the Creator of all that has been made (*Noet.* 12, 17).

Christ is indeed God over all (*Noet.* 6, 13; see Rom 9:5; cf. Acts 10:36), but he also is the divine person who became incarnate and suffered for our salvation—Christ is therefore both God and man (*Noet.* 6, 8, 17–18). In the flesh—that is, in Christ—the impassible God suffered (*Noet.* 15), taking on himself our infirmities (*Noet.* 18). We therefore must appreciate the mystery of the economy of salvation—it was the Word who was made flesh (*Noet.* 4, 16), and we find in the economy Father, Son, and Spirit (*Noet.* 8, 14). Yet Hippolytus is clear that there is only one God, though three persons: the Father commands, the Son obeys, and the Spirit enlightens (*Noet.* 14). *Contra haeresin Noeti* ends with a rhetorical flourish on the mysterious, tragic irony of the death of Christ, resembling that of Melito. In a similar context we find a fitting summary of the work of Christ for salvation:

59. For the Greek and Latin texts, see PG 10:803–30.

60. See Papandrea, *Novatian*, 38–40.

> Let us believe then, blessed brethren, according to the tradition of the apostles, that God the Word came down from heaven, (and entered) into the holy Virgin Mary, in order that, taking the flesh from her, and assuming also a human, by which I mean a rational soul, and becoming thus all that man is with the exception of sin, He might save fallen man, and confer immortality on men who believe on His name. (*Noet.* 17)[61]

Refutation of All Heresies also aids our understanding of Christology in the pre-Nicene era.[62] The Word of God is himself God (*Haer.* 10.33.8), the firstborn child of the Father (ὁ προτόγονους πατρὸς παὶς), whose voice was from before the morning star (*Haer.* 10.33.11; see also Ps 110:3).[63] This Word was incarnate in the last times for the salvation of humanity (*Haer.* 10.33.13–14). Invoking second-Adam Christology, the Word was born of a virgin and renews humanity: he passed through every stage of life, providing humanity a standard (νόμος) and a goal—and showing us we have the power to do good or evil (*Haer.* 10.33.15; see also *Noet.* 17).[64]

EARLY LATIN CHRISTOLOGY

Tertullian of Carthage

A KEY WRITER ON CHRISTOLOGY from the Latin-speaking church in the early centuries is Tertullian of Carthage (d. c. 225). Here I will consider four pertinent works for Christology: *Against Marcion*, *Against Praxeas*, *Prescription against Heretics*, and *On the Flesh of Christ*.

In *Against Marcion* Tertullian defends the integrity of Luke's Gospel and Paul's letters, and rebuts the argument that the Old Testament and New Testament attest different gods.[65] Christ is the Son of the Creator—thus the same God of the Old Testament is the God of the New Testament (*Marc.* 2.27; 3.1; 4.3). He appeared in the Old Testament, for he is the image of the invisible God (*Marc.* 2.27; 3.9, 16, 24; 4.10; 5.19; see Col 1:15). Not only

61. Translation modified from *ANF* 5:230.

62. For a critical edition see M. David Litwa, ed. and trans., *Refutation of All Heresies*, Writings from the Greco-Roman World 40 (Atlanta: SBL, 2016), whose translation (and numbering) I follow.

63. Note the alliteration: ἡ πρὸ ἑωσφόρου φωσφόρος φωνή.

64. See Litwa, *Refutation of All Heresies*, 757n142.

65. For the Latin and English, see Ernest Evans, ed. and trans., *Tertullian: Adversus Marcionem*, 2 vols. (Oxford: Clarendon, 1972).

is the same God—the Creator—the Father of Christ, but the Son himself is the Word by whom the world was created, and he is divine (*Marc.* 2.16, 27; 4.9, 25; 5.19), and he can therefore forgive sins (*Marc.* 4.10). It is proper for Jesus to work on the Sabbath, because divine works are not outlawed, only human works (*Marc.* 4.12). The Son himself spoke in the prophets and predicted his own coming (*Marc.* 4.11, 13–14). The Son is not less than the Father (*non minori se*), for by the Son, who is the Word, all things have been created (*Marc.* 4.25).

This preexistent, divine Son became a man, by being born of a virgin (*Marc.* 3.12–13; 4.10) and taking real flesh in the incarnation (*Marc.* 3.11), thus becoming the second Adam (*Marc.* 3.8–9). He is the seed of David, full of the Holy Spirit (*Marc.* 5.8). In this flesh he fulfilled the law and prophets (including Isa 53; *Marc.* 3.17; 4.2, 7–8), died, and rose from the dead (*Marc.* 3.8)—by his death he has destroyed death (*Marc.* 3.9). Yet he remains God in the incarnation: forgiving sins (*Marc.* 4.10) and healing the leper without fearing defilement (*Marc.* 4.9). Even the bleeding woman recognized that Jesus was God and thus beyond defilement (*Marc.* 4.20). The Son of God, who descended for us and died for us, is God; Tertullian even says that God died (*Marc.* 2.16, 27), though in other writings he clarifies what this means (e.g., *Prax.* 27, 29). Jesus will come again: his first advent was in obscurity, though his second advent will be in glory (*Marc.* 3.7).

In *Against Praxeas* Tertullian argues against misunderstandings about the unity of God: though God is indeed one, this one God exists in three persons: Father, Son, and Holy Spirit (*Prax.* 1–2).[66] Along with this, Tertullian outlines the commonly held views about Jesus in the *regula fidei*: the Son is the Word of God, who proceeds from the Father and created all things; he was sent by God to be born of a virgin, suffered, died, and was raised. He is both God and man (*Prax.* 2, see also 9, 11). Christ is God overall, which is shown from Romans 9:5 (*Prax.* 13). Further supporting the preexistence of the Son is Tertullian's use of prosopological exegesis—a method of reading the Old Testament in which distinct Trinitarian persons converse with one another. Thus, he argues in *Against Praxeas* 11–12 that in some texts the Father speaks to the Son (Ps 2:7; Isa 42:1; 49:6), and the Son speaks to the

66. For Latin and English, see Ernest Evans, ed. and trans., *Tertullian's Treatise against Praxeas* (London: SPCK, 1948).

Father (Ps 3:1; 71:18; Isa 61:1).[67] Though the Son is a distinct person, he is not separate from the Father (*Prax.* 8–9, 23); there is one divine essence (*substantiae ... unitatem*)—which is indivisible (*indivisae substantiae*)—but an economy (οἰκονομίαa) of operations (*Prax.* 2, 9, 11, 13). When Jesus says he and his Father are one (John 10:30), it means one essence (Latin: *unum*; Gk. ἕν), not one person (Latin: *unus*; Gk. εἵς; *Prax.* 22). The Son is eternally the Son (*Prax.* 7–8, 10).

Tertullian also reflects on how Jesus can be both God and man: this does make Jesus become something different—a "third thing" (*tertium quid*)—but the properties of each nature are preserved, and actions are appropriate for one of the two natures (*Prax.* 27). Thus, miracles are attributed to his deity and hunger to his humanity. It was not the Father who died on the cross (i.e., patripassianism) but the Son who died (*Prax.* 30). Further, though Christ died on the cross, that is not to say that he died with respect to his divine nature (*ex divina [substantia]*), for the divine nature is immortal. He thus died with respect to his human nature (*ex humana substantia*; *Prax.* 29). This sort of thinking became foundational for the *communicatio idiomatum* ("communication of properties") in subsequent theological discussions.

In his *Prescription against Heretics* Tertullian contrasts those who hold to the rule of faith with the heretics who introduce novel doctrines (*Praescr.* 13). Tertullian argues that Christ is God incarnate (*Praescr.* 13).

Tertullian discusses the nature of the incarnation further in *On the Flesh of Christ* (*De carne Christi*).[68] Jesus Christ is our God, who was truly born of a virgin and truly rose from the dead (*Carn.* 1–2, 5). By his flesh, he restores our flesh, for he loves his creatures (*Carn.* 4, 14). Tertullian also speaks of "inseparable operations." As God and man he is both born and unborn, fleshly and spiritual, weak and strong, dying and living (*Carn.* 5). For Tertullian, in contrast to Marcionistic teachings, it is crucial that Jesus was truly born in flesh: to die for us, he had to be a true man who was really born, and his flesh had to be like ours (*Carn.* 6). Jesus was born from the substance of Mary and shared in our human nature, though Jesus's flesh

67. He also argues that the Spirit speaks of the Father and the Son in the voice of a third person (Ps 110:1) and that the Spirit speaks to the Father about the Son (Isa 53:1–2).

68. The Latin text, edited by Aem. Kroymann, can be found in vol. 2 of *Tertulliani Opera*, ed. E. Dekkers et al., CCSL 1–2 (Turnhout: Brepols, 1954).

was without sin (*Carn.* 12, 16–17, 20, 22). Christ was not sinful flesh, for he did not receive any corruption from Adam. Instead, Christ was able to abolish sin in the flesh because he was entirely without sin in the flesh (*Carn.* 16; see also *Marc.* 5.14). As Adam shared our flesh without a human father, so Christ shared our flesh without a human father (*Carn.* 16–18, 22). Christ is the seed of David via Mary, but he is also the second Adam (*Carn.* 22).

In addition to Christ as second Adam, Tertullian also speaks of Jesus as prophet, who spoke already in the Old Testament (e.g., *Marc.* 4.13–14); high priest (*Carn.* 5), even during the days of his humiliation (*Marc.* 4.35; see also 4.9); and king, who rules spiritually and reigns from God's right hand (*Marc.* 4.20; 5.9).

Tertullian's Christology adheres to the rule of faith. Those who read the Scriptures rightly—as taught by Christ and the apostles—hold rightly to the Son of God, who is God incarnate (*Praescr.* 13, 20–21, 37). The heretics twist the real thing by picking and choosing from the Scriptures, thus perverting the true meaning of the texts (*Praescr.* 17). Tertullian's teaching has been found to support several theological points that are important for later theological discussions, including inseparable operations of the Trinity, the eternal generation of the Son, and divine simplicity.[69]

Novatian

Though he proved to be a controversial figure in the early church given his rigorous views on ecclesiology, Novatian's On the Trinity is a significant work for early Christology that anticipated later discussions.[70] Written in the mid-third century, *On the Trinity* speaks also of the rule of truth (i.e., rule of faith) and its common belief among the churches (*Trin.* 1, 9, 29).[71] This rule of truth also speaks of Jesus, the Son of God (*Trin.* 9). The Son of God's coming was promised in the Old Testament and fulfills the shadows and figures of all sacraments (*Trin.* 9). For example, he fulfills Isaiah 53 (*Trin.* 9, 28).

On the one hand, the Son's incarnation is real, and he really came in flesh and has healed us by his resurrection (*Trin.* 10–11, 13). On the other hand, Novatian explains at length how the Son is not only man, but is

69. Papandrea, *Novatian*, 29–30.

70. See the helpful assessment of Papandrea, *Novatian of Rome*.

71. For the Latin, see *Novatiani Opera*, ed. G. F. Diercks, CCSL 4 (Turnhout: Brepols, 1972).

truly God (*Trin.* 11). In fact, much of the rest of the discourse is devoted to demonstrating the divinity of the Son. He is Immanuel, God with us, who is always present in prayer, for God is everywhere (*Trin.* 12, 14). He is the Creator of all things, the image of the invisible God, and as God he can grant salvation (*Trin.* 13–18). Elsewhere the Son is described as being in the form of God (Phil 2:6), which attests his divinity (*Trin.* 22). Like Tertullian, Novatian appeals to John 10:30 to defend the unity of the Father and the Son: they are not one person (*unus*) but one in relationship to each other (*unum*; *Trin.* 13, 15, 27). If his sufferings show his humanity, his miracles show his divine power (*Trin.* 11).

Jesus Christ is both God and man (*Trin.* 11, 15). This enables Novatian to answer the question of whether God can die. His answer is that Christ is not only man but also God. Though with respect to divinity he is impassible (*impassibilis*) and immortal (*immortale*), human weakness (*humana fragilitas*) is susceptible to suffering (*passibilis*, *Trin.* 25). It was not the divinity in him that died but his humanity (*Trin.* 25). This is also similar to Tertullian's anticipation of the *communicatio idiomatum* in *Against Praxeas* 29.

Novatian concludes with a majestic discussion of the Father-Son relationship in On the Trinity 31.[72] The Son was begotten from the Father before all time and is always in the Father; he is not unborn but born. The Father is always the Father, and the Son came forth from the Father—he is before all things but after the Father. The Son is God from God, and he is the Son of the Father, but he does not derive his divinity from the Father. If the Son was not born, then the danger would be to have two Gods. Here Novatian shows the contours of eternal generation, though Novatian's way of framing things would need to be refined by later theologians. Yet it has been argued that Novatian is a forerunner in understanding the need for eternal generation that appreciates divine immutability and assures there never was a time the Son did not exist as a distinct person from the Father.[73]

72. Compare Douglas F. Kelly, "Novatian," in *New Dictionary of Theology*, ed. Sinclair B. Ferguson and David F. Wright (Downers Grove, IL: InterVarsity, 1988), 472.

73. Papandrea, *Novatian*, 85–92. Papandrea lists other ways Novatian anticipated later developments (p. 119), including the later teaching on the hypostatic union and the *communicatio idiomatum*—topics I will cover in later chapters.

CONCLUSION

One of the great chimeras of contemporary "popular" theology is that Jesus was only considered to be divine later in church history—perhaps after a (close) vote at the Council of Nicaea in the fourth century. The fantastical nature of this claim is evident not only from the biblical texts themselves but also from the abundant primary sources of early Christianity. The divinity of Jesus was never seriously questioned by the orthodox, nor was his humanity—though both these tenets had to be explained carefully and defended against those who posited different gods in the Bible and something less than the full humanity of Jesus. The heretics tended to focus on only one explanation for Christ: he is God, or he is man, or he is something else.[74]

But for the orthodox in the pre-Nicene period, Jesus was already understood to be both God and man. This has been the standard position since the earliest recoverable days of the church.[75] The preexistence of the divine Son of God was commonly held—his true coming in the flesh from the family of David, his real suffering for our salvation, and his bodily resurrection from the dead. Even so, there is also a noticeable lack of precision and uniformity in some of the statements we have considered. Further reflection, articulation, and ecclesiastical labors were needed to keep the church's Christology from veering into subordinationism[76]—the notion that the Son is somehow less than the Father in his essential being—or from so emphasizing the divinity of the Son that his full humanity was effectively denied. At the same time, this survey has shown a clear and consistent chorus affirming both the divinity and humanity of the Son. We should therefore agree with John Calvin that pre-Nicene theology leads to Nicene theology rather than to Arian theology.[77]

Though the main contours of Christology were clear among the orthodox in the first few centuries, questions about how to put all the pieces together remained to be teased out in more detail in the major creeds of the

---

74. Behr, *Way to Nicaea*, 78.

75. See Warfield, "'Two Natures,'" 213–14, 236–38, 250.

76. See, e.g., Leo Donald Davis, SJ, *The First Seven Ecumenical Councils (325–787): Their History and Theology*, Theology and Life 21 (Wilmington, DE: Glazier, 1987), 39, 45–47; Wellum, *God the Son*, 272, 275, 277.

77. Calvin, *Inst.* 1.13.27–28, noted in Muller, *PRRD* 4:204.

early church, especially at Nicaea/Constantinople, Ephesus, and Chalcedon. We turn now to them.

FURTHER READING

The Ante-Nicene Fathers. Edited by Alexander Roberts and James Donaldson. 1885–1887. 10 vols. Reprint, Peabody, MA: Hendrickson, 1994. Though these are not the best critical editions of the included writers, these ten volumes provide accessible and handy translations of key works of early Christianity, including Irenaeus, Justin Martryr, Tertullian, Athenagoras, Origen, Theophilus, and others. Nothing replaces reading the primary sources themselves.

Behr, John. *The Way to Nicaea*. The Formation of Christian Theology 1. Crestwood, NY: St. Vladimir's Seminary Press, 2001. Behr provides a selective introduction to key figures and christological issues in the pre-Nicene era.

Grillmeier, Aloys. *Christ in Christian Tradition*. Vol. 1, *From the Apostolic Age to Chalcedon (451)*. 2nd ed. Translated by John Bowden. Atlanta: John Knox, 1975. This book provides a sweeping survey of Christology in the early Christian church.

Holmes, Michael W., ed. *The Apostolic Fathers: Greek Texts and English Translations*. 3rd ed. Grand Rapids: Baker Academic, 2007. This useful collection of early Christian writings includes, among others, the letters of Ignatius and Polycarp, 1–2 Clement, Epistle of Barnabas, Epistle to Diognetus, and the Didache.

Kelly, J. N. D. *Early Christian Doctrines*. 5th rev. ed. Peabody, MA: Prince, 2007. This is a classic synthesis of early Christian theology.

VII

CREEDAL, CONCILIAR, AND MODERN CHRISTOLOGY

FROM NICAEA TO THE TWENTY-FIRST CENTURY

We move now to the further development of Christology. In this chapter I focus especially on some major creeds (and confessions) of the church.[1] Though early Christians consistently affirmed the full divinity and full humanity of Jesus, more precision and agreement was needed to articulate the truths about Christ from Scripture, to avoid confusion, and to counter unbiblical views. In the creeds we begin to see the language become standardized. Though creedal language is often not found in Scripture, or is used in ways that are sometimes different from Scripture, it is legitimate and often helpful to use nonscriptural terms to articulate of scriptural truths.[2]

Yet the councils that gave rise to the creeds wrestled with more than only language; they also wrestled with the concepts: What is true about Christ? In what sense is he God? What does it mean for him to be fully man? How can both be true? The creeds promote greater understanding about Christ in the church as they wrestle with the proper language to explain the rich, wonderful mystery of Christ, who is fully God and fully man. This

1. On the differences in creeds and confessions, see Fairbairn and Reeves, *Story of Creeds and Confessions*, 7–9.

2. See especially Calvin, *Inst.* 1.13.3 (1:123–24); Turretin, *Inst.* 1.1.3 (1:1).

chapter covers an enormous range of material, and I do not aim to give a thorough discussion of church history or the creeds. Instead, I sketch some key developments and issues relating to creedal Christology in the context of church history.

CHRISTOLOGY IN THE NICENE AND POST-NICENE ERA

Christology and the Nicene and Constantinopolitan Creeds (AD 325, 381)

Arianism and the Council of Nicaea (AD 325)

The first major creed to address Christology is the Nicene Creed (AD 325), which was affirmed and finds fuller articulation in the Constantinopolitan Creed (AD 381).[3]

One of the key issues addressed by the Council of Nicaea was how to articulate the full divinity of the Son. It would not, however, be best to say the council had to decide whether the Son was to be considered divine; for as we saw in the previous chapter, that was already well-established. What needed still to be established was the nature of the Son's divinity—was it entirely the same as the Father, or was there some subtle difference between the divinity of the Father and the Son?

One of the most famous debates leading to Nicaea centered on the controversy surrounding Arius, a presbyter in the Alexandrian church, whose controversial views about the Son would be deemed heretical.[4] Arius held that the Son does not share exactly the same nature with God. According to the Council of Nicaea, Arius taught that there was a time when the Son was not, that he did not exist before he was begotten, and the Son was a work of God.[5] Athanasius of Alexandria also records some of Arius's teachings, including that the Son was created, was adopted by God, and does not share the same essence with God; the Son is not God's equal (*Syn.* 15). Athanasius

3. For the pre-Reformation creeds in this chapter, I use the English translations (which also include Greek and Latin texts) of Norman P. Tanner, ed., *Decrees of the Ecumenical Councils*, 2 vols. (Washington, DC: Georgetown University Press, 1990).

4. See the helpful summary in Phillip Schaff, *History of the Christian Church* (New York: Scribner's Sons, 1885–1910), 3:618–21.

5. See the Nicene Creed, along with the letter from the synod to the Egyptians (Tanner, *Decrees* 1:5, 16–*19). For a more recent caution, see Oliver D. Crisp, *The Word Enfleshed: Exploring the Person and Work of Christ* (Grand Rapids: Baker Academic, 2016), 3.

frequently refers to the well-known teaching of Arius that there was a time when the Son was not (see, e.g., *C. Ar.* 1.5). In sum, Arius taught an ontological distinction between the Father and the Son. He may have been trying to reconcile how a transcendent God could suffer and therefore spoke of the incarnation (and suffering) of the Logos as the incarnation of a lesser divinity.[6] Further, the popular ontology of Middle Platonic thought was conducive to postulating a higher God (the Father) and a lower, derived Son who was a lesser divinity.[7]

Where did this teaching originate? Philip Schaff points to the possibility, in part, of the influence in Alexandria of the "contradictory elements" in Origen's Christology.[8] Yet Origen himself held to a higher Christology than Arius, and Origen's complicated legacy in the early church makes this connection difficult to substantiate.[9] According to Athanasius, Arian theology seemed to depend, for example, on an exegesis of Proverbs 8:22–25 that spoke of Wisdom's creation. The Son was understood to be the Wisdom of God spoken of in Proverbs 8; therefore, Arius understood the Son to be created.[10]

In contrast to this Arian approach, Athanasias argued that the Son's begetting did not indicate the Son's creation.[11] Athanasius distinguished between the Son's begetting, which was eternal, and the Arian argument that the Son was created—which does not accurately describe the Son. The Son is not a creature, nor is he changeable, for the divine Trinity is always perfect (*C. Ar.* 1.17). Nor is there ever a time when the Son is not the Son (*C. Ar.* 1.11–16); he is eternally the Son, lest we suppose that God's essence or the Son himself changes (*C. Ar.* 1.35–36; see also Heb 13:8). The Father and the Son share the same essence (e.g., *C. Ar.* 1.9, 14–16). In contrast to

6. See Gerald Bray, *God Has Spoken: A History of Christian Theology* (Wheaton, IL: Crossway, 2014), 243–46.

7. Thanks to John McClean for his observation on this point; see also Bray, *God Has Spoken*, 243.

8. Schaff, *Church History* 3:619–20.

9. See Lewis Ayres, *Nicaea and Its Legacy: An Approach to Fourth-Century Trinitarian Theology* (Oxford: Oxford University Press, 2004), 21.

10. Athanasius countered this Arian exegesis at length in *C. Ar.* 2.31–82 (*NPNF*[2] 4:357–93). For a critical edition of orations 1–3, see Karin Metzler, ed., *Athanasius Werke*, vol. 1, part 1, issues 2–3 (Berlin: de Gruyter, 1998–2000). I use the numbering of this edition.

11. *C. Ar.* 2.57–72 (*NPNF*[2] 4:379–88).

the Arian reading of Proverbs 8 (and other texts),[12] the Son's divinity was well-established in orthodox Christian tradition and coheres with the rule of faith. For Athanasius, Proverbs 8:22, which speaks of wisdom as the first of God's works, does not refer to the Son's creation as the Wisdom of God. Rather, it refers to the incarnation of the Wisdom of God, when he took a created nature (*C. Ar.* 2.44–56). This is the theology of the incarnation of the second Adam (*C. Ar.* 2.51, 61, 67, 69). We must distinguish between the Son in his divine essence and the Son's role in the economy of redemption as an incarnate man.

The real issue was not simply how the Arians interpreted a handful of texts; it was the theological commitments manifested in the Arians' exegetical approach. Certainly Proverbs 8 is not the clearest text in the Bible about the divinity of Jesus,[13] but as I argued in part 1 of this volume, the New Testament provides plenteous support for the full divinity of the Son. Athanasius found ample support for the Son's divinity in texts such as John 1:1; 14:6, 9–10; 10:30; 8:12; Philippians 2:6–7; Colossians 1:15 (e.g., *C. Ar.* 1.37–45; 2.54, 57–65; 3.3–6, 29; 4.1). For example, the Son is in the Father and the Father is in the Son "because the whole Being of the Son is proper to the Father's essence" (ἐπειδὴ συμπᾶν τὸ εἶναι τοῦ υἱοῦ τοῦτο τῆς τοῦ πατρὸς οὐσίας ἴδιόν ἐστιν, *C. Ar.* 3.3).[14] The Son is not a man who became God but God who became man (*C. Ar.* 1.39; see also Phil 2:6–11). Further, Athanasius makes it clear that if the Son were only a creature, he would not have been able to undo the curse of God against sin; but the divine Son of God, who condemned humanity in the beginning, is the same one who undoes the condemnation of humanity (*C. Ar.* 2.67). And if anyone would truly honor the Father, they must honor the Son truly as the divine Son of God (*C. Ar.* 2.43).

Athanasius's views reflect the conclusions of the Nicene Creed itself. The Son is from the same essence or substance of the Father (ἐκ τῆς οὐσίας). The Son is not merely of a similar substance (ὁμοιούσιος) to the Father, but the Nicene Creed affirms that the Son is of the same substance (ὁμοούσιος).

---

12. Beyond Prov 8, the Arians misread other key texts, such as Acts 2:36 and Phil 2:9–10, to which Athanasius also responds. See, e.g., *C. Ar.* 1.37–45; 2.11–18 (*NPNF*[2] 4:327–33, 354–57).

13. As Athanasius himself admits; see *C. Ar.* 2.44 (*NPNF*[2] 4:372).

14. Trans. *NPNF*[2] 4:395; Greek text from Metzler, *Athanasius Werke* 1.1.3:309.

The language of "essence" or "substance" (οὐσία) reflected in these terms refers to the divine nature. The Son is God of God, Light of Light. Indeed—the Son is true God of true God (θεὸν ἀληθινὸν ἐκ θεοῦ ἀληθινοῦ). Thus the Nicene Creed argues that the Son, in his essence, differs in no way from the Father. The Son is begotten, but this does not mean he was created; begottenness does not mean that the Son is in any way a creature (thus γεννηθέντα οὐ ποιηθέντα ["begotten not made"]). Further, the Son's begetting does not mean that the Son is "subject to change or alteration" (τρεπτὸν ἢ ἀλλοιωτόν); he is unchangeable.

Similarly, in Gregory of Nazianzus's famous *Five Theological Orations* (*Or.* 27–31) he speaks of the divine Trinity and the eternal generation of the Son. The Son is begotten, but not physically and without respect to time (*Or.* 29.2). Thus, there never was a time when the Father was not the Father, nor a time when the Son was not the Son (*Or.* 29.3, 5, 17). The Son is from the Father but is not temporally after the Father (*Or.* 29.4). Sonship does not entail a distinction in essence but an identity of essence (*Or.* 29.16; 30.20). Similar to Athanasius's interpretation of Proverbs 8:22, Gregory argues that anything that has been caused—such as "he created me" in this passage—must refer to the Son's incarnation (since God is uncaused; *Or.* 30.2). If the Son does not know the future, that lack of knowledge must be attributed to his humanity, not his divinity (*Or.* 30.15).

Council of Constantinople (AD 381)

The Constantinopolitan Creed (or the Niceno-Constantinopolitan Creed) confirms the Nicene Creed about the Son, but adds that the Son was "begotten before all the ages" (γεννηθέντα πρὸ πάντων τῶν αἰώνων). It also adds more details about the incarnate ministry of the Son, including his birth of Mary, his suffering, and his resurrection on the third day.[15]

In addition to Arianism, the Constantinopolitan Creed identifies other theological errors, such as the theology of Paul of Samosata.[16] Paul was the bishop of the major city Antioch in the third century and argued for an

15. Fairbairn and Reeves note three ancient accounts of this council (*Story of Creeds and Confessions*, 71n33): Socrates, *Ecclesiastical History* 5.8; Sozomen, *Ecclesiastical History* 7.7; Theodoret of Cyrus, *Ecclesiastical History* 5.8, which can all be found in *NPNF*[2] vols. 2–3.

16. See the letter from the bishops gathered at Constantinople in Tanner, *Decrees* 1:25–*30.

adoptionistic Christology in which Jesus became God's Son when the Logos rested on him (see Eusebius, *Hist. eccl.* 7.27–30). His theology was already condemned by AD 268, but canon 19 of the Council of Nicaea responded to the followers of Paul who persisted into the fourth century. Further, canon 1 from Constantinople anathematizes Sabellianism, which stated that God was modalistic and the persons of the Trinity were confused. Athanasius argues against both Arianism and Sabellianism in short scope: "For thus [Jesus] overthrows both Sabellius, in saying, 'I am' not, 'the Father,' but, 'the Son of God;' and Arius, in saying, 'are One' " (*C. Ar.* 4.17).[17]

Another christological error identified in canon 1 from Constantinople was Apollinarianism, which taught that Jesus did not have a human mind or human soul.[18] This teaching derived from Apollinarius of Laodicea—a defender of the Nicene faith whose teaching fell out of favor and was opposed at Constantinople.[19] Apollinarius stated, "It is inconceivable that the same person should be both God and an entire man."[20] The upshot of Apollinarianism is that Jesus is not fully human, since all people have a human mind.

In contrast to Apollinarius, the bishops' letter from Constantinople states of Christ that "the economy of his flesh was not soulless nor mindless nor imperfect" (οὔτε ἄψυχον οὔτε ἄνουν ἤ ἀτελῆ τὴν τῆς σαρκὸς οἰκονομίαν). To be sure, parsing this out proves to be a difficult matter, as will be evident later (see below on the Council of Ephesus).

Gregory of Nazianzus speaks to the Apollinarian controversy in more detail in his letters. Gregory observes three grievous errors of Apollinarius: he taught that the flesh of Christ was preexistent, he denied the Son had a human mind in the incarnation, and (most grievously of all) he taught that the Son died with respect to his divinity (*Ep.* 202 [to Nectarius]). Especially

---

17. Trans. *NPNF*[2] 4:439.

18. Sometimes Apollinarius speaks of Christ not having a human soul, and sometimes he speaks of Christ not having a human mind. See Christopher A. Beeley, "The Early Christological Controversy: Apollinarius, Diodore, and Gregory Nazianzen," *VC* 65 (2011): 378–85, esp. 382n34.

19. Concise discussions of Apollinarius's theology can be found in Davis, *First Seven Ecumenical Councils*, 103–8; John Behr, *The Nicene Faith*, part 2, *One of the Holy Trinity*, Formation of Christian Theology 2 (Crestwood, NY: St. Vladimir's Seminary Press, 2004), 379–401.

20. Fragment 9 in Norris, *Christological Controversy*, 108. See also, e.g., fragments 25, 45 (pp. 108–9).

noteworthy is the teaching that in place of the human mind of Christ was the divine mind (Ep. 102 [second letter to Cledonius]; 202; see also Or. 30.12). In opposition to this, Gregory underscores the unity of the person in the incarnation: it is the impassible Son of God who became perfect man to redeem fallen humanity (Ep. 101 [first letter to Cledonius]). Gregory emphatically denies that the Savior is two persons (Ep. 101). He sums it up: if Christ has not assumed a human mind, then there is no salvation for us, "For that which he has not assumed He has not healed" (Ep. 101).[21] Since our minds are sinful and fell in Adam, we need a Savior with a human mind to sanctify our minds and remove our condemnation (Ep. 101). This reflects the Bible's clear emphasis on the full humanity of the Son.

Christology and the Council of Ephesus (AD 431)

The next key council is the Council of Ephesus (AD 431).[22] The flashpoint of this controversy dealt with whether it was appropriate to identify Mary as "God-bearer" (ϑεοτόκος), which was really a discussion about the number of "subjects" in Christ.[23] On one side of the debate was Nestorius, bishop of Constantinople. On the other was Cyril, bishop of Alexandria—and one of the towering figures in the development of orthodox Christology.[24]

Nestorius denied that it was proper to call Mary "God-bearer," but instead she should be called "Christ-bearer"[25] (Χριστοτόκος). For Scripture does not speak of the Son of God suffering but of his humanity suffering; the Word of God is not the Son of David. J. N. D. Kelly comments that for Nestorius, "God cannot have a mother ... and no creature could have engendered the Godhead; Mary bore a man, the vehicle of divinity, but not God."[26] Nestorius's theology was significantly influenced by another

---

21. Trans. *NPNF*[2] 7:440.

22. In what follows I have especially benefited from John A. McGuckin, *St. Cyril of Alexandria and the Christological Controversy: Its History, Theology, and Texts* (repr., Crestwood, NY: St. Vladimir's Seminary Press, 2004).

23. As McGuckin has noted, Nestorius's denial that Mary was "God-bearer" was addressed by a council that met at *Ephesus*—the traditional city where Mary lived her final years—did not bode well for Nestorius (*St. Cyril*, e.g., 26–28, 40–41, 47).

24. On this debate, see McGuckin, *St. Cyril*.

25. Here I draw from Nestorius, *Second Letter to Cyril*, available in Tanner, *Decrees* 1:40–*44.

26. Kelly, *Early Christian Doctrines*, 311.

feature I have yet to discuss, which is the theology of the Antiochene school prominent in early Christianity (such as Diodore of Tarsus and Theodore of Mopsuestia), which was often viewed with suspicion from those with ties to Alexandrian school of early Christianity.[27]

Though Nestorius's theology is hard to pin down these many centuries later, he appears effectively to have denied one (or the proper) "subject" in Christ and emphasized "the abiding distinctive relationship of the two fully enduring spheres of reality (or 'natures') in the incarnate Lord."[28] Nestorius apparently thought that Cyril so stressed the unity of Christ that he veered into Apollinarianism by denying a human mind in Christ.[29] Nestorius himself taught that there was a conjunction (rather than a union) of natures in Christ, which resulted in a new "person" (πρόσωπον) that was identical neither with the Word nor with humanity.[30] Instead, "'the man' ... was the temple in which 'the God' dwelt."[31] Thus, for Nestorius: "The πρόσωπον of union, not the Logos or Word, was thought to be the subject of the incarnate Christ."[32] This also means that Nestorius did not employ the *communicatio idiomatum* ("communication of properties"), which states that both divine and human properties could be attributed to the single subject of Christology—not that the natures are confused, but that what is proper to each nature can be attributed to the person of the Son.[33] But in Nestorius's account, both divine and human characteristics could be attributed "indifferently" to the πρόσωπον of Christ in the incarnation.[34]

For his part, Cyril emphasized the unity of Christ.[35] Though Cyril did, like Apollinarius, affirm one subject in Christ, he distinguished himself

---

27. See McGuckin, *St. Cyril*, 20–23, 48–49; Fairbairn and Reeves, *Story of Creeds and Confessions*, 84–91.

28. McGuckin, *St. Cyril*, 131.

29. Noted by McGuckin, *St. Cyril*, 131–32.

30. See Kelly, *Early Christian Doctrines*, 314–15; Davis, *First Seven Ecumenical Councils*, 146–47; Letham, *Systematic Theology*, 492; Fairbairn and Reeves, *Story of Creeds and Confessions*, 90.

31. Kelly, *Early Christian Doctrines*, 314, noting Nestorius's comments on John 2:19. For Nestorius's own words, see his *Second Letter to Cyril* in Norris, *Christological Controversy*, 135–40. See also Schaff, *History* 3:718–19.

32. Letham, *Systematic Theology*, 492.

33. See McGuckin, *St. Cyril*, 153.

34. Kelly, *Early Christian Doctrines*, 316; see also McGuckin, *Saint Cryil*, 155.

35. See, e.g., his *Second Letter to Nestorius* and *Third Letters to Nestorius*. Also important is his commentary on John, which has been produced in a modern English translation: see

from Apollinarianism by affirming a human soul in Christ and denied the natures are confused.[36] The Word of God (i.e., the Logos) "appropriates" human nature in the incarnation.[37] Cyril's christological argument in the Nestorian controversy can be summarized:

> The human nature is ... not conceived as an independently acting dynamic (a distinct human person who self-activates) but as the manner of action of an independent and omnipotent power—that of the Logos: and to the Logos alone can be attributed the authorship of, and responsibility for, all its [i.e., the human nature's] actions. ... There can only be one creative subject, one personal reality, in the incarnate Lord; and that subject is the divine Logos who has made a human nature his own.[38]

This realization is massively significant for one's Christology, as we will see in subsequent chapters. The personal subject in the incarnation is not equally divine and human. Instead, the personal subject is always the divine Son of God, though in the incarnation we must understand the Son of God as God-in-flesh and all that entails—which is more than a body, but includes all that it means to be fully human.[39] In contrast to Nestorius, the *communicatio idiomatum* was important for Cyril and in many ways summed up his theology of the incarnation: "human nature is appropriated by God."[40]

Cyril spoke of the divine Word who "united to himself hypostatically flesh enlivened by a rational soul, and so became man and was called son of man, not by God's will alone or good pleasure, nor by the assumption of a person alone. Rather did two different natures come together to form a unity, and from both arose one Christ, one Son."[41] Cyril refers to this as a "hypostatic union" (τὴν καθ' ὑπόστασιν ἕνωσιν)—the union is key.[42] Two natures (human and divine) are united in one Christ. Cyril writes,

Cyril of Alexandria, *Commentary on John*, trans. Maxwell.

36. McGuckin, *St. Cyril*, 183.
37. McGuckin, *St. Cyril*, 184–85.
38. McGuckin, *St. Cyril*, 186.
39. See McGuckin, *St. Cyril*, 186.
40. McGuckin, *St. Cyril*, 192.
41. Cyril of Alexandria, *Second Letter to Nestorius* (trans. Tanner, *Decrees* 1:*41).
42. Tanner, *Decrees* 1:43.

"It was not as though the distinctness of the natures was destroyed by the union, but divinity and humanity together made perfect for us one Lord and one Christ."[43] Further, Cyril is clear that this does not entail change or suffering in the divine nature, but the Word was "begotten according to the flesh" for us and for our salvation. It is thus proper to speak of Mary as the mother of God: she did not give birth to the Godhead, but the Son's rational, ensouled body was born from her, and was hypostatically united to the divine Word of God. Cyril insists that the Son of God must not be divided. The human and divine expressions in Scripture refer to the same person.[44] That person is the "hypostasis of God in the flesh."[45] Yet Cyril also argues that because the divine Son of God is now God-in-flesh, no incarnate action is either purely divine or purely human—every incarnate action is the action of the God-man.[46] This will have significant implications for how we think of the work of Christ in later chapters.

The Council of Ephesus sided with the theology of Cyril, and Nestorius's theology was condemned.[47] Later, in AD 433, the so-called Formula of [Re] Union between Cyril of Alexandria and John of Antioch affirmed a union of two natures in one Christ, affirmed Mary as the God-bearer, and affirmed a rational soul in Christ who is perfect God and perfect man.[48] By this point the relationship between the two natures of Christ was becoming clearer and better defined, but the classic exposition of the two natures came later, at the Council of Chalcedon.

---

43. Cyril of Alexandria, *Second Letter to Nestorius* (trans. Tanner, *Decrees* 1:*41).

44. See Cyril of Alexandria, *Third Letter to Nestorius* in Tanner, *Decrees* 1:50–*61.

45. McGuckin, *St. Cyril*, 149–50.

46. McGuckin, *St. Cyril*, 200.

47. This phrasing papers over the complexities and competing events surrounding the Council of Ephesus. For discussions see McGuckin, *St. Cyril*, 53–107; Davis, *First Seven Ecumenical Councils*, 153–60; Fairbairn and Reeves, *Story of Creeds and Confessions*, 89–95.

48. Available in Tanner, *Decrees* 1:69–*70.

Christology at the Council of Chalcedon (AD 451)

Eutychianism and the Second Council of Ephesus (AD 449)

THE CHRISTOLOGY OF CYRIL OF Alexandria continued to prove influential in subsequent councils, including the Second Council of Ephesus (AD 449) and the massively significant Council of Chalcedon in AD 451.[49] Just prior to Chalcedon the error of Eutychianism was addressed at the Second Council of Ephesus in AD 449 (a.k.a. "the robber council"). Eutyches was a monk who purported to follow Cyril's Christology, but had a confused understanding that Christ had two natures before his incarnation and one nature after the incarnation.[50] This is also known as monophystism (μόνος ["one"] + φύσις ["nature"]), whereby "the Logos absorb[s] the human nature."[51] This new nature is sometimes understood as a "third thing" (*tertium quid*), though some other christological errors we have addressed might be categorized in similar terms.[52] Part of the confusion surrounding Eutyches, it seems, stemmed from what one meant by the Greek term φύσις—did it mean "person," as Cyril often used it, or "nature," as it came to be used in the Formula of [Re]Union and later?[53] It is correct to affirm one person in Christ, but the term φύσις after the First Council of Ephesus had come to be used as nature. This was further clarified at the Council of Chalcedon.

The Council of Chalcedon (AD 451)

THE CLASSIC DISCUSSION OF THE relationship between the two natures (φύσεις) of Christ and the one person (πρόσωπον) of Christ came at the Council of Chalcedon. Those gathered at Chalcedon affirmed the decision of the Councils of Nicaea, Constantinople, and (first) Ephesus. They also denied Eutychianism, by denying that there is "a single nature of the flesh

49. See here McGuckin, *St. Cyril*, 108.

50. See Pope Leo's Letter to Flavian (in Tanner, *Decrees* 1:81–*82); Davis, *First Seven Ecumenical Councils*, 170–71; Wilhite, *Gospel according to Heretics*, 169–78.

51. Schaff, *History* 3:735. Reeves and Fairbairn observe that this language comes from Theodoret of Cyrus, who opposed Eutyches (*Story of Creeds and Confessions*, 98–99).

52. Compare Tertullian, *Prax.* 27.

53. See Fairbairn and Reeves, *Story of Creeds and Confessions*, 98.

and the divinity."[54] The Chalcedonian Definition affirmed the impassibility of the divinity of the only-begotten Son (μονογενής) and rejected any teaching that suggested the confusion or the mixture of the two natures of Christ. Positively, Chalcedon stated that Christ is perfect in divinity and perfect in humanity. In terms of his divinity, he is begotten before all ages and consubstantial with the Father. This means that there is no difference in the divine essence between the Father and the Son. In terms of his humanity, Christ has a body and a rational soul, differing from us only in that he was sinless (Heb 4:15). The two natures "undergo no confusion, no change, no division, no separation,"[55] and at no point is the difference between the two natures taken away in the union of the two natures. Rather, what is proper to each nature remains and comes together in one person: Jesus Christ. Crucially, Christ is not two persons but one person with two natures. Our Savior is not simply an exalted man, but is the eternal Son of God who has come down to save us.[56] This is the classic definition of the hypostatic union: in the incarnation two natures (divine and human) are united in one person (Jesus Christ). I will discuss the hypostatic union further in chapter 9.

If the full divinity of Christ was clarified at Nicaea and Constantinople, and the full humanity of Christ clarified at Constantinople and Ephesus, Chalcedon provided further clarity into the relationship of the divine nature and human nature of Christ: the natures remain distinct, but are united in the one person. This provided the theological framework for the *communicatio idiomatum* ("communication of properties"), which emerged as crucially important in Chalcedonian Christology.[57] It is always the Son of God who acts, but since in the incarnation the Son has two natures, then what is proper to each nature can be attributed to the one person of Christ. Further, we will discuss later that Christ's natures do not abstractly "act." Instead, in the incarnation it is always the person of Christ who acts according to what is proper to each nature. This is crucial for construing Christology correctly.

---

54. Tanner, *Decrees* 1:*84.
55. Tanner, *Decrees* 1:86–*86. Greek: ἀσυγχύτως, ἀτρέπτως, ἀδιαιρέτως, ἀχωρίστως.
56. This is emphasized in Fairbairn and Reeves, *Story of Creeds and Confessions*, 104.
57. See Pope Leo's letter to Flavian (in Tanner, *Decrees* 1:79–*80).

Post-Chalcedonian Christology

WE HAVE LOOKED BRIEFLY AT the first four ecumenical creeds, which are generally considered to be the most important.[58] Yet the Council of Chalcedon was not the final word on Christology. But given the space constraints in this volume, only a select set of later developments must suffice. Though Chalcedon clarified the one person and two natures of Christ, some issues remained unresolved. One of the most important debates dealt with the number of wills in Christ: Did Christ have one will (monothelitism), or did he have two wills (dyothelitism)? If he had two wills, did this threaten the unity of the person? If he had one will, did this lead back to Apollinarianism, which denied a human mind in Christ?

A key figure in these debates is Maximus the Confessor. Though rejected in his own lifetime for teaching that Christ had two wills, Maximus's defense of dyotheletism was eventually vindicated. For Maximus, wills are the functions of natures, not of persons (for the three persons of the Trinity have one divine will).[59] Maximus points especially to the Gospel accounts where Jesus prays in the garden of Gethsemane as a place where we see "two wills (θελήσεις) and two operations (ἐνεργείαι) respective to the two natures," and these are not opposed (*Opusculum* 6).[60] Here we see Christ's obedience as a man for us and for our salvation (*Opusculum* 6). This language of two wills and two operations—though crucially, the human will is not opposed to the divine will—was later codified by the Third Council of Constantinople in AD 680–681 ("we proclaim equally two natural volitions or wills in him and two natural principles of action").[61] If that which is not assumed is not healed, then it was necessary for Christ to have a human will to save us entirely.[62]

---

58. E.g., Schaff, *Creeds of Christendom* 1:44.

59. Fairbairn and Reeves, *Story of Creeds and Confessions*, 150; Adonis Vidu, *The Same God Who Works All Things: Inseparable Operations in Trinitarian Theology* (Grand Rapids: Eerdmans, 2021), 75.

60. St. Maximus the Confessor, *The Cosmic Mystery of Jesus Christ*, trans. Paul M. Blowers and Robert Louis Wilken, PPS 25 (Crestwood, NY: St. Vladimir's Seminary Press, 2003), 174. See also *SPT* 25.31 (2:82–85).

61. Quotation from Tanner, *Decrees* 1:*128. See further Maximus the Confessor, "Introduction," in *Cosmic Mystery*, 14–16; Tanner, *Decrees* 1:128–*30. The council cites Pope Leo's letter to Flavian from the Chalcedonian context, invoking the *communicatio idiomatum*, as support; they also cite Gregory of Nazianzus in his *Or.* 30.

62. Fairbairn and Reeves, *Story of Creeds and Confessions*, 150–51.

As we conclude this section on the Christology of early ecumenical councils, it is important to emphasize that their insights are, at root, attempts to do justice to the biblical accounts of who Christ is. The New Testament already teaches that Jesus is the fully divine Son of God and that he is fully human. Both of these must be emphasized, but as this historical survey has suggested, it can be extremely difficult to articulate exactly what this means in practice. This is where creeds prove to be so beneficial: while they do not solve every aspect of the mystery of the incarnation, they provide clarifications and guardrails in our understanding of who Christ is according to Scripture. While the creeds are not infallible, their insights into the person of Christ have proven to be reliable guides in how best to interpret Scripture.

CHRISTOLOGY IN THE REFORMATION AND POST-REFORMATION ERAS

The Christology of Rome and the Reformers

Surely much more could be said about Christology from the seventh to the sixteenth centuries, but regrettably, space in this volume is limited, and I have to be selective in the survey of church history. Thus, without denying that the importance of the medieval period, we move ahead now to the sixteenth-century context of the Reformation (which indeed builds on medieval theology, as I seek to illustrate in following chapters). In this section I will look at the crucial period from around 1500–1700, especially the Reformers (such as Luther and Calvin) and their heirs. Though the Reformation did occasion debate on the person of Christ—perhaps most notably with respect to questions about the human nature of Christ and the Lord's Supper—much of the debate, like the Reformation itself, focused on the work of Christ.

The context of the Reformation and post-Reformation developments is one that struggled to avoid two extremes. On the one hand, though the Reformation sought to submit the claims of tradition to the norming norm of Scripture, the Reformers recognized the importance of the church's historic confessions, and they viewed themselves as heirs to Christology that had been professed for ages. On the other hand, some pushed for a radical break with tradition, seen, for example, in the rise of Socinianism, which I discuss below. Whereas the Reformers continued to affirm traditional beliefs like the Trinity and the preexistence of Christ as fully according with Scripture, the Socinians challenged such views on the basis of a more atomistic approach to Scripture that did not read Scripture in light of the church's catholic tradition. The appeal of Socinianism may have been in part its radical approach that purported to follow the principle of "no creed but the Bible" in a way that was not beholden to any tradition. This, however, went too far for the Reformers and their heirs, who understood (rightly) that our interpretation of the Bible must accord with the faith confessed through the ages. Instead, the Reformers and their heirs sought to cling both to the church's tradition and to Scripture—though Scripture itself had the final word.

The Righteousness of Christ

In terms of the work of Christ, the Reformed emphasis on justification by faith alone ensured that the foundation of justification was understood to be the obedience of Christ and not the obedience of believers. The Reformers emphasized the effectual work of Christ's obedience—that is, his righteousness—which is imputed to believers. Calvin memorably states, "How has Christ abolished sin, banished the separation between us and God, and acquired righteousness to render God favorable and kindly toward us? To this we can in general reply that he has achieved this for us by the whole course of his obedience."[63] Since the righteousness that counts for justification remains Christ's righteousness, it must be imputed—that is, legally reckoned—to believers by faith alone. No believer's imperfect obedience suffices to meet the standard of perfect obedience necessary for eternal life. Though believers' obedience is necessary, it does not count for justification (instead, believers' obedience correlates to the category of sanctification). In contrast, the Roman Catholic teaching codified at the Council of Trent (1564) argues that righteousness is infused in justification. Though this debate about righteousness veers into the application of salvation, it also relates to the efficacy of Christ's work and is a telling example of how one's view of Christ affects many other doctrines.

63. Calvin, *Inst.* 2.16.5 (1:507).

The Person of Christ and the Lord's Supper

Another aspect of the Reformation era that was the focal point of intense debate was the way in which Christ is present in the Lord's Supper. The Roman Catholic doctrine of transubstantiation, in which the bread and wine actually become the body and blood of Jesus in the Mass, was rejected by the Reformers. Christology was crucial to this debate: if Jesus has provided a once-for-all sacrifice, then it is wrong to "resacrifice" Christ in the Mass. Nor do the bread and wine actually become the body of Christ.[64]

Yet the Lutherans and Reformed differed among themselves as to how Christ was present in the Supper.[65] For Lutheranism, the elements did not actually become the body and blood of Jesus, but Jesus was bodily present in the elements (often mislabeled "consubstantiation"). This seems to require the omnipresence of Christ's human nature—something to which the Reformed objected. It also requires a distinctive perspective on the *communicatio idiomatum*—in the Lutheran understanding of the Supper, divine qualities are now attributed to the human nature of Christ (for the death of Christ, which is commemorated in the Supper, speaks to the human suffering of Christ).[66] This attribution is not merely in a semantic sense (*genus idiomaticum*), but is a real interchange of properties (*genus maiestaticum*). This explains the omnipresence of Christ's human nature and thus how he can bodily be present in the sacrament of the Lord's Supper.

In contrast, the Reformed tradition held to the real, Spiritual presence of Christ in the Supper. The elements do not become the body and blood of Jesus. Nor is the human nature of Christ omnipresent—the body of Christ is in heaven. Instead, following Calvin, the Reformed spoke about the special presence of Christ in the celebration of the Supper by means of the

---

64. See Turretin, *Inst.* 19.27 (3:488–505).

65. See Robert Kolb and Carl R. Trueman, *Between Wittenberg and Geneva: Lutheran and Reformed Theology in Conversation* (Grand Rapids: Baker Academic, 2017), 59–86, 175–205.

66. For this and the following sentences, see Steven D. Paulson, "Christology," in *Dictionary of Luther and the Lutheran Traditions*, ed. Timothy J. Wengert (Grand Rapids: Baker Academic, 2017), 142–45; Muller, *Dictionary of Latin and Greek*, 70–71. See also K. J. Drake, *The Flesh of the Word: The Extra Calvinisticum from Zwingli to Early Orthodoxy*, Oxford Studies in Historical Theology (Oxford: Oxford University Press, 2021), 218–20. For Luther's own discussion, see *LW*, 37:215–20; see also the Formula of Concord, article 7.

Holy Spirit—not physically[67]—thus understanding the *communicatio idiomatum* to mean that divine attributes can be predicated on the person of Christ, without confusing the boundary between the Christ's true humanity and his true divinity, between the finite and the infinite.

Extreme Christological Responses to the Reformation

The Reformation not only ushered in a new appreciation for the Scriptures and the work of Christ, but also opened up the door for many others who shirked the authorities of Christian tradition and ventured boldly (and often heretically) into new theological directions. In Calvin's own day the conflict with Michael Servetus, who was eventually condemned to death, has taken on a life of its own. Yet it is important to understand that Servetus apparently went looking for trouble and continued to push his heretical views that denied the Trinity.[68] Part of Servetus's errors were christological: he argued that Christ "was not the eternal Son of God but a form taken by God to come to earth. And that was only the beginning."[69]

Such christological (and Trinitarian) errors were not limited to Servetus, but proved to be the hobgoblins of the Reformation heritage. Another theological bogey was the Socinian challenge. The Socinians drew their name from Laelius Socinus (1525–1562)—who rubbed shoulders with Reformers such as Melanchthon and Calvin—and especially his nephew, Faustus Socinus (1539–1604).[70] The Socinians—forerunners of Unitarians—denied the Trinity, the preexistence and deity of Christ, and the substitutionary work of Christ.[71] In Socinian teaching we are not saved by Jesus's representative, atoning work but by our faithfulness and obedience.[72] As should be apparent by this juncture, these Socinian emphases were significant deviations from scriptural teaching and the church's established,

67. See, e.g., Calvin, *Inst.* 4.17.10. I discuss the doctrine often known as the *extra Calvinisticum*, which addresses the omnipresence of the Son of God, in the following chapter.

68. See Bruce Gordon, *Calvin: A Biography* (New Haven: Yale University Press, 2011), 217–24. See also Calvin, *Inst.* 2.14.5; Turretin, *Inst.* 3.25.3 (1:266).

69. Gordon, *Calvin*, 218.

70. On these figures, see F. L. Cross, ed., *The Oxford Dictionary of the Christian Church*, 3rd ed., ed. E. A. Livingstone (Oxford: Oxford University Press, 2005), 1523.

71. See Muller, *PRRD* 4:91–99.

72. See the Socinian Racovian Catechism 2.2; 5.8–9.

creedal heritage. The Socinians provide a stark example of how the person and work of Christ are related: to misunderstand the person of Christ means one will likely also misunderstand the work of Christ. A Jesus who is not fully divine does not fully save; downplaying the divinity of Christ necessarily downplays the saving efficacy of his work.

Post-Reformation Christology

THE DECADES FOLLOWING THE MAGISTERIAL Reformation brought a proliferation of creeds and confessions, along with post-Reformation dogmatic works, that congealed the Reformation emphases relating to the person and work of Christ. The post-Reformation era is marked by greater clarity and precision on both the person and work of Christ. This is the era, for example, in which we find classic creedal statements such as the Heidelberg Catechism and Westminster Confession of Faith, a wealth of detailed works of Reformed dogmatics (e.g., Polanus, Owen, Turretin, Mastricht),[73] and the articulation of such doctrines related to Christology as the covenant of works, the covenant of grace, and the covenant of redemption (i.e., the *pactum salutis*). This era is also marked by a more concerted emphasis on Christ as prophet, priest, and king.[74]

The covenant of works states that God entered into a covenant relationship with Adam in his upright, created state and offered him permanent, eternal life on the contingency of perfect obedience. Adam was not in a position to earn eternal life; he was but a creature. But God condescended by means of a covenant and offered Adam more than he could ever earn. In this, Adam failed, but Christ came as Mediator of the covenant of grace to fulfill what Adam failed to do. Christ is, as Paul states in the New Testament, the second man and last Adam (Rom 5:12–21; 1 Cor 15:22–28, 45–49), and his perfect obedience realizes the requirement for eternal life that Adam failed to achieve. The covenant of grace therefore refers to the divine plan of salvation to save fallen humanity by faith in the Mediator.[75] All humanity from

---

73. See Muller, *PRRD*.

74. Though this is apparent already in the Bible and the patristic era, it became particularly prevalent with Calvin (*Inst.* 2.15). On the development of this theme in Luther and Calvin, see Bray, *God Has Spoken*, 535–41. The emphasis on Christ's threefold office was also necessary given the Socinian emphasis on (and distinctive theology of) Christ as prophet, priest, and king. Thanks to Todd Rester for this latter observation.

75. See WCF 7.

Adam onward relates to God by means of one of these two covenants: those who rely on their own works are under the covenant of works and thus required to meet the unattainable goal of perfect obedience themselves for eternal life. In contrast, all those who live by faith in the Son of God relate to God by means of the covenant of grace and rely on the perfect obedience of the Mediator for eternal life.[76] This applies both to Old Testament and New Testament believers. This means that there is only one Mediator for both old covenant and new covenant believers, who was already present and active in the old covenant. This is another way the Bible emphasizes the preexistence of the Son and his work already in the old covenant.

A related concept is the covenant of redemption (or the *pactum salutis*).[77] This concept refers to an eternal, intra-Trinitarian "covenant" by which the Son freely agreed to serve as the Mediator of the covenant of grace for the redemption of his people. Biblical support for this doctrine is marshaled from texts that speak of the Son's coming to accomplish salvation (e.g., John 6:38–40; 17:4), of things that were granted to the Son (e.g., Luke 22:29), of the Son's being chosen (e.g., 1 Pet 1:20), and of the preexistent work of the Son in the Old Testament.[78] This does not entail subordination in the Godhead nor the division of the will of God, since Father and Son share the same will and Christ's obedience is the obedience of the economy of redemption, which does not entail any sort of subordination of essence of the Son to the Father.[79] This means our Savior is fully God who became a man and obeyed for us—not because he was required to but because of his love for us (see Rom 5:8).

76. "The covenant of grace is, however, not the discarding or annihilating but rather the fulfilling of the covenant of works. The difference between the two is mainly that in our stead Christ fulfills the requirement which God, by reason of the covenant of works can bring to bear on us." Bavinck, *Wonderful Works of God*, 391.

77. See Turretin, *Inst.* 12.2.7, 13–14 (2:175, 177–78); 14.13.16 (2:450); Bavinck, *RD* 3:212–16, 365; Muller, *PRRD* 4:265–67.

78. In addition to the previous note, see Owen, *Works* 1:54–64; Scott R. Swain, "Covenant of Redemption," in *Christian Dogmatics: Reformed Theology for the Church Catholic*, ed. Michael Allen and Scott R. Swain (Grand Rapids: Baker Academic, 2016), 107–25, esp. 118–20; Berkhof, *Systematic Theology*, 265–71.

79. Bavinck argues that whereas a covenant between God and humanity is a διαθήκη, the *pactum salutis* is a συνθήκη, in which "the greatest freedom and the most perfect agreement coincide" (*RD* 3:214–15).

CHRISTOLOGY IN THE MODERN ERA

Rejections of Chalcedon

Though most Christians continue to hold to the Christology of the Chalcedonian Definition, it has also proven to be open for further discussion and challenges in the centuries that have followed. Indeed, it has often been observed that the Chalcedonian Definition does not elaborate on the meaning of some of its key terms—such as "person" (ὑποστάσις) and "nature" (φύσις).[80] Thus, Chalcedon does not say everything that could be said. While most Christian traditions still find Chalcedon binding, some modern theologians—whose influence may be traced back to G. W. F. Hegel and Friedrich Schleiermacher—argue that we need to revisit Chalcedon.[81] For some, the terminology is problematical, reveals a shift away from the biblical realities, and derives more from the "Hellenized" or philosophical world of the early Christians.[82] It has also been observed that kenotic Christologies, for example, speak of the divine Son in some way divesting himself of (or refusing to "utilize") some of his divine attributes in the incarnation.[83] Kenoticism has been one approach to deal with the apparent paradox of Chalcedon—that is, the paradox of how one who is fully God can also be fully man.[84] But it runs afoul of the church's creedal traditions and does not do justice to the Son's never-changing divinity, as I argue further in chapters 8–9.

We ought not to overlook the significant influence of Karl Barth's Christology as well. According to Bruce McCormack, Barth's "is a post

80. E.g., Sarah Coakley, "What Does Chalcedon Solve, and What Does It Not? Some Reflections on the Status and Meaning of the Chalcedonian 'Definition,'" in *The Incarnation: An Interdisciplinary Symposium on the Incarnation of the Son of God*, ed. Stephen T. Davis, Daniel Kendall, SJ, and Gerald O'Collins, SJ (Oxford: Oxford University Press, 2002), 158–59, 162–63.

81. See Bruce L. McCormack, "The Person of Christ," in *Mapping Modern Theology: A Thematic and Historical Introduction*, ed. Kelly M. Kapic and Bruce L. McCormack (Grand Rapids: Baker Academic, 2012), 149–73; Mark S. G. Nestlehutt, "Chalcedonian Christology: Modern Criticism and Contemporary Ecumenism," *Journal of Ecumenical Studies* 35 (1998): 175–96.

82. See, e.g., the view of Ernst Troeltsch, among others, discussed in Nestlehutt, "Chalcedonian Christology."

83. Compare Oliver D. Crisp, *Divinity and Humanity: The Incarnation Reconsidered*, Current Issues in Theology, ed. Iain Torrance (Cambridge: Cambridge University Press, 2007), 141.

84. See James Anderson, *Paradox in Christian Theology: An Analysis of Its Presence, Character, and Epistemic Status*, Paternoster Theological Monographs (Milton Keynes, UK: Paternoster, 2007), 81–90.

metaphysical Christology that finds its focus in narrated history of Jesus of Nazareth as attested in the New Testament and never looks away from it."[85] Put differently, Barth "dispense[s] with the metaphysical conception of the 'person' of Christ altogether. ... The two 'natures'—really, divine and human *being*—are made one in a single human history."[86] Yet McCormack also argues that Barth "upheld the logic of Chalcedon."[87] The christological contribution of Barth to ongoing theological conversations is significant, but I am not able to address Barth's complex theology at any length in the present volume.

The "Historical Jesus" Movement

ANOTHER CHALLENGE TO CHALCEDON IS the reevaluation of the divinity of Christ in the academic study of "the historical Jesus." In the wake of the Enlightenment influential thinkers began to doubt faith and elevate reason in the church, which has often led to questioning the church's historic teaching on Christology. The "historical Jesus" movement—or the "quest of the historical Jesus," as it is often known[88]—began to use reason to reconstruct who Jesus "really" was and what he "really" claimed about himself. Since theological claims could not be verified, those must be set aside and the tools of historical criticism employed instead. These can be summed up in the threefold method of Ernst Troeltsch: correlation, analogy, and criticism.[89] In a nutshell, this meant that biblical claims (especially to the miraculous) require an explanation of natural causation, we must understand historical claims to have an analogy in our own days, and we must weigh claims with critical reason. Relying on the tools of historical criticism led to a watered-down, noncreedal, reconstructed Jesus that differed from the biblical witness: the "Jesus of history" was divorced from the

85. McCormack, "Person of Christ," 170.

86. McCormack, "Person of Christ," 171, emphasis original.

87. McCormack, "Person of Christ," 171.

88. Albert Schweitzer, *The Quest of the Historical Jesus*, trans. W. Montgomery (New York: Collier, 1968). B. B. Warfield observes that Schweitzer begins this famous book by casting off the constraints of Chalcedon. See Warfield, "'Two Natures,'" in Craig, *Person and Work of Christ*, 212–13. Schweitzer himself argues, "This dogma [i.e., the two natures of Chalcedon] had first to be shattered before men could once more go out in quest of the historical Jesus" (*Quest of the Historical Jesus*, 3).

89. See, e.g., Van A. Harvey, *The Historian and the Believer: The Morality of Historical Knowledge and Christian Belief* (London: SCM, 1967).

"Christ of faith."[90] This approach also introduced an unbiblical dichotomy between history and theology. Though this approach claims to be "neutral," it is anything but neutral, as it allows some types of evidence and disallows other types by way of presupposition. Even so, the historical Jesus movement has impacted the church, and its tendrils continue to reach for many today who are confronted with seemingly new challenges to Jesus's identity—but are instead old challenges that have already been sufficiently answered.

The historical Jesus movement is widely considered to have begun with Herman Samuel Reimarus in the eighteenth century, who argued that Jesus came to start a political revolution.[91] The continued influence of Reimarus is evident in the popular book by Reza Aslan, *Zealot: The Life and Times of Jesus of Nazareth*,[92] which makes a similar argument to Reimarus. Both authors must subject the Gospels to a method of weighing and sifting evidence, with Reimarus even attributing dishonesty to Jesus.[93]

Perhaps the most influential writing of this era (from the late seventeenth century to the onset of World War I in the early twentieth century) was David Strauss's *The Life of Jesus Critically Examined*—a book that Albert Schweitzer considered "one of the most perfect things in the whole range of learned literature."[94] Strauss, following Hegel, believed that both supernatural approaches to the Gospels and naturalistic explanations were inadequate. Instead of approaching the Gospels as historical, we must approach them as "myth." That is, we must understand the message of the Gospels to be what really matters, not their historicity. Thus, for example, Strauss argues, "The supernatural birth of Christ, his miracles, his

---

90. This was already critiqued by Martin Kähler, *The So-Called Historical Jesus and the Historic, Biblical Christ*, trans. Carl E. Braaten (Philadelphia: Fortress, 1964) (originally written in 1896); see also, e.g., Luke Timothy Johnson, *Living Jesus: Learning the Heart of the Gospel* (San Franciso: HarperOne, 2000); Dale C. Allison Jr., *The Historical Christ and the Theological Jesus* (Grand Rapids: Eerdmans, 2009).

91. See G. E. Lessing, ed., *Fragments from Reimarus*, ed. C. Voysey (repr., Lexington: American Theological Library Association, 1962).

92. Reza Aslan, *Zealot: The Life and Times of Jesus of Nazareth* (New York: Random House, 2013).

93. Lessing, *Fragments from Reimarus*, 12.

94. David Friedrich Strauss, *The Life of Jesus Critically Examined*, ed. Peter C. Hodgson, trans. George Eliot (repr., Mifflintown, PA: Sigler, 1994); Schweitzer, *Quest of the Historical Jesus*, 78.

resurrection and ascension, remain eternal truths, whatever doubts may be cast on their reality as historical facts."[95] Thus the ideas of the Gospels matter more than supposed historical events.

Strauss denied the authority of the Gospels, and his solution of "myth" was driven more by Hegelianism than Scripture.[96] Scripture affirms the historicity of the work of Christ, and without that historicity, the message is devoid of significance. Yet Strauss's basic approach continues to be influential even today, as some scholars insist that the historicity of Jesus from the Gospels is not recoverable, whereas the "message" remains the most important aspect. This is evident in the theology of Rudolf Bultmann—perhaps the most influential New Testament scholar of the twentieth century—who argues that it is the message (κήρυγμα) of Jesus that matters, since we can know very little of Jesus himself.[97] Strauss's views also persist in a range of other studies as well, including Aslan's *Zealot* and the arguments one may encounter in New Testament scholarship whereby the spiritual message of the Gospels is true, whatever the merits of their historical claims about Jesus.[98]

Understanding the Person of Jesus

One of the significant errors of the historical Jesus movement is the misguided notion that a purely "human" Jesus is who Jesus really was. This is a view that has consistently been rejected by the church. As we saw earlier, the church rejected any approach to Christology that did not understand the eternal Son of God to be the personal subject of the incarnation. The incarnation is not about a man who becomes God but about God who becomes man.[99] The historical Jesus movement—both in the past and

95. Strauss, *Life of Jesus*, lii, emphasis added.

96. See Robert B. Strimple, *The Modern Search for the Real Jesus: An Introductory Survey of the Historical Roots of Gospels Criticism* (Phillipsburg, NJ: P&R, 1995), 32; see also Stephen Neill, *The Interpretation of the New Testament, 1861–1961* (London: Oxford University Press, 1964), 16.

97. See, e.g., Rudolf Bultmann, *Jesus and the Word*, trans. Louise Pettibone Smith and Erminie Huntress Lantero (New York: Scribner, 1958), 8, 12.

98. See, e.g., Francis Watson, *Gospel Writing: A Canonical Perspective* (Grand Rapids: Eerdmans, 2013), 510–52. Though admittedly he is professedly following Origen, Watson's belief that the Gospels cannot be correlated to extratextual historical realities (see 550) arguably resembles a modern, Straussian approach.

99. See also Fairbairn and Reeves, *Story of Creeds and Confessions*, 77, 90, 104.

today—often misses this and ends up with a Jesus that aligns more closely with heretical views of Jesus than orthodox views.

For example, it is common to read in historical Jesus scholarship of a Jesus who did not claim to be the Messiah and/or who is not the eternal Son of God. But this reflects a Nestorian Christology whereby Christ is divided into two persons. At the very least, it drives an unworkable wedge between the two natures of Christ that threatens the unity of the person. For in the incarnation there is one person, and the human nature of Jesus is not a different person from the eternal Son of God. McGuckin observes similarly, "The widespread distinction in contemporary biblical interpretation between the Jesus of History and the Christ of Faith frequently betrays ... an undisclosed christological anthropology that is more like that of Nestorius than it is of Cyril."[100] Even so, we also must not hesitate to affirm that Jesus is fully man: "all that man as man is, that Christ is to eternity."[101] In chapter 9 I will discuss in more detail the mysterious relationship of the human and divine natures of Jesus to the one person.

Some studies venture even more boldly into Arianism and adoptionism. Some, for example, consider New Testament Christology to be adoptionistic, whereby Jesus became Son of God at his baptism or resurrection.[102] But we have seen in this and the previous chapter that orthodoxy has always affirmed the full divinity of the Son. Any scholarly approach that argues Jesus became divine, or is in some way less divine than the Father, is to be rejected.

In the end, we must affirm with Chalcedon that Jesus is Christ is both fully man and fully God, though the implications of this are difficult to work out and require us to tread carefully.

What about the Atonement?

I WILL ADDRESS THE ATONEMENT in more detail in chapter 10, but it is relevant at this point to note that the historical Jesus movement as a whole has little

100. McGuckin, *St. Cyril*, 190.

101. Benjamin B. Warfield, "The Human Development of Jesus," in *Selected Shorter Writings*, 2 vols, ed. John E. Meeter (Phillipsburg, NJ: P&R, 1970–73), 1:162.

102. See, e.g., Philipp Vielhauer, "On the 'Paulinism' of Acts," in *Studies in Luke-Acts: Essays Presented in Honor of Paul Schubert*, ed. Leander E. Keck and J. Louis Martyn (Nashville: Abingdon, 1966), 44.

substantial to say about the saving work of Christ on behalf of sinners. If Jesus came to start a political revolution, he did not come to give his life as a substitutionary atonement for sin. For example, Albert Schweitzer famously concludes the first edition of his *Quest of the Historical Jesus* with a crucified, nonresurrected Jesus who was wrong about his mission but was courageous enough to stand up and face the consequences of his errors.[103] Others argued that Jesus was a great moral teacher and encouraged humanity to reach its highest ideals. One popular book from the nineteenth century portrays a purely natural Jesus who is nevertheless the object of the faith of humankind.[104]

Again, as throughout church history, we must recognize the need to keep the person and the work of Christ united. Who is it who saves us? Is it a man who enables us to reach God? Or is it the Son of God himself, who came down and took a human nature to redeem fallen humanity? The former view has been consistently and roundly rejected by orthodox Christianity—yet this was often the approach of the historical Jesus movement. The latter is Christianity. I will explain how this all fits together in the following chapters.

The "Historical Jesus" Is a Noncreedal Jesus

THERE IS NOTHING NEW UNDER the sun. Though we will continue to face challenges to Jesus, most of the challenges we will face on the identity of Jesus have already been posed somewhere in the past and have been sufficiently answered. For example, J. Gresham Machen already countered many of these arguments in his 1923 book *Christianity and Liberalism*,[105] which highlights the need for a proper

103. Schweitzer, *Quest of the Historical Jesus*, 370–71. Dunn et al. note that in later editions of this book Schweitzer excised this passage. See James D. G. Dunn, *Jesus Remembered*, Christianity in the Making 2 (Grand Rapids: Eerdmans, 2003), 47n101.

104. Ernest Rénan, *Life of Jesus*, ed. Joseph Henry Allen (Boston: Roberts Brothers, 1896), 77. See also Neill, *Interpretation of the New Testament*, 193–94. Rénan in one sense acknowledges that Jesus is divine, but he reimagines it: "This sublime Person ... may well be called divine,—not in the sense that Jesus has absorbed all that is divine, or was one with it; but in the sense that he is the one who has impelled his fellow-men to take the longest step towards the divine" (*Life of Jesus*, 420).

105. This section is adapted from Brandon D. Crowe, "Christianity and Liberalism and the Gospels," in *Christianity and Liberalism: Legacy Edition*, by J. Gresham Machen (Philadelphia: Westminster Seminary Press, 2019), 260–62. Used with permission.

understanding of the person of Jesus. Several aspects of Machen's thought are relevant today.

First, the Gospels—and the other New Testament writings—are not first of all about grand ideas, but they are about Jesus—about who he really is and what he really did. Jesus cannot be understood simply as a great moral teacher, for he claimed much more than that about himself. He is the supernatural Son of God who came to accomplish salvation. Nonhistorical readings of the Gospels devolve into mysticism. The message of the New Testament is rooted in what Jesus has actually done (Luke 1:1–4).

Second, it is not our task to sift the Gospels to identify what the historical Jesus "really" said or did. A reconstructed (and nonsupernatural) Jesus is not the Jesus of history, nor is it the Jesus of the Gospels. To put one's faith in a reconstructed Jesus is to put one's faith in the subjective principles and methods used by fallible revisionists. The inspired texts must be our authorities, not reformatted texts that distort the picture of the evangelists. Though his point is a bit different, Irenaeus warns about those who misinterpret the Scriptures and turn a beautiful mosaic of a king into a picture of an ugly dog—they are weaving ropes of sand (*Haer.* 1.8.1). So it is with those who cut and paste from the Gospels.

Third, the Gospels are supernatural documents, and Jesus is a supernatural Savior who came to save sinners. Jesus explicitly states that he has come to give his life as a ransom (Matt 20:28; Mark 10:45). The atonement only makes sense if Jesus is divine, for what good does the self-sacrifice of a noble man do if that sacrifice is merely an example that cannot save another? There must be something different about Jesus that enables his sacrifice to be efficacious and salvific.

This means the Gospels are good news. Machen argues that the substitutionary death of Christ is predicated on the uniqueness of Christ himself, and this anticipates the great miracle of the resurrection. To be sure, one might be surprised to hear that a man has been raised from the dead. But Jesus is no mere man (though he is truly man)—he is the divine Son of God who came to deal with the real problem of our sin in a way that only he could do. The biblical Jesus is the answer that a sinful world needs. This is the Savior we meet in the Gospels.

CONCLUSION

Though the orthodox always agreed on the divinity and humanity of Christ, it took time for these to be worked out with precision. Christ is fully divine and fully human. He is one person who has two natures in the incarnation. The human nature does not act on its own, nor does the divine nature negate the need for a human soul in in the incarnation. Though these parameters were established by Chalcedon, further articulation with respect both to the ontology and the economy of redemption proved to be necessary.

In the modern era, the elevation of reason and the throwing off of "dogma" (which is never actually possible) led not to greater clarity on the person and work of Christ but to a greater proliferation of divergent opinions. The incarnation is a mystery that cannot be explained fully using the tools of human logic. We should not try to overexplain the ineffable, but we should follow trusted guides to help us find our way and keep us from christological errors. The rule of faith and the church's creedal articulations guide the way and provide guardrails for scholarly study of Jesus. Put simply, the creeds show us the right way to read Scripture, while modern reconstructions are vacuous.

This chapter has been largely descriptive. In the following three chapters I will set out a more positive case for how we today should understand the person and work of Christ.

FURTHER READING

Fairbairn, Donald, and Ryan M. Reeves. *The Story of Creeds and Confessions: Tracing the Development of the Christian Faith*. Grand Rapids: Baker Academic, 2019. Fairbairn and Reeves provide helpful context for the material covered in this chapter and explains the background and theology of various creeds from the early church to the twentieth century.

McGuckin, John Anthony. *St. Cyril of Alexandria: The Christological Controversy. Its History, Theology, and Texts*. Reprint, Crestwood, NY: St. Vladimir's Seminary Press, 2004. McGuckin provides a historical treatment of the Nestorian controversy (including the First Council of Ephesus), the Christologies of Nestorius and Cyril, and a collection of relevant primary texts.

Muller, Richard A. *Post-Reformation Reformed Dogmatics.* 2nd ed. 4 vols. Grand Rapids: Baker Academic, 2003. Muller provides a discussion of the development of doctrine in the post-Reformation period. Volume 4 is particularly relevant, as it includes discussions of the Trinity, the persons of the Trinity, development of the *pactum salutis*, and so forth.

Tanner, Norman P., SJ, ed. *Decrees of the Ecumenical Councils.* 2 vols. Washington, DC: Georgetown University Press, 1990. This is a compendium of major creeds, in original languages and translation, from the Council of Nicaea in the fourth century to Vatican II in the twentieth century.

Wilhite, David E. *The Gospel according to Heretics: Discovering Orthodoxy through Early Christological Conflicts*. Grand Rapids: Baker Academic, 2015. Wilhite introduces controversial figures and issues from a sympathetic viewpoint in order to foster greater understanding.

VIII

THE MEDIATOR OF THE COVENANT OF GRACE

THE ETERNAL SON

THE DEBATES OF THE PREVIOUS chapter highlight the importance of properly identifying the person of the incarnation. Put simply, it is the eternal Son of God who takes on flesh in the incarnation. In this chapter I address in more detail that person—the Second Person of the Trinity, who is eternally the Son of God. I will then address his role as the Mediator of the covenant of grace—a concept that became more fully articulated in the post-Reformation era, as noted in the previous chapter. Jesus Christ, the eternal Son of God, is the one Mediator of the covenant of grace.

ETERNAL, DIVINE SONSHIP

BEFORE THE INCARNATION IN THE economy of redemptive history, the Son was already Creator and Mediator of the covenant of grace. Indeed, the Second Person of the Trinity is the eternal Son of God—he never came into being, nor is he in any way "less divine" than the Father. The Son is fully God. The divinity of the Son is well-attested in Scripture, as I argued in part 1—he is the eternal Logos (John 1:1) who is God over all (Rom 9:5), and this has been the conviction of orthodox Christian believers from the earliest recoverable days of the church, as I argued in chapters 6–7.

Eternal Generation Speaking of the eternality of the divine Son requires us to consider the often misunderstood concept of eternal generation (i.e., being eternally begotten).[1] Many find this topic to be overly speculative and perhaps do not see the need to discuss the nature of the Son's begetting in such detail. But it matters a great deal, and it is not as speculative as it may seem at first.

The distinctions between the persons of the Trinity are not between levels of deity, for all three persons are equally God, "the same in substance, equal in power and glory" (WSC 6). Instead, the distinctions among the persons of the Trinity are often known as personal properties: the Father begets, the Son is begotten, and the Spirit proceeds from the Father and the Son.

So, to speak of the eternal generation of the Son is to speak of what is proper to the Son of God: he is begotten.[2] But, as we saw with Athanasius's argument in the previous chapter, *begotten* does not mean *created*. To be begotten means that the Son receives his personal subsistence from the Father.[3] Further, some Reformed speak of eternal generation as an act "*passively accomplished* in the Son," while others demur at this language.[4] Eternal generation speaks not of generation of the Son's divine *essence* but of the generation of an uncreated, divine *person*.[5] In eternal generation the Father begets the Son, communicating the divine essence to the Son so that both Father and Son possess the same essence, without change.[6] However,

1. Portions of section originally appeared as "God the Son," *TableTalk* 43.12 (2019): 12–15. Used with permission.

2. Turretin, *Inst.* 3.29.14 (1:298); see also the Chalcedonian definition of the faith, in Tanner, *Decrees* 1:86–*86.

3. Berkhof, *Systematic Theology*, 93–94; see also Mastricht, *Theoretical-Practical Theology* 2:230–31, 556; Muller, *PRRD* 4:283–88.

4. Muller, *PRRD* 4:287, emphasis added. Turretin is one who demurs, e.g., *Inst.* 3.29.5 (1:293).

5. Turretin, *Inst.* 3.29.6, 21, 23 (1:293, 300–301); Mastricht, *Theoretical-Practical Theology* 2:231, 556; Owen, *Works* 1:218.

6. See Turretin, *Inst.* 3.28.3 (1:282); 3.29.4, 6 (1:292–93); Mastricht, *Theoretical-Practical Theology* 2:231; *SPT* 8.7 (1:204–5); Owen, *Works* 1:218; Berkhof, *Systematic Theology*, 93. See also the Irish Articles (1615): "9. The essence of the Father does not beget the essence of the Son; but the person of the Father begetteth the person of the Son, by communicating His whole essence to the person begotten from eternity" (Dennison, *Reformed Confessions* 4:92). See also James Ussher, *A Body of Divinitie, or The Summe and Substance of Christian Religion: Catechistically propounded, and explained, by way of Question and Answer: Methodically and familiarly handled* (London: Downes & Badger, 1645), 79–80. These references to Ussher and the Irish Articles are indebted to Harrison Perkins, *On the Nature and Kingdom of God:*

some who follow Calvin may not find "communication of essence" to be the most felicitous language.[7] Calvin emphasized the Son's aseity (that, is his self-existence) as a necessary entailment of the Son's full divinity. Calvin thus denied a communication of essence in eternal generation, which he believed would threaten the aseity of the Son.[8] In Calvin's view, the Son is *autotheos* ("God from himself") when considered as to his divinity, and eternally begotten when considered as to his personal subsistence.[9]

It is indeed proper to affirm the aseity of the Son with respect to his essential being,[10] but historically for the Reformed, aseity has been understood as something communicated from Father to Son (see John 5:26).[11] Further, the communication of essence in eternal begetting does not entail the ontological subordination of the Son, but ensures the essential equality of Father and Son.[12] In light of Calvin's influence, relating the Son's aseity to eternal generation has proven to be a tricky question in the post-Reformation period. Chad Van Dixhoorn argues for three approaches to the issue of aseity and eternal generation among the early modern Reformed that are consistent with the Westminster Confession of Faith, as they wrestled with Calvin's position: tradition A, which finds the divine essence communicated by means of eternal generation; tradition B, which understands the divine essence to belong inherently to the Son (and therefore is not

---

James Ussher's Theological Manuscripts, Historical Texts in Reformed Theology (Philadelphia: Westminster Seminary Press, forthcoming 2023). Compare also Vos, *Reformed Dogmatics* 1:60. In Latin "communication" (*communico/communicatio*) of essence does not mean "production" (*productio*) of essence. See Chad Van Dixhoorn, "Post-Reformation Trinitarian Perspectives," in Sanders and Swain, *Retrieving Eternal Generation*, 191–93, 196.

7. See Brannon Ellis, *Calvin, Classical Trinitarianism, and the Aseity of the Son* (Oxford: Oxford University Press, 2012), esp. 62, 99–102, 197–227.

8. Scott R. Swain, "B. B. Warfield and the Biblical Doctrine of the Trinity," *Them* 43 (2018): 16–17; Ryan M. McGraw and Scott Cook, "Charles Hodge on the Trinity: Personhood and Subordination Language," in *Charles Hodge: American Reformed Orthodox Theologian*, ed. Ryan M. McGraw (Göttingen: Vandenhoeck & Ruprecht, forthcoming).

9. Calvin, *Inst.* 1.13.25 (1:153–54), a passage noted in McGraw and Cook, "Hodge on the Trinity," forthcoming; see also Muller, *PRRD* 4:325–26; Maresius, *Theologiae elenchticae* 3.2 (p. 88).

10. Turretin, *Inst.* 3.28.40 (1:291–92), *SPT* 8.18 (1:214–15); Mastricht, *Theoretical Practical Theology*, 2:231; see also Muller, *PRRD* 4:324–32. This point was especially pertinent for the Reformed and post-Reformed in discussions in which the full divinity of the Son was under attack, such as with the Socinians, or Arminians who did not affirm the aseity of the Son. Thanks to Todd Rester for this latter observation.

11. Swain, "Warfield and the Biblical Doctrine," 17.

12. Swain, "Warfield and the Biblical Doctrine," 16–18.

communicated); and tradition C, which focuses on the generation of the person of the Son, which also entails a communication of essence.[13] Calvin's view best fits with tradition B, whereas traditional trinitarianism teaches some combination of tradition A and C. Whichever view one holds on this issue, eternal generation is best understood not as speaking of levels of divinity or of divinity somehow given to the Son in a way that threatens his essential coequality with the Father (and Spirit), but it speaks instead of the eternal "order of subsistence" of Trinitarian persons.[14]

Further, this generation must be eternal. The generation of the Son could not happen at a moment in time, for if it did, then the Son would not be eternally the Son—nor would the Father be eternally the Father.[15] If the Son's generation were a singular event, this would mean that God in some sense changes. That is, if the Father ever became the Father, or the Son ever became the Son, then God would not be immutable.[16] Because the Son of God never changes, his begetting must be an eternal begetting—it is not something that happened a long time ago or once for all. Nor does eternal generation entail any division in God, as though the divine essence were divided between the three persons or multiplied from one person to another.[17] For God is indivisible as well as immutable.[18] Each person of the Godhead possesses the same divine essence and the fullness of the divine essence. Eternal generation is also a necessary act, which means that it always is and could not be otherwise.[19] Eternal generation is a timeless, placeless, and changeless reality.[20]

---

13. Van Dixhoorn, "Post-Reformation Trinitarian Perspectives," 205–207. Thanks also to Ryan McGraw for this observation and for helpful feedback on these issues.

14. See Turretin, *Inst.* 3.29.6, 21, 25 (1:293, 300–301). See also Muller, *PRRD* 4:253: "The Father, as the Reformed orthodox argue, is *not* first in duration, nature or causality, dignity or excellence, but rather in subsistence and operation" (emphasis original).

15. E.g., Maresius, *Theologiae elenchticae* 3.2 (pp. 87–90).

16. See Athanasius, *C. Ar.* 1.35–36.

17. Maresius, *Theologiae elenchticae* 3.2 (pp. 89–90); Turretin, *Inst.* 3.29.4 (1:293); Vos, *Reformed Dogmatics* 1:60.

18. See Athanasius, *C. Ar.* 1.28; see also *C. Ar.* 1.14–22.

19. Turretin, *Inst.* 3.29.22 (1:301).

20. See Turretin, *Inst.* 3.29.5, 7 (1:293–94), who also notes here that the internal works of the Trinity are eternal and unceasing. See also Berkhof, *Systematic Theology*, 94; Mastricht, *Theoretical-Practical Theology* 2:230; SPT 8.5–20 (1:204–17); Maresius, *Theologiae elenchticae nova synopsis* 3.2 (pp. 87–90); Owen, *Works* 1:19, 218.

Admittedly, even if we can explain eternal generation accurately, we cannot understand it fully. It is ineffable, but is not for that reason to be rejected.[21]

Where is eternal generation found in Scripture? As with so many important doctrines, it cannot be gleaned from a handful of prooftexts.[22] It is rather the "good and necessary consequence" of the teaching of Scripture as a whole. It likely finds support from the traditional rendering of μονογενής as "only begotten" in John (see 1:14, 18; 3:16, 18; also 1 John 4:9), which I noted in chapter 3. Yet the concept of eternal begetting is not dependent on how one translates μονογενής, but derives from what Scripture reveals more holistically about the Son's preexistence and the eternal relationship between the Father and the Son (e.g., John 17:5, 24; see also Col 1:15–20; Heb 1:1–3). The Father has always been the Father, and the Son has always been Son of the Father (John 1:1–2; see also Matt 11:25–27; Luke 10:21–22). Further, as noted in chapter 3, the "life in himself" that is granted to the Son in John 5:26 likely supports eternal generation quite directly.

Historically, support for eternal generation has also been gleaned from the Old Testament. Richard Muller notes that the Socinians opposed eternal generation on the basis of four key prooftexts, each of which they denied taught eternal generation: Psalms 2:7; 110:3; Proverbs 8:23; Micah 5:2.[23] Yet again it is important to note that eternal generation does not rely on these four texts but on the teaching of Scripture as a whole. For example, though Psalm 2:7 is used in the New Testament to refer to the resurrection of Jesus (e.g., Acts 13:33), the sonship declared and vindicated in the resurrection is grounded on preexistent sonship.[24] The resurrection is emphatically not the means by which Christ becomes the Son of God, properly speaking.[25] Indeed, as I argued in chapter 2, the portrait of the king in Psalm 2:7 transcends what was true of the created, Davidic king (see Ps 2:12), and Acts

21. Mastricht, *Theoretical-Practical Theology* 2:547; Gregory of Nazianzus, *Or.* 29.8.

22. Compare Muller, *PRRD* 4:284–87.

23. Muller, *PRRD* 4:284.

24. Mastricht, *Theoretical-Practical Theology* 2:530, 542; see also Maresius, *Theologiae elenchticae* 3.1 (p. 81).

25. See Mastricht, *Theoretical-Practical Theology* 2:551–53.

4:25–27 makes it clear that the key referent of this passage is Christ.[26] Given this greater sonship in the progression of revelation, it also makes sense that the begetting in view (see Ps 2:7) of the true Son of God is also a greater begetting than what was true for the Davidic king. The "today" of Psalm 2:7 is thus clearly fulfilled in the resurrection (Acts 13:33; Heb 1:5),[27] which seems to be firmer exegetical ground than finding an eternal "today" in Hebrews[28] (see, e.g., Heb 3:12–15; Diogn. 11.4–5).

As for Micah 5:2, John Owen responded to the Socinians that Micah 5:2 is only part of the biblical teaching on eternal generation—it speaks specifically of the eternal aspect.[29] I argued in chapter 2 that Micah 5:2 does appear to allude to the eternal origins of the greater Son of David. Proverbs 8 reflects on the importance of wisdom in creation and has often been taken to refer to the Son's eternal generation.[30] However, this is an unnecessary conclusion, though Proverbs 8 does play an important role in anticipating New Testament teaching on Christ as the wisdom of God (e.g., 1 Cor 1:30; Col 1:15–20; maybe Matt 11:19, 28–30).[31]

In sum, the Socinians were incorrect to find eternal generation only from a handful of prooftexts.

Avoiding Subordinationism

Since the Son is fully divine, eternal generation does not imply eternal subordination of the Son to the Father. One of the problems with some of the forebears of the doctrine of eternal generation[32] is the teaching that the Son is somehow intrinsically subordinate to the Father. Before we

26. Muller, *PRRD* 4:285; Mastricht, *Theoretical-Practical Theology* 2:543, 547, 551; see also Muller, *PRRD* 4:260.

27. See Crowe, *Hope of Israel*, 58–61; R. B. Jamieson, *The Paradox of Sonship: Christology in the Epistle to the Hebrews*, Studies in Christian Doctrine and Scripture (Downers Grove: IVP Academic, 2021), 17–20, 104–7.

28. Madison N. Pierce, "Hebrews 1 and the Son Begotten 'Today,'" in Sanders and Swain, *Retrieving Eternal Generation*, 117–31; Bauckham, "Divinity of Jesus," 251–52.

29. Muller, *PRRD* 4:284.

30. See Matthew Y. Emerson, "The Role of Proverbs 8: Eternal Generation in Hermeneutics Ancient and Modern," in Sanders and Swain, *Retrieving Eternal Generation*, 44–66.

31. See Bavinck, *RD* 2:274; Bruce K. Waltke, *The Book of Proverbs: Chapters 1–15*, NICOT (Grand Rapids: Eerdmans, 2004), 127–32, 409n104.

32. See ch. 6.

consider the Son's role as Mediator of the covenant of grace and his work of humiliation, it is important to appreciate the doctrine of the Trinity and the full divinity of the Son to guard against subordinationism.[33] The Son is not somehow less divine than the Father; the Son of God is himself God no less than the Father is God.

It is further helpful to consider the principle of the unity of the external works of the Trinity—that is, inseparable operations—which was one of the key principles of those who promoted Nicene theology.[34] Stated simply, inseparable operations states that where one person of the Trinity is active *in ad extra* works (that is, works external to God's intrinsic being), all the persons are active. The Son does nothing in the incarnation apart from the Father and Spirit, for all three are equally God, even though it is indeed fitting that it is the Son who is incarnate.[35] That is, the incarnation terminates on the Son, though the Son does not act independently in the incarnation.[36] The Son's actions *ad extra* are not independent, but are a distinct, personal (i.e., filial) mode of actions inseparable from the unified, Trinitarian operations.[37] For example, we see a glimpse of the way each person of the Trinity harmoniously works *ad extra* in a text such as 1 Peter 1:2, which speaks of the foreknowledge of God the Father, the obedience of the Son, and the sanctification of the Holy Spirit.

However, some have argued for the Son's eternal submission (or subordination) to the Father in light of the Bible's teaching about the Son's obedience to the Father. But the full divinity of the Son warns against positing degrees of divinity or rank in God's being. Though some actions are appropriated by or fitting for particular persons of the Trinity (i.e., the doctrine of appropriations),[38] a right understanding of the Trinity is crucial to guard against filial subordinationism. The Son submits in the economy

33. See, e.g., Robert Letham, *The Holy Trinity: In Scripture, History, Theology, and Worship*, 2nd ed. (Phillipsburg, NJ: P&R, 2019), 451–92.

34. See Ayres, *Nicaea and Its Legacy*, e.g., 280–82, 296–300; see also D. Glenn Butner, *The Son Who Learned Obedience: A Theological Case against the Eternal Submission of the Son* (Eugene, OR: Pickwick, 2018), 141–42; Vidu, *Same God*, esp. 52–90.

35. See Turretin, *Inst.* 13.4 (2:304–6).

36. See Muller, *PRRD* 4:255–60; Turretin, *Inst.* 3.27.16–20 (1:280–82).

37. Vidu, *Same God*, 82, 103.

38. Muller, *PRRD* 4:267–74; Letham, *Systematic Theology*, 610, 939–40.

of redemption; ontologically, he is not eternally subordinate to the Father. Further, we run astray if we posit separate wills of the Father and the Son.[39]

In this light we can understand 1 Corinthians 15:28: "When all things are subjected to him, then the Son himself will also be subjected to him who put all things in subjection under him, that God may be all in all." This text has often been understood to refer to the eternal subordination of the Son to the Father. However, 1 Corinthians 15 has the economy of redemption in view; it does not speak of an eternal—or everlasting—subordination of the Son. The Leiden Synopsis explains carefully:

> Although the Son of God is less than the Father because of that mediation, he is not therefore less than him in his deity. For he accepted his mediatorial task from the Father by a dispensation that was shared and willed by the Trinity as a whole—and that included himself. ... In the age that is to come he will lay aside his office of Mediator when he will hand over his scepter to the Father; yet he will hold on to his divinity with the Father unchanged forever and ever.[40]

John Owen speaks of Christ's subjection to the Father only in his human nature.[41] Similarly, Turretin understands 1 Corinthians 15:28 to refer to either the church, the humanity of Christ, or his office of mediation.[42] Similar views have been argued more recently by (among others) Oliver Crisp, R. B. Jamieson, Glenn Butner, and Adonis Vidu.[43] Bavinck is characteristically nuanced, arguing for an end to the mediatorial role of Christ's humiliation as prophet, priest, and king, but not to "the mediatorship of union," which means Christ as head of the church remains prophet, priest, and king with respect to his human nature, for he is the perfect image of God.[44]

---

39. For further discussions see, e.g., Letham, *Holy Trinity*, 461–64; Barrett, *Simply Trinity*, 213–59.

40. *SPT* 26.29 (2:114–17).

41. Owen, *Works* 1:236–37; see also 1:271–72.

42. Turretin, *Inst.* 14.17.11 (2:493).

43. Crisp, *Word Enfleshed*, 6; R. B. Jamieson, "1 Corinthians 15.28 and the Grammar of Paul's Christology," *NTS* 66 (2020): 187–207; Butner, *Son Who Learned Obedience*, 162–72; Vidu, *Same God*, 266n48.

44. Bavinck, *RD* 3:482; see also Letham, *Work of Christ*, 208.

THE MEDIATOR OF THE COVENANT OF GRACE

THIS ETERNAL SON OF GOD is the Mediator of the covenant of grace.[45] As noted in the previous chapter, the covenant of grace is a way to refer to God's one plan of salvation by grace that applies to both Old Testament and New Testament believers. Put simply, all of God's people are saved by faith in the Mediator of the covenant of grace, whether they lived before or after the coming of Christ.

The covenant of grace can be seen in the Bible's first promise of redemption in Genesis 3:15 that the seed of the woman would crush the serpent's head (BC 17). Though Adam sinned in the beginning, God intervened to offer forgiveness and restoration by faith, and later Adam and Eve are portrayed as faithful covenant keepers.[46] All subsequent Old Testament covenants were built on this promise in Genesis 3:15 and can be subsumed under covenant of grace.[47] The covenant of grace speaks of God's provision to cover humanity's sin through the work of the Mediator. In the covenant of works in the beginning, Adam was offered glorious, permanent, eternal life contingent on his perfect obedience (see WCF 19; WLC 30). Though Adam failed, Christ the Mediator came as the Last Adam, with a pure human nature, to realize the internal and external obedience required of Adam in the beginning, that he might deliver us from sin, overcome the devil, and secure eternal life. The covenant of grace is God's single plan of redemption to save all those who are "in Adam" who look in faith to the last Adam.[48]

Thus, in the covenant of grace faith is directed toward the Mediator (WCF 7.3; WLC 32). This means that already in the Old Testament, the Son of God is the Mediator between God and humanity. It also means that the entire Old Testament after Adam recounts this single covenant of grace—this includes the Mosaic covenant.[49] Though his final sacrifice was yet future, the efficacy of his future sacrifice applied to true believers already in the Old Testament (WCF 7.5; WLC 33–34). Thus, the Mosaic covenant and its litany of sacrifices were not ways that sinful people were to make themselves right before God. Instead, though some have argued that we should

---

45. See further Bavinck, *RD* 3:196–228; Turretin, *Inst.* 12.5–9 (2:174–247).
46. See Crowe, *Path of Faith*, 17–21.
47. See Owen, *Works* 1:120–34.
48. See the helpful discussion of Bavinck, *RD* 3:222–28.
49. See Turretin, *Inst.* 12.12 (2:262–69).

understand the Mosaic covenant in some sense to be a republication of the covenant of works, it is more prudent to focus on the Mosaic covenant as fundamentally part of the one covenant of grace.[50] Its sacrifices anticipated the final sacrifice of Christ, and the participants in those sacrifices were to look in faith to the provision of God to take away their sin.[51] For example, when Paul speaks of justification by faith in Romans 4, he points to two Old Testament believers: Abraham (see Gen 15:6) and David (see Ps 32:1–2). Justification was already a reality in the Old Testament.

It is crucial that we appreciate the person who is the Mediator—he is always the divine Son of God—the true prophet, priest, and king (WCF 8.1; WLC 31, 36). Francis Turretin explains that the divinity of Christ is seen in the efficacy of his threefold office: for as a prophet he illumines our minds and inclines our hearts to what is right, as king he rules the church and defends us against the devil, and as a priest he satisfies divine justice and purchases eternal redemption. No mere man could do these things.[52] John Owen puts it simply, “Upon the glory of this divine person of Christ depends the efficacy of all his offices.”[53] He is Mediator already in the Old Testament, and from the time of the New Testament until today is the Mediator who has permanently taken to himself a human nature in the incarnation. Yet the personal agent, as we saw in the previous chapter, is always the Son of God.

Despite the continuity of the covenant of grace, we do indeed encounter remarkably new developments in the administration of the covenant of grace when the Son took on flesh in the incarnation. In the hypostatic union, the eternal Son of God took to himself a human nature in a personal and permanent union and definitively accomplished salvation. Though his work applies to all believers in the covenant of grace (OT and NT), his coming in redemptive history was the climactic, final act of redemption that brought the full flowering of the plan of God. We thus ought not to flatten distinctions between the Old Testament and the New Testament, even though there is indeed a unity of the covenant of grace. The new covenant

50. See also Letham, *Systematic Theology*, 447–61.

51. See further Crowe, *Why Did Jesus Live a Perfect Life?*, 59–84.

52. Turretin, *Inst.* 3.28.30 (1:290).

53. Owen, *Works* 1:20, see also 1:85–100.

administration of the covenant of grace is fuller and richer than the old covenant administration of the covenant of grace—though both covenants have the same Mediator (WCF 7.5–6; WLC 34–36).

CONCLUSION

The person of Son of God is eternal and fully divine. He is the Word of God who reveals the Father and is the one Mediator of the unified covenant of grace. In the incarnation the eternal Son of God is united hypostatically to a human nature, with the result that from the time of the incarnation he is not only fully God, but also fully man. With the incarnation comes a new era in the Son's mediatorial work—the climactic accomplishment of redemption, including the definitive sacrifice for sin.

Once we are clear as to the person of the Mediator, we can best think about the natures of the Mediator, which is the topic of the next chapter.

FURTHER READING

Bavinck, Herman. *Reformed Dogmatics*. Vol. 2, *God and Creation*. Edited by John Bolt. Translated by John Vriend. Grand Rapids: Baker Academic, 2004. Bavinck provides a standard discussion of the person of the Son in Trinitarian perspective in volume 2; he says more about his role in the covenant of grace in volume 3 (See especially chapter 6).

Mastricht, Petrus van. *Theoretical-Practical Theology*. Vol. 2, *Faith in the Triune God*. Translated by Todd M. Rester. Edited by Joel R. Beeke. Grand Rapids: Reformation Heritage, 2019. This wide-ranging volume covers the nature of faith but also the persons of the Trinity. Chapter 26, which focuses on the Son of God, is particularly relevant.

Owen, John. *The Works of John Owen*. Edited by William H. Goold. 16 vols. Reprint, Edinburgh: Banner of Truth, 1965–1968. See especially volume 1 (*The Glory of Christ*), which contains both Owen's ΧΡΙΣΤΟΛΟΓΙΑ [*Christologia*] and his *Meditations and Discourses on the Glory of Christ*. Interested readers will also find christological insights in other volumes of Owen's collected works.

Turretin, Francis. *Institutes of Elenctic Theology*. Translated by George Musgrave Giger. Edited by James T. Dennison Jr. 3 vols. Phillipsburg, NJ: P&R, 1992–1997. Turretin's work is marked by clarity and precision, which are important for the topics covered in this chapter. He has much to say about the eternal sonship of Christ (see 1:253–302) and the covenant of grace (see 2:169–269).

IX

THE MEDIATOR BETWEEN GOD AND MAN

ONE PERSON, TWO NATURES

Understanding that the Mediator of the covenant of grace is the person of the Son of God is crucial for understanding the topics covered in this present chapter. In what follows I discuss Christ's two natures (divine and human), which are united hypostatically in one person. This raises a host of issues: How should we understand the human nature assumed in the incarnation? Was it fallen or sinless? How do the two natures relate to each other? Can we apply some actions to one nature and some to another? Or is this out of bounds, since it is always one person who acts? What about Jesus's temptations? Was it possible that he could sin? Further, is it permissible to say that the Son of God died? Such questions require a discussion of the *communicatio idiomatum*, which will help us think rightly about the incarnation.

One important, preliminary point is needed here: when discussing the hypostatic union, we are seeking to describe faithfully issues that often appear to be incompatible and paradoxical. Our task is not to solve every mystery (indeed, we cannot!), but to speak carefully and faithfully about the reality of Christ's one person and two natures.

THE HYPOSTATIC UNION

Defining the Hypostatic Union

Crucial for constructing orthodox Christology is an appreciation of the hypostatic union, which is often considered to be one of the two great mysteries of Christianity (along with the Trinity).[1] In theological terms, ὑποστάσις (Latin *subsistentia*, *persona*) typically refers to a person (whereas the Gk. οὐσία, φύσις, and the Latin *substantia*, *essentia*, refer to God's essential being).[2] The hypostatic union speaks of the union of two natures (divine and human) in one person (ὑποστάσις) in the incarnation. These natures are not confused or mixed, nor do the natures act independently of the person. The Son of God is always the person who acts. He never ceases to be fully divine, even as he takes to himself a fully human nature.

The Westminster Confession of Faith 8.2 summarizes the hypostatic union:

> The Son of God, the second person in the Trinity, being very and eternal God, of one substance and equal with the Father, did, when the fulness of time was come, take upon Him man's nature, with all the essential properties, and common infirmities thereof, yet without sin; being conceived by the power of the Holy Ghost, in the womb of the virgin Mary, of her substance. So that two whole, perfect, and distinct natures, the Godhead and the manhood, were [inseparably] joined together in one person, without conversion, composition, or confusion. Which person is very God, and very man, yet one Christ, the only Mediator between God and man.[3]

The hypostatic union thus speaks of the one person of Christ who is fully God and fully man. Two natures does not mean two persons. Instead, in the hypostatic union only one, divine person takes a human nature and acts in the incarnation.[4] The debates between Cyril of Alexandria and

---

1. E.g., Turretin, *Inst.* 13.6.1 (2:310).

2. See, e.g., Muller, *Dictionary of Latin and Greek*, 346; Letham, *Systematic Theology*, 942; John M. Frame, *Systematic Theology: An Introduction to Christian Belief* (Phillipsburg, NJ: P&R, 2013), 482.

3. Reading "inseparably" in place of "inseparately," in line with the wording adopted by the Presbyterian Church in America.

4. This is not to deny inseparable operations, noted in the previous chapter. See further Turretin, *Inst.* 13.4.2, 7–8 (2:304–5).

Nestorius are particularly relevant for these issues, for Cyril appreciated the unity of the person of Christ, whereas Nestorious's Christology divided the person of Christ and denied a union of natures in one person (he preferred "conjunction").

John Owen points out four aspects entailed in the hypostatic union: (1) the assumption of human nature into personal subsistence with the Son of God, (2) the union of the two natures (divine and human) in a single person, (3) the mutual communication of the two natures by virtue of the union, and (4) the predications of the person of Christ that follow on that union and communion.[5]

Crucially, the Son of God is immutable; he does not change, even in the incarnation. However, in the incarnation something new happens: the eternal, unchangeable Son of God takes to himself a human nature. The Son thus becomes what he was not (a man), while never ceasing to be what he was (divine Son of God).[6] The human nature is assumed (that is, "taken on") in the incarnation; the same cannot be said of the divine nature, since the Son is eternally and unchangeably the divine Son of God.[7]

This brings us to an important distinction between *anhypostasia* and *enhypostasia*. *Anhypostasia*, which was an implication of Chalcedon, means that Christ's human nature has no personal existence apart from the incarnation.[8] The doctrine of *enhypostasia*—articulated by Leontius of Jerusalem[9] and codified at the Second Council of Constantinople (AD 553; see, e.g., canons 5–6)—states that in the incarnation, it is the person of the Son of God who is united to a human nature; the human nature does not act on its own, but "the Son of God provides the personhood for

5. This is a close paraphrase of Owen, *Works* 1:224.

6. See Owen, *Works* 1:326–27; see also Turretin, *Inst.* 13.6.25 (2:317).

7. See also Owen, *Works* 1:226.

8. For discussions, see Letham, *Systematic Theology*, 501–2, 939; Donald Macleod, *The Person of Christ*, CCT (Downers Grove, IL: InterVarsity Press, 1998), 201–3, 199–201; Wellum, *God the Son Incarnate*, 316–17.

9. There has often been confusion between Leontius of Jerusalem with Leontius of Byzantium on this point. For a discussion, see Dennis M. Ferrara, "'Hypostasized in the Logos': Leontius of Byzantium, Leontius of Jerusalem and the Unfinished Business of the Council of Chalcedon," *Louvain Studies* 22 (1997): 311–27; see also Aloys Grillmeier, *Christ in Christian Tradition*, vol. 2, part 2, *From the Council of Chalcedon (451) to Gregory the Great (590–604)*, trans. John Cawte and Pauline Allen (Louisville: Westminster John Knox, 1995), 282–86; Letham, *Systematic Theology*, 501–2.

the assumed human nature."[10] Fred Sanders summarizes these concepts simply: "The human nature of Christ … is both anhypostatic (not personal in itself) and enhypostatic (personalized by union with the eternal person of the Son)."[11] These two concepts help to guard us from thinking of Christ as two persons in the incarnation or from misconstruing the relationship between the two natures. The principle is that natures do not act, but persons act. It is thus the person of the Son of God who acts in the incarnation.

The Necessity of the Hypostatic Union for Redemption

A PROPER UNDERSTANDING OF THE hypostatic union will greatly affect our understanding of the work of Christ: the person who acts is always the Son of God, and in the incarnation every act is the act of the God-man (θεάνθρωπος).[12] This is important because our redemption requires both the work of God and the work of man. This is also why it is important that the two natures are not confused or mixed: for the divine nature cannot change, but if the human nature of Christ were something other than our nature—or if he were less than fully human—then we would not have a Savior who could save we who are by nature fully human. Let us look briefly at the importance for each of the two natures of our one Mediator.

Why is it necessary that the Mediator should be God?[13] In short, the problem of sin is so great that only God can appease the wrath of God against sin.[14] Further, only God can give life (see Deut 32:39), so it is necessary for our Redeemer to restore humanity to new life through life-giving

---

10. See Letham, *Systematic Theology*, 501, 941 (quotation from 941); Davis, *First Seven Ecumenical Councils*, 233–34; Macleod, *Person of Christ*, 201–3; Thomas F. Torrance, *Incarnation: The Person and Life of Christ*, ed. Robert T. Walker (Downers Grove, IL: IVP Academic, 2008), 84, 211–12, 228–30; Wellum, *God the Son Incarnate*, 318–24. Thanks also to John McClean for his insights on the issues covered in this paragraph.

11. Fred Sanders, "Introduction to Christology: Chalcedonian Categories for the Gospel Narrative," in *Jesus in Trinitarian Perspective: An Introductory Christology*, ed. Fred Sanders and Klaus Issler (Nashville: B&H Academic, 2007), 30–32

12. Owen, *Works* 1:234.

13. See HC 17; WLC 38; *SPT* 25.41 (2:90–91). Portions of the next three paragraphs are adapted from Crowe, *Why Did Jesus Live a Perfect Life?*, 139–42.

14. See, e.g., Mastricht, *Theoretical-Practical Theology* 2:515; Vos, *Reformed Dogmatics* 3:24–25.

power, seen preeminently in his resurrection from the dead.[15] Further, no mere human can ever truly merit anything before God, but all people remain "unworthy servants."[16] Strictly speaking, only the actions of God can attain eternal life.[17] Thus, the work of the Mediator must be infinitely valuable.[18] Further, Christ's obedience as Mediator benefits others. This also points to his divinity.[19] The Mediator who accomplishes salvation is the Mediator who applies salvation.[20]

Why is it necessary that the Mediator should be man?[21] In short, since the problem of sin originated with a man, it was necessary for a man to render the obedience to God that has been necessary from the beginning, thus realizing the design for humanity as the crown of creation. As a man he also raises human nature and enables a more intimate access before the throne of God, for our great high priest shares our nature. And, as we have seen, Christ's entire sinlessness as a man benefits those who are born with fallen, corrupted natures.

In sum, only a Mediator who is both fully God and fully man could free us from the tangled knot of sin's curse.[22] Only a man can render the obedience due from humanity to God, and only God can grant eternal life. Turretin makes the point poignantly:

> The work of redemption could not have been performed except by a God-man (*theanthrōpon*) associating by incarnation the human nature with the divine by an indissoluble bond. For since to redeem us, two things were most especially required—the acquisition of salvation and the application of the same; the endurance of death for satisfaction and victory over the same for the enjoyment of life—our mediator ought to be God-man (*theanthrōpos*) to accomplish these things: man to suffer, God to overcome; man

15. Turretin, *Inst.* 13.17.8 (2:366). See also Bauckham, *Testimony of the Beloved Disciple*, 246–48.

16. See, e.g., Turretin, *Inst.* 17.5.20 (2:716); Bavinck, *RD* 2:570; WCF 16.5.

17. Compare Owen, *Works* 1:201–2.

18. See, e.g., Vos, *Reformed Dogmatics* 3:48; Berkhof, *Systematic Theology*, 319; Hodge, *Systematic Theology* 2:395; Turretin, *Inst.* 13.3.20 (2:303); CD 2.3.

19. Vos, *Reformed Dogmatics* 3:21–22.

20. Turretin, *Inst.* 13.3.19 (2:302); Berkhof, *Systematic Theology*, 319; Richard B. Gaffin, "The Work of Christ Applied," in Allen and Swain, *Christian Dogmatics*, 269–70.

21. See HC 16; WLC 39; *SPT* 25.40 (2:90–91).

22. See also Anselm, *Cur Deus Homo?* 2.6–7; Polanus, *Syntagma* 6.12.H (p. 362).

> to receive the punishment we deserved, God to endure and drink it to the dregs; man to acquire salvation for us by dying, God to apply it to us by overcoming; man to become ours by the assumption of flesh, God to make us like himself by the bestowal of the Spirit. This neither a mere man nor God alone could do. For neither could God alone be subject to death, nor could man alone conquer it. Man alone could die for men; God alone could vanquish death.[23]

True, Sinless Human Nature

True Humanity

It was necessary for the Son of God to assume a true human nature in order to save sinful human beings. We considered in chapter 7 Gregory of Nazianzus's famous dictum about the incarnation: "For that which he has not assumed He has not healed."[24] If Christ did not assume a human nature like ours—if he were not a real human—then he would be in a different category from us and could not save us. But praise be to God that Christ shared in our humanity (Heb 2:14). As a human he is like us in every way—he shares our "essential properties" and our "common infirmities" (WCF 8.2) with only sin excepted (see also BC 18). The incarnation underscores the goodness of creation and the unity of the Testaments. Contrary to Gnosticism, creation is not inherently evil, and this is most dramatically seen in the union of the eternal Son of God to a created, human nature. In fact, Bavinck argues that "the denial of the true and complete human nature always results from a certain dualism."[25]

To be clear, Christ had to be fully human, which means that he had not only a true human body but also a true (or "reasonable") soul (WLC 37). As we saw in chapter 7, the incarnation necessarily means that the Son of God is fully human. Our Savior must be fully a human no less than we are fully human in order to save humanity imprisoned by sin. This requires a real body and a real soul. For indeed, sin is a problem not only in our bodies but also in our minds (see, e.g., Matt 5:28). We therefore need a Savior who can save us not only from external deeds we have committed

23. Turretin, *Inst.* 13.3.19 (2:302–3).

24. *Ep.* 101 (trans. *NPNF*[2] 7:440).

25. Bavinck, *RD* 3:297.

but even from sinful minds. This is why it is so important that our Savior have a true body and a reasonable soul.

Biblical teaching on the true humanity of Christ is seen in a multitude of ways. As we saw in the discussion of chapter 3 on the Gospels, Jesus was truly born of Mary (Matt 1:16–25; Luke 1:31–35; Gal 4:4); he grew from a child into a man (e.g., Luke 2:52; 3:23); he had physical needs, such as hungering (Matt 4:2), thirsting (John 19:28), and sleeping (Mark 4:38); he experienced human emotions, such as compassion (Matt 9:36), amazement (Mark 6:6), grief (John 11:33–35), and anger (Mark 3:5);[26] he suffered in body and soul (Matt 26:38; Mark 14:34; Luke 22:44,[27] 63; John 19:1; Heb 2:18; 5:7–8); and he died (Mark 15:16–39; Gal 3:13). He also rose again as a man and ate with his disciples in his resurrected state (Acts 10:41). His authority in the resurrected state is that of the Son of Man (e.g., Matt 28:18–20, echoing Dan 7:13–14)—he is thus the true man who realizes the dominion designed for humanity from the beginning (e.g., Gen 1:26–28; see also Ps 8).[28] Even in his resurrected state he is a man—the true, eschatological man (1 Cor 15:45–49). We thus see Christ's true humanity in his perfect obedience, which humanity owes to God. Though Christ, as one who was by nature God, did not owe obedience for himself, he came as a man and willingly placed himself under the law (Gal 4:4–5) in order to redeem his people.[29]

Sinless, Unfallen Humanity

ANOTHER IMPORTANT POINT IS THAT the human nature of Christ was not preexistent. It was created in and from the womb of the virgin Mary. This was a work of new creation—not creation *ex nihilo* (i.e., from nothing) but *de novo* (i.e., something new).[30] The notion that Christ's human nature was created in the womb of Mary has often been debated—it was denied by Apollinarians, Eutychians, and some Anabaptists.[31] In contrast, the

26. See Benjamin Breckinridge Warfield, "The Emotional Life of Our Lord," in Craig, *Person and Work of Christ*, 91–145.

27. This verse is textually uncertain, but on balance, it seems likely to be original. At the very least, it reflects the widespread belief in the early church that Jesus suffered in the garden. See further comments in ch. 3 of this study.

28. On Son of Man, see also Turretin, *Inst.* 13.5.4 (2:307).

29. See also Calvin, *Inst.* 2.13 (1:474–81); Owen, *Works* 1:206–23.

30. See Ferguson, *Holy Spirit*, 38–39.

31. See, e.g., Turretin, *Inst.* 13.5 (2:306–10); Polanus, *Syntagma* 6.14.E (page 365).

Reformed creeds affirm that Jesus's human nature is "of the substance" of Mary (see WCF 8.2; WLC 37; HC 35). This means he has a human nature exactly like ours—only sin excepted.[32] Bavinck even argues that the belief in Christ's preexistent human nature views matter as evil and resembles Gnosticism more than biblical religion.[33]

As a work of new creation, Jesus's humanity was pure; it was not sinful human nature. Yet in recent years some among the Reformed have argued that Jesus took a fallen human nature—thereby emphasizing the real solidarity with the sinners he came to save—yet without being himself a sinner.[34] By this, perhaps confusingly, is often meant that Jesus had a fallen human nature but not a sinful human nature.[35] However, despite how popular this view has become in some circles, it entails exegetical and theological problems. I list several here:[36]

1. It is a fool's errand to try to divide fallenness from sinfulness. If Jesus had a fallen human nature, then he had a sinful human nature, for fallenness is a consequence of Adam's sin. Some terms from historical theology help here. Two effects of sin are (a) guilt (*reatus*)—which makes one subject to fault (*culpa*) and punishment (*poena*)—and (b) the corruption of the soul (*macula*, including *deformitas naturae*, or the defilement of nature).[37] As John Owen argues, these cannot be divided, as though Christ could take the guilt of punishment (*reatus poenae*) without the guilt of fault (*reatus*

32. "If another human nature had been created anew, either out of the earth or out of nothing, such a man, having merely a similar nature, could not be surety, not having the identical nature. Such a man would not have transgressed, and thus could also not bear the punishment. The surety had to come forth from the human nature which had sinned" (à Brakel, *Christian's Reasonable Service*, 481; see also 500).

33. Bavinck, *Wonderful Works of God*, 307.

34. E.g., Edward Irving, "The Doctrine of the Incarnation Opened: In Six Sermons," in *The Collected Writings of Edward Irving*, ed. G. Carlyle (London: Strahan, 1865), 5:115–46, 421, 440; Karl Barth, *Church Dogmatics*, trans. and ed. Geoffrey W. Bromiley and T. F. Torrance (Edinburgh: T&T Clark, 1956), e.g., IV.1:165; Torrance, *Incarnation*, 61–65, 195, 212; 231–32; Thomas F. Torrance, *The Trinitarian Faith: The Evangelical Theology of the Ancient Catholic Church* (Edinburgh: T&T Clark, 1995), 161–68; see also John C. Clark and Marcus Peter Johnson, *The Incarnation of God: The Mystery of the Gospel as the Foundation of Evangelical Theology* (Wheaton, IL: Crossway, 2015), 103–25; see also Bavinck, *RD* 3:313n226.

35. See Wellum, *God the Son*, 232–35.

36. After writing this section, I discovered that some similar points have been made by Crisp, *Divinity and Humanity*, 90–117.

37. Following Muller, *Dictionary of Latin and Greek*, 207, 306–7.

culpae).[38] If Jesus somehow took or inherited a fallen human nature, that would be an imperfect human nature that would render him subject to the guilt (*reatus*) and corruption (*macula*) of sin. But Jesus's human nature is an act of new creation, and new creation does not entail fallenness. Jesus was in no way subject to the guilt of Adam's first sin (see WLC 25).[39]

2. Though Mary was a sinner, and Christ's humanity is derived from Mary, the Holy Spirit preserved the holiness of the incarnation. This is stated explicitly in Luke 1:35: "And [Gabriel] answered [Mary], 'The Holy Spirit will come upon you, and the power of the Most High will overshadow you; therefore the child to be born will be called holy—the Son of God.' "[40] Further, Luke's terminology for the Spirit's overshadowing (ἐπισκιάζω) Mary recalls the holiness of God's presence overshadowing the tabernacle and the temple (e.g., Exod 40:34–35).[41] Thus, a body was prepared for Christ suitable to his full and perfect obedience to serve as the final, great high priest (Heb 10:5).[42] Christ was born "free from all taint of sin."[43]

3. The New Testament's two-Adam structure (e.g., Luke 3:38; Rom 5:12–21; 1 Cor 15:45–49) attests Christ's sinless and unfallen human nature. The last Adam was not represented by the first Adam and thus was not implicated in Adam's first sin. This is part of the rationale for the virginal conception of Jesus. Jesus is thus free from both inherent and imputed (i.e., legally reckoned) sin.[44] Put differently, the virginal conception speaks of Christ's true humanity—and even as a descendant of Adam—without including Jesus in the covenant of works. Calvin relates the sinless humanity of Christ to this two-Adam structure,[45] and Turretin is characteristically nuanced:

38. Owen, *Works* 5:196–99; see also Turretin, *Inst.* 9.3.6 (1:595–96). Thanks to Todd Rester for insights on this point.

39. The Latin translation of WLC 25 expressly speaks of *reatus* as an effect of Adam's first sin. See *Confessio fidei in conventu theologorum authoritate Parliamenti Anglicani indicto elaborata; eidem Parliamento postmodum exhibita; quin & ab eodem, deindeque; ab Ecclesia Scoticana cognita & approbata; una cum Catechismo duplici, Majori, Minorique; e sermono Anglicano summa cum fide in Latin versa* (Cambridge: Johannes Field, 1659), 93.

40. See also Bavinck, *RD* 3:292.

41. See Ferguson, *Holy Spirit*, 38–39; Turretin, *Inst.* 13.11.9 (2:341–42).

42. See Turretin, *Inst.* 13.11.11 (2:342).

43. Turretin, *Inst.* 13.11.3 (2:340); see also 13.11.10 (2:342).

44. Turretin, *Inst.* 13.11.15 (2:343).

45. See Calvin, *Inst.* 2.13.4 (1:480–81).

> although Christ sprang from Adam, a sinner, still he did not draw from him sin either imputed or inherent because he did not descend from him in virtue of the general promise—"increase and multiply." Rather he descended from him in virtue of the special promise concerning the seed of the woman [Gen 3:15]. And although he was in Adam as to nature, yet not as to person and moral state or federal relation, by which it happens that all the posterity of Adam (Christ excepted) partake of his sin.[46]

Bavinck clarifies that the virginal conception is not the ultimate cause of Jesus's sinlessness, "but it was the only way in which he who already existed as a person and was appointed head of a new covenant could now also in a human way—in the flesh—be and remain who he was: the Christ, Son of God the Most High."[47] This is also important for understanding the hypostatic union and the human nature of Jesus (see point 6 below). If someone argues that Jesus took a fallen human nature, we need to probe the same person's view about Adam's federal headship. Was Adam the first person and the progenitor of sin? Was Christ somehow "in Adam"? Such questions cannot be avoided if one argues that Christ had a fallen human nature.

4. A fourth reason why Jesus did not take a fallen human nature is that Jesus is the perfect man. A perfect man is not a sinful man, since there was no sin originally in creation. Jesus assumed a true, full, integrated human nature in its substance and accidents; the only exception was sin and those accidental properties associated with sin.[48] Put simply, an imperfect human nature is not true human nature.[49] Similarly, John Anthony McGuckin writes on Cyril of Alexandria's understanding of Christ's perfect humanity:

> He did not displace a human fetus that had a human hypostatic reality of its own, because there was never an instant when this human fetus existed independently of his personal creative act. It was a human fetus within

46. Turretin, *Inst.* 13.5.19 (2:310); see also Vos, *Reformed Dogmatics* 3:22, 25–26, 47–48.

47. Bavinck, *RD* 3:294–95.

48. Polanus, *Syntagma* 6.15.F–G (p. 367): "*Assumsit perfectam naturam humanam tum quoad substantiam tum quoad accidentia ejus, excepto peccato et accidentibus illis quae cum peccato connexa; sic ut non tantum perfectos sit Deus, sed etiam perfectus homo*" (6.15.F, emphasis original). For more on substance and accident see Muller, *Dictionary of Latin and Greek*, 4, 346.

49. Polanus, *Syntagma* 6.15.G (p. 367): "*Quia veram naturam humanam assumsit: vera autem non esset, si perfecta non esset.*"

> Mary because it was created in the perfect attributes applicable to the human genus, and within a human womb, but it was unique in that it was the direct and personal presence of the Logos on which it depended for the inception of its existence, not on human insemination.[50]

Yet if this is true, we must wrestle with the meaning of Romans 8:3, which states that Christ came in the likeness of sinful flesh (ἐν ὁμοιώματι σαρκὸς ἁμαρτίας). This cannot mean Christ was a sinner, for in addition to the texts we have already seen, 1 John 3:5 makes it clear that in Christ is no sin, but he came to take away sin. First John assumes that Christ would not be able to take away sin if he himself were sinful. Thus Romans 8:3 is more likely speaking about the weakness of the flesh, as is suggested from the first part of Romans 8:3, when Paul speaks of the law weakened by the flesh. Further, the text does not say "in sinful flesh" but "in the likeness [ὁμοιώματι] of sinful flesh."[51] Christ's human nature is like our human nature essentially, but it was unlike ours in being sinless. He was "without fault or corruption [*absque vitio et corruptela*]."[52] Christ did not assume an immortal human nature but a human nature "susceptible to suffering and death ... in flesh that was in the same form and appearance as sinful flesh."[53] This was different from Adam before the fall, in that Adam was created without a nature weakened by sin. However, this does not mean that Christ had a fallen human nature.[54] It is instead to say he came into a world, as a real man, that had been affected by sin.

5. As our Savior, Christ had to be fully, vicariously obedient in every way—internally as well as externally. His internal holiness required a pure, perfect human nature free from sin. As noted above, one cannot separate sin and guilt. If Jesus in any sense bore the guilt of Adam's first sin, then he would be in need of deliverance, and this would be inconsistent with the Bible's view of Christ's vicarious satisfaction (see ch. 10). If Christ had a

50. McGuckin, *St. Cyril*, 215.

51. So, e.g., John Murray, *The Epistle to the Romans*, NICNT (Grand Rapids: Eerdmans, 1959–1965), 1:279–80; contrast C. E. B. Cranfield, *A Critical and Exegetical Commentary on the Epistle to the Romans*, ICC (Edinburgh: T&T Clark, 1975–1979), 1:379–82.

52. Calvin, *Inst.* 2.13.4 (1:481; my insertion of the Latin from the 1559 edition). See also *Inst.* 2.16.12 (1:518–19); Polanus, *Syntagma* 6.15 (pp. 368–69).

53. Bavinck, *RD* 3:309–10.

54. See also Warfield, "Emotional Life," 144–45.

fallen human nature, it would be a human nature inclined toward sin (compare Jas 1:13–15). The Reformed creeds speak of sin as a power that binds us, rendering us incapable of anything truly good (CD 3.3), and this corruption spread by natural birth, descending from Adam (CD 3.2). If Jesus's human nature were fallen, he would be incapable of doing anything truly, spiritually good (see WLC 25). No one who descends naturally from Adam is free from the bondage of sin (WLC 26), and no sinner could never pay the price of redemption (HC 16). Heidelberg Catechism 36 puts it starkly: "What benefit do you receive from the holy conception and birth of Christ? That He is our Mediator (Heb 2:16–17), and with His innocence and perfect holiness covers, in the sight of God, my sin, wherein I was conceived (Ps 32:1)."[55] Similarly, Polanus argued that an aspect of the righteousness of Christ that covers us is not only his obedience to the law of God but also his innocence and holiness from the moment of his conception, when he took a human nature.[56]

This assumes that sin is not merely external but internal as well. The law of God requires not just external obedience but internal obedience.[57] If Jesus were born with a fallen human nature, he would have been prone toward sin and tempted internally as well as externally. But, as I will argue below, the temptation of Jesus was purely external given the holiness of his person. It is difficult to see how Jesus could have overcome the disparity between sacrifice and heartfelt obedience (Heb 10:5–7; see Ps 40:6–8) if he were himself inclined toward sin, due to a fallen nature. For Jesus to be a perfect human priest and perfect sacrifice required him to be free from original sin.[58] Further, if Jesus had a nature affected by sin, then he would owe obedience for himself, to atone for his imperfection.[59] If he had a fallen human nature, then something in his human nature would need to be fixed or rectified, which means his obedience would be for himself and not for

55. Dennison, *Reformed Confessions* 2:778.

56. Polanus, *Syntagma* 6.14.C–D (p. 365), and 6.14.F (p. 366): "*Justitia Christi quae nobis à Deo Patre imputatur, pars est innocentia et sanctitas inde à prima origine et momento conceptionis naturae humanae inhaerens.*"

57. Polanus, *Syntagma* 6.14.G–H (p. 366). See also Charles Octavius Boothe, *Plain Theology for Plain People* (Bellingham, WA: Lexham, 2017), 47.

58. Polanus, *Syntagma* 6.14–15.H–K (p. 367).

59. See Owen, *Works* 1:206–8.

us in some ways. But this is foreign to Scripture, which instead speaks of Christ as holy (ὅσιος) and unstained (ἀμίαντος; Heb 7:26).

In this light, John Owen argues effectively,

> This nature of ours, wherein the work of our recovery and salvation is be wrought and performed, was not to be so derived from the original stock of our kind or race as to bring along with it the *same taint of sin*, and the same *liableness unto guilt*, upon its own account, as accompany every other individual person in the world. ... For, if this nature in him were so *defiled* as it is in us ... it could do nothing that should be acceptable unto him. And if it were *subject unto* guilt on its own account, it could make no satisfaction for the sin of others.[60]

Owen continues, "It was necessary ... that he by whom the work of our recovery was to be wrought should be a man, partaker of *the nature that sinned*, yet *free from all sin*, and all the consequents of it."[61]

Christ is an obedient representative who obeys freely for others, not out of compulsion or due to any imperfection in his own human nature that has to be overcome.

6. The hypostatic union disallows the possibility that Jesus assumed a fallen human nature. As we have seen, in Christ's incarnation his human nature was united hypostatically to his divine nature, but there remains only one person: the eternal, immutable, omnipotent, holy Son of God. The human nature the Son assumed did not create a problem for the hypostatic union, for creation is good and people are created in the image of God; therefore it was fitting for the Son to take to himself a human nature. But this was not fallen or sinful human nature, for it was not possible for the divine Son of God to be united to a sinful nature.[62]

We could further relate Christ's sinless humanity to the special anointing of the Holy Spirit throughout the life of Christ.[63] Not only did the Holy

---

60. Owen, *Works* 1:199, emphasis original.

61. Owen, *Works* 1:200, emphasis original.

62. See, e.g., Owen, *Works* 1:215; WCF 8.2; WLC 38; Turretin, *Inst.* 13.11 (2:340–47); Vos, *Reformed Dogmatics* 3:47. This point stands, though proponents of the fallen nature view often argue that in the assumption of fallen nature, it is immediately sanctified.

63. For this point, see Bavinck, *RD* 3:292–93, 366.

Spirit sanctify Christ's human nature in his conception and birth, but the Spirit was Christ's constant companion throughout his life, sanctifying his human nature every step of the way (see WLC 42).[64] Bavinck is helpful:

> In Christ the human nature had to be prepared for union with the person of the Son, that is, to a union and communion with God as that to which no other creature had ever been dignified. If humans in general cannot have communion with God except by the Holy Spirit, then this applies even more powerfully to Christ's human nature, which had to be unified with the Son in an entirely unique manner. This special union, which far exceeds and differs essentially from the immanence of God in his creatures, the manifestation of God in his people, makes a priori probable and even necessary a very special activity on the part of the Holy Spirit.[65]

Put simply, Scripture never speaks of Christ's humanity as sinful or fallen, and this would not be possible in light of the hypostatic union of the divine and human natures in the person of the Son of God.

7. The view that Christ had a sinful or fallen human nature is a comparatively novel position, whereas the orthodox christological position has traditionally been that Christ's humanity was sinless and unfallen. To include a handful of examples, Tertullian relates the virginal conception of Jesus to his perfection as a man, which cleanses us from all pollution (*Carne Christi* 20). Tertullian also argues that Romans 8:3 means that the flesh of Christ "resembled that which had sinned—resembled it in its nature, but not in the corruption it received from Adam" (*Carne Christi* 16).[66] Athanasius, like Cyril of Alexandria, is representative of those who see Christ as a new Adam who washes us by his holiness (*C. Ar.* 1.47; 2.65; 3.33; maybe also 3.23.8).[67] Christ's baptism is often related to his cleansing of his people, as it is already in Ignatius of Antioch (Ign. *Eph.* 18.2). The letter of Pope Leo to Flavian, adopted by the Council of Chalcedon, states comprehensively,

---

64. See also Jones, *Knowing Christ*, 53–61.

65. Bavinck, *RD* 3:292.

66. Trans. *ANF* 3:535.

67. For Cyril's view, see Kelly, *Early Christian Doctrines*, 317–18; McGuckin, *St. Cyril*, 225–26.

> Thus was true God born in the undiminished and perfect nature of a true man, complete in what is his, and complete in what is ours [*In integra ergo veri hominis perfectaque natura verus natus est deus, totus in suis, totus in nostris*]. ... There was in the Saviour no trace of the things which the Deceiver brought upon us, and to which deceived humanity gave admittance. His subjection to human weaknesses in common with us did not mean that he shared our sins. He took on the form of a servant without the defilement of sin [*sine sorde peccati*], thereby enhancing the human and not diminishing the divine. ... What was taken from the mother of the Lord was the nature without the guilt [*Adsumpta est de matre domini natura, non culpa*].[68]

A similar emphasis on Jesus's sinless human nature is seen also in Thomas Aquinas[69] and in later, Reformed creeds, such as the Heidelberg Catechism (e.g., Q&A 36) and the Leiden Synopsis. The latter states that the Son of God did not take flesh that was corrupted: "For it was not fitting that the human nature that is subject to sin be united with the Son of God."[70] This is consistent with many other Reformational and post-Reformational theologians we have seen, including Calvin, Polanus, Owen, Turretin, Bavinck, and (more recently) Robert Letham and Douglas Kelly.[71]

8. We must beware of the modern danger that seeks to explain scientifically the virginal conception, the creation of Jesus's human nature, or the hypostatic union. This is not possible. T. F. Torrance helpfully points out, "If you ask biological questions of the virgin birth you will only get biological answers, and to ask biological questions only is to presuppose from the start that there is nothing more here than normal biological process."[72] Some have argued that Jesus's full humanity requires him to share the same process of evolution as other people in order to be fully human.[73] But this approach purports to understand and explain scientifically the

68. Latin text and translation from Tanner, *Decrees* 1:78–*79.

69. E.g., *Summa theologiae* 3a, quest. 4, art. 6, resp. 1–2.

70. *SPT* 25.18 (2:74–2:77), quotation from 2:77.

71. Letham, *Systematic Theology*, 526–30; Douglas Kelly, *Systematic Theology: Grounded in Holy Scripture and Understood in the Light of the Church*, vol. 2, *The Beauty of Christ: A Trinitarian Vision* (Fearn, UK: Mentor, 2014), 309–15.

72. Torrance, *Incarnation*, 95.

73. E.g., Andrew T. Lincoln, *Born of a Virgin? Reconceiving Jesus in the Bible, Tradition, and Theology* (Grand Rapids: Eerdmans, 2013).

means by which the Son took to himself a true body and reasonable soul. Yet if we cannot understand the way that any child comes to be in the womb (see Eccl 11:5), then surely we cannot understand the hypostatic union scientifically. Further, on an evolutionary theory of human origins (and the incarnation!), no adequate explanation is given for the universality of sin intruding in God's good, created order. This view also does not sufficiently account for the person of the divine Son who takes a human nature. The hypostatic union was not a natural process by which the Son of God was born but a supernatural, monadic, nonrepeatable event in the history of the universe.

Summing Up Though Gregory's maxim that the "unassumed is the unhealed" is valuable, it can be taken in unbiblical directions, which is what happens when it is used to argue that Jesus must have assumed fallen human nature; this is a point that Scripture does not support.[74] By this statement Gregory meant Christ assumed every part of what makes us human (including a human soul); he did not mean that Christ took a fallen human nature. Sinfulness does not belong properly to human nature, but is a result of the fall into sin. It is certainly biblical and necessary to affirm the solidarity of Christ with his people (e.g., Heb 2:14), but Scripture does not speak of Christ's human nature as fallen or sinful. Further, this point is theologically contradictory and problematic. How could Christ be a spotless substitute if he were born under the guilt of sin? How could he do what Adam failed to do as a new Adam if he were represented by Adam's federal headship? How could he deliver incorruptibility if he were born with a corrupted nature? It is better to understand the human nature of Christ to have limitations, but this is not to be described as sinful or fallen.

74. For further assessments, see Letham, *Systematic Theology*, 526–33; Rafael Noguira Bello, *Sinless Flesh: A Critique of Karl Barth's Fallen Christ*, Studies in Historical and Systematic Theology (Bellingham, WA: Lexham, 2020); Macleod, *Person of Christ*, 221–29; William Duncan Rankin, "Carnal Union with Christ in the Theology of T. F. Torrance" (PhD diss., University of Edinburgh, 1997).

THE HYPOSTATIC UNION AND THE COMMUNICATION OF PROPERTIES

Defining the Communicatio Idiomatum

Having established that Christ has two natures, we turn now to a consideration of how the two natures relate to each other in the hypostatic union. This has often been a contested point of Christology. Again the Westminster Confession of Faith explains the concept concisely: "Christ, in the work of mediation, acts according to both natures, by each nature doing that which is proper to itself; yet, by reason of the unity of the person, that which is proper to one nature is sometimes in Scripture attributed to the person denominated by the other nature" (WCF 8.7).[75] This is known as the "communication of properties" (*communicatio idiomatum*).[76] Put simply, some works are proper to Christ's divine nature, some to his human nature. Even so, either sort of work is a work of the one person, the God-man, since it is always he who works (not a nature that works).[77] This does not, however, entail a confusion or mixing of the natures, for they remain distinct. The human nature retains its finite characteristics (for example, the human nature is neither omnipresent nor omniscient), and the divine nature retains its characteristics (for example, omnipresence and omniscience).

Indeed, one of the debated issues relating to the *communicatio idiomatum* is the question of the omnipresence of Christ's human nature. On the one hand, since the Son of God is immense and omnipresent, he cannot be limited in his essence to physical body. In this sense, the Son of God is present everywhere. This is the teaching often known as the *extra Calvinisticum*—it was often associated with Calvin and the Reformed, though its presence appears much earlier than Calvin in Christian tradition (e.g., Athanasius, *Inc.* 8, 17).[78] But the Reformed have argued that this

75. Trans. from Dennison, *Reformed Confessions* 4:245.

76. For a discussion and explanation, especially with respect to the difference between communication of *properties* to communication of *attributes*, see Turretin, *Inst.* 13.8 (2:321–27); see also Bavinck, *RD* 3:308–16.

77. This was important for Cyril of Alexandria: "In Cyril's hands the exchange of properties is like an intellectual firework, a condensed cipher of all that he holds to be important in christology and faith" (McGuckin, *St. Cyril*, 191).

78. A common text to prove this doctrine has been John 3:13, which in many manuscripts reads ὁ ὢν ἐν τῷ οὐρανῷ ("who is in heaven") at the end of the verse. So, e.g., John Chrysostom,

omnipresence of the Son of God does not apply to his human nature in the incarnation, which remains limited and finite. This debate has often centered on the role of the presence of Christ in the Lord's Supper, as I discussed in chapter 7. Whereas Lutheran and Roman Catholic Christology argue for the bodily presence of Christ in the Supper, the Reformed have maintained the finitude of Christ's human nature since the attributes of divinity cannot be communicated to the finite human nature.[79]

The Communicatio Idiomatum *and Christ's Humanity*

UNDERSTANDING THE *COMMUNICATIO IDIOMATUM* PROPERLY helps us parse rightly the relationship between the divine and the human natures of Christ in the hypostatic union. Christ's human nature remains human, and thus finite, created nature; his human nature does not have divine characteristics. Even so, the glorious nature of the hypostatic union means that some impressively unique things can be predicated of the human nature of Christ. Such predications reflect the communion of natures (*communio naturarum*), which states that in the hypostatic union, Christ's two natures have fellowship with each other, and "the disposition of one nature depends on and corresponds to their other."[80] Two related categories to consider are the grace of union and habitual graces.[81]

First, the grace of union, or the grace of eminence, refers to the dignity of Christ's human nature above all other creatures, due to the union of the divine and human natures in the one person of Christ.[82] Thus, it is appropriate to worship Jesus Christ (Phil 2:6–11), the one who is an exalted man, because of the union of the human nature with the divine Logos.[83]

Homilies on John 27 (*NPNF*[1] 14:94); Owen, *Works* 1:92–93. However, though the doctrine is valid and can be demonstrated from good and necessary consequence of Scripture, this phrase in John 3:13 presents a difficult textual question, and its originality, while possible, is by no means certain. See also Wellum, *God the Son*, 332–38. For a contemporary discussion of the *extra* from Zwingli to the period of early Reformed orthodoxy, see Drake, *Flesh of the Word*.

79. See further Bavinck, *RD* 3:256–59.

80. *SPT* 25.29 (2:83).

81. Here I draw significantly from Turretin, *Inst.* 13.8.1 (2:321).

82. See Owen, *Works* 1:227–28; see also WLC 39; Thomas Aquinas, *Summa theologiae* 3a, ques. 2, art. 10, resp.; Thomas Joseph White, OP, *The Incarnate Lord: A Thomistic Study in Christology* (Washington, DC: Catholic University of America Press, 2015), 87.

83. See Vos, *Reformed Dogmatics* 3:56.

Second, habitual graces refer to "those remarkable gifts which the divine nature bestowed upon the human, which although the highest and most perfect in their own order, still were not simply infinite, but according to the capacity of the recipient in the order of created gifts."[84] Vos writes that they were "extraordinary gifts of knowledge, will, and power [which] were communicated to the human nature, which it did not possess in itself."[85] Drawing from the anointing of the Spirit on the Messiah in Isaiah 11:1–2, these can be categorized as gifts of holiness, wisdom, and power.[86] In other words, habitual graces refer to the special dispensation given to Christ's human nature for the accomplishment of his work (see also WCF 8.3).[87]

In the hypostatic union, we should also consider the lifelong anointing of the Holy Spirit on Christ (see WCF 8.3). As a child who grew into a man, Jesus grew in wisdom and benefited from the anointing of the Spirit (e.g., Luke 2:40, 52; 4:14, 18).[88] Since it is not possible for the divine Son of God to change in himself, these statements are proper to the humanity of Jesus.[89] As a man, Christ grew and was more and more equipped for his work, which helps explain the special anointing of the Spirit at his baptism for his public ministry.[90] As a man, he was anointed with the Spirit beyond measure (John 3:34).[91] By means of the Holy Spirit Christ, in his human nature, was equipped for his work.[92] Yet this is not to be construed in such a way as to divinize Christ's human nature; his human nature remained a finite, human nature.[93] It is also in this light that it is appropriate to speak of Christ having faith (see, e.g., Heb 12:2). As a man, Jesus walked by faith,

84. Quoting Turretin, *Inst.* 13.8.1 (2:321). See also *SPT* 25.30 (2:82–83); Thomas Aquinas, *Summa theologiae* 3a, ques. 7, art. 9, resp.; White, *Incarnate Lord*, 87.

85. Vos, *Reformed Dogmatics* 3:56; see also Owen, *Works* 1:93

86. Vos, *Reformed Dogmatics* 3:58. Turretin provides a more extensive list: "wisdom, understanding, counsel, might, knowledge, fear [of the Lord]" (*Inst.* 13.12.4 [2:347–48]).

87. See also Turretin, *Inst.* 13.8.12 (2:325).

88. This point, and these texts, are noted by Vos, *Reformed Dogmatics* 3:58.

89. See, e.g., Muller, *PRRD* 4:319; Turretin, *Inst.* 13.6.25 (2:317); see also Athanasius, *C. Ar.* 3.51–52.

90. Vos, *Reformed Dogmatics* 3:57

91. See Turretin, *Inst.* 13.12.2 (2:347); *SPT* 25.30 (2:82–83).

92. See Vos, *Reformed Dogmatics* 3:56.

93. E.g., Owen, *Works* 1:93, 345.

with the assurance of things unseen, and trusted in God (Heb 11:1), though he did not need saving faith since he was not a sinner.[94]

Appreciating that some actions are proper to Christ's humanity and some to his divinity—while maintaining the unity of the person—requires careful terminology. Theologians often speak of "attribution" to reflect the biblical teaching that some things are "proper" only to a nature but are nevertheless true of the Son of God as they are attributed to the person as a whole, and are not acts of a nature alone.[95] For example, one might say that in the economy of redemption the Son died as he is man but not in his divinity, since God cannot die; what is "attributed" to the person as a whole is that he died. Attribution is important because it helps us recognize that certain things are true of Christ because of his divine nature or human nature, without implying that the natures are divided or that the natures act when it is Christ, the person, who acts.

Similarly, an exegetical method known as "partitive exegesis" interprets potentially confusing scriptural passages about the Son's actions by speaking of some actions that are true by virtue of the divinity of Jesus and some that are true only by virtue of his taking on a human nature in the incarnation[96]—though one must never lose sight of single-subject Christology that appreciates it is always the person of the Son of God who acts. Thus, the Son's ignorance of the future (Matt 24:36) is understood in relation to his humanity, not to his divinity. Again the principle: persons act according to natures; natures as such do not act. Put another way, Christ the Mediator acts personally as the God-man (θεάνθρωπος). Actions are attributed to the one Mediator, not to the natures per se.

In sum, as the God-man (θεάνθρωπος), Christ acts according both to his divine nature and his human nature to accomplish his salvific work

94. See Turretin, *Inst.* 13.12.5-8 (2:348); Vos, *Reformed Dogmatics* 3:60; see also Bavinck, *RD* 3:312.

95. "Reduplication" (a term taken from medieval logic) is another common approach. See J. David Moser, "Tools for Interpreting Christ's Saving Mysteries in Scripture," *SJT* 73 (2020): 284–94, esp. 287, 292. See also Wellum, *God the Son Incarnate*, 439–40, 452. Thanks to John McClean and Mark Garcia for their insights on this paragraph.

96. See, e.g., Matthew R. Crawford, *Cyril of Alexandria's Trinitarian Theology of Scripture*, Oxford Early Christian Studies (Oxford: Oxford University Press, 2014), 13–14, noting also, e.g., Behr, *Nicene Faith*, 208–15.

(*apotelesma* = ἀποτέλεσμα).[97] This is sometimes called the *communicatio apotelesmatum* ("communication of [mediatorial] effects") or *communicatio operationum* ("communication of [mediatorial] operations").[98] We thus affirm that it is the one, divine person of the Mediator who accomplishes his unified work of salvation as the God-man, while recognizing it is important to parse out carefully the way each nature contributes to this unified work.

Miracles A RIGHT UNDERSTANDING OF THE hypostatic union is also important for interpreting miracles of Jesus. The habitual graces help us understand the power communicated by the Holy Spirit to the human nature of Jesus. Jesus was the supremely authoritative man, and much of his ministry can be understood as the authority of a new Adam ruling over God's creation (i.e., the Son of Man; see Gen 1:26–28; Ps 8; Dan 7:13–14). Yet the incarnation also entailed a voluntary emptying of the Son (Phil 2:7) whereby he took on a human nature with its limitations.[99] Even so, we must reject kenotic Christology that claims in the incarnation the Son of God divested himself of (at least some of) his divine attributes.[100] The Son of God is immutable, even in the incarnation.

This brings us to the relationship of the divine Son's agency or causality with respect to his finite human nature in the incarnation—an issue not directly addressed by the church's creeds.[101] One important voice in this conversation is John Owen, who "clarifies that even the assumption [of human nature] is 'the act of the divine nature, and so, consequently, of the *Father*, *Son*, and *Spirit*,' but 'as unto the *term of the assumption*, or the taking of our nature unto himself, it was the peculiar act of the person of the Son.' "[102] By this Owen helpfully guards the principle of inseparable operations in

97. See *SPT* 25.31(2:82–85); Turretin, *Inst.* 14.2.3 (2:379–80).

98. See also Muller, *Dictionary of Latin and Greek*, 35, 71; Wellum, *God the Son*, 326; Kelly, *Systematic Theology*, 242–46.

99. Warfield observed that Christ emptied himself by *adding* a human nature in "Person of Christ according to the New Testament," 42; see also Turretin, *Inst.* 13.9.8 (2:334). Polanus, *Symphonia Catholica seu Consensus*, 239–42, situates this emptying in the economy of redemption and illustrates it from the *consensus Patrum*.

100. A lengthy discussion can be found in Wellum, *God the Son*, 355–419.

101. So, e.g., Vidu, *Same God*, 181.

102. Adonis Vidu, "Trinitarian Inseparable Operations and the Trinity," *Journal of Analytic Theology* 4 (2016): 106–27, quoting Owen, *Works* 1:225 (I have retained Owen's original italics).

God's works *ad extra*: the Son did not act independently in the incarnation.[103] Owen further argues that all other works in the incarnation entail Christ working by means of the Holy Spirit mediately on his human nature, for the Holy Spirit is "the *immediate, peculiar, efficient cause* of all external divine operations."[104] Owen's viewpoint has, however, sometimes been taken to imply that the Son's mighty acts were acts of the Spirit working in and through Christ's human nature in a way that would downplay the divine Son's agency in his incarnate works, or which would at least give us pause before identifying an incarnate work of Christ as proof of his divinity.[105] Such options, however, may not adequately account for Owen's view of the agency of the Son of God in the incarnation.[106] Owen himself observes, "Whatever the Son of God wrought in, by, or upon the human nature, he did by the Holy Ghost, who is his Spirit, as he is the Spirit of the Father."[107] Owen thus affirms that the Son himself acts in the incarnation but that he acts by the Spirit "in, by, or upon" his human nature. Owen further affirms that "the *immediate actings* of the Holy Ghost are not spoken of him *absolutely*, nor ascribed unto him *exclusively*."[108] Thus again Owen guards the principle of inseparable operations. A helpful, balanced perspective on this issue from the same era as Owen is found in the Westminster Confession of Faith, which guards the unity of the person who acts in the incarnation (8.7), while also affirming the special anointing of the Holy Spirit on Christ's humanity (8.3).[109]

The emphasis on the Holy Spirit in the incarnate works of Christ is salutary and reflects numerous biblical passages on the role of the Spirit

---

103. See also Vidu, *Same God*, 163–71 (who distinguishes *acts* from *states*, and sees Owen doing something similar, even in the widely discussed passage in Owen, *Works* 3:160 ["The only singular immediate *act* of the person of the Son on the human nature was the *assumption* of it into subsistence with himself"; emphasis original]); Kolb and Trueman, *Between Wittenberg and Geneva*, 78 n. 50; Wellum, *God the Son*, 327–28, 410, 432–33; cf. 382.

104. Owen, *Works* 3:161, emphasis original; compare also Jones, *Knowing Christ*, 53–61, 135–42.

105. On this latter option, see Myk Habets, *The Anointed Son: A Trinitarian Spirit Christology*, Princeton Theological Monographs (Eugene, OR: Pickwick, 2010), 211. He also notes the likelihood that Owen was responding to Socinian approaches (209).

106. See Tyler R. Wittman, "The End of the Incarnation: John Owen, Trinitarian Agency and Christology," *IJST* 15 (2013): 284–300. Thanks also to Blair Smith for feedback on this point.

107. Owen, *Works* 3:162. My point follows Wittman, "End of the Incarnation," 299.

108. Owen, *Works* 3:162, emphasis original; see similarly Vos, *Reformed Dogmatics* 3:59.

109. Thanks to Chad Van Dixhoorn for this observation. Compare also *SPT* 25.30 (2:82–83).

in the miracles of Jesus (e.g., Matt 12:28). Even so, it would not be appropriate to deny the personal agency of the Son in his powerful deeds, nor should we simply equate Christ's miraculous works with what would have been suitable for any Spirit-empowered prophet. The powerful deeds of Christ are the Spirit-empowered actions of the God-man.[110] In the incarnation the Son does not divest himself of or limit his "access to" his divine attributes, but the limitations of Christ's human nature are evident in his state of humiliation.[111]

It is again to be emphasized that in the incarnation it is always the person of the Son of God who acts (WCF 8.7), though he does so as the God-man. Neither the human nature nor the divine nature as such works on its own, for it is the person who acts, and that according to the natures. Several points bear mention in this respect. First, Jesus's powerful deeds are often works reserved for God alone—such as raising the dead (e.g., Matt 9:23–26; Mark 5:35–43; Luke 7:11–17; John 11:1–44; see also Deut 32:39), forgiving sins (e.g., Mark 2:1–12), walking on the sea (theophany), and ruling over creation (e.g., Matt 8:23–27; 14:22–33; see also Job 9:8; Pss 77:16–20; 107:28–30; Isa 43:16; see also Ps 44:23).[112] Indeed, Christ's accomplishment of divine actions is one way we know he is God.[113] We must not consider these works to be "only" works of the Holy Spirit on Christ's humanity in a way that would threaten the unity of the Mediator.[114]

Second, Jesus's miracles often fulfill scriptural promises of what God himself will do in the new age.[115] For example, Isaiah 35 speaks of the God who comes to save his people (see 35:4)—including the benefits of the lame leaping, the blind seeing, and the deaf hearing (35:5–6). This is exactly what Jesus told the disciples of John the Baptist that he himself did in Matthew

110. See also Bavinck, *RD* 3:315–16; compare *RD* 3:338: "He not only performs miracles but in his person is himself the absolute miracle. … He is himself the greatest miracle, the center of all miracles."

111. Compare Crisp, *Divinity and Humanity*, 152.

112. On Deut 32:39, see Bauckham, *Testimony of the Beloved Disciple*, 246–48. The possible allusion to Ps 44:23 comes from Marcus, *Mark 1–8*, 338.

113. E.g., WLC 11; Turretin, *Inst.* 14.7.16 (4:401–2); Muller, *PRRD* 4:245–46, 302; see also Crisp, *Divinity and Humanity*, 141.

114. See also Vos, *Reformed Dogmatics* 3:58–59; Letham, *Work of Christ*, 69.

115. Thanks to Blake Franze for sparking my thinking on this point.

11; Luke 7. In Isaiah 35, the implication is that God will make these things happen.

Third, even in his state of humiliation, Christ acted on his own authority.[116] Whereas the apostles were sent forth to do mighty works in Christ's name (e.g., Matt 10:1–42; Luke 10:1–20) and invoked Christ's name in their miracles (e.g., Acts 3:6, 12–16; 9:34), Christ performed his miracles and cast out demons on his own authority (e.g., Mark 1:34; 5:41; see also Jude 9).[117] Yet he also acted authoritatively as a Son (John 5:17–47), in fellowship with and dependent on his Father and empowered by the Holy Spirit (e.g., Matt 12:28; see also Luke 11:20). The Son's actions are always the actions of the God-man in the incarnation, even as the external works of God are undivided.

Fourth, historically miracles have been commonly understood as signs of divinity. Gregory of Nazianzus notes the interplay of the divine and human in Jesus's raising of Lazarus: "He asks where Lazarus was laid, for He was Man; but He raises Lazarus, for He was God," and again, "He was baptized as Man—but He remitted sins as God."[118] Athanasius likewise states that Jesus's miracles and exorcisms demonstrated his divinity (*Inc.* 16, 18). Pope Leo's letter to Flavian adopted by the Council of Chalcedon, addressing the concept of the *communicatio idiomatum*, speaks of the miracles as proper to divinity.[119] This was also Calvin's view.[120] Turretin argues, "He who works miracles by a proper and physical virtue ought to be omnipotent. But Christ as man did not work them by his own power, but after the manner of a moral instrument. Therefore he ought to concur to a miraculous work by contributing what is his own, but the infinite virtue by which properly the miracle was produced belonged to the divinity alone (Mk. 5:30). The miracles are ascribed to Christ in the concrete, not to humanity in the abstract."[121] This is the implication of texts that say (miraculous) power

116. See Vos, *Reformed Dogmatics* 3:58–59; Bauckham, "Mark's Christology of Divine Identity."

117. When Jesus does pray before a miracle (e.g., John 11:41–42), it is for the benefit of others. See Calvin, *Inst.* 1.13.13; Turretin, *Inst.* 3.28.23 (1:288).

118. Gregory of Nazianzus, *Or.* 29.29 (trans. *NPNF*[2] 7:308–9). See similarly Athanasius, *C. Ar.* 3.32.

119. See Tanner, *Decrees,* 1:79–*79. See also the affirmation of this at the Third Council of Constantinople (in Tanner, *Decrees*, 1:129–*30).

120. See Calvin, *Inst.* 1.13.13 (1:136–38).

121. Turretin, *Inst.* 13.8.35 (2:331).

flowed from Christ (e.g., Luke 6:19; 8:46).[122] Here we may appreciate the wisdom of affirming (in the spirit of the WCF and Owen) that the miracles of Jesus, as actions of the God-man, are both divine actions of the Son and Spirit-empowered actions worked through his human nature.

Yet at the same time, in the incarnate economy, Christ willingly limited himself and did not rely on his divine power to avoid or assuage his human suffering.[123] To do so was a temptation, as we see in the devil's request for Jesus to turn the stones into bread.[124] This seems to have been particularly true for works that would have benefited Christ himself[125] or caused him to deviate from his work of redemption.

In sum, it is always the divine Son of God who acts in the incarnation (WCF 8.7), though as the God-man he acts instrumentally through his human nature by the power of the Spirit. (Though we must not think of this "instrumentality" in a way that would deny the enhypostatic reality of Christ's human nature.) David Moser provides a helpful summary and illustration:

> As the paralytic laid before his feet, God the Word forgave his sins. He did this in two ways: as God authoritatively and as a human being instrumentally. Though both of his natures retained their proper energies, each doing what is proper to it, *he* forgave the man's sins. God himself in the flesh did this; that we can utter such a sentence remains astoundingly difficult to grasp but beautiful in its glory.[126]

Three Debated Issues

A CONSIDERATION OF THE RELATION of the two natures brings up a number of debated issues, but at this juncture I will engage three specific issues that have often been debated in the history of the church: impeccability, ignorance, and the death of Christ.

---

122. Turretin, *Inst.* 3.28.23 (1:288); see also à Brakel, *Christian's Reasonable Service* 1:497.

123. See, e.g., Macleod, *Person of Christ*, 169.

124. See Warfield, "Historical Christ," 17. Warfield also recognizes that Christ's teaching and his powerful deeds revealed a supernatural person (e.g., 17–18, 30–31).

125. See Macleod, *Person of Christ*, 220.

126. Moser, "Tools for Interpreting," 294, emphasis original.

Could Jesus Have Sinned?

The question has often arisen: Could Christ have sinned in his state of humiliation? That is, was he peccable (able to sin), or was he impeccable (not able to sin)?[127] Making this question particularly difficult is the statement in Hebrews that Christ was tempted in every way just as we are (Heb 4:15). Many see in this text the implication that Christ could have indeed sinned, for his temptations were just like ours.[128] For example, one approach, recognizing the reality of the human experience of Christ with respect to his human nature (which nature is not impeccable) and perhaps relating this to the need to succeed as a man where Adam failed, affirms the reality of Christ's sinlessness, but stops short of saying that Christ was impeccable with respect to his humanity.

This is a difficult issue, yet it is important to consider again the implications of the hypostatic union. If we have established that it is the single person of the Son of God who acts, then we must ask whether the holy, sinless Son of God could sin—for the human nature of Christ is not an independent agent. Asking this question clarifies the issue. For since it is always the Son of God who acts and since it is not possible for God to sin, then we must say that Jesus was impeccable in his state of humiliation. In the hypostatic union there exists an asymmetry between the divine and human natures. This cautions us from thinking of the human and divine natures of Christ as being absolutely equivalent. The divine nature in a sense takes priority over the human nature, for the person of the divine Son in the incarnation becomes what he was not formerly (a man)—though without the human nature mixing with or morphing into the divine nature. As with so much in the incarnation, this is a great mystery.

Bavinck reflects starkly on Christ's impeccability: "He is the Son of God, the Logos, who was in the beginning with God and himself God. He is one with the Father and always carries out his Father's will and work. For those

127. This question is similar to the question of whether the Son assumed a fallen human nature, but is distinct enough to warrant its own discussion. For example, even among those who affirm Jesus assumed an unfallen human nature, one encounters differing views as to whether Jesus was peccable or impeccable in the state of humiliation.

128. See, e.g., Cullmann, *Christology of the New Testament*, 94; Hodge, *Systematic Theology* 2:457. Hodge's view is noted by William S. Plumer, *The Person and Sinless Character of our Lord Jesus Christ* (Richmond, VA: Presbyterian Committee of Publication; New York: Randolph, 1876), 26–27.

who confess this of Christ, the possibility of him sinning and falling is unthinkable."[129] Likewise Owen: "The subsistence of the human nature in the person of the Son of God, rendered the least sin utterly impossible unto him; for all the moral operations of that nature are the acts of the person of the Son of God."[130] When we ask whether Jesus could have sinned, the question ultimately is: Could the holy Second Person of the Trinity have sinned? The answer is an emphatic "no!"

Even so, Scripture does not deny the reality that Christ was tempted. But in what way was he tempted? We must understand both solidarity and distinction between Christ's temptations and ours. Solidarity, on the one hand, because he knows what it is like to suffer when tempted, and he can help us when we are tempted (Heb 2:18). He came in the likeness of sinful flesh (Rom 8:3), which though it does not entail fallenness or peccability, does entail a nature susceptible to death, weakness, and suffering.[131] Yet there is a distinction as well. Whereas all of us who descend from Adam in an ordinary manner inherit a corrupt nature and are tempted inwardly by desires that deviate from God's perfect will (Jas 1:14–15), God is not tempted by evil (Jas 1:13). Because Christ is the divine Son who did not inherit a sinful nature, he was not inclined toward evil in his heart, as we are, but temptations were for him entirely external.[132]

Yet this does not negate the reality of his temptations, nor does it downplay the reality of his godly choices as fully human.[133] Jesus knows what it is to face suffering on account of temptation, and because he never succumbed to temptation, he knows what it is like to resist each step of the way and can help those who are being tempted.[134] Indeed, "it is completely misguided to imagine that the agony of temptation overcome is less than the agony of the

129. Bavinck, *RD* 3:314; see also Vos, *Reformed Dogmatics* 3:48, 58.

130. Owen, *Works* 1:215. See also Turretin, *Inst.* 10.3.5–6 (1:666); Letham, *Systematic Theology*, 520–26; Macleod, *Person of Christ*, 229–30; Wellum, *God the Son*, 459–65.

131. See Bavinck, *RD* 3:309–11.

132. Bavinck, *RD* 3:315.

133. See Plumer, *Person and Sinless Character*, 59, 66–67. This is one of the objections of Hodge, *Systematic Theology* 2:457.

134. Further, impeccability does not necessarily entail Christ's full knowledge of this reality according to his human nature. See Macleod, *Person of Christ*, 230; Donald Macleod, *From Glory to Golgotha: Controversial Issues in the Life of Christ* (Fearn, UK: Christian Focus, 2021), 38.

temptation yielded to."[135] Hebrews leaves no doubt that Christ is uniquely a sympathetic and powerful great high priest (e.g., Heb 2:14–18; 4:14–5:10).

In sum, since in the incarnation the divine Son of God takes a (pure) human nature while remaining the divine Son of God, it is not proper to say that Jesus could have sinned.[136]

Did Jesus Know the Future?

Carefully considering the relationship of the two natures in the hypostatic union also helps us with another difficult question: How could Christ not know something about the future (Matt 24:36; Mark 13:32)?[137] If Jesus is divine, and if he therefore knows all things, how can Jesus be ignorant of anything? This was a significant issue in the Arian controversy, for the objection to Christ's divinity arose that this statement proved Jesus is not fully God (e.g., Athanasius, *C. Ar.* 3.26).

The answer comes from a proper understanding of the relationship between Jesus's divine and human natures. Athanasius addresses this issue by arguing that some things (such as ignorance) are spoken from Christ's human nature. While the divine Son of God knows all things, his humanity is limited and ignorant of some things (*C. Ar.* 3.42–43). This has been a standard approach in Christian theology: statements about Christ's ignorance must be spoken with respect to his humanity, for while the Son of God knows all things exhaustively by virtue of his divinity, the human nature of Christ is not omniscient.[138] This lack of knowledge of the future was particularly fitting during Christ's state of humiliation, in which his

---

135. Macleod, *From Glory to Golgotha*, 38.

136. This issue also bears on whether it is appropriate to make images of Christ and whether the second commandment is understood differently in light of the incarnation. That is, if we are not to make images of God, but in the incarnation the Son of God takes a real, visible human body, is it appropriate to make images of the Second Person of the Trinity? The Reformed have often answered "no," for it is the Son of God we meet in the incarnation, and we cannot divide him so as to make a picture, for example, of only his human nature. Further complicating this is the impossibility of capturing the present glory of Christ, in his state of exaltation, with a picture. Instead, we walk by faith, not by sight (2 Cor 5:7). See, e.g., HC 97–98; WLC 109; Owen, *Works* 1:346, 380, 392–95, 409–10; Jones, *Knowing Christ*, 204–6. For a different view, see St. John of Damascus, *Three Treatises on the Divine Images*, trans. Andrew Louth, PPS (Crestwood, NY: St. Vladimir's Seminary Press, 2003); Second Council of Nicaea (AD 787), definition and anathemas 1–3 (in Tanner, *Decrees* 1:135–*137).

137. I take the phrase οὐδὲ ὁ υἱός ("nor the Son") in Matt 24:36 to be original.

138. See Owen, *Works* 1:93.

divinity was "veiled."[139] And yet we must be careful here, for the Son of God remained omniscient even in his state of humiliation, for he did not divest himself of his divine attributes. When speaking of his divine knowledge Christ was also speaking as the God-man, and thus all statements were spoken via Christ's human nature and thus cannot be "solely" categorized as divine or human. For these are united in the actions of the God-man.[140]

Christ's lack of specific knowledge about the future is also consistent with the point noted earlier, that in the incarnation, the Son of God could grow in his knowledge according to his human nature. Yet, as with the questions of Jesus's miraculous works, this by no means solves all the difficult questions. Was Jesus's knowledge as a man evidence of his divine knowledge as Son of God, or was it given by revelation from the Father by the Holy Spirit?[141] Here it may be helpful to differentiate between (1) beatific knowledge, (2) infused knowledge, and (3) acquired knowledge of Christ's soul.[142] Beatific knowledge refers to the blessed heavenly vision, "face-to-face," which Christ did not experience on earth.[143] Infused knowledge refers to the special endowment of Christ's humanity by the Spirit, and acquired knowledge refers to the things Christ learned as a man—drawing on his infused knowledge. In these latter two categories, Christ as a man was able to grow and increase in knowledge, for he was not omniscient in his humanity.[144] It is further helpful to remember that Christ had a work to accomplish as Mediator, and what was revealed to him in his humanity must have served to further this work. Further, since the acting person was the divine, omniscient Son of God, any lack of knowledge must have been voluntary and served specifically his work as Mediator. As fully man, Christ "had a human intellect. Not only a human intellect but also a human

139. See also the discussion in Crisp, *Divinity and Humanity*, 148–52.

140. Compare Thomas Aquinas, *Summa theologiae* 3a, quest. 9, art. 1.

141. So Wellum, *God the Son*, 213, 456–58; Macleod, *Person of Christ*, 166–67.

142. See, e.g., Thomas Aquinas, *Summa theologiae* 3a, quest. 9–12; Bavinck, *RD* 3:312; Turretin, *Inst.* 13.8.19 (2:327); 13.13 (2:348–52); Owen, *Works* 1:93; Muller, *PRRD* 4:320. For an assessment and critique of Bavinck's view of development in Christ's humanity, see Bruce R. Pass, *The Heart of Dogmatics: Christology and Christocentrism in Herman Bavinck*, Forschungen zur systematischen und ökumenischen Theologie 169 (Göttingen: Vandenhoeck & Ruprecht, 2020), 99–112.

143. Contrast Thomas Aquinas, *Summa theologiae* 3a, quest. 9, art. 2.

144. See also Jones, *Knowing Christ*, 88, 102.

intellect."[145] Yet even though the human mind of Jesus was limited, his knowledge as the divine Son extended "'beyond' his brain."[146]

When discussing the hypostatic union, we must resist the pull toward Nestorianism, as though there were two persons speaking in Christ.[147] One could thus say that Jesus both knew and was ignorant of the future at the same time—depending on the nature that is in view in the statement.[148] But the unity of the person must not be in doubt. As God, he knows all things; as a man, he had to learn and grow in knowledge. Since the Son always remains the omniscient Son of God, the relative ignorance of Christ's human nature must not be taken absolutely, but as that lack of knowledge that was fittingly veiled, by virtue of his humanity, in the state of humiliation.

Could the Son of God Die?

Perhaps the starkest example of the importance of rightly relating the two natures to the one person of Christ is how to deal with the question of the death of the Son of God. Can we say the Son of God died? On one hand, it is not possible for the Son of God to die by virtue of his divinity; God cannot die. However, it is possible for the Son of God to die by virtue of his human nature, for his human nature is weak and mortal. Though the Son of God never ceases to exist, he does die in the economy of redemption with respect to his human nature that he took in the incarnation.[149]

This position has likewise been firmly established in the history of Christian theology. Athanasius argues that the Son of God could not suffer or die in his essence but only in his humanity (*C. Ar.* 2.16; 3.56). As divine, the Son of God is impassible; as a man, he is passible (*C. Ar.* 3.31–34; Gregory of Nazianzus, *Or.* 30.16). Gregory of Nazianzus explains that Jesus's cry of dereliction on the cross ("My God, my God, why have you forsaken me?" [Ps 22:1]) does not refer to the divine Son's being abandoned by his Father or by the Godhead in his suffering (for that is not possible), but it was Christ, in his person, representing us: "For we were the forsaken and despised

145. Macleod, *From Glory to Golgotha*, 20.

146. This last phrase comes from Daniel J. Treier, "Incarnation," in Allen and Swain, *Christian Dogmatics*, 239.

147. See also Warfield, "Person of Christ," 66–68.

148. See Turretin, *Inst.* 13.13.5 (2:349–50); Athanasius, *C. Ar.* 3.42.

149. See, e. g., Polanus, *Syntagma* 6.13.B–C (page 363).

before, but now by the Sufferings of Him Who could not suffer, we were taken up and saved."[150] This is an important point given how much popular misunderstanding there is about Christ's abandonment on the cross: this emphatically cannot mean that the Trinity was somehow "ripped apart" at the cross, for God *qua* God cannot suffer, and the Trinity can never be severed. Instead, this must refer to the Son's suffering as a man in the state of humiliation in the economy of redemption.

In this vein, Cyril of Alexandria distinguishes between the Son of God absolutely and as he is in the economy of redemption. Thus, suffering applies to God in the flesh, and this is an economic rather than absolute reality for Cyril.[151] Cyril speaks, by the doctrine of appropriations, that Christ "suffers impassibly"—that is, the divine Son really suffers as (*qua*) man.[152] The Belgic Confession makes a similar point (BC 19), as do many post-Reformed dogmaticians.[153]

Even so—though we must distinguish between the divine and human natures in Christ's death—this does not mean that it is the "human nature" of Christ that died in the abstract.[154] Given the *communicatio idiomatum*, actions proper to one of the natures can be predicated of the person. In this sense, we must affirm that on the cross the Son of God died. Failure to appreciate this was a key issue in the Theopaschite Controversy, addressed at the Second Council of Constantinople (AD 553), which affirmed a strict identity between the person of Christ incarnate and the Word of God.[155]

CONCLUSION

THE HYPOSTATIC UNION IS A unique phenomenon that is one of the great mysteries of the universe; we have not been able to plumb its depths in this brief discussion. We must affirm that Christ is fully God and, from the time of the incarnation, fully man. Further, it is one of the astonishing realities of the universe that from

150. Gregory of Nazianzus, *Or.* 30.5 (trans. *NPNF*² 7:311).

151. McGuckin, *St. Cyril*, 201–3, 222.

152. McGuckin, *St. Cyril*, 202. McGuckin invokes Cyril's *Second Letter to Nestorius* and his letter to John of Antioch (203).

153. E.g., Mastricht, *Theoretical-Practical Theology* 2:158; Turretin, *Inst.* 13.7.9 (2:320); 13.8.20 (2:327); Hodge, *Systematic Theology* 3:143–44.

154. See Wellum, *God the Son*, 438–39.

155. See Fairbairn and Reeves, *Story of Creeds and Confessions*, 144–49.

the time of the incarnation, the Son of God never ceases to be a man, but the hypostatic union continues forever. Yet the hypostatic union neither limits the divine nature of the Son of God, nor does it divinize the human nature of the Son. But it does explain the wonders of our salvation, that Christ, in the work of mediation, acts according to both natures—doing what is appropriate as God to save sinners and doing what is appropriate as a perfect man to render the obedience from humanity that has always been required (see WCF 8.6).

FURTHER READING

Jones, Mark. *Knowing Christ*. Edinburgh: Banner of Truth, 2015. Written with minimal footnotes and including questions for discussion, this topically arranged study builds on many of the best Puritan voices, such as John Owen and Thomas Goodwin. Jones provides a theologically sensitive introduction to the mysteries of the incarnate life of the Lord Jesus for nonspecialists.

Macleod, Donald. *The Person of Christ*. CCT. Downers Grove, IL: InterVarsity, 1998. Macleod's book is a solid introduction to difficult issues relating to the person of Christ—though it may suggest revisiting divine impassibility in the final pages. For a more accessible contribution covering similar terrain, see Macleod's *From Glory to Golgotha: Controversial Issues in the Life of Christ* (Fearn, UK: Christian Focus, 2021).

Vos, Geerhardus. *Reformed Dogmatics*. Edited and translated by Richard B. Gaffin Jr. 5 vols. Bellingham, WA: Lexham, 2012–2016. Volume 3 on Christology is a concise but trenchant discussion of many key issues related to the person and natures of Christ. Vos's portions on the work of Christ are also quite helpful.

Wellum, Stephen J. *God the Son Incarnate: The Doctrine of Christ*. FET. Wheaton, IL: Crossway, 2016. In this contemporary discussion of the person of Christ, Wellum engages kenotic Christology to a significant degree.

X

THE MEDIATOR'S WORK

HUMILIATION AND EXALTATION

OUR MEDIATOR IS THE DIVINE Son of God who acts according to his divine nature and according to his human nature. He is uniquely able to save us from our sins because he acts as God to save us and as man to rectify the disobedience of humanity. We have also seen, especially in part 1 of this book, manifold ways that Christ acts as prophet, priest, and king.

In the present chapter I look in more detail at the work of Christ under two major headings: his state of humiliation and his state of exaltation. Along with these I again employ Christ's threefold office as prophet, priest, and king. This threefold approach to Christ's work helps us appreciate his multifaceted work, including both his life and his death, both his humiliation and exaltation, in ways that will discourage us from facile or oversimplified categorizations.

PROPHET, PRIEST, AND KING

WE HAVE SEEN THE THREEFOLD office (*munus triplex*) of Christ in various ways throughout this study. This has been a standard way of speaking about Christ's work since the days of Eusebius of Caesarea (*Hist. eccl.* 1.3—though we saw even earlier evidence in ch. 6) and later in the work of John Calvin (*Inst.* 2.15) and the broader Reformed tradition. We need to consider in more detail the reasons why it is fitting for our Mediator to be a prophet, priest, and king, which we will then relate to the two states of Christ. The threefold office of Christ, our Mediator, not only recalls the three anointed offices of the Old Testament, but also looks back to Adam himself, who was the prototypical prophet, priest, and king.[1] Indeed, Christ was appointed prophet, priest, and king from eternity and was already active in his threefold office in the Old Testament.[2]

Prophethood, priesthood, and kingship overlap, and it is difficult to separate them. Bavinck observes, "[Christ] does not just perform prophetic, priestly, and kingly activities but is himself, in his whole person, prophet, priest, and king. And everything he is, says, and does manifests that threefold dignity."[3] I will address each of these briefly, generally following the explanations of Westminster Larger Catechism 43–45.

First, as a prophet, Christ declares to us the word of God. He is the authoritative interpreter of Scripture, for he is himself the eternal Word of God (John 1:1) and the climactic revelation (Heb 1:2). One could also include here Christ's miracles, which are prophetic sign-acts that demonstrate and support his oral message, and Christ's pouring out of the Spirit, for the sake of understanding the truth.[4] As the final prophet, Jesus brings the full-flowered word of God and enables us to understand the truth.

Second, as a priest, Jesus offers himself as the final sacrifice for sins, he intercedes for his people, and he blesses his people. One might also include here Christ's healing ministry, as noted in several church fathers, at least with respect to cleansing lepers (e.g., Irenaeus, *Haer*. 4.8.2)—where purity language is tied to Jesus's miraculous healing (e.g., Matt 11:5; Mark 1:42). As noted in chapter 3, restorative miracles can also be understood in priestly terms.[5] His priesthood benefits us by taking away our sins, enabling access to the throne of God, and providing divine blessing for we who are unworthy. This means that Christ's obedience throughout his life is also a priestly act, for our forgiveness and righteous standing before God rest

1. See similarly Bavinck, *RD* 3:331, 367-68; Bavinck, *Wonderful Works of God*, 316.

2. Bavinck, *RD* 3:365.

3. Bavinck, *RD* 3:367; see also *RD* 3:337.

4. See, e.g., Herman Ridderbos, *The Coming of the Kingdom*, trans. H. de Jongste, ed. Raymond O. Zorn (Philadelphia: Presbyterian and Reformed, 1962), 115–21; Owen, *Works* 1:95. Bavinck (*RD* 3:367) notes that often miracles are often discussed in theological works under the heading "Prophet."

5. Bavinck, *Wonderful Works of God*, 325–27.

on the entire work of Christ—including both his obedience and his final sacrifice (see WCF 8.5). We are reconciled by his obedience no less than by his death and resurrection. Christ is therefore now a perfected, glorified, heavenly priest, and his ongoing priestly ministry means that our salvation is secure, for he intercedes for us.

Third, as a king, Jesus inaugurates and rules over the kingdom of God, subduing his and our enemies, ruling over the church, bestowing salvation, rewarding obedience, directing the world, and pouring out his wrath on the disobedient. Here we can also consider Christ's powerful miracles as royal acts of the inbreaking kingdom of God, along with the outpouring of the Spirit, which is closely tied to Christ's victory as the heavenly king (e.g., Acts 2:33–35; Eph 4:7–14; see also Ps 68:18). The kingship of Christ also points us to Christ's divinity, for the universality of Christ's kingship exceeds the rule of any created being.[6] Christ's kingship benefits his people by fighting the battles we cannot fight and ensuring that we are led to the promised land of everlasting rest. He is the Captain of his people, who has all authority over every spiritual power and will protect his church to the end, for he rules over all history.

HUMILIATION AND EXALTATION

CHRIST'S THREEFOLD OFFICE IS CLOSELY related to his two states: humiliation and exaltation.[7] This general schema has been known from the days of the early church. For example, I noted in chapter 6 that Justin spoke of two advents of Christ: one in obscurity and one in glory. In brief, Christ's state of humiliation consists in (1) his lowly birth, (2) his submission to the law, (3) the sufferings of his life, (4) bearing the wrath of God, (5) his cursed death on the cross, (6) his burial, and (7) remaining under the power of death after his crucifixion (WSC 27; see also WLC 46–50). Christ's exaltation consists in (1) his resurrection from the dead on the third day, (2) his ascension into heaven, (3) his heavenly session at God's right hand, and (4) his coming again to judge the world (WSC 28; see also WLC 51–56).

---

6. Owen, *Works* 1:96–99.

7. Helpful discussions of prophet, priest, and king in the two states are found in Bavinck, *RD* 3:364–68 (humiliation); 3:475–82 (exaltation), and Bavinck, *Wonderful Works of God*, 322–29 (humiliation); 355–66 (exaltation).

It is crucial to affirm that Christ is a prophet, priest, and king in both these states (WLC 42; WSC 23). This is particularly important when speaking of the priestly aspects of Christ's work, since it has often been argued that Christ is a priest only in heaven. The Socinians, for example, denied the substitutionary work of Christ and thus argued that Christ is primarily a priest in heaven.[8] And, as we saw briefly in chapter 5, it is common today to argue that in Hebrews—the text that addresses the priesthood of Christ most explicitly—Christ is only a priest in heaven. Though Hebrews clearly emphasizes Christ's priesthood in his heavenly state of exaltation, limiting Christ's priesthood to his heavenly state is insufficient in light of the concepts of priesthood pertaining to Christ's earthly state of humiliation in Hebrews. Thus I argue that the death of Christ (e.g., Heb 1:2; 9:26, 28), along with the earthly prayers of Christ and his obedience (e.g., Heb 5:7–9; 10:5–7), are priestly actions, and these apply to Christ's state of humiliation. In Bavinck's words, "Precisely because Christ brought this one perfect sacrifice on the cross, He can as High Priest take His place at the right hand of God (Heb 8:1)."[9]

Moreover, though Hebrews is distinctive in the amount of space devoted to specific language of Christ's priesthood, the priesthood of Christ is evident in manifold ways throughout Scripture apart from the explicit title "priest." Further supporting this is the common trope of the church fathers who find Christ to be a priest during his days of humiliation. I gave several examples in chapter 6. To recapitulate three examples: Justin speaks of Christ's priestly death on the cross (e.g., *Dial.* 96, 116) and more broadly of all the things accomplished by our high priest (*Dial.* 115); Irenaeus speaks of Christ's healing ministry as a priestly activity (*Haer.* 4.8.2); and Tertullian clearly speaks of Christ as high priest even during his days of humiliation (*Carn. Chr.* 5; *Marc.* 4.35). Added to these, Athanasius speaks of Christ becoming a merciful and faithful high priest when he became incarnate and in sacrificing himself for us (*C. Ar.* 2.9).

Christ's role as prophet, priest, and king in his state of humiliation and exaltation underscores the unity of Christ's work. Though Christ has

8. Ribbens cautions that the Socinians did not *entirely* deny that Christ was a priest on earth, but that "they clearly diminish Christ's earthly priesthood and sacrifice in order to emphasize the heavenly" ("Ascension and Atonement," 8–9).

9. Bavinck, *Wonderful Works of God*, 360.

now entered his state of exaltation, he is the same Christ who acted on our behalf during the days of his humiliation. Christ is now who he was during his life of suffering and humiliation—though now he is glorified. Christ is a priest who has now been made perfect (Heb 5:9–10).

There is therefore a close relationship between the two states of Christ, such that the state of exaltation may even be described as a reward for Christ's obedience in the state of humiliation. One of the clearest places we see this is in Philippians 2:9, where the servant who was humble unto death is therefore exalted. Bavinck captures the matter characteristically well: "The preposition διο (therefore) in Philippians 2:9 refers ... specifically to the meritorious cause of the exaltation. Because Christ humbled himself so deeply, therefore God has so highly exalted him."[10] These two states can further be related to the work of Christ to accomplish the debt owed by humanity (humiliation) and the outpouring of gifts of grace toward God's people (exaltation).[11]

STATE OF HUMILIATION

We have seen that our Mediator is the eternal, divine Son of God, in need of nothing. Yet the wonderfully good news of the gospel is that the eternal Son became incarnate "for us and for our salvation," as the Nicene Creed puts it. The Son of God became man to pay humanity's debt by obeying as a fully human representative, which required his positive obedience to God's law and his suffering the penalty for sin. Put simply, he was not obligated to obey for his own sake but for our sake.[12] We need someone to satisfy God's justice and wrath toward sin and secure the obedience required of humanity.[13] The language of satisfaction has been helpfully used to address this in the history of exegesis.[14]

10. Bavinck, *RD* 3:434, emphasis original. On the important concept of *meritum ex pacto* ("merit from the covenant"), see Bavinck, *RD* 2:544, 569–71.

11. See, e.g., Turretin, *Inst.* 13.9 (2:332–34)

12. See Owen, *Works* 1:201.

13. See further Owen, *Works* 1:178–205, esp. 194–95.

14. See, e.g., Turretin, *Inst.* 14.10–14 (2:417–82); Bavinck, *RD* 3:393–98.

The Representative Obedience of Christ

Obedience and Satisfaction

Influenced especially by Anselm of Canterbury's *Why the God-Man?* (*Cur Deus Homo?*), the language of satisfaction speaks to a vicarious work of Christ whereby he meets God's demands for humanity.[15] Anselm argues that only a God-man can save us from our sin. For on the one hand, humanity owes a debt to God because of sin, yet humanity has always owed obedience, so we can never offer enough obedience to pay the debt (1.11, 19–20; 2.4). This means that only God can save us (1.4–5; 2.5), but it remains that a man must make restitution for human sin (1.22–24). Anselm thus explains that something more is needed to satisfy God's honor and justice: "So, then, everyone who sins must repay to God the honor that he has taken away, and this is the satisfaction [*satisfactio*] that every sinner ought to make to God" (1.11; see also 1.21; 2.18).[16] That something more is the obedience and death of the God-man, who voluntarily gave his life as a man in order to save his people (1.8–10, 25). Christ paid what he did not owe, resulting in salvation for his people (2.18–19). Anselm summarizes, "No one but God can make this satisfaction [*satisfactionem*]. ... But no one ought to make it except man"; therefore, "it is necessary for a God-Man [*deus homo*] to make it" (2.6).[17] Further, to make satisfaction for sin ultimately requires Christ to die (2.11).

Though Anselm's argument required further nuancing, his basic framework for understanding the biblical concept of satisfaction took root.[18] Language of "satisfaction" is seen, for example, in Calvin: "Our Lord came in order to take Adam's place in obeying the Father, to present our flesh as the price of satisfaction to God's righteous judgment, and, in the same flesh, to pay the penalty that we had deserved."[19] Likewise, the Canons of Dort

---

15. For an accessible edition of this work, see Eugene R. Fairweather, ed. and trans., *A Scholastic Miscellany: Anselm to Ockham* (Philadelphia: Westminster, 1956), 100–183. The Latin text can be found in S. Anselmi, *Cur Deus Homo*, ed. Franciscus Salesius Schmitt, Florilegium Patristicum tam veteris quam medii aevi auctores complectens 18 (Bonn: Petri Hanstein 1929).

16. Trans. Fairweather, *Scholastic Miscellany*, 119.

17. Trans. Fairweather, *Scholastic Miscellany*, 151.

18. See also Benjamin Breckinridge Warfield, "The Chief Theories of the Atonement," in Craig, *Person and Work of Christ*, 353–54.

19. Calvin, *Inst.* 2.12.3 (1:466).

2.2 speaks of the satisfaction of Christ: "Since, therefore, we are unable to make that satisfaction in our own persons, or to deliver ourselves from the wrath of God, He has been pleased of His infinite mercy to give His only begotten Son for our Surety, who was made sin, and became a curse for us and in our stead, that He might make satisfaction to divine justice on our behalf."[20]

Similar language is found in Heidelberg Catechism 56 and Westminster Confession of Faith 8.5: "The Lord Jesus, by His perfect obedience, and sacrifice of Himself, which He through the eternal Spirit, once offered up unto God, hath fully satisfied the justice of His Father; and purchased, not only reconciliation, but an everlasting inheritance in the kingdom of heaven, for all those whom the Father hath given unto Him."[21] Likewise John Owen: "For, by the obedience and sufferings of the Son of God incarnate, there was full satisfaction made unto the justice of God for the sins of man, a reparation of his glory, and an exaltation of the honour of his holiness."[22] Such statements reflect the biblical teaching discussed in part 1, especially texts that speak of Jesus laying down his life as a substitute to bear the wrath of God against sin (e.g., Matt 20:28; Rom 3:24–26; 8:32; 2 Cor 5:21; 1 Pet 2:24; 3:18; 1 John 2:2; 4:10).

Christ's obedient work meets God's demands, atoning for sin. It is therefore fitting to speak of Christ's work in his state of humiliation to be vicarious satisfaction—representative obedience on behalf of others—and this must include both his passive obedience and his active obedience.[23] Both are necessary for our salvation. The active obedience refers to Christ's positive accomplishment of what God's law requires; passive obedience refers to Christ's bearing the penalty due to sin throughout his life. I will explain these in more detail in what follows, but Bavinck provides a helpful orientation:

> Scripture regards the entire work of Christ as a fulfillment of God's law and a satisfaction of his demand. As prophet, priest, and king, in his birth and in his death, in his words and in his deeds, he always did God's will. He

20. Trans. Dennison, *Reformed Confessions* 4:130. See also WCF 11.1, 3; 15.3; 16.5.
21. Trans. Dennison, *Reformed Confessions* 4:245.
22. Owen, *Works* 1:217.
23. See Bavinck, *RD* 3:376, 393–98; Muller, *Dictionary of Latin and Greek*, 321–23.

> came into the world to do his will. The law of God is within his heart [Ps 40:8]. His entire life was a life of complete obedience, a perfect sacrifice, a sweet odor to God. That will of God was one, as was the obedience with which Christ submitted to it and the righteousness he accomplished in it.[24]

Unified Obedience CHRIST'S OBEDIENCE MOST CERTAINLY EXTENDS to the cross, but before we consider his death, it is important to consider his obedience throughout his life.[25] This brings us to the traditional distinction between the active obedience of Jesus and the passive obedience of Jesus.[26] These terms do not refer to two stages of Christ's obedience (that is, the active obedience refers to Christ's life, whereas the passive obedience refers to his death), though these terms have often been taken this way.[27] Instead, a more satisfying approach is to see these referring to two aspects of Christ's integrated, unified obedience: Christ's active obedience refers to his positive accomplishment of righteousness in accord with God's law, whereas the passive obedience refers to Christ's obedience of suffering.[28] The latter certainly includes preeminently the cross, but is not limited to the cross. Instead, Christ's unified obedience can be understood from two angles: positively obeying God (even on the cross) and suffering the penalty as a sin-bearing representative (even during his life, prior to the cross). These are two aspects of the unified work of Christ for us. In both these ways, in his state of humiliation Christ obeyed for us, procuring salvation. Forgiveness of sins is correlated to Christ's passive obedience, and the right to eternal life is correlated to Christ's active obedience.

One place we see this unified obedience of Christ, yielding eternal life, is in Romans 5:12–21, where Paul contrasts the death and condemnation that came through Adam with the life and justification that come through Christ. A key text is Romans 5:18–19: "Therefore, as the trespass of one man

---

24. Bavinck, *RD* 3:394.

25. For fuller discussions, see Crowe, *Why Did Jesus Live a Perfect Life?*

26. For an insightful study of the history of this doctrine, see Heber Carlos de Campos Jr., *Doctrine in Development: Johannes Piscator and Debates over Christ's Active Obedience*, Reformed Historical-Theological Studies (Grand Rapids: Reformation Heritage, 2017).

27. See, e.g., Muller, *Dictionary of Latin and Greek*, 237.

28. The term "passive" derives from the Latin *patior* (= Greek πάσχειν), and is best correlated to the meaning "to suffer."

led to condemnation for all men, so the righteous act of one man leads to justification and life for all men. For as by the one man's disobedience the many were constituted sinners, so by the one man's obedience the many will be constituted righteous."[29] Here the representative obedience of Christ is referenced compactly as his (singular) righteous act, and this is contrasted with the representative disobedience of Adam.[30] Paul does not identify any particular act of Christ, and it is unlikely his comments here are limited to only one act of Christ (such as his death on the cross). For in this passage, the life and justification that flow from Christ's obedience require more than only one righteous deed.[31] Thus it is more likely that the entirety of Christ's work for us is summarized as a singular righteous act, which would include both Christ's active and passive obedience. Yet even if the death of Christ alone is in view, it would entail both his active and passive obedience, since these are not temporal distinctions but logical distinctions, focusing on two aspects of Christ's obedience; in reality, they always coincide.

A similar insight comes from John's Gospel, where Christ's multifaceted ministry is summarized as one work (e.g., John 4:34; 7:21; 10:32; 17:4). That is, in John the plurality of Jesus's works (5:20; 9:3–4; 10:25, 32, 37–38; 14:10–12; 15:24) were ultimately part of one integrated work.[32] To be sure, the focal point of that one work was the "exaltation" or "glorification" of the Son (which includes his death and the resurrection/ascension, e.g., John 12:23; 13:31–32; 17:1–5), but that one work includes all that Jesus did to accomplish salvation.

To state the matter simply, Christ's multifaceted work of representation can be summarized by New Testament authors as one work or one righteous act, which summarily points to the unity of his vicarious obedience in the state of humiliation.

---

29. Author's translation, modified from the ESV.

30. "One" (ἑνός) most likely refers to one *man* in 5:18 (rather than one *righteous act*) in light of the passage's sustained focus on the representative actions of Adam and Christ and the statements in 5:12, 15–17, 19. See further Crowe, *Why Did Jesus Live a Perfect Life?*, 45–46.

31. See also Turretin, *Inst.* 14.13.17 (2:450).

32. See further Crowe, *Last Adam*, 126.

Saving Obedience

CHRIST'S REPRESENTATIVE OBEDIENCE IN THE state of humiliation is therefore saving obedience. For first of all, as a true man, Christ's obedience is true, perfect human obedience, which fulfills what was originally intended of Adam. In the beginning, Adam was required to love and obey God fully. As noted earlier, Adam was tested by God to see whether he would choose to listen to God's word and obey him, but Adam failed that test. Yet eternal life, according to God's covenantal arrangement, has always required perfect obedience. This is evident in the use, for example, of Leviticus 18:5; Deuteronomy 27:26 in the New Testament (see, e.g., Luke 10:25–37; Rom 10:5–12; Gal 3:10–12). Eternal life is contingent on someone keeping the commands of God perfectly.

No natural person since Adam was able to meet that demand, but Christ is the second and last Adam, the holy Son of God born of a virgin, and he has faithfully kept the entire moral law of God and thus realizes the requirement of humanity for eternal life. To benefit from this, we look to him by faith rather than our own works. We do not have to ascend into heaven or descend to the depths of the earth; we instead must trust in the Messiah, who has obeyed on our behalf (Rom 10:6–13). By faith we benefit from the righteousness of his perfect obedience, which is required by the law of God.[33]

Second, not only is Christ's obedience human obedience, but it is also the obedience of the God-man and is therefore the obedience of a divine person.[34] This renders Christ's obedience qualitatively different from any merely human obedience—it is instead infinitely valuable and able to withstand the judgment of God.[35] As man, Christ was subjected to suffering and the penalty of sin; as God, he overcame sin and grants us salvation.[36] If Christ were a mere man he would have been subject to the law on his own account. But as one who is by nature God, he was above

---

33. Following closely Polanus, *Syntagma* 6.14.F–G (page 366).

34. See also WLC 38–40; Turretin, *Inst.* 12.2.11 (2:176–77); 13.3.19–20 (2:302–3); 14.2 (2:379–84); 14.12.7 (2:440); Hodge, *Systematic Theology* 2:395; 3:143–44; Berkhof, *Systematic Theology*, 319.

35. See, e.g., HC 14; CD 2.3; WLC 38.

36. See Turretin, *Inst.* 13.3.19 (2:302–3).

the law by nature and thus could voluntarily place himself under the law as a man for our sake.[37]

Since Christ has provided the perfect satisfaction, there is nothing left for believers to do to gain eternal life.[38] The penalty has been paid entirely; our sins are fully covered. To understand this more fully, we turn our attention to the question of the death of Christ and what it accomplished.

The Death of Christ and the Question of Atonement

I HAVE ARGUED THAT THE work of Christ is best understood as a unified whole: his entire life was active and passive and was vicarious satisfaction. Even so, the death of Christ stands out as a diamond among jewels, and it merits further consideration as part of his state of humiliation. For indeed, in many ways the wonderful mystery of the gospel is summed up in the death of Christ for sinners. This also brings us to the oft-debated issue of the atonement and which theory/theories of the atonement best account for the biblical evidence.[39] This concept, however, is a modern one, and one that may not be all that helpful.[40] On the one hand, atonement is often related particularly to the death of Christ, which is an appropriate way to speak (see HC 37). On the other hand, I have argued that the work of Christ (and thus atonement) entails much more than only the death of Christ, so atonement requires more than only the death of Christ.

Be that as it may, it appears that the traditional way of framing the issue as theories of the atonement may be so ingrained that we cannot avoid it entirely. While not all the models of the atonement are equally valid (e.g., the moral), and some authors have overemphasized one side of the evidence,[41] some of the so-called theories coexist quite well with one another.

37. See Owen, *Works* 1:200–201.

38. See Turretin, *Inst.* 14.12.5–6 (2:439).

39. Examples include the moral, mystical, governmental, ransom, and penal substitutionary models. For concise discussions, see Warfield, "Chief Theories," 351–69; Henri A. G. Blocher, "Atonement," in *Dictionary for Theological Interpretation of the Bible*, ed. Kevin J. Vanhoozer (Grand Rapids: Baker Academic, 2005), 72–76.

40. See Adam J. Johnson, "Theories and *Theoria* of the Atonement: A Proposal," *IJST* 23 (2021): 92–108.

41. See, e.g., the much-discussed work of Gustaf Aulén, *Christus Victor: An Historical Study of the Three Main Types of the Idea of the Atonement*, trans. A. G. Hebert (London: SPCK, 1931). For one critique, see Kelly, *Systematic Theology* 2:437–39. See also Alan Spence, "A Unified

For example: Christus Victor (understood properly) fits well with penal substitution. Even though vicarious satisfaction or penal, substitutionary atonement is the most helpful category to encompass the various facets of Christ's work,[42] it is best to understand the death of Christ specifically to reflect his threefold office as prophet, priest, and king, which helps us avoid reductionism.[43]

In sum, I have argued that the work of Christ entails much more than just the death of Christ. Even so, this broader understanding of the work does not obviate the need to think carefully about the role of Christ's death and the nature of the atonement.

Prophet, Priest, and King in His Death

We already saw in chapter 6 that the descriptions of the death of Christ in the church fathers are multifaceted, including imagery of prophet, priest, and king. In the same spirit, the Reformed creeds that employ the offices of prophet, priest, and king to explain the work of Christ also reflect a multifaceted approach—though admittedly much more emphasis falls on priestly and royal dimensions.[44] In practice, various theories of the atonement often coincide, and the multifaceted descriptions of Christ's death help us see in greater depth the richness of the work of Christ for us.[45]

As a prophet on the cross, Christ most fully revealed the love and wrath of God, and he was crucified primarily for his prophetic speech, especially his prophetic speech that he was the king(!). Further, the greatest prophetic sign of Christ was his lifting up on the cross, so that all who look to him may have eternal life (John 3:14–17). In typical Johannine fashion, this lifting up certainly includes his glorification on the other side of the crucifixion, but the crucifixion is an irreducible part of that movement for John.

Theory of the Atonement," *IJST* 6 (2004): 404–20; Henri Blocher, "Biblical Metaphors and the Doctrine of the Atonement," *JETS* 47 (2004): 629–45.

42. So also Warfield, "Chief Theories," 351.

43. Further, the English term "atonement" was coined in the sixteenth century (*Oxford English Dictionary*, 2nd ed., 20 vols. [Oxford: Oxford University Press, 1989], 1:754–55); we must beware the possibility of anachronism—using a later English term to limit the Bible's multifaceted teaching. See also Johnson, "Theories," 100–1.

44. E.g., HC 1; 31; WCF 20.1; WLC 44–45.

45. See Bavinck, *RD* 3:383–84; also *RD* 3:366–67.

As priest, Jesus's death sums up and seals the obedience of his entire life for us. His death is therefore the final, perfect sacrifice for sin that does not need to be repeated (Heb 7:27; 9:26–28; 10:10). It is the substance to which all prior sacrifices pointed (10:1). He is the propitiation for our sins and those of the whole world (1 John 2:2), for his blood alone suffices to take away our sin and bear the wrath of God. Christ's propitiatory sacrifice is necessary because sin is subject to the wrath of God. This is visibly represented in the Old Testament by the sacrificial system, which is summarized in Hebrews: without the shedding of blood there is no remission of sins (9:22). Only Christ is a sufficient substitute who can truly bear the penalty for sins. Sin brings death, and to free us from the curse of ultimate death Christ had to give his own life as our Passover Lamb. He has effected a true, lasting exodus for his people. We celebrate and remember his sacrifice in the Lord's Supper, but his sacrifice never needs to be repeated.

Further, Jesus's kingship is seen preeminently on the cross. Christ was crucified as a royal threat, and the charge above him read "King of the Jews." Further, this was given in three languages (John 19:20), denoting that he is the king of the whole world. It was by being lifted up that this king drew all people to himself (John 12:32). By his entire obedience, and especially by his death and resurrection, Christ bound the strong man and plundered the devil (Matt 12:29). Christ is thus the Victor who frees his people from the power, bondage, and tyranny of the devil.[46] There is no need to divide between Christ as the penal substitute for sin and Christ as the victorious king; these are held together on the cross.[47] Not only has he thus paid for all our sins with his precious blood, but he has set us free from the tyranny of the devil (HC 1). To be clear, this is not to say that Christ pays a ransom to the devil in his death. For indeed, Scripture instead speaks of the devil being plundered, bound, and conquered, not paid.[48] While it is true that

---

46. Polanus (*Syntagma*, 6.12.I [page 362]) correlates freedom from the devil to adoption.

47. See also Sinclair B. Ferguson, "*Christus Victor et Propitiator*: The Death of Christ, Substitute and Conqueror," in *For the Fame of God's Name: Essays in Honor of John Piper*, ed. Sam Storms and Justin Taylor (Wheaton, IL: Crossway, 2010), 171–89; Henri Blocher, "*Agnus Victor*: The Atonement as Victory and Vicarious Punishment," in *What Does It Mean to Be Saved? Broadening Evangelical Horizons of Salvation*, ed. John G. Stackhouse Jr. (Grand Rapids: Baker, 2002), 67–91.

48. See, e.g., Owen, *Works* 1:197; Garland, *Theology of Mark's Gospel*, 477; see also Anselm, *Cur Deus Homo?* 2.19.

the devil holds the power of death (Heb 2:14–15),[49] the devil is conquered by the work of Christ. Indeed, for Christ to overcome on our behalf he must also free us from sin, guilt, and death, which requires a penal substitute.[50]

It may be possible to see all three offices of Jesus challenged during his passion.[51] Those who ridiculed and beat Jesus taunted him to prophesy. They did not realize he was the greatest prophet (Matt 26:67–68; Mark 14:65). Those who blasphemed and goaded Jesus to save himself did not realize that he was offering the final sacrifice (Matt 27:42; Mark 15:29–31). Those who mocked Jesus's kingship did not realize that he was truly the king of the world (Matt 27:37–43; Mark 15:32; Luke 23:35; John 19:19–22). Yet in all these ways Jesus proved faithful as prophet, priest, and king, which is demonstrated by his resurrection from the dead.

The Logic of the Cross

As Bavinck argues, the atonement is the chief benefit of Christ's death.[52] It therefore behooves us to consider this in more detail. We will not understand the cross if we do not understand the holiness of God and his righteous anger against sin. We also will not understand the cross if we do not grapple with the penalty of destruction that every person deserves for his or her sin. Further, we will not understand the cross if we do not grasp its role as the focal point of God's grace, mercy, and love in Christ. After addressing those issues, I will say more about what Christ's work on the cross actually accomplished.

The triune God is holy: Father, Son, and Spirit. We catch glimpses of this in Scripture where even the heavenly beings must shield their faces from the self-existent source of all life and goodness, and this is even a greater threat for sinful people (e.g., Isa 6:1–7; see also Luke 5:8). He is eternally perfect and is not in need of humanity, but he created people for his own glory. Sin assaults the character of God and interjects chaos and disorder into the cosmos. Sin is rebellion against God's authority and law, and it cannot go

---

49. See R. B. Jamieson, *Jesus' Death*, 110–14 and 111n50.

50. See Richard B. Gaffin Jr., *No Adam, No Gospel: Adam and the History of Redemption* (Phillipsburg, NJ: P&R; Philadelphia: Westminster Seminary Press, 2015), 20, noted in Crowe, *Last Adam*, 210.

51. Following Jones, *Knowing Christ*, 124, 228–29.

52. Bavinck, *RD* 3:447, 449–50.

unaddressed. Yet all humans owe God obedience by nature since he is our Creator. Obedience is not "extra" but is required of all people, created in the image of God.

Since sin is an affront to God's holiness, even one sin deserves the wrath of God (Rom 3:23; Jas 2:10). If God requires perfect obedience, then no natural person stands a chance on the basis of his or her own works. All are condemned before him (e.g., Rom 2:1), and justly so (3:4–6). He owes us nothing, for God is self-existent and complete in himself. On the other hand, all people owe God love and obedience. God is not in our debt, and he is not required inherently to bestow salvation on those who have broken his law.

We must linger over this point. God owes us nothing. He is under no obligation to rescue a sinful, rebellious people. No one deserves salvation. We have forfeited our right to eternal life and blessedness by our rebelliousness.

But this understanding of human sinfulness and God's lack of compulsion enables us to appreciate the love, grace, and mercy of God more profoundly, especially in light of the cross of Christ. For the good news of the gospel is that God did for us what only he could do, and he did this out of his abundant love, not because of any obligation. This is grace, in spite of our sin.

Yet we must not stop with generic statements; we must understand the horrors of the cross to see the drastic nature of God's love for us. Crucifixion was one of the most gruesome ways to torture and murder a person. One can imagine the deterrent public crucifixions would have been to those who saw the victims slowly suffocate over the course of hours and days, while their bodies hung precariously and they fought to win the small, Pyrrhic victories for each breath, which only prolonged inevitable death. The physical excruciation is difficult to fathom. Yet the physical pain was by no means all that Christ endured, for he also faced the unprecedented experience of separation from God as a consequence of the unthinkable burden of bearing the holy wrath of God against sin (more on this below). It is on the cross that his wrath bearing was focused most intently, and this likely explains why Christ died comparatively quickly, surprising even Pontius Pilate. He was crucified for our sins, bearing our penalty.

It is this shocking portrait of a holy Savior savagely, publicly murdered that highlights most dramatically the holiness of God and his anger toward sin. Yet we also need to see by faith this crucified Savior to appreciate what it took to procure our forgiveness. For surely Jesus meant it when he said "it is finished" (τετέλεσται, John 19:30). He did not merely make us "savable" by his death on the cross, as if we needed to supplement Christ's work; the cross actually accomplished salvation. He actually bore the penalty for his people's sins in a way that guarantees they will not have to bear that penalty. This is what is often known as "limited atonement"—though ironically, this view does not limit the power of Christ's atonement. Limited or "particular" atonement teaches the precious truth that Jesus truly gave his life as a wrath-bearing substitute for his people (see, e.g., Matt 20:28; John 10:11; Acts 20:28; Rom 8:32; Eph 5:25; WCF 8.5, 8).[53] There is no lack in Christ's death for those who look to him by faith.

The horrors of the cross are at the same time the proof of God's rich love for us, that justice and mercy have met in Christ and that our Savior has done all that is needed for salvation. Yes, the cross is difficult to think about, but we must, for it brings us face to face with both our sinfulness and God's immeasurable love to do for us what we could not do for ourselves. For those who look to Christ, their sins are as dead as the reality of Christ's death on the cross, and their new life is as certain as his resurrection from the dead. God does not simply overlook or forget our sins; where would the lasting peace be in that? For if we are really guilty and no penalty has been paid, our sins would hang over us like the sword of Damocles. Instead, Christ as our priest has taken our sins on himself and fully discharged the penalty we have accrued. If Christ has taken them away, they cannot be brought back on us.[54]

Further, it is no mere man we meet on the cross, but the one who was rich beyond all splendor, who suffered so that we may be rich in him (2 Cor 8:9). This is the eternal Son of God, who not only took a human nature, but also suffered in that human nature in order that he might render perfect human obedience and pay the penalty owed by humanity for sin that he himself did not commit. Who can fathom these things? How can we plumb not just the depths but even the beginnings of so great a love for those who are so underserving?

53. For a fuller discussion, including discussions of relevant (and difficult) biblical texts, see Gibson and Gibson, *From Heaven He Came*, esp. 227–397. A classic work is John Owen, *The Death of Death in the Death of Christ* (repr., Edinburgh: Banner of Truth, 1959), which is also included in volume 10 of Owen's *Works*.

54. Here I am following Martin, *Atonement*, 136–38 (including the Damocles reference).

It is no wonder that this unmerited work of God on our behalf, focused in his Son on the cross, is the topic of so many hymns of praise:

> O sacred Head, now wounded,
> with grief and shame weighed down,
> now scornfully surrounded
> with thorns, thine only crown!
> O sacred Head, what glory,
> what bliss till now was thine!
> Yet, though despised and gory,
> I joy to call thee mine.[55]

In sum, as I argued in chapter 4, the cross of Christ effects reconciliation: removing enmity between a holy God and sinful people. On the cross our debts of sin were canceled (Col 2:13–14), and Christ became sin for us so that we might become in Christ the righteousness of God (2 Cor 5:21).

Paul wants only to know Jesus and him crucified (1 Cor 2:2), and he boasts only in the cross (Gal 6:14). Why? Because the cross brings us to the heart of the work of Christ. It assaults our pride to think that we are not worthy of salvation. It assaults our pride to think that we are not smart enough or good enough for God to save us (see 1 Cor 1:18–25). If we were, then there would have been no need for the Son of God to come and suffer as he did for us. We boast in the cross because it assures us of God's love. It shows us the dramatic steps taken by God to take our sins away. It warns us that we can do nothing to add to or supplement the work of Christ. By looking to the cross, we look away from ourselves to the one who has done for us what we could not do for ourselves. If we have been crucified with Christ, then we will also live and reign with him (Rom 6:3–4; Gal 2:20). Our reconciliation is as certain as Christ's new life from the dead, for Christ was justified from death (1 Tim 3:16). Our justification rests on his death and resurrection, and we benefit from this by union with Christ by faith. Because of the cross of Christ we can have peace with God.

55. Bernard of Clairvaux, "O Sacred Head, Now Wounded," trans. Paul Gerhardt (1656) and James W. Alexander (1830), included in *Trinity Hymnal* (Philadelphia: Great Commission, 1990), 247.

Dereliction, Burial, and the Question of the Descent

Christ's state of humiliation also entails his death and burial, along with the traditional statement "he descended into hell."

We begin by looking at the cry of dereliction, when Jesus cried out, "My God, my God, why have you forsaken me?" (Ps 22:1 in Matt 27:46; Mark 15:34). This is a moment of great mystery. Mark Jones cautions, "Only one person has understood these words ... Christ himself."[56] On the one hand, we must not posit a view that would somehow break apart the Trinity, as if the immutable, eternal coinherence of the persons of the Trinity were somehow made null at the cross. Further, we must not posit a view that ascribes suffering to God as God. Though it has been increasingly popular to doubt God's impassibility in recent years, it is right and proper to resist this trend and continue to affirm that God in himself is impassible. This means he is not subjected to any force outside himself (WCF 2.1). This is not, however, the same thing as saying God is not compassionate or that God is devoid of emotions or affections (understood appropriately).[57] For indeed, the Bible often speaks of God's love, delight, anger, pity, and so forth (e.g., Exod 34:6–7; Judg 2:18; Zeph 3:17). It is, however, to affirm that in the crucifixion it was specifically the Son of God, by virtue of his human nature, who suffered for us.

With these caveats in place, we can consider Christ's cry of dereliction on the cross. The cry of dereliction must have corresponded to a subjective experience in Christ. However, the cry of dereliction points beyond this to some mysterious, objective reality, which corresponds to the wrath-bearing nature of Jesus's death. As Bavinck argues, following Calvin:

> In the cry of Jesus we are dealing not with a subjective but with an objective God-forsakenness: He did not feel alone but had in fact been forsaken by God. His feeling was not an illusion, not based on a false view of his situation, but corresponded with reality. On the other hand, this must not be understood in the sense that the Father was personally angry with Christ. Calvin puts it very correctly: "Yet we do not suggest that God was ever inimical or angry toward him. How could he be angry toward his beloved Son, 'in whom his heart reposed' [cf. Matt 3:17]? How could Christ by his

56. Jones, *Knowing Christ*, 146.

57. See Bavinck, *RD* 2:99–101.

> intercession appease the Father toward others, if he were himself hateful to God? This is what we are saying: he bore the weight of divine severity, since he was 'stricken and afflicted' [cf. Isa. 53:5] by God's hand, and experienced all the signs of a wrathful and avenging God." Also on the cross Jesus remained the beloved Son, the Son of his Father's good pleasure (Matt. 3:17; 17:5).[58]

This is consistent with the struggle of Christ in Gethsemane: he did not doubt, but trusted his Father as the Son, aligning his human will with the divine will—and never were the two out of accord.[59]

Yet there is another angle here as well, arguably a more prominent angle. In the cry of dereliction Jesus does not say "My Father, my Father" but "My God, my God." Though the Trinitarian dimensions of the Father-Son dynamic are often discussed with respect to the cry of dereliction, it seems to be significant that Jesus avoids using "my Father" in this statement and instead (following Ps 22:1) says "my God." In other words, the Father-Son relationship is not so much emphasized as is the God-man relationship. Jesus bore the penalty for sin as a cursed man (see Gal 3:13); this statement does not reveal to us the immanent life of the Trinity. The best lens for understanding the cry of dereliction appears to be Jesus, as the last Adam and greater David, bearing the weight of sin as a covenant representative.[60]

At this moment we catch a glimpse of Christ bearing the wrath of God against sin as our substitute. For this reason, given the gravity of this event and the truth of the cry of dereliction, it has been traditional in Reformed thought to understand Christ's descent into hell to refer to this moment, when Christ figuratively descended into hell by bearing the wrath of God against sin on the cross. This, for example, is Calvin's take on that debated portion of the Apostles' Creed,[61] and Heidelberg Catechism 44 takes a

---

58. Bavinck, *RD* 3:389, quoting Calvin, *Inst.* 2.16.11. See also Macleod, *From Glory to Golgotha*, 64, 70; à Brakel, *Christian's Reasonable Service*, 579–80.

59. See also Warfield, "Emotional Life," 133–34n109.

60. Thanks to Mark Garcia for suggesting this perspective, who also pointed me to Fred Sanders's post, https://scriptoriumdaily.com/godforsaken-for-us/. See also Colin E. Gunton, *Christ and Creation* (Grand Rapids: Eerdmans, 1992), 26–27.

61. See Calvin, *Inst.* 2.16.8–12. Calvin argues that "he descended into hell" follows the mention of burial because the creed moves from what happened visibly to the invisible judgment of God he endured (*Inst.* 2.16.10).

similar view. This is a truth not to be missed, for it highlights for us the role of Christ as a representative, wrath-bearing substitute on the cross, bearing the pains of hell for his people.

Christ's humiliation also entails his burial, showing that Christ was truly dead (HC 41) and that he remained under the power of death until the third day (WLC 50). Indeed, WLC 50 relates "he descended to hell" to Christ's remaining under the power of death. The death of Christ was no mere swoon, but it was true, bodily, human death experienced by the Son of God in the incarnation.

This brings us to one of the most difficult and controversial aspects of the humiliation of Christ: whether Christ's descent into hell should be understood as a "local" descent (for lack of a better term) in which Christ descended to the abode of the dead. And if so, what did he do there?

Much of the Reformation tradition, tracing its roots back to Calvin, understands Christ's descent to be the hellish torments experienced by Jesus on the cross. Yet another, more ancient tradition, understands this to be a local descent of Christ's soul to hell—that is, to Hades, the realm of the dead. This later became associated with another doctrine, the *limbus patrum* ("border of the fathers"), which speaks of the way that by his descent, Christ opened up heaven for departed believers who were imprisoned or perhaps waiting in the realm of the dead. This is sometimes further related to doctrine of purgatory, which is found in Roman Catholic tradition and speaks of postmortem need to make some sort of payment or restitution for some types of sins. Though to be clear, not all who hold to a local descent hold to all these doctrines.

Christ's descent is included in the Apostles' Creed, which means this is supposedly something all Christians can agree on. Some evangelicals, however, demur at this phrase and argue it should be excised. Others argue that we ought to recover the early church's understanding of this phrase, which could be summarized that Jesus descended to the realm of the dead both to proclaim his victory and to open up the way to heaven for those who were awaiting him by faith.[62] Notably, Christ's descent is also codified in

62. See Matthew Y. Emerson, *"He Descended to the Dead": An Evangelical Theology of Holy Saturday* (Downers Grove, IL: IVP Academic, 2019), 103.

the Reformed tradition (e.g., HC 44; WLC 50), so confessionally Reformed must wrestle with what it means to affirm the clause.

How shall we understand this debated phrase? I am not able to answer these questions definitively, but I give a sketch here of a way forward. To anticipate my conclusion: while there is widespread historical support for the idea of a "local" descent, I remain unconvinced that there is sufficient exegetical warrant for it. Instead, the phrase speaks of Christ's real experience of death for his people as a representative.

1. On this issue, as with all theological questions, our final authority must be Scripture itself. I remain unconvinced exegetically that the doctrine is taught in Scripture or is a good and necessary consequence that is to be deduced from Scripture. If there is no scriptural foundation, then despite its antiquity, it is not binding.[63] The proposed interpretations of biblical texts often marshaled in support of the geographical descent of Christ are unpersuasive.[64]

For example, though Ephesians 4:9–10 mentions Christ descending to the lower regions of the earth (κατέβη εἰς τὰ κατώτερα μέρη τῆς γῆς), the syntactical role of the genitive (τῆς γῆς) is best taken as an example of apposition, whereby the lower regions are equated with the earth.[65] It is also possible this is a reference to Christ's burial.[66] Either way, "lower regions of the earth" is not clear evidence for the descent of Christ's soul into the realm of the dead, much less does it address what may have happened there. One's reading of Ephesians 4 likely will also color one's reading of Romans 10:7, which refers to Christ descending to the abyss. However, though it is possible that Paul refers here to the abyss as the realm of departed souls, this abyss need only refer to Christ's burial and the reality of his death, for the answer to the abyss is Christ's resurrection.[67]

---

63. It may be significant that both Justin and Irenaeus invoke a spurious text from Jeremiah to defend the descent.

64. For Reformed discussions of key texts, see Polanus, *Syntagma* 6.21 (pp. 410–15); Mastricht, *Theoretico-Practica Theologia*, rev. ed. (Utrecht: Gerardum Muntendam, 1698), 5.13.4–8 (1:560–61); Turretin, *Inst.* 13.15.9–14 (2:359–61); Bavinck, *RD* 416; à Brakel, *Christian's Reasonable Service* 1:584.

65. So, e.g., Wallace, *Greek Grammar*, 99–100; Turretin, *Inst.* 13.15.8, 10 (2:359).

66. Mastricht, *Theoretico-Practica Theologia* 5.13.12 (1:563).

67. Emerson argues that the plural ἐκ νεκρῶν refers to the *place* of the dead ones (*"He Descended,"* 47–48, 58). Yet this need only mean that Jesus rose from the experience of death and the grave represented by the biblical Sheol. On Rom 10:7, see also Polanus, *Syntagma*

The sign of Jonah (Matt 12:38–42; see also Luke 11:29–32), which speaks of Christ remaining in the belly of the earth for three days, is often understood to refer to Christ's descent.[68] However, the sign of Jonah is best understood as Christ's resurrection for several reasons. First, the *sign* of Jonah is primarily about Christ's (public) resurrection. Jesus himself was the sign of Jonah to his generation, which speaks of his deliverance from death and his presence among them.[69] Second, the sign of Jonah was a sign specifically to Jesus's generation. It is difficult to see how Jesus's descent to the realm of the dead—with particular focus perhaps on departed believers—would be a sign to Jesus's generation. Third, there is ample tradition from the early church that the sign of Jonah was understood to refer primarily to Christ's resurrection.[70]

Similarly, Acts 2 ("you will not abandon my soul to Sheol") speaks much more clearly about Christ's resurrection than his supposed local descent of soul to the realm of the dead.[71] Hebrews 2:14–15 speaks of Christ defeating the one who has the power of death, and some even see here an echo of Heracles/Hercules, who conquered in the underworld.[72] Yet despite whatever possible echoes we may find to Heracles for the audience of Hebrews, we must be cautious of importing too much from the Greek pantheon in this particular way. Just as there may be parallels between Jesus and Heracles, there are many differences as well. It is not clear that Hebrews 2:14–15 teaches that Jesus went to the realm of the dead actively to conquer.[73] The resurrection is much more clearly taught in Hebrews. Likewise, "the

---

6.21.B–E (p. 412). Bavinck writes of Christ: "Though as a deceased person belonging to Hades [= Sheol], in terms of his soul, he was in paradise (Luke 23:43)" (*RD* 3:410). See also *RD* 4:605; *SPT* 27.31 (2:152–55).

68. Emerson, *"He Descended,"* 35–39.

69. See further Crowe, *Hope of Israel*, 156–58.

70. Justin, *Dial.* 107; Athanasius, *C. Ar.* 3.25.23; Cyril of Jerusalem, *Catechetical Lectures* 4.12; see also Irenaeus, *Haer.* 4.9.2; 4.33.4; 5.5.2, noted in Crowe, *Hope of Israel*, 157n17.

71. Crowe, *Hope of Israel*, 24–27. Justin W. Bass believes that Rom 10:7 and Acts 2:27, 31 provide the strongest NT evidence for Christ's descent. See Bass, *The Battle for the Keys: Revelation 1:18 and Christ's Descent into the Underworld*, Paternoster Biblical Monographs (repr., Eugene, OR: Wipf & Stock, 2014), 77. For an alternative view, see Polanus, *Syntagma* 6.21.H (p. 412), who argues that Acts 2:31 makes it clear Jesus's body is in Hades, and the soul is used in 2:27 by way of synecdoche.

72. E.g., Lane, *Hebrews 1–8*, 56–57.

73. Mastricht observes of Heb 2:14–15 (and Col 2:14–15) that Jesus already defeated the devil on the cross (*Theoretico-Practica Theologia*, 5.13.12 [1:562–63]).

keys of death and Hades" in Revelation 1:18 has been taken as a reference to Christ's descent.[74] Yet here again Christ's resurrection victory is clearly in view, whereas one can only infer a local descent. In Philippians 2:10 those "under the earth" may well describe all those who are buried in the earth, awaiting the resurrection, without implying that their souls are indiscriminately in a shared experience of the intermediate state.[75] Alternatively, Paul's threefold phrasing (heaven, earth, and under the earth) could be a way to refer all rational creatures.[76]

Finally 1 Peter 3:18–22 (esp. vv. 19–20) is sometimes taken as evidence for Christ's local descent. If so, this passage would also speak of Christ preaching to spirits in prison during the time of his descent. However, I argued in chapter 5 that the announcement in view in this passage is more likely a reference to Christ's resurrection.

In sum, despite the prevalence of tradition, nowhere does Scripture clearly teach a local descent of Christ, nor does Scripture teach that Christ was actively conquering during the time in which his body lay buried in the grave.

2. We must consider the phrase itself, which is varied, but a standard form in Latin reads *descendit ad inferna* ("he descended to the lower regions") or perhaps better *descendit ad inferos* ("he descended to the dead [ones]"). While the English form of the phrase "descended into hell" carries connotations of punishment, this is not necessary with the Latin phraseology.[77] The Latin simply refers to the place of dead souls, reflecting the biblical concept of Sheol. Yet because the phrase speaks of death, "the final enemy" (1 Cor 15:26), it de facto also connotes suffering and anguish.[78]

Further, though this phrase has sometimes been dismissed as a later addition to the Apostles' Creed that appeared only in the fourth century and was not common until later, and though it does not appear in early

74. See Bass, *Battle for the Keys*, 97–114; Emerson, *"He Descended,"* 50–53.

75. Bavinck, *RD* 4:604–6. The passage in 1 Sam 28 in which Samuel appears from below to the witch of Endor is fraught with difficulty. It is difficult to put too much stock in this passage either way. See also Polanus, *Syntagma* 6.21.D–E (p. 414).

76. Polanus, *Syntagma* 6.21.A (p. 413).

77. For the state of the question, see Emerson, *"He Descended,"* 3–4, 66–103, who prefers *inferos*, which is also the form in which Polanus interacts with it. See also Jeffrey Hamm, "*Descendit*: Delete or Declare? A Defense against the Neo-Deletionists," *WTJ* 78 (2016): 93–116.

78. So, e.g., WLC 50; Vos, *Reformed Dogmatics* 3:216; Mastricht, *Theoretico-Practica Theologia* 5.13.9 (1:561).

iterations of the creed (e.g., Irenaeus, *Haer*. 1.10.1), this objection is a red herring. Ample evidence exists for belief in a local descent by at least the middle the second century (Justin Martyr, Irenaeus, Melito), and perhaps as early as Ignatius of Antioch.[79] It will not do to dismiss the phrase as a later concept, for it does indeed reflect a much earlier tradition.

3. We must admit there are a range of views about the descent of Christ. Reformed theologians have typically rejected the local descent of Christ, whereas it is more commonly affirmed in Roman Catholic and Lutheran theology.[80] The Reformed's denial is not only because of its lack of explicit scriptural warrant but also (crucially for this volume) because of christological concerns: it is difficult to reconcile the descent with a Reformed understanding of the *communicatio idiomatum* and the limitations of Christ's human nature. On the one hand, though Christ's body and soul were separated in the humiliation of the duration of the time his body lay in the grave, the hypostatic union was not undone during that time.[81]

We therefore must ask in what way Christ could have gone to the place of the dead. It could not have been locally in his body, for his body was in the grave. Neither could it have been with respect to his divine nature, which is omnipresent and does not "move" anywhere. It must then have been with respect to his human soul, but there are still problems with this.[82] Jesus committed his soul into the hands of his Father when he died (Ps 31:5 in Luke 23:46), and Christ's human soul is not omnipresent. Thus, Jesus's promise to the repentant thief on the cross that he would be with

---

79. Justin, *Dial.* 72; Irenaeus, *Haer.* 4.22.1; 4.27.2; 5.31.1–2; *Epid.* 78; Melito, *Peri Pascha*, 55, 100–102. Some of these are noted by Charles E. Hill, "'He Descended into Hell,'" *Reformed Faith and Practice* 1.2 (2016): 3–10. For early examples of the rule of faith (*regula fidei*), see Ferguson, *Rule of Faith*, 3–15. See Ign. *Magn.* 9.2 (though see Matt 27:52–53); Ign. *Trall.* 9.1. See also Clement of Alexandria, *Strom.* 6.6; Origen, *Cels.* 2.43; Athanasius, *C. Ar.* 3.23. An extensive discussion of Christ's descent is found in the Gospel of Nicodemus (or Acts of Pilate B) 21–26, but this text is difficult to date. The editors of a recent edition suggest it may be from the fifth or sixth century. See Bart D. Ehrman and Zlatko Pleše, *The Apocryphal Gospels: Texts and Translations* (Oxford: Oxford University Press, 2013), 465.

80. See, e.g., Bavinck, *RD* 3:410–17; Turretin, *Inst.* 13.15–16 (2:356–64); Vos, *Reformed Dogmatics* 3:206–9; Mastricht states: "*Reformati omnem localem descensum negant*" (*Theoretico-Practica Theologia* 5.13.12 [page 562]).

81. E.g., BC 19; Owen, *Works* 3:180; Vos, *Reformed Dogmatics* 3:204; Maresius, *Theologiae elenchticae nova synopsis* 4.8 (pages 108, 115); Emerson, "*He Descended*," 162, 204.

82. See Mastricht, *Theoretico-Practica Theologia* 5.13.12 (1:562). This same point is made by Berkhof, *Systematic Theology*, 342.

Jesus "today" in paradise (Luke 23:43) assumes Jesus speaks with respect to his humanity about the paradise of heaven.[83] One difficulty with this view, however, may arise if "paradise" is understood not as heaven but as a section of Sheol reserved for the righteous—perhaps the same place as "Abraham's bosom" (Luke 16:22).[84] This location would have housed the souls of the departed righteous, who were awaiting the coming of Christ. Even so, on balance "paradise" is best understood as a heavenly state. As many have noted, Elijah and Enoch were translated into a blessed state.[85] Elijah was seen ascending into heaven on a fiery chariot (e.g., 2 Kgs 1:1), which we can presume transported him to paradise.[86] Most crucially, in the New Testament Paul clearly refers to paradise as the "third heaven" (2 Cor 12:2, 4).[87]

For these reasons, while it is true that Jesus experienced death as a representative and overcame death (in his resurrection!), the Reformed have often understood Christ's descent into hell as a state rather than a place.[88] His descent was a relatively passive act in which he resigned himself to his Father.[89]

4. We are on much firmer exegetical and theological ground to understand the time of Christ's burial to refer to his state of humiliation rather than his state of exaltation. The Reformed have consistently maintained

83. See Turretin, *Inst.* 13.15.5 (2:357).

84. E.g., Emerson, *"He Descended,"* 133; Ed Christian, "The Rich Man and Lazarus, Abraham's Bosom, and the Biblical Penalty *Karet* ('Cut Off')," *JETS* 61 (2018): 513–23. For a response that anticipates modern discussions, see Polanus, *Syntagma* 6.21.A–D (p. 414).

85. E.g., Polanus, *Syntagma* 6.21.B, D, G (p. 415); Mastricht, *Theoretico-Practica Theologia* 5.13.12 (1:562). The Gospel of Nicodemus (or Acts of Pilate B) 25 refers to Christ leading souls out of the lower regions into paradise. See also Charles E. Hill, Regnum Caelorum*: Patterns of Millennial Thought in Early Christianity*, 2nd ed. (Grand Rapids: Eerdmans, 2001), 22–23, 47–50, 65–66, 246, 271–72. He notes various views, including the view that paradise was experienced by those who were translated, not experiencing death (e.g., 2 Bar. 4.1–7; 46.7; 48.30 59.8; 76.2; 4 Ezra 4.7–8; 6.26; 7.36; LAB 48.1; Irenaeus, *Haer.* 5.5.1–2).

86. See also 1 Macc 2:58, noted in Polanus, *Syntagma* 6.21.G (p. 414).

87. See, e.g., *SPT* 27.28–29 (2:150–53); Bavinck, *RD* 4:605; Daniel J. Hyde, *In Defense of the Descent: A Response to Contemporary Critics*, Explorations in Confessional Theology (Grand Rapids: Reformation Heritage, 2010), 30.

88. So Mastricht, *Theoretico-Practica Theologia* 5.13.2.1–2 (1:558–59), 5.13.9 (1:561); Polanus, *Syntagma* 6.21.H–I (p. 410). Vern Poythress commented to me in personal correspondence, "The Bible uses the terminology of Hades, paradise, and (by association) heaven in connection with the intermediate state. But it does not develop this into a univocal geography."

89. So Vos, *Reformed Dogmatics* 3:215; Berkhof, *Systematic Theology*, 342.

this position,[90] though it is common among those who hold to a local descent of Christ to view the descent of Christ as the beginning of his exaltation.[91] During the time of his burial, Christ's soul was separated from his body, which is a disruption of the creation pattern.[92] Further, the Bible clearly speaks of Christ's glorification in tandem with his resurrected, glorified body. Apart from Christ's body being revived, there is no eschatological renewal of humanity in Christ. Christ's body lying in the grave means it remains under the power of death (WLC 50). Indeed, Scripture is clear that the resurrected Christ is the firstfruits of new creation (1 Cor 15:21–23).[93] To be sure, there is a sense in which Jesus's lifting up on the cross was his glorification, as we see in the Gospel of John (12:23; 13:31–32; 17:1–5), and there is a close relationship between Christ's states of humiliation and exaltation.[94] But Jesus's state of exaltation commenced with his breaking the bonds of death in his glorious resurrection. This is clearly taught in Scripture. Therefore, we ought not to consider the descent of Christ to be the first stage in his exaltation.[95]

5. Another difficulty of the local descent is the view of many that Christ descended to the dead to free the souls of departed saints who were awaiting a glorious experience of postmortem life.[96] In addition to the lack of scriptural warrant for this view, Reformed theology has understood an essential unity of the experience of eternal life in the intermediate state (i.e., eternal life before the final resurrection) for both Old Testament and

---

90. E.g., Mastricht, *Theoretico-Practica Theologia* 5.13.12 (1:562); Turretin, *Inst.* 13.15.7–8 (2:359); Bavinck, *RD* 3:417, 433–38; à Brakel, *Christian's Reasonable Service* 1:583; Vos, *Reformed Dogmatics* 3:201–3.

91. Emerson, *"He Descended,"* 56–57, 64–65, 118, 136.

92. See also *SPT* 27.27 (2:150–51); Vos, *Reformed Dogmatics* 3:202–3.

93. See also Turretin, *Inst.* 13.15.14 (2:361): "The triumphal song which Paul sings (after Hosea, 1 Cor 15:54, 55) is rightly referred to the resurrection of Christ, by which he began to triumph over sin, death and hell. But it cannot pertain to a descent into hell, which was the lowest degree of his humiliation."

94. See Bavinck, *RD* 3:432.

95. See also the suggestive comments of Treier: "A proper response to such exegetical complexities, however, affirms the creedal phrase while noticing its location: at the extreme point emphasizing Christ's humiliation unto death, leading into resurrection and exaltation" ("Incarnation," 245).

96. Hyde interacts briefly with the view that paradise is *now* in heaven after the coming of Christ (*Defense*, 30–31). For examples of this view, see Bass, *Battle for the Keys*, 55–56; Emerson, *"He Descended,"* 134–35.

New Testament believers. Those who departed this life before the coming of Christ already experienced "a blessed rest and happiness."[97] Owen states, "It is contrary unto all notions and revelations of the respect of God unto his people ... that those who have passed through their course of obedience in this world, and finished the work given unto them, should not enter, upon their departure, into blessed rest in the presence of God. Take away the persuasion hereof, and the whole nature of faith is destroyed."[98] Commenting on the notion that the souls of departed believers may have been in imprisoned (see interpretations of 1 Pet 3:19), Turretin writes, "Nowhere in Scripture is any place called a prison where happy spirits are contained."[99] Indeed, as noted above, the examples of Enoch and Elijah seem to provide examples of Old Testament believers who were transported to the heavenly paradise.[100] The unity of eternal life among Old Testament and New Testament believers is a hallmark of Reformed theology and is supported by texts such as Hebrews 12:23.[101] Such evidence further corroborates that "paradise" throughout the New Testament refers not to the shadowy realm of the dead where Old Testament believers dwelled but to the place of heavenly reward.[102]

In sum, while there is great mystery on this point, it seems best to affirm that the descent of Christ (1) refers to the hellish torments of Sheol he endured for the sake of his people—it was a state rather than a place,[103] and (2) more certainly, affirms that Christ was truly dead and that he experienced, as Mediator, the separation of the soul from his body, as do all

---

97. So John Owen, *Works* 1:262–66.

98. Owen, *Works* 1:264.

99. Turretin, *Inst.* 13.15.12 (2:360).

100. See similarly Mastricht, *Theoretico-Practica Theologia* 5.13.12 (1:562–63). For the view that the OT already envisions hope for the righteous experiencing eternal life upon death, see T. Desmond Alexander, "The Old Testament View of Life after Death," *Them* 11 (1986): 41–46.

101. Bavinck, *RD* 3:410. Hill, writing from a confessional Reformed perspective, argues that Heb 12:23, along with Heb 11:39–40, teaches a change in status for departed saints in light of the completed work of Christ ("'He Descended into Hell,'" 9–10). On the unity of eternal life among OT and NT believers, see, e.g., Calvin, *Inst.* 2.10.7–14; Turretin, *Inst.* 12.7.45 (2:231–32); see also 12.10 (2:247–57); Bavinck, *RD* 3:223; WCF 32.1.

102. See Bavinck, *RD* 4:301, 604–6.

103. See also *SPT* 27.25; 27.30–32 (2:148–49, 152–55); à Brakel, *Christian's Reasonable Service* 1:583.

who die (see WLC 50).[104] Admittedly, the Reformed understanding of the descent clause is difficult to reconcile with the view of the early church, which provides the impetus for the phrase.[105] It may indeed be possible to understand the descent of Christ locally in a way that coheres with confessional Reformed theology. But in the end, the local descent view suffers from lack of scriptural support.

Whatever view one takes on this debated issue, the good news is the burial is not the end of the story. Christ emerged victorious from the grave, overcoming death by means of his resurrection, which begins his state of exaltation.

STATE OF EXALTATION

Closely related to his state of humiliation, Christ's exaltation commenced with his resurrection from the dead.[106] This, no less than his humiliation, constitutes the work Christ for us. For our resurrection and justification depend on the resurrection and justification of Christ from the dead (1 Tim 3:16).[107] At the same time, whereas Christ's state of humiliation correlates more to the accomplishment of salvation, his state of exaltation correlates more to the application of salvation. Christ procured salvation in his state of humiliation; he applies it to his people in his state of exaltation.[108] When Christ said "it is finished" on the cross, this did not mean his work had entirely come to an end. Instead, it means his active work of humiliation was finished.[109] In the words of Bavinck, "In the state of exaltation there still remains much for Christ to do."[110] Turretin explains the logic of why Christ's exaltation is necessary:

104. Mastricht, *Theoretico-Practica Theologia* 15.13.10 (1:562); Bavinck, *RD* 3:416; Turretin, *Inst.* 13.16.5, 7–8 (2:363); Berkhof, *Systematic Theology*, 342–43.

105. See also Vos, *Reformed Dogmatics* 3:216.

106. So, e.g., WLC 51; Turretin, *Inst.* 13.17.1 (2:364).

107. See Gaffin, *Centrality of the Resurrection*.

108. See Turretin, *Inst.* 13.9.5 (2:334); Gaffin, "Work of Christ Applied," 269. The accomplishment of salvation and the application of salvation should not be divorced from each other, for we receive the benefits of salvation in union with Christ himself. See "Work of Christ Applied," 274–75, 278–79, 283–90.

109. Bavinck, *Wonderful Works of God*, 344.

110. Bavinck, *RD* 3:568, noted in Gaffin, "Work of Christ Applied," 268–69.

> To reconcile God to us and to obtain the fruits of saving grace, two things were to be done: first, satisfaction was to be made to offended justice by the suffering and death of Christ; second, the gifts of grace were to be poured out upon men (which was done in the exaltation, Eph. 4:8). ... In respect of the former, he must act for us with God by doing and suffering all that we owed. In respect of the latter, he must act in the name of God towards us that by imparting to us the benefits of the covenant he might draw us into communion with him. His threefold office also demanded this.[111]

In what follows I discuss four aspects of Christ's exaltation: his resurrection from the dead, his ascension into heaven, his heavenly session at God's right hand, and his future return in glory. This section will not be as extensive as the section on Christ's humiliation; to counterbalance this, I have discussed aspects of Christ's exaltation earlier in this volume, especially in chapters 4–5.

The Resurrection of Christ

One of the clearest passages where we see the relationship between Christ's two states is in Philippians 2:5–11, especially the "therefore" (διό) in 2:9. Precisely because Jesus humbled himself in obedience unto death, therefore he has been highly exalted.[112] The resurrection is the reward for Christ's perfect obedience, including his obedience unto death.[113] By being raised from the dead, Christ was fully vindicated, emerging victorious over death (1 Tim 3:16). Geerhardus Vos explains two effects of Christ's resurrection:

> a) In coming out from under the curse and wrath of God, under which the Mediator had been in the state of His humiliation. This was followed by an entrance into the favor and full good pleasure of God that rested on Him as Mediator. The opposite of curse is blessing, and He is the Blessed of the Father.

111. Turretin, *Inst.* 13.9.3 (2.333).

112. Bavinck, *RD* 3:434.

113. The term "unto" (μέχρι) in Phil 2:8 most likely has Jesus's entire obedience in view, not only his death on the cross. See Crowe, *Why Did Jesus Live a Perfect Life?*, 133–37.

> b) In a change of condition coinciding with this exchange of legal position. Both in body and in soul it must be made clear that the curse had ceased and that the Mediator found Himself basking in the good pleasure of the Father. His exaltation is therefore at the same time glorification, just as the humiliation was also at the same time a shattering for Him.[114]

Jesus's resurrection was thus a judicial declaration that Jesus was "in the right," and this in turn provides the basis for the justification of all who trust in him (see Rom 4:24–25).[115] Christ's resurrection was also the firstfruits of the resurrection of all believers (1 Cor 15:20–23)—his resurrection realized Israel's hope of resurrection, and those in Christ will share in a resurrection like his (see, e.g., Acts 4:2; 26:6–8, 23).

Christ's resurrection therefore marked a transition from humiliation to glory. But the resurrection also demarcates two ages of redemptive history: Christ's resurrection marks the turning of the ages, from the age of anticipation to the age of fulfillment.[116] This helps us understand some of the difficult passages in Jesus's Farewell Discourse (John 13:31–16:33). Why did Jesus say that the Father was greater than he was (John 14:28), when earlier he said that he and the Father are one (10:30)? In the Farewell Discourse Jesus explained the transition that was coming when he, as the suffering servant (see 13:1–2), would be glorified on the other side of the cross.[117] When Jesus said that it would be good for his disciples if he went away, this was because he was about to emerge victorious over the grave and be exalted in heaven. When Christ was glorified, then he would pour out the Spirit (7:39; see also 20:22). This would usher in the greater age, which correlates to Christ's exaltation at the Father's right hand. This is why the disciples could do greater works than Jesus (14:12)—the greater works refer to the greater era of redemptive history contingent on Christ's resurrection and ascension.[118]

---

114. Vos, *Reformed Dogmatics* 3:219.

115. See, e.g., Turretin, *Inst.* 16.9.11 (2:685).

116. See Vos, "Eschatological Aspect of the Pauline Conception," 96, 107; Ridderbos, *John*, 512.

117. See Ferguson, *Lessons from the Upper Room*, 61–83.

118. See also Luke 20:34–35 (discussed in Crowe, *Hope of Israel*, 111); Turretin, *Inst.* 3.25.12 (1:269).

Paul makes a similar point. In Romans 1:3–4 the resurrection of Christ is correlated to the era of the Holy Spirit.[119] Likewise, in 1 Corinthians 15:44–47, Christ as resurrected last Adam is also characterized as life-giving Spirit (πνεῦμα ζῳοποιοῦν, 15:45) since there is such a close relationship between the Spirit and Christ in his resurrected state.[120] Thus, at Pentecost Peter explains that the outpouring of the Holy Spirit is proof that God has made (ἐποίησεν) Jesus both Lord and Christ (Acts 2:36). This "making" does not refer to any change in the essence of the Son of God but to a change in redemptive history: Christ has been raised from the dead and rules over the world (see Ps 110:1).[121] The Spirit's outpouring is therefore proof that Christ has risen and the eschatological age has arrived. From this point on there is a new aspect to Christ's lordship beyond what was true prior to the completion of his work of humiliation.[122]

The Rule of Christ: The Exaltation and Heavenly Session

Sometimes when Scripture speaks of Christ's exaltation, it is difficult to determine whether resurrection, ascension, or enthronement is in view (see, e.g., Acts 3:13). This reflects the close relationship between the aspects of Christ's state of exaltation.

Heidelberg Catechism 49 helpfully elaborates on Christ's ascension. First, as the ascended Lord is our advocate before the Father in heaven (1 John 2:1; see also Gregory Nazianzus, *Or.* 30.14). Second, Jesus, as a risen and glorified man, is present bodily in heaven as a guarantee that where he is, there we will one day be. Third, as noted in the previous section, the resurrected Lord pours out his Spirit. He also reigns from heaven over the whole world as the ascended priest-king after the order of Melchizedek, as Hebrews makes clear. This principle invokes Psalm 110:1, perhaps the most-quoted Old Testament passage in the New Testament.

In chapter 5, I argued that it is reductionistic to understand Jesus's priestly ministry in Hebrews to be entirely in heaven. But it is prudent to emphasize that Hebrews does indeed teach that Christ is presently and

119. Vos, "Eschatological Aspect of the Pauline Conception," 103–5; Gaffin, *Centrality of the Resurrection*, 98–113

120. Gaffin, *Centrality of the Resurrection*, 62–66.

121. See Turretin, *Inst.* 3.28.31 (1:290); Athanasius, *C. Ar.* 1.41.

122. Crowe, *Hope of Israel*, 114.

properly a priest in heaven (e.g., Heb 6:19–20; 7:25; 8:1–2; 10:12). It is as our exalted priest that Christ appears bodily in heaven, "in the merit of his obedience and sacrifice on earth," quieting our consciences and providing access to the throne of grace (4:14–16).[123] Indeed, Christ serves permanently in the heavenly sanctuary (7:16–17), the true holy of holies, which provided the pattern for the earthly tabernacle (Heb 1:3; 10:12).

Further, as priest-king Jesus reigns over a worldwide kingdom as the final Son of David. This point is emphasized in Acts, which says much about the role of Christ as exalted Lord over all (e.g., Acts 10:36; 17:30–31). His kingdom shall never end, for he reigns as the resurrected one who inherits the promise to David's offspring of an everlasting kingdom (2 Sam 7:12–16; Luke 1:31–33; see also Acts 15:15–18).

The Return of Christ THE EXALTATION OF CHRIST ALSO entails his future return as judge of the world. The one who was judged unjustly will return (visibly) in power and with a full display of his glory to judge the world in righteousness (WLC 56). It is worth observing that Scripture teaches Christ will return once and visibly—it does not teach discrete returns that include a secret rapture of the church.

Scripture says much about the return of Christ.[124] In the Gospels the return of Christ is sometimes mentioned explicitly (e.g., Matt 24:29–31, 36–44; 26:64; Luke 17:24), but is also anticipated in Christ's transfiguration (Matt 17:1–8; see also 2 Pet 1:16–19), which unveiled his divine glory and anticipates the glory that will be manifested when Christ returns.[125] Jesus's return in Acts is said to be on the clouds, just as he ascended into heaven (Acts 1:11; see also Luke 24:50). His return will result in the renewal of all things (Acts 3:20–21; see also Matt 19:28).

Likewise Paul clearly believes Christ will return (1 Cor 15:23; 1 Thess 4:15–16; 5:23; 2 Thess 1:7, 10; 2:1–9; see also Acts 17:30–31), and the author of Hebrews writes that our great high priest will return from heaven to save those who await him (Heb 9:28). The Catholic Epistles give a great deal of attention to the return of Christ. James speaks of Christ's return as the

---

123. Following WLC 55.

124. Some of these passages come from Berkhof, *Systematic Theology*, 695–707.

125. See also Poythress, *Theophany*, 385.

coming of the Lord and judge (Jas 5:7–9). Peter encourages his readers to persevere in faithfulness until the revelation of Jesus Christ, which will be a day of grace for his people (1 Pet 1:7, 13; 2:12; 4:13). Second Peter was written in large measure to encourage professing believers to live consistently with the path of righteousness because Jesus really is coming back to restore all things (2 Pet 1:19; 3:3–13). Jude mentions the coming of the Lord and warns that it will be a day of punishment for the ungodly (Jude 14–15) but a day of mercy for his people (21). The book of Revelation, though it is about much more than only the return of Christ, does indeed help us focus on Christ's return as well. Jesus will return to execute judgment on his enemies and deliver his people (Rev 19:11–16; 21:1–22:5). We do not know when he is coming back (Matt 24:36; Mark 13:32), but we know he is coming soon (ταχύ, Rev 22:7, 20).

CONCLUSION

One can summarize the work of Christ in a number of ways; in this chapter I have considered Christ's threefold office as prophet, priest, and king in relation to his two states (humiliation and exaltation). In the incarnation Christ has done for us what we could not do for ourselves. Having humbled himself in obedience unto death (state of humiliation), he has been vindicated and raised as our prophet, priest, and king (state of exaltation). He has come in the fullness of time and redeemed us from the curse of the law, yet as the one Mediator between God and humanity his work also applies trans-testamentally, covering both Old Testament believers and New Testament believers (see WCF 11.4, 6). In both cases the way we benefit from Christ's work is by faith, resting on his work alone for salvation.

FURTHER READING

Anselm of Canterbury. *Cur Deus Homo? [Why the God-Man?]*. Pages 100–183 in *A Scholastic Miscellany: Anselm to Ockham*. Edited and translated by Eugene R. Fairweather. Philadelphia: Westminster, 1956. Anselm's work explains the logic of why a God-man must make satisfaction for sins. It was foundational for later discussions of vicarious satisfaction.

Bavinck, Herman. *Sin and Salvation in Christ*. Vol. 3 of *Reformed Dogmatics*. Edited by John Bolt. Translated by John Vriend. Grand Rapids: Baker Academic, 2006, esp. part 3 (323–482). Bavinck writes with a wide knowledge of the history of Christian theology and is also a sensitive exegete. His discussion of the unified obedience of Christ is excellent. For a more concise discussion, see Bavinck, *The Wonderful Works of God: Instruction in the Christian Religion according to the Reformed Confession*, trans. Henry Zylstra (repr., Glenside, PA: Westminster Seminary Press, 2019).

Letham, Robert. *The Work of Christ*. CCT. Downers Grove, IL: InterVarsity Press, 1993. Letham considers the work of Christ as prophet, priest, and king and shows the relationship of Christ's entire work—his death and resurrection as well as his obedient life—to our justification.

Packer, J. I. "What Did the Cross Achieve? The Logic of Penal Substitution." *TynBul* 25 (1974): 3–45. Packer provides a comparably brief but compelling articulation and defense of substitutionary, penal atonement, written with an eye to personal application as well. See also Packer's introductory essay to John Owen, *The Death of Death in the Death of Christ* (Edinburgh: Banner of Truth, 1959).

XI

THE CENTRALITY OF CHRISTOLOGY FOR CHRISTIAN DOGMATICS

SUMMING UP ALL THINGS IN CHRIST

The Christian faith hinges on Christ himself: who he is and what he has done. He is the central focus of Scripture and the only Mediator for all humanity. In this final chapter on Christ in dogmatic perspective, it is appropriate to consider briefly the priority and centrality of Christ in Scripture and in theology. In what follows I illustrate first the centrality of Christ in Scripture and second the centrality of Christ in systematic-theological constructions.

CHRIST-CENTERED BIBLICAL THEOLOGY

It is no imposition on Scripture to posit that Christ is central to Scripture; Jesus himself and the apostles make this point on numerous occasions. After his resurrection Luke's Gospel includes two explanations from Jesus about how it was necessary (δεῖ) for him to fulfill the Old Testament by suffering and rising again and that this message must go forth from Jerusalem (Luke 24:25–27, 44–47). First Peter 1:10–11 makes a similar point: the Old Testament prophets inquired about the manner and time of the coming Christ's suffering and his subsequent glory. In Luke Jesus critiques his disciples for being slow to understand that the Scriptures were about him. Similarly, in John 5 Jesus tells his religious opponents that the Scriptures bear witness to him and that Moses wrote about him (John 5:39, 46). If they believed Moses, they ought to believe Jesus himself, for the prophets in the holy Scriptures promised beforehand the gospel of God's Son (Rom 1:1–2). For indeed, the prophets already bore witness to forgiveness of sins through him (Acts 10:43). He is the preexistent Word of God to whom and by whom Scripture in its entirety testifies.

This point was widely appreciated by the church fathers. Irenaeus saw Scriptures held together in Christ (*Haer.* 4.2.3; 4.33.10).[1] Brevard Childs writes, "Origen assumes that all of Scripture is about the presence of the Logos that defines its content."[2] Of Cyril of Alexandria, Robert Louis Wilken observes: "The Bible is a book about God's revelation in Christ, hence the interpreter must set the ancient stories within a frame of reference that includes Christ."[3]

Thus, when at the conclusion of the Bible Jesus speaks of himself as the Alpha and the Omega, the first and the last, the beginning and the end (Rev 22:13), he emphasizes his own role as the divine Son of God who is eternal and supreme in all things. He is supreme not just at the polarities of the beginning and the end but at the beginning, the end, and everything in between. This statement applies generally to the Son of God, but it can also apply to Scripture itself. If the Son is supreme over all creation, he is also supreme in Scripture itself.

At the same time, we must appreciate that the New Testament is clearer and fuller than the Old Testament in its witness to Christ. This is where biblical theology makes an important contribution. Reformed biblical theology understands the Old Testament and New Testament to be fundamentally unified, testifying to the one covenant of grace (see the next section), but it also allows for real development as well. After Adam's failure in the covenant of works, the Lord was gracious to Adam and Eve and promised that the woman's offspring would come and crush the head of the serpent (Gen 3:15). This promise is progressively fulfilled in Scripture, especially

---

1. Noted in Osborn, *Irenaeus of Lyons*, 183–85.

2. Brevard Childs, *The Struggle to Understand Isaiah as Christian Scripture* (Grand Rapids: Eerdmans, 2004), 68–69.

3. Wilken, "St. Cyril of Alexandria," 461; see also 478.

through the covenants God makes with key representatives.[4] God made a covenant with Noah (Gen 6:18; 9:1–17), which included the re-creation of the world and the repetition of commands given to Adam (9:7; see also 1:28). Next comes God's covenant with Abraham, in which he promised Abraham a land and many descendants (e.g., Gen 12:1–3; 13:15–16; 15:5; 17:7–8)—yet Paul makes it clear that ultimately the promise to Abraham is focused on a single descendant, Jesus Christ (Gal 3:16). In the Mosaic covenant God gave his people his law (Exod 19–23) and set forth Moses as the paradigm of prophet (Deut 18:15, 18) and mediator (Exod 33:12–23). Later God made a covenant with David (2 Sam 7:12–16), promising him an everlasting kingdom and setting the stage for understanding the kingly work of Christ, who reigns over a worldwide, everlasting kingdom.

Christ is the Mediator of the new covenant—the everlasting covenant (Heb 9:15; 12:24; 13:20)—which brings the fulfillment of the promises to the patriarchs. He is the prophet like Moses (see Luke 9:35), and the one who reigns over the house of David forever (1:31–33), also fulfilling Jacob's prophecy of a ruler from Judah (Gen 49:10). Further, as the last Adam, Christ is the seed of the woman who crushes the head of the serpent (compare Gen 3:15; Rom 16:20). The new covenant has been inaugurated and is already here in principle, though its consummation and perfection lie in the future. The new covenant is new, but it is not entirely without precedent, as it builds on the covenants that came before.

Further, already in the Old Testament God's people were saved by faith rather than works. New Testament examples of justification, for example, include Abraham and David, who were saved by faith alone (Gen 15:6; Ps 32:1–2; Rom 4:1–25; Heb 11:1–40). The New Testament thus does not set forth a fundamentally different way of salvation, but speaks of an essential unity between God's covenant dealings with humanity in both the Old Testament and New Testament. This reflects what Vos refers to as the "organic nature" of biblical theology, in which later revelation assumes and builds on prior revelation.[5] Beyond this, all of revelation focuses on Jesus Christ himself,

4. For concise introductions, see Richard P. Belcher Jr., *The Fulfillment of the Promises of God: An Explanation of Covenant Theology* (Fearn, UK: Mentor, 2020); Thomas R. Schreiner, *Covenant and God's Purpose for the World*, Short Studies in Biblical Theology (Wheaton, IL: Crossway, 2017); Crowe, *Path of Faith*.

5. Vos, *Biblical Theology*, 7–8.

who is present as the Son of God in the shadows of the Old Testament—for indeed, he was already Mediator in the Old Testament (e.g., 1 Tim 2:5)—and is more fully revealed in the New Testament in conjunction with his once-for-all incarnate work.

Biblical theology therefore should draw attention to the unity of God's covenantal dealings with humanity across the ages, even as it appreciates the glorious, climactic work of the triune God in the incarnation of the Son of God. The coming of Christ excels the glories of the Old Testament, for in Christ we see the glory of God with unveiled face (2 Cor 3:7–18). We do injustice to the biblical texts if we deny Christ's presence and activity already in the Old Testament, yet we also do injustice to the biblical texts if we deny that a greater, fuller glory came when the Son of God took on flesh. We must have a theological system that appreciates both the preexistent work of the Son and also his role as the goal of biblical theology.[6] Put differently, Christ must be central in our theology, even as we must appreciate the various ways we see Christ in Scripture.

We must have a trans-testamental hermeneutic that allows for the presence and activity of the Son of God already in the Old Testament portions of redemptive history prior to his unique work in the incarnation. This approach is problematic for those who deny the preexistence of Christ and the supernatural character of Scripture. Scripture itself compels us to understand the one who came for us and for our salvation to be the eternal Son of God active already in the Old Testament.

CHRIST-CENTERED SYSTEMATIC THEOLOGY

Given the primacy of Adam and Christ in the Bible's understanding of God's covenants with humanity, another approach to Christ-centered interpretation is to organize all of the Bible under two, overarching covenants: the covenant of works made with Adam (WLC 20) and the covenant of grace made with Christ (WLC 31).[7] This approach is established in Reformed covenant theology, but it also reflects a long history of biblical interpretation that sees Christ's role as the second and last Adam to be programmatic for all of

6. See also Barrett, *Canon, Covenant, and Christology*, 20, 45, 47.

7. For a chart, see Crowe, *Path of Faith*, 20.

Scripture: the latter days are like the beginning but better.[8] Thomas Goodwin memorably states that Paul, in texts such as Romans 5, speaks as if there had only been two men (Adam and Christ), and all people hang either from the belts of one or the other.[9] This approach appreciates that God's covenant with Adam was distinct from later covenants, because only with Adam in his state of integrity was eternal life possible by means of perfect obedience, according to God's covenantal design. In that created state it was possible for Adam not to sin (*posse non peccare*), but it was also possible for him to sin (*posse peccare*). After Adam's sin it was not possible for humankind not to sin (*non posse non peccare*). When Christ came as the incarnate Mediator in the fullness of time, he took on the mantle of perfect obedience required of Adam in the beginning and ushered in the eschatological age of the Spirit, which will consummate in the glorious state, in which it will not be possible to sin (*non posse peccare*).[10]

This overarching, bicovenantal schema holds many advantages for appreciating the Christ-centeredness of Scripture. This structure highlights the unity of God's plan of salvation across the Testaments and explains how Old Testament believers can be saved by Christ prior to his incarnation—it is because Christ was already the Mediator in the Old Testament, and the work of Christ is applied to all believers from the beginning of the world onward (WCF 8.6). His work is seen in the types, promises, and sacrifices of the Old Testament, which pointed to the coming offspring of the woman who would crush the serpent's head. Thus, Old Testament believers were saved by faith in Christ just as New Testament believers are; there is fundamental (i.e., essential) unity of the means and substance of salvation between the Old Testament and New Testament, even as we find real distinctions with respect to knowledge, fullness, experience, and so forth.[11] This schema also guards the uniqueness of Christ's work, for only

8. See Crowe, *Last Adam*, 7–11.

9. Thomas Goodwin, *Christ Set Forth*, vol. 4 of *The Works of Thomas Goodwin* (Edinburgh: James Nichol, 1862), 31. See also F. F. Bruce, *Romans*, 2nd ed., TNTC (Grand Rapids: Eerdmans, 1985), 120.

10. See Marianne Djuth, "Liberty," in *Augustine through the Ages: An Encyclopedia*, ed. Allan D. Fitzgerald (Grand Rapids: Eerdmans, 1999), 495–98; Muller, *Dictionary of Latin and Greek*, 200, 233–34, 269.

11. See Calvin, *Inst.* 2.10–11 (1:428–64); Turretin, *Inst.* 12.7–8 (2:216–40).

Christ, the last Adam, can meet the requirements of perfect obedience for eternal life.

Put simply, if Christ is central in Scripture, then Christ must be central in our systematic theology. The traditional loci of systematic theology—such as the doctrines of revelation, God, creation, humanity, salvation, church, sacraments, and last things—must all be understood in relation to Christ himself. To illustrate:

> Scripture/revelation: Christ is the one Mediator for Old Testament and New Testament believers, and the Old Testament speaks already of him. The Son is the Word of God who preeminently makes God known—both in Old Testament and more fully in the New Testament.
>
> God: we do not understand God abstractly, but the biblical God is the triune God, whom we meet face-to-face in Jesus Christ.
>
> Creation: the Son is the agent of creation and is indeed the goal of creation (Col 1:16).
>
> Humanity: Jesus Christ is the true human who is the standard for all others—he was perfectly sinless and realizes the full dignity of our nature, raising it to new heights (WLC 39).
>
> The church: the church is the people of God, which has its foundation not merely in the assembly of the Lord in the Old Testament but in the core group of apostles chosen by Christ himself.
>
> The sacraments: Further, it is Christ himself who instituted the two sacraments of baptism and the Lord's Supper, which are to mark the New Testament church.
>
> Last things: Finally, the world will be consummated when Christ himself returns as Lord and Judge of all.

This is not an exhaustive survey, much less discussion, of how Christ relates to some key loci of systematic theology, but it illustrates how Christ must be central in dogmatics.

CONCLUSION

Put simply, Christ is the high point and focal point of God's special revelation in Scripture.[12] To read Scripture rightly we must never lose sight of Christ, and thus we must also ensure that our theological formulations, which reflect Scripture, never lose sight of Christ either. For all things are summed up in him (Eph 1:10).

FURTHER READING

Barrett, Matthew. *Canon, Covenant, and Christology: Rethinking Jesus and the Scriptures of Israel.* NSBT 51. Downers Grove, IL: IVP Academic, 2020. Barrett considers the centrality of Christ in Scripture and its implications for the doctrine of Scripture.

Belcher, Richard P., Jr. *The Fulfillment of the Promises of God: An Explanation of Covenant Theology*. Fearn, UK: Mentor, 2020. This introductory survey of confessional Reformed covenantal theology explains difficult issues with clarity and interacts with other views of covenant theology as well.

Pass, Bruce R. *The Heart of Dogmatics: Christology and Christocentrism in Herman Bavinck*. Forschungen zur systematischen und ökumenischen Theologie 169. Göttingen: Vandenhoeck & Ruprecht, 2020. Pass's monograph addresses the role of Christology in Bavinck's theology.

Webster, John. "The Place of Christology in Systematic Theology." Pages 611–27 in *The Oxford Handbook of Christology*. Edited by Francesca Aran Murphy. Oxford: Oxford University Press, 2015. Contextualizes the role of Christology in systematic theology, focusing on theology and economy.

12. See Bavinck, *RD* 1:347; Bavinck, *Wonderful Works of God*, 20.

PART 3

TRUTH FOR WORSHIP, LIFE, AND MISSION

XII

THE GOSPEL OF GRACE

LIFE IN THE SON

We come now to part 3 of this book, where I consider briefly some additional practical implications of the person and work of Christ. Here in chapter 12, I consider the relationship of Christ himself to the gospel message. In short, we cannot separate the gospel message from Christ himself, nor can we add anything to his work. Instead, we must be united to him by faith, and in that context we discuss a range of redemptive benefits. Further, the gospel is a message that must be proclaimed, for it indeed is a message of good news.

CHRIST-CENTERED GOSPEL

The good news of the gospel is that Jesus Christ does for us what we cannot do for ourselves. No person in Adam can perfectly obey the law of God, yet perfect obedience was never rescinded as the means of inheriting eternal life. Further, sin deserves the wrath of God, and no sinner is able to escape this wrath by personal obedience, for no human obedience is sufficient to withstand the wrath of God. This is why it is also necessary for our redeemer to be divine, to withstand the wrath of God and grant us eternal life. This was at stake in so many of the early church controversies: Is our Redeemer a man who by apotheosis became God? Or is he God who became man? The orthodox are clear that our Savior is God who became human, thus descending to do for us what we could not do for ourselves.

The beauty of the gospel, which we do well to linger over, is that Jesus Christ, who is fully God and fully man, is our Mediator. He is the truly faithful man, and as the divine Son, his work is sufficient to bear the wrath of God against sin and lift us to heaven. Jesus is our wisdom, righteousness, sanctification, and redemption (1 Cor 1:30). Further, we will not appreciate the good news of the gospel if we do not appreciate that this is the free grace of God—there was no compulsion for Christ to become a man and suffer for us. His obedience was rendered for us, not for himself. He was under no compulsion; he did it out of his own love and good pleasure.[1]

The good news of the gospel thus entails both the person of Christ and his work. There is nothing for us to add to his work, for it is perfect. This is why understanding faith appropriately is so important: too often faith is misconstrued as a work, as though we could add something to what Christ has done. But there is no supplementing the work of Christ; it is perfect, complete, and unique. We therefore must understand faith as an instrument, the means by which we benefit from Christ's work.[2] His obedience for us is the obedience of the God-man, and it delivers us from our inability to obey God's law perfectly, yielding forgiveness of sins and eternal life.

It is a liberating reality to understand that Christ has done all that is necessary for salvation, for we too often think that we can somehow supplement the work of Christ.[3] Paul struggles against this perversion of the gospel in Galatians. Anytime we posit that the gospel is Christ plus anything we misconstrue and twist the gospel of free grace. Our works are never good enough or pure enough to contribute in any way to our justification before God. The gospel teaches us that we instead find our solace and comfort in our Savior, who loved us and gave himself for us (Gal 2:20).

This means that when we speak of the gospel of Jesus Christ, we must never divorce the message from the person of Christ himself. When we come to the gospel, we come to Christ. We are not saved because of our faith, but our faith unites us to Christ himself. To believe the gospel is to

---

1. See Owen, *Works* 1:333–39, 355.

2. For further discussion and defense, see Crowe, *Why Did Jesus Live a Perfect Life?*, 159–62.

3. See Sinclair B. Ferguson, *The Whole Christ: Legalism, Antinomianism, and Gospel Assurance—Why the Marrow Controversy Still Matters* (Wheaton, IL: Crossway, 2016).

believe in Christ himself.[4] There can be a subtle pull away from Christ himself when we begin to talk about the gospel and think of the wonderful benefits that salvation entails. However, we must not abstract these benefits from Christ himself, for it is Christ entirely who is our hope. Bavinck explains:

> The righteousness which justifies us, therefore, is not to be separated from the person of Christ. ... There is no possibility of sharing in the benefits of Christ without being in fellowship with the person of Christ. ... In order to stand before the judgment of God, to be acquitted of all guilt and punishment, and to share in the glory of God and eternal life, we must have Christ, not something of Him, but Christ Himself. ... The crucified and glorified Christ is the righteousness which God grants us through grace in the [*sic*] justification. ... And then we can stand before His presence as though we had never had sin, or done sin, indeed, as though we had ourselves achieved the obedience which Christ has achieved for us.[5]

If Christ himself is the gospel, then we must give due attention to this good news of Christ throughout all of Scripture. We don't simply find the gospel in the letters of Paul; we find it in the Old Testament. For the Old Testament prophets prophesied of Christ by the Spirit of Christ (1 Pet 1:10–12), and all the Scriptures point to Christ, in whom there is life (John 5:39–40). The way of salvation by grace through faith is not only found in the New Testament, but began already with the institution of the covenant of grace in the Old Testament (e.g., Gen 3:15; John 1:16). Attention to the good news of Christ in Scripture should also account for the good news of the Gospels themselves, in which we find a sustained focus on Christ himself. To whatever texts we turn in Scripture, we must always ask how they speak of Christ himself and his work for us. The themes of prophet, priest, and king are quite helpful in this regard.

UNION WITH CHRIST AND FULL SALVATION

WHEN WE SPEAK OF THE obedience of Christ for us and how we are made right with God by faith alone, we are

4. See Owen, *Works* 1:127–31.
5. Bavinck, *Wonderful Works of God*, 436; see also Bavinck, *RD* 4:263.

speaking particularly of justification. Crucially, the foundation of our justification before God is not our own works, a combination of our works and Christ's work, or even our faith. May it never be! Instead, the foundation of our justification is the perfect obedience of Jesus Christ, in both its active and passive dimensions. This means that the righteousness that is counted for believers in justification is in no way the believer's own righteousness, but is the entire, perfect righteousness of Jesus Christ. This is what is intended by the term "imputation": the righteousness counted to the believer in justification remains the righteousness of Christ (i.e., it does not bring into view the believer's growth in holiness), and this righteousness is legally reckoned to believers by faith alone. This guards the unique obedience of Christ that is the foundation for our acceptance before God, which is at the heart of the good news of the gospel. When we are united to Christ by faith, his righteousness is counted to us, and we are therefore counted righteous in Christ.

Further, to speak of faith in Christ as central to the gospel message is to speak of union with Christ by faith. Union with Christ is not one-dimensional, but brings into view a range of redemptive benefits comprising salvation: justification, adoption, sanctification, glorification, and so forth.[6] All these benefits find their context in union with Christ.[7]

Christ himself is our salvation. And just as surely as he has risen from the dead, justified from death, he provides the certainty of our future, resurrection, and eternal life. To look at Christ is to see the one who lived the life of perfect conformity to the law of God. It is also to look on the one who has risen triumphant over sin and death and lives now in a glorified body. In this way also Christ is a pattern for us: he saves not only our souls but also our bodies. For creation is good, and our bodies are part of God's good creation. Though we have been corrupted by sin in body and soul, Christ redeems us in body and soul so that we will live forever in the new heavens and new earth in glorified bodies.

---

6. See especially John Murray, *Redemption Accomplished and Applied* (Grand Rapids: Eerdmans, 1955).

7. See the programmatic comments of Calvin, *Inst.* 3.1.1 (1:537–38). See also Gregory of Nazianzus, *Or.* 30.19 (*NPNF*[2] 7:317).

GOSPEL MISSION

The gospel is good news, and we are commanded to proclaim this good news to the end of the earth (Acts 1:8). Two passages here illustrate the centrality of the Christ-centered gospel message that we are to take to the end of the earth.

First is 2 Corinthians 5:17–21, a text that speaks of Christ's substitutionary death on our behalf (5:21). Christ became sin so that we might become the righteousness of God in him. This statement is best taken as a discussion of justification, and the righteousness of God is thus best taken as our status in God's sight. We have been reconciled and have been given the ministry of reconciliation (5:18), which includes the message of reconciliation (5:19). Though Paul is speaking primarily about his apostolic task in this text, the apostolic focus on the gospel message is equally suitable for all those who are part of God's new creation in Christ (5:17). Together with the realities of reconciliation through Christ, then, comes the spreading of that message as ambassadors on Christ's behalf (5:20). The two go hand in hand, for hearing and responding to the message of reconciliation is the ordinary means by which people are reconciled to God. Again in 2 Corinthians 5:17–21 Paul emphasizes that this reconciliation occurs "in him," that is, in Christ.

The emphasis on the necessity of the message of salvation is also in view in Romans 10:1–21. As I argued in chapter 10, in this passage Paul contrasts the path of righteousness by works, which is impossible (Rom 10:5; see Lev 18:5), with the righteousness that comes by faith (Rom 10:6). Crucially, that righteousness finds its focus in Christ himself (10:6–10). We are not to ascend into heaven ("that is, bring Christ down"), nor descend into the abyss ("that is, to bring Christ up from the dead"), for Christ has already done these things for us (Rom 10:6–7). To be saved we simply must confess with our mouths and believe in our hearts that Jesus is Lord (10:9–13).

But for someone to call on Christ for salvation, that person must know about Christ. Paul asks rhetorically a series of questions in Romans 10:14–17:

> How then will they call on him in whom they have not believed? And how are they to believe in him of whom they have never heard? And how are they to hear without someone preaching? And how are they to preach unless they are sent? As it is written, "How beautiful are the feet of those who preach the good news!" [Isa 52:7] But they have not all obeyed the gospel.

> For Isaiah says, "Lord, who has believed what he has heard from us?" [Isa 53:1] So faith comes from hearing, and hearing through the word of Christ.

In other words, salvation comes by faith in Christ, but for someone to believe in Christ, that person must know about Christ. Therefore, we must labor to ensure that preachers are being sent forth to tell people about Christ. This provides crucial logic for missions and provides a framework for the spread of the gospel message: this good news that comes by faith in Christ and not by works of the law entails a message that must be proclaimed. Certainly that message must remain a Christ-centered message, for Paul's point here and throughout Romans is that Christ has done for us what we could not do by our own obedience to the law. For Christ is the end or goal of the law (Rom 10:4), so we only truly understand the law if we understand its relationship to Christ himself. To be clear, Paul speaks not of faith in an abstract sense that yields salvation but specifically of faith in Christ himself. Our faith must be directed toward the proper object—the person of Jesus Christ himself.

This also assumes that what Jesus did for us really matters. The apostolic preaching in Acts is not generic but specifically about Christ himself and what he did. Jesus from Nazareth, though he was crucified, has been resurrected as both Lord and Christ (Acts 2:32–36). As the resurrected Lord over all (10:36), Christ is returning to judge all people (17:30–31). Just as all people come from one man (17:26; see also Luke 3:38), so in Christ, the last Adam, salvation is offered to all people through Jesus Christ. No matter our past, no matter what we have done, the call is to receive forgiveness of sins and new life through Christ. In a striking example, this message was even offered to those in some way culpable for the murder of Christ (Acts 2:36–40). Yet there was nothing they could do to earn forgiveness; instead, the call was to receive Christ by faith by turning to him, which entails turning away from sin. Those who turn to Christ are promised forgiveness of sins and the Holy Spirit. Though it took different forms, in Acts this message was preached to audiences all over the ancient world, including Jerusalem, Samaria, Philippi, Athens, Corinth, Ephesus, and Rome.

We today are likewise called to proclaim unceasingly this message of salvation by grace through faith and support others in this task as well. This good news is not only for one group or nation, but it is for all people.

For Christ reigns now from heaven over the entire world, and the message about Christ is a message for the whole world.

CONCLUSION

THE FOCUS OF THIS BOOK on the person and work of Christ provides the proper context for the gospel message. The gospel is not a transactional message about abstract concepts but a message about Jesus Christ and our relationship to him. He himself is our Savior, and he invites us to come to him to find life (Matt 11:28–30; John 20:30–31).

FURTHER READING

Ferguson, Sinclair B. *The Whole Christ: Legalism, Antinomianism, and Gospel Assurance—Why the Marrow Controversy Still Matters*. Wheaton, IL: Crossway, 2016. Ferguson considers how Christ himself is the answer to the dangers of both antinomianism and legalism.

Köstenberger, Andreas J., with T. Desmond Alexander. *Salvation to the Ends of the Earth: A Biblical Theology of Mission*. 2nd ed. NSBT 53. Downers Grove, IL: IVP Academic, 2020. This biblical-theological study of mission in the Bible includes significant discussion on mission's relation to Christ.

Murray, John. *Redemption Accomplished and Applied*. Grand Rapids: Eerdmans, 1955. Murray's work is a classic, expounding the work of Christ and its benefits to the believer.

XIII

PLURALISM AND THE UNIQUENESS OF CHRIST

NO OTHER NAME

In this chapter, I turn to some other issues in applying Christology to our world today: How does the distinctiveness of Christ relate to all people? How is one to think of the gospel in a world of so many competing claims? How do we understand claims of exclusivity with respect to Christ, and how do we adjudicate the view that there are multiple paths to God (i.e., pluralism)? This chapter will venture a brief discussion of such issues.

CHRIST THE ONLY SAVIOR

The Bible teaches that there is only one Mediator between God and humanity—the man Christ Jesus (1 Tim 2:5). There is no other name given among humankind by which we can be saved (Acts 4:12). Jesus is the way, the truth, and the life, and the only way to the Father in heaven (John 14:6). Such exclusive claims often sound arrogant in a pluralistic world. But if the Bible's explanation about the plight of humanity is correct (which it is), and if the Bible is correct about the unity of humanity (which it is), and if the Bible is correct about who God is (which it is), then the exclusivity of Jesus as the way to salvation makes perfect sense. Additionally, it is not arrogant to say that the personal God who created us can speak to us in ways we can understand, and if he speaks, then we must listen. It is not up to us to determine what is proper and improper for God, but we must submit to what he has revealed. Indeed, one might argue instead that it is arrogant to think that God cannot speak to us and that, if he did, we would not be able to understand. This also brings us back to the doctrine of Scripture, which is a necessary presupposition for understanding the logic of the exclusivity of Christ.

In sum, the one true God over all the world—for he created the entire world—is triune: Father, Son, and Spirit. No other religion affirms this; if one does not affirm the biblical God, we must conclude that one is not affirming who God truly is. The true God is the Creator of all people, and all people naturally owe obedience to him. Yet God is also a covenantal God and offered humanity a reward for obedience, through the headship of Adam in the beginning. When Adam failed, it affected all people, for all people descend from Adam as the first man (e.g., Acts 17:26). The unity of the human race is part of the logic for why there is only one way to the Father: there are no other human persons who exist outside the realm of God's covenant dealings with Adam. Only Christ, as a divine person who became a true man, stands outside of the covenant of works with Adam. Only Christ has emerged victorious over death and ushers in the realm of new creation, which is seen in his resurrection from the dead, and will consummate in the new heavens and the new earth.

This risen Christ rules over the entire world; he is not simply the Messiah of one nation (see Acts 10:36). When Christ as the last Adam came, his work was rendered for those who are naturally in Adam. This does not, however, mean that all persons are automatically saved because of what Christ has done. The New Testament would not make sense if this were our perspective, for faith in Christ is required for salvation, and there are plenty we meet and read about in the New Testament who do not have true, saving faith in Christ.

Thus, Christ is the only Savior because only Christ is the God-man who came to do for us what we could not do for ourselves. He is God come down to save us, not a man who became God (see, e.g., Athanasius, *C. Ar.* 1.39). Christianity teaches that because of our sin, we are unable to save ourselves; sin is a universal human condition that renders us unable to do any truly good, saving work. Yet the good news of the gospel is that Christ has come to do for us what we could not do for ourselves.

CHRIST THE SAVIOR FOR ALL

Perhaps surprisingly, the logic of the exclusivity of Christ also points to the relevance of Christ for all people: Christ is the Creator of all people, he is the true human being, and he rules from heaven over the entire world—he is the one Savior for all people. In this sense, all people are invited to come to Christ; there is no other way for anyone to be saved apart from Christ.

That Jesus is the one Savior for all people is especially clear in Acts, where the movement from Jerusalem to all Judea and Samaria and to the end of the earth (Acts 1:8) also illustrates the relevance of the gospel of Christ for all people. Yes, Christ is the hope of Israel (28:20), but the prophets of Israel also spoke of an age when the nations would come to the light of Jerusalem (Isa 2; Mic 4). And already in the Gospels we see anticipations of the work of Christ beyond Israel to the nations (e.g., Matt 2:1–12; 8:5–13; 28:18–20; Mark 7:24–30; John 12:19–26).

And as we saw in the previous chapter, there is no one good enough on one's own to come to Jesus; for all have sinned and fall short of the glory of God (Rom 3:23). We misunderstand the gospel if we seek to limit it to one people group or one special faction in the church. This was one of the problems of the Pharisees in the New Testament (e.g., Luke 7:36–50) and also appears to have been one of the problems of the schismatics in 1 John who claimed special insight. In response, the apostle John insisted that Jesus is the Savior for the whole world (e.g., 1 John 2:2); the apostle Paul makes a similar point (1 Tim 4:10). Yet in both cases faith in Christ is also emphasized—for only those who trust in Christ receive forgiveness and truly have Christ as Savior (see also 1 John 5:13)

Jesus Christ is the Savior of the whole world: and the offer of the gospel is to be freely extended to all who would come. All are invited to come to Christ; there is no prior accomplishment, background, pedigree, sin, ethnicity, religious commitment, or any other factor that either qualifies or disqualifies someone from coming to Christ. Jesus is not just the Savior for Westerners, as the wonderful growth of Christianity in the Global South in recent years has made increasingly obvious. Jesus of Nazareth came as the Jewish Messiah from Galilee. But this true Son of David is the Savior of Jews and gentiles, as Paul labored so assiduously to make clear (e.g., Gal 3:26–29; Eph 2:11–22).

Indeed, the book of Acts that insists Jesus is the only Savior (Acts 4:12) is the same book that finds the spread of the gospel to the whole world: the message about Christ as Savior is not only for the religious of Jerusalem but for the lost sheep of Samaria, for the Roman centurion Cornelius, for the Philippian jailer and Lydia of Philippi, for the council of the Areopagus in Athens, for both Jews and Greeks in Ephesus, and for those in Rome itself. In other words, the claim in Acts 4:12 is complemented by the missions to the end of the earth we see in foundational form in Acts, illustrating that the message about Christ's exclusivity is to be taken to all people, in order that they might turn and be saved.

THE GOSPEL FOR A PLURALISTIC WORLD

If Christ is therefore the Savior of the whole world, we must take the message to all parts of the world. This message is relevant for all people, but it is also a different message from all other religions. For only Christianity teaches that God the Son himself came down and became a true man, without ceasing to be God, to grant eternal life in fellowship with the triune God.

This point must be emphasized, for in popular sentiment it is common to hear that all religions teach the same basic truths and/or that all roads lead to God (i.e., pluralism). While there is a universal *sensus divinitatis* ("sense of the divine") in all people, this does not mean that all religions teach the same thing. In reality, religious beliefs are often mutually exclusive and offer competing visions of reality. The more one knows about these various religions, the more difficult it is to conclude that they teach basically the same thing.

Either the true God exists eternally in three persons, or he does not. Both cannot be true.

Either the second person of the Trinity has taken a human nature and conquered sin, rising to eternal life, and grants life to all who believe in him, or he has not. Both cannot be true.

Either Jesus is the way, the truth, and the life, and the only way to the Father, or he is not. Both cannot be true.

The Scriptures teach that God is triune, that Christ is the eternal Son of God who has taken a human nature and accomplished salvation as the God-man, and that he is the way, the truth, and the life. This is true no matter where one lives.

It is easy to grow lethargic in our understanding of Christ and his work and assume that it really does not matter what we believe as long as we are sincere. Interestingly, something like this appears already to have been a problem addressed in the New Testament, for as William Lane argues with respect to the Christology of Hebrews, "the readers' lethargy derives from their failure to grasp the full significance of Christ."[1] Hebrews makes it clear that we cannot live as though Christ has not come, for if we do, there remains no sacrifice for sins (Heb 10:26–31).

The Bible is thus clear that we must hold fast to Christ, even when it is difficult. And it is indeed difficult to maintain the universality of Christ's claims for all people in a pluralistic world that so often tells us that any absolute claims are suspect. Yet the great irony not always appreciated is that disallowing all absolute claims is itself an absolute claim that reflects a particular worldview that is antithetical to the Christian worldview; at some level, making absolute claims is inescapable. And as soon as someone claims that Christianity is not commensurate with or compatible with a pluralistic worldview, that person has manifested an exclusive worldview that maintains some beliefs are appropriate and other are not.

Such is the reality we face in the twenty-first century. We live in a world of competing truth claims, though a great many people view their modern beliefs as self-evident when in fact they are imbibing more than they know from the philosophical and religious beliefs of many forbearers.[2] In such a world it is crucial to understand with clarity what the Bible teaches about salvation in Christ and the importance of loving our neighbors as ourselves. A claim that Christ is the only Savior must not be misconstrued as belief in our own inherent wisdom or stubborn personal preferences but in the revealed truth of God in Scripture. It is a belief in the universal problem of sin that overpowers all of us, and the universal solution for

1. Lane, *Hebrews 1–8*, cxxxviii.

2. See Carl R. Trueman, *The Rise and Triumph of the Modern Self: Cultural Amnesia, Expressive Individualism, and the Road to Sexual Revolution* (Wheaton, IL: Crossway, 2020).

all who would embrace it—Jesus Christ, the Son of God, in whom we have life by believing in his name (John 20:30–31).

THE CONSUMMATION

Though we do not always see it with our eyes in this age, the end of the Bible shows us a glorious picture of people from every tribe, tongue, people, and nation gathered around the throne of God (Rev 5:9–10; 7:1–17). This is not the patriotic or religious rally of one nation or ethnic group; this is the fruit of the ingathering of the nations from all over the world—those who come by the blood of their crucified and risen Savior to heavenly worship. This apocalyptic vision pulls back the curtain and offers us a peek into heavenly realities. Revelation encourages us that in the end, Christ will indeed build his church, and not even the gates of hell can oppose it (see Matt 16:18). For Christ has defeated the devil and bound him from deceiving the nations (Rev 20:2–3). Not only do the nations gather in worship of Christ, but his work enables this glorious vision.

CONCLUSION

We do not pick the times in which we live, but Jesus Christ is the same yesterday, today, and indeed forever (Heb 13:8). The clash of worldviews facing the church today is not so different from the issues facing the church in the first few centuries. It was countercultural then to claim exclusive devotion to Jesus and maintain a biblical ethic in the first century, and it is countercultural to claim the same today. Yet we are guided not by the winds of the age but by God's inspired words in the Scriptures. Those Scriptures show us that in whatever age we live, and wherever we live, Jesus Christ is our loving and gracious Savior who alone has proven victorious over sin and offers us eternal life, that where he is we may be also (John 14:3).

FURTHER READING

Edwards, James R. *Is Jesus the Only Savior?* Grand Rapids: Eerdmans, 2005. Edwards considers the exclusivity of Christ in light of contemporary challenges, such as historical-critical biblical studies, pluralism, and postmodernism.

Piper, John. *Jesus the Only Way to God: Must You Hear the Gospel to Be Saved?* Grand Rapids: Baker, 2010. Piper's book is a straightforward, clear, and urgent pastoral call to understand the significance of Christ as the world's only Savior and the need to proclaim him throughout the world.

Rowe, C. Kavin. *One True Life: The Stoics and Early Christians as Rival Traditions*. New Haven: Yale University Press, 2016. Rowe shows the distinctiveness of Christianity in the ancient world by contrasting it with Stoicism.

Strange, Daniel. *Their Rock Is Not Like Our Rock: A Theology of Religions*. Grand Rapids: Zondervan, 2014. Strange argues, from a Reformed perspective, that non-Christian religions are idol atrous responses to divine revelation that are opposed to, yet dependent on, the truth of a Christian worldview and are "subversively fulfilled" in the gospel of Christ (see, e.g., p. 42).

CONCLUSION

SEVEN THESES ON THE PERSON AND WORK OF CHRIST

THERE IS MUCH MORE TO say on the person and the work of Christ than we have been able to cover in this volume. If all the world could not contain the books that could be written about all the marvelous deeds Christ accomplished (John 21:25), then surely the present volume is but an overview of issues that merit continued reflection and further study. In that spirit, I include here seven summative but nonexhaustive theses on the person and work of Christ:

1. The Son of God is eternally the Son of God, the Second Person of the Trinity.
2. In the fullness of time, the Son of God took to himself a true body and a reasonable soul for us and for our salvation.
3. The hypostatic union must be affirmed rightly, though mystery will always remain.
4. The gospel is good news about this Son of God.
5. All the Scriptures cohere in and bear witness to Jesus himself.
6. Church history and the great creeds and confessions of the church are not infallible, but they are invaluable guides to understanding and articulating the biblical portrait of Christ.
7. Jesus, the Son of David, is the one Savior for the whole world.

SEVEN THESES

1. The Son of God is eternally the Son of God, the Second Person of the Trinity.

We do not first encounter the Son of God in the New Testament, but the Son is active already in the Old Testament. Indeed, he is eternally the Son of God—uniquely, eternally begotten of the Father. This does not mean the Son himself is in any sense created. Instead, he is the Creator and the one Mediator between God and humanity across the ages. In Johannine terms, the Son is the Logos. We therefore also must expect to hear the voice of the Logos in the Old Testament. This is a corollary of inspiration: the Scriptures are divinely inspired, and the Old Testament is a prophetic book that both speaks about Christ and is spoken as the revelation of Christ himself. For the Old Testament prophets prophesied by the Spirit of Christ (1 Pet 1:10–12). The lenses of prophet, priest, and king are especially helpful in understanding how the Old Testament points to Christ. A biblically sensitive Christology is not merely a New Testament Christology—it must be a whole Bible Christology.

2. In the fullness of time, the Son of God took to himself a true body and a reasonable soul for us and for our salvation.

Even though the Son was present and active in the Old Testament, it was not until the fullness of time that he became incarnate for us and for our salvation. In the incarnation the eternal Son of God continues to be what he always was while becoming what he was not: true man. The incarnation was accomplished not because of any need or compulsion in God but because of his own will and love for us. The incarnation itself is not redemption as such, but is a constituent aspect and *sine qua non* of redemption. Not only must our Redeemer be truly God, but he also must be truly man.

3. The hypostatic union must be affirmed rightly, though mystery will always remain.

To explain the incarnation accurately, we must speak of one person (the divine Son of God) who takes to himself a pure, human nature. Thus two natures (divine and human) are united in one person. The human nature always remains (and retains the characteristics of) human nature, and the divine nature always remains (and retains the characteristics of) divine nature. Nor can the divine nature of Christ be limited to the human body of Christ, for the Son never ceases to be omnipresent with respect to his divinity. We must always work to understand the relationship of these two natures carefully, but the mystery of the unparalleled and unprecedented reality known as the hypostatic union must also be recognized.

4. The gospel is good news about this Son of God.

THE CHRISTOLOGICAL REALITIES DISCUSSED IN this book are not something different from the gospel, but they are ways that the gospel is guarded and propagated. Christological heresies often misconstrue the nature of the gospel. The good news of the gospel is the good news about this Son of God—the eternal Son of God who became a man without ceasing to be the Son of God. He is the second Adam and true man; he is the final prophet, priest, and king, who was made low and suffered yet was raised to glorious new life. The gospel is about both what Christ has done for us in his state of humiliation and what he continues to do in his state of exaltation. In our desire to know more of the gospel, we must always seek to know more of Christ himself, that we may be united to him by faith.

5. All the Scriptures cohere in and bear witness to Jesus himself.

THIS IS THE POINT OF texts such as Luke 24:44–47 and John 5:39. We do not read the Scriptures correctly if we do not read them in relation to Christ himself. This applies, *mutatis mutandis*, to dogmatic constructions as well. For if we have not understood the Scriptures, if we have not understood their relation to Christ himself, then neither have we properly construed the loci of systematic theology.

6. Church history and the great creeds and confessions of the church are not infallible, but they are invaluable guides to understanding and articulating the biblical portrait of Christ.

WE NEED THE CREEDS. THEY are not impositions on the text of Scripture, but are the fruit of intense wrestling with the Scriptures. We neglect the creeds to our own great peril. If those who do not know history are doomed to repeat history (as the saying goes), then those who do not know the heresies addressed by the creeds seem doomed to repeat those heresies. To this end, we should promote knowledge of the creeds themselves. They are not typically so long as to be inaccessible, but they also reward careful consideration and reflection. At the same time, we must recognize that creeds have not said all that it is possible to say about Christology, and it may be that in the future additional statements will be needed to address unforeseen issues that are consistent with but not directly addressed by the church's great christological affirmations.

7. Jesus, the Son of David, is the one Savior for the whole world.

The gospel speaks about the fulfillment of the covenant promises of God, not least with respect to the coming of the true Davidic king, who will reign over the kingdom of David forever (2 Sam 7:13–15; Luke 1:31–33). Jesus is the Son of David who rules over the kingdom of David and reunites the scattered people under one king. Yet this Son of David is also the son of Adam (Luke 3:38), and is not simply the Savior of Israel but is also the Savior for the whole world. Those who worship Christ from all over the world today are fulfillments of the prophetic hopes that the nations would come to the light of Jerusalem (Isa 60:1–3). We worship Jesus not as the Savior of a provincial people but as the ascended Lord of all who reigns over the universe. He has come, he has conquered, and he has ascended. But his present reign also reminds us that he is coming again, and he is coming soon.

THE GRACE OF OUR LORD JESUS CHRIST

The gospel of Jesus Christ, which is set forth in Scripture and defended in the church's creedal traditions, is about the eternal Son of God who came to us for our salvation. Without ceasing to be God, he became a man to live an obedient human life and grant us eternal life. This is described in Scripture in various ways. Sonship is central to the story line of Scripture, and this prepares us for and terminates on the divine sonship of Christ himself. He leads to a heavenly promised land, which is another way of speaking of a new exodus, and he is both the shepherd who leads us and the lamb who has been slain for our sins. As our Mediator he is our prophet, priest, and king. He is the Word of God who reveals to us the will of God; he is our priest who offers the final, definitive sacrifice for sins and continually intercedes for us; and he is the king over the everlasting, gracious kingdom of God, comprising people from every tribe, tongue, people, and nation. He was all these things during the days of his humiliation, and he continues to be our prophet, priest, and king in his glorified, resurrected state.

These categories help us understand what is beyond our understanding; there are limits to what we can understand. Should this be surprising? Should we expect to understand exhaustively the wonders of the infinite God taking to himself a finite human nature? Mystery will always remain. Yet these mysteries, which must be maintained, provide some of the richest material for spiritual nourishment. Precision matters because in the precision we guard the realities of what has been revealed to us in Scripture: Jesus Christ is truly and fully God and truly and fully human.[1]

We have seen in the final few chapters more clearly why this is not abstract, but is good news for sinners who struggle and doubt on this present new exodus journey of life. Jesus Christ is our hope and our life. The Heidelberg Catechism's opening question and answer present an abiding encouragement about our life in Christ:

> Q. What is your only comfort in life and in death?
>
> A. That I am not my own, but belong— body and soul, in life and in death— to my faithful Savior Jesus Christ. He has fully paid for all my sins with his precious blood, and has set me free from the tyranny of the devil. He also watches over me in such a way that not a hair can fall from my head without the will of my Father in heaven: in fact, all things must work together for my salvation. Because I belong to him, Christ, by his Holy Spirit, assures me of eternal life and makes me wholeheartedly willing and ready from now on to live for him.[2]

It is most fitting that the Bible ends with the abiding grace of Jesus Christ. I know of no better way to leave our discussion than with the way John

1. "The creeds do not solve riddles; they preserve mysteries" (Jamieson, *Paradox of Sonship*, 152–53).

2. From the translation adopted by the Christian Reformed Church in 1975 and approved in 1988, https://www.crcna.org/sites/default/files/HeidelbergCatechism.pdf.

ends his vision of the risen Christ: "The grace of the Lord Jesus be with everyone. Amen" (Rev 22:21 CSB).

GLOSSARY[1]

anhypostasia: the teaching that apart from the incarnation, the human nature of Christ had no personal existence.

Apollinarianism: teaching derived from Apollinarius of Laodicea that in the incarnation the Son of God did not have a human soul. This was condemned at the Councils of Constantinople (AD 381) and Ephesus (AD 451).

apposition: two terms standing in close proximity (where relevant, in the same grammatical case) that are mutually interpretive.

Arianism: teaching deriving from Arius that stated the Son was less than fully divine; this was condemned especially in the Nicene and Constantinopolitan Creeds (AD 325, 381).

communicatio idiomatum: "communication of properties"; in the incarnation, some actions and properties are proper to Christ's divinity and some to his humanity. Even so, actions proper to one nature can be attributed to the person given the unity of the person.

covenant of grace: the Trinitarian work of redemption, by which true covenant members are granted eternal life by faith in the Mediator. This applies to all of God's elect people throughout history.

1. The following definitions are not exhaustive and are focused especially on the topics included in this volume. These definitions are my own summaries, though they inevitably draw on a range of sources. Helpful sources include Muller, *Dictionary of Latin and Greek*; Letham, *Holy Trinity*, 577–85; Barrett, *Simply Trinity*, 319–25.

covenant of redemption: a.k.a. *pactum salutis*, "covenant of peace," "counsel of peace," et al. eternal, intra-Trinitarian covenant whereby the Son freely agrees to accomplish redemption on behalf of the elect; this does not imply any division in the divine will.

covenant of works: a.k.a. "covenant of life," "covenant of nature," et al. The covenantal arrangement given to Adam in his created state whereby eschatological, eternal life was offered to him upon condition of his perfect obedience—though without implying that Adam's obedience would autonomously earn him a reward.

economy of redemption: the work of God *ad extra* to accomplish salvation; this economy is often distinguished from God as he is in himself.

enhypostasia: the teaching that in the incarnation (and only in the incarnation) the human nature of Christ has personal existence.

essence (Latin *essentia*, *substantia*; Gk. οὐσία, φύσις): God's singular, essential being. In Trinitarian terms, there is no distinction in essence between Father, Son, and Spirit (is to be distinguished from subsistence).

eternal generation: the orthodox Christian teaching that the Son of God is eternally the Son; he never becomes the Son of God but always exists in a filial relationship to the Father.

Eutychianism: see monophysitism.

historia salutis: "history of salvation," i.e., accomplishment of salvation.

hypostatic union: the orthodox Christian teaching that two natures (divine and human) are united in the one person (ὑποστάσις) of Christ.

inclusio: "bookend" literary structure in a text, which features a parallel beginning and ending.

limbus patrum: "border of the fathers"; the so-called limbo of the fathers, referring to the imprisonment of believing saints who were freed when Christ descended "locally" to Hades.

locus (Latin): in theological discussions, refers to a text or a (theological) topic.

logos: (= Gk. λόγος), "word"; term with a long history in philosophy, especially Stoicism, and used in early Christianity (following the Gospel of John) to speak of Christ, often as Creator and Wisdom.

modalism: Trinitarian heresy that denies God is eternally Father, Son, and Spirit, but the three persons are instead three successive "modes" of God.

monophysitism: the christological error that views Christ as having only one nature; for Eutyches, this mean the Logos somehow "absorbed" Christ's human nature.

munus triplex: threefold office (of Christ): prophet, priest, king.

nature: essence, being; the Son is by nature eternally God. In the incarnation, the Son has two natures: he retains his divine nature and takes on a created, human nature.

opera trinitatis ad extra indivisa sunt: "the external works of the Trinity are undivided"; underscores the unity of the Trinitarian works in relation to creation.

ordo salutis: order (or application) of salvation.

pactum salutis: see covenant of redemption.

partitive exegesis: exegetical method that distinguishes between statements that are true of Jesus by virtue of his divinity and statements that are true by virtue of his taking on a human nature in the incarnation.

patripassianism: "the suffering of the Father": that is, the modalistic approach to God that reimagined the Trinity. By denying God is eternally three persons, it thus denied distinct persons in the economy of redemption (so, e.g., Praxeanism; Sabellianism). Thus patripassianism teaches that the Father suffered on the cross. See also modalism.

person: in the Trinity are three eternal persons: Father, Son, and Spirit, who are distinguished by their "personal properties." It is the person of the Son who becomes incarnate. See also subsistence; hypostatic union.

Praxeanism: see modalism; patripassianism.

prosopological exegesis: interpretive approach common in the early church that identifies specific, divine persons speaking in Old Testament texts.

regula fidei: "rule of faith," a.k.a. "rule of truth," "canon of truth," etc. Trinitarian summary of normative Christian doctrine dating back to the earliest decades of the church; closely resembles what we know today as the Apostles' Creed.

Sabellianism: see modalism; patripassianism.

subordinationism: erroneous christological view that refers to the notion that the Son is eternally subordinate to the Father in his essential being. See also economy of redemption.

subsistence (Latin *subsistentia*; Gk. ὑποστάσις): the specific or personal mode of being for each person of the Trinity (to be distinguished from essence).

substance (Latin *substantia*): see essence.

BIBLIOGRAPHY

Abbott, Thomas Kingsmill. *A Critical and Exegetical Commentary on the Epistles to the Ephesians and to the Colossians*. ICC. New York: Scribner's Sons, 1909.

Abernethy, Andrew T. *The Book of Isaiah and God's Kingdom: A Thematic-Theological Approach*. NSBT 40. Downers Grove, IL: InterVarsity, 2016.

Achtemeier, Paul J. *1 Peter: A Commentary on First Peter*. Hermeneia. Minneapolis: Fortress, 1996.

Alexander, T. Desmond. "The Old Testament View of Life after Death." *Them* 11 (1986): 41–46.

Allison, Dale C., Jr. *A Critical and Exegetical Commentary on the Epistle of James*. ICC. New York: Bloomsbury T&T Clark, 2013.

———. *The Historical Christ and the Theological Jesus*. Grand Rapids: Eerdmans, 2009.

———. *The New Moses: A Matthean Typology*. Minneapolis: Fortress, 1993.

Andersen, Francis I., and David Noel Freedman. *Micah: A New Translation with Introduction and Commentary*. AB 24E. New York: Doubleday, 2000.

Anderson, James. *Paradox in Christian Theology: An Analysis of Its Presence, Character, and Epistemic Status*. Paternoster Theological Monographs. Milton Keynes, UK: Paternoster, 2007.

Anselmi, S. *Cur Deus Homo*. Edited by Franciscus Salesius Schmitt. Florilegium Patristicum tam veteris quam medii aevi auctores complectens 18. Bonn: Petri Hanstein, 1929.

Aquinas, Thomas. *Summa theologiae: Latin Text and English Translation, Introduction, Notes, Appendices and Glossaries*. Edited by Thomas Gilby, OP, et al. 60 vols. New York: McGraw-Hill, 1964–1973.

Aslan, Reza. *Zealot: The Life and Times of Jesus of Nazareth*. New York: Random House, 2013.

Aulén, Gustaf. *Christus Victor: An Historical Study of the Three Main Types of the Idea of the Atonement*. Translated by A. G. Hebert. London: SPCK, 1931.

Ayres, Lewis. *Nicaea and Its Legacy: An Approach to Fourth-Century Trinitarian Theology*. Oxford: Oxford University Press, 2004.

Baldwin, Joyce G. *Daniel: An Introduction and Commentary*. TOTC 23. Downers Grove, IL: IVP Academic, 1978.

Barrett, C. K. *A Critical and Exegetical Commentary on the Acts of the Apostles*. 2 vols. ICC. Edinburgh: T&T Clark, 1994–1998.

———. *The Gospel according to St. John: An Introduction with Commentary and Notes on the Greek Text*. 2nd ed. London: SPCK, 1978.

Barrett, Matthew. *Canon, Covenant, and Christology: Rethinking Jesus and the Scriptures of Israel*. NSBT 51. Downers Grove, IL: IVP Academic, 2020.

———. *Simply Trinity: The Unmanipulated Father, Son, and Spirit*. Grand Rapids: Baker, 2021.

Barth, Karl. *Church Dogmatics*. Translated by Geoffrey W. Bromiley. 14 vols. Edinburgh: T&T Clark, 1956–1977.

Barth, Markus. *Ephesians 1–3: A New Translation with Introduction and Commentary*. AB 34. Garden City, NY: Doubleday, 1974.

Bass, Justin W. *The Battle for the Keys: Revelation 1:18 and Christ's Descent into the Underworld*. Paternoster Biblical Monographs. Reprint, Eugene, OR: Wipf & Stock, 2014.

Bauckham, Richard. *The Climax of Prophecy: Studies on the Book of Revelation*. London: T&T Clark, 1993.

———. "Confessing the Cosmic Christ (1 Corinthians 8:6 and Colossians 1:15–20)." Pages 139–71 in *Monotheism and Christology in Greco-Roman Antiquity*. Edited by Matthew V. Novenson. NovTSup 180. Leiden: Brill, 2020.

———. "The Divinity of Jesus in the Letter of the Hebrews." Pages 233–53 in *Jesus and the God of Israel: God Crucified and Other Studies on the New Testament's Christology of Divine Identity*. Milton Keynes, UK: Paternoster, 2008.

———. *God Crucified: Monotheism and Christology in the New Testament*. Grand Rapids: Eerdmans, 1999.

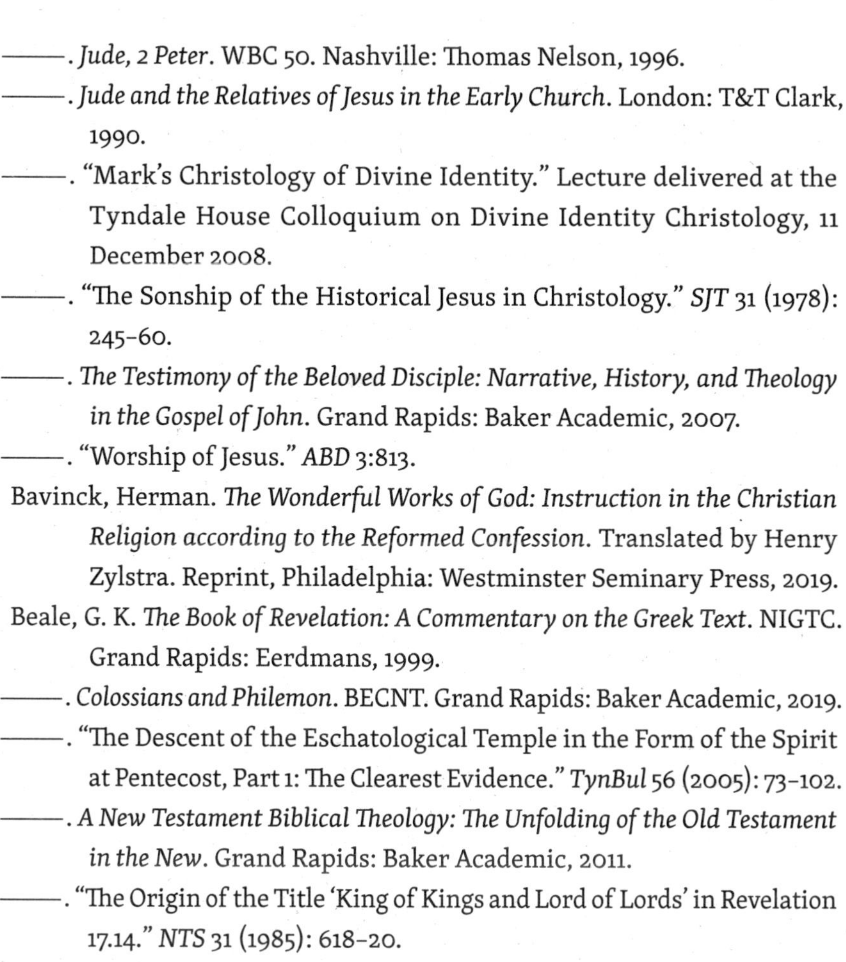

———. *Jude, 2 Peter*. WBC 50. Nashville: Thomas Nelson, 1996.

———. *Jude and the Relatives of Jesus in the Early Church*. London: T&T Clark, 1990.

———. "Mark's Christology of Divine Identity." Lecture delivered at the Tyndale House Colloquium on Divine Identity Christology, 11 December 2008.

———. "The Sonship of the Historical Jesus in Christology." *SJT* 31 (1978): 245–60.

———. *The Testimony of the Beloved Disciple: Narrative, History, and Theology in the Gospel of John*. Grand Rapids: Baker Academic, 2007.

———. "Worship of Jesus." *ABD* 3:813.

Bavinck, Herman. *The Wonderful Works of God: Instruction in the Christian Religion according to the Reformed Confession*. Translated by Henry Zylstra. Reprint, Philadelphia: Westminster Seminary Press, 2019.

Beale, G. K. *The Book of Revelation: A Commentary on the Greek Text*. NIGTC. Grand Rapids: Eerdmans, 1999.

———. *Colossians and Philemon*. BECNT. Grand Rapids: Baker Academic, 2019.

———. "The Descent of the Eschatological Temple in the Form of the Spirit at Pentecost, Part 1: The Clearest Evidence." *TynBul* 56 (2005): 73–102.

———. *A New Testament Biblical Theology: The Unfolding of the Old Testament in the New*. Grand Rapids: Baker Academic, 2011.

———. "The Origin of the Title 'King of Kings and Lord of Lords' in Revelation 17.14." *NTS* 31 (1985): 618–20.

———. *The Temple and the Church's Mission: A Biblical Theology of the Dwelling Place of God*. NSBT 17. Downers Grove, IL: InterVarsity, 2004.

Beeley, Christopher A. "The Early Christological Controversy: Apollinarius, Diodore, and Gregory Nazianzen." *VC* 65 (2011): 376–407.

Begg, Alistair, and Sinclair B. Ferguson. *Name above All Names*. Wheaton, IL: Crossway, 2013.

Behr, John. *The Nicene Faith*. The Formation of Christian Theology 2. Crestwood, NY: St. Vladimir's Seminary Press, 2004.

———, ed. and trans. *Origen: On First Principles*. 2 vols. Oxford Early Christian Texts. Oxford: Oxford University Press, 2017.

———, trans. *St. Irenaeus of Lyons: On the Apostolic Preaching*. PPS 17. Crestwood, NY: St. Vladimir's Seminary Press, 1997.

———. *The Way to Nicaea*. The Formation of Christian Theology 1. Crestwood, NY: St. Vladimir's Seminary Press, 2001.

Belcher, Richard P., Jr. *The Fulfillment of the Promises of God: An Explanation of Covenant Theology*. Fearn, UK: Mentor, 2020.

———. *Prophet, Priest, and King: The Roles of Christ in the Bible and Our Roles Today*. Phillipsburg, NJ: P&R, 2016.

Bengel, J. A. *Gnomon of the New Testament*. 5 vols. 3rd edition. Translated by Andrew R. Fausset. Edinburgh: T&T Clark, 1860.

Bello, Rafael Noguira. *Sinless Flesh: A Critique of Karl Barth's Fallen Christ*. Studies in Historical and Systematic Theology. Bellingham, WA: Lexham, 2020.

Berkhof, Louis. *Systematic Theology*. 4th ed. Grand Rapids: Eerdmans, 1996.

Bieneck, Joachim. *Sohn Gottes als Christusbezeichnung der Synoptiker*. Abhandlungen zur Theologie des Alten und Neuen Testaments 21. Zürich: Zwingli-Verlag, 1951.

Blocher, Henri A. G. "Agnus Victor: The Atonement as Victory and Vicarious Punishment." Pages 67–91 in *What Does It Mean to Be Saved? Broadening Evangelical Horizons Of Salvation*. Edited by John G. Stackhouse Jr. Grand Rapids: Baker, 2002.

———. "Atonement." Pages 72–76 in *Dictionary for Theological Interpretation of the Bible*. Edited by Kevin J. Vanhoozer. Grand Rapids: Baker Academic, 2005.

———. "Biblical Metaphors and the Doctrine of the Atonement." *JETS* 47 (2004): 629–45.

Boice, James Montgomery. *Psalms 1–41: An Expositional Commentary*. Grand Rapids: Baker Books, 2005.

Boothe, Charles Octavius. *Plain Theology for Plain People*. Bellingham, WA: Lexham, 2017.

Brakel, Wilhelmus à. *God, Man, and Christ*. Vol 1 of *The Christian's Reasonable Service*. Edited by Joel R. Beeke. Translated by Bartel Elshout. Grand Rapids: Reformation Heritage, 1992.

Bray, Gerald. *God Has Spoken: A History of Christian Theology*. Wheaton, IL: Crossway, 2014.

Brennan, Nick. *Divine Christology in the Epistle to the Hebrews: The Son as God*. LNTS 656. London: T&T Clark, 2021.

Brown, Raymond E. *The Gospel according to John: Introduction, Translation, and Notes*. 2 vols. AB 29–29A. New York: Doubleday, 1966–1974.
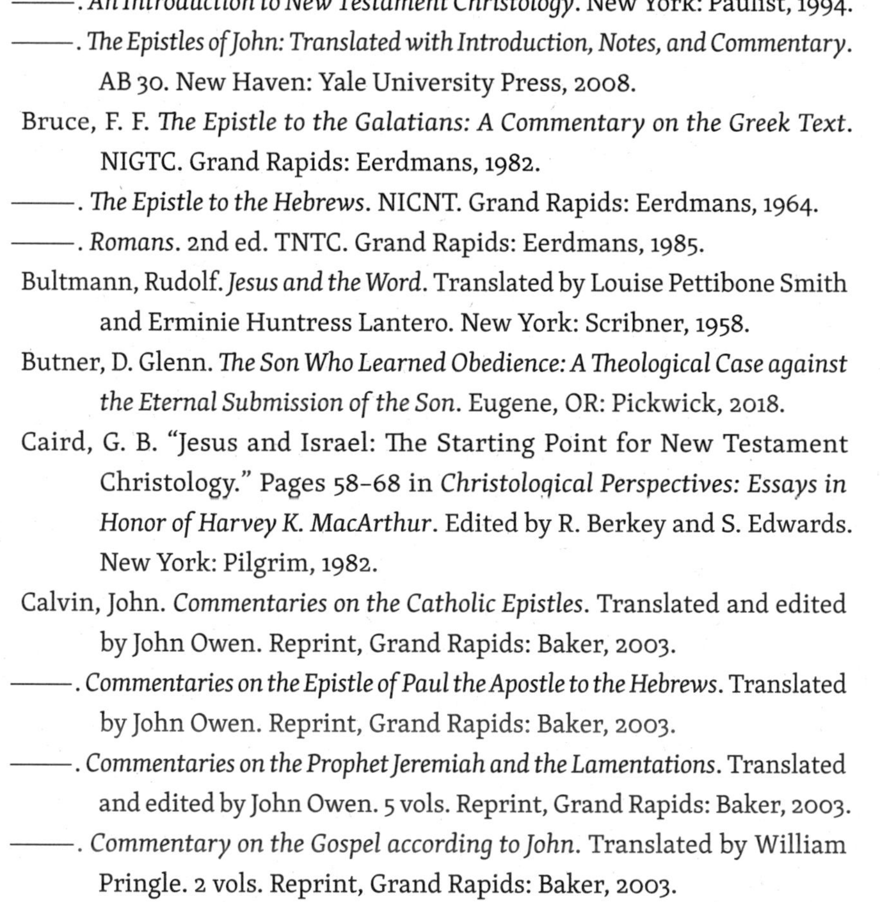
———. *An Introduction to New Testament Christology*. New York: Paulist, 1994.
———. *The Epistles of John: Translated with Introduction, Notes, and Commentary*. AB 30. New Haven: Yale University Press, 2008.
Bruce, F. F. *The Epistle to the Galatians: A Commentary on the Greek Text*. NIGTC. Grand Rapids: Eerdmans, 1982.
———. *The Epistle to the Hebrews*. NICNT. Grand Rapids: Eerdmans, 1964.
———. *Romans*. 2nd ed. TNTC. Grand Rapids: Eerdmans, 1985.
Bultmann, Rudolf. *Jesus and the Word*. Translated by Louise Pettibone Smith and Erminie Huntress Lantero. New York: Scribner, 1958.
Butner, D. Glenn. *The Son Who Learned Obedience: A Theological Case against the Eternal Submission of the Son*. Eugene, OR: Pickwick, 2018.
Caird, G. B. “Jesus and Israel: The Starting Point for New Testament Christology.” Pages 58–68 in *Christological Perspectives: Essays in Honor of Harvey K. MacArthur*. Edited by R. Berkey and S. Edwards. New York: Pilgrim, 1982.
Calvin, John. *Commentaries on the Catholic Epistles*. Translated and edited by John Owen. Reprint, Grand Rapids: Baker, 2003.
———. *Commentaries on the Epistle of Paul the Apostle to the Hebrews*. Translated by John Owen. Reprint, Grand Rapids: Baker, 2003.
———. *Commentaries on the Prophet Jeremiah and the Lamentations*. Translated and edited by John Owen. 5 vols. Reprint, Grand Rapids: Baker, 2003.
———. *Commentary on the Gospel according to John*. Translated by William Pringle. 2 vols. Reprint, Grand Rapids: Baker, 2003.
———. *Commentary on the Prophet Isaiah*. Translated by William Pringle. 4 vols. Reprint, Grand Rapids: Baker, 2003.
———. *Commentary upon the Acts of the Apostles*. Edited by Henry Beveridge. 2 vols. Reprint, Grand Rapids: Baker, 2003.
Campos, Heber Carlos de, Jr. *Doctrine in Development: Johannes Piscator and Debates over Christ’s Active Obedience*. Reformed Historical-Theological Studies. Grand Rapids: Reformation Heritage, 2017.
Capes, David B. *Old Testament Yahweh Texts in Paul’s Christology*. WUNT 2/47. Tübingen: Mohr Siebeck, 1992.
Cara, Robert J. *Hebrews: A Mentor Commentary*. Fearn, UK: Mentor, forthcoming.

Carraway, George. *Christ is God Over All: Romans 9:5 in the Context of Romans 9–11*. LNTS 489. London: Bloomsbury, 2013.

Carson, D. A. *The Gospel according to John*. PNTC. Grand Rapids: Eerdmans, 1991.

———. "John 5:26: *Crux Interpretum* for Eternal Generation." Pages 79–97 in *Retrieving Eternal Generation*. Edited by Fred Sanders and Scott R. Swain. Grand Rapids: Zondervan, 2019.

———. "Matthew." Pages 1–599 in *Matthew, Mark, Luke. Vol. 8 of The Expositor's Bible Commentary*. Edited by Frank A. Gaebelein. Reprint, Grand Rapids: Zondervan, 1995.

———. *The Son of God: A Christological Title Often Overlooked, Sometimes Misunderstood, and Currently Disputed*. Wheaton, IL: Crossway, 2012.

———. "The Three Witnesses and the Eschatology of 1 John." Pages 216–32 in *To Tell the Mystery: Essays on New Testament Eschatology. Festschrift for Robert H. Gundry*. Edited by Thomas E. Schmidt and Moisés Silva. Journal for the Study of the New Testament Supplement Series 100. Sheffield: JSOT, 1994.

Childs, Brevard S. *The Book of Exodus: A Critical, Theological Commentary*. OTL. Louisville: Westminster, 1974.

———. *Isaiah: A Commentary*. OTL. Louisville: Westminster John Knox, 2001.

———. *The Struggle to Understand Isaiah as Christian Scripture*. Grand Rapids: Eerdmans, 2004.

Chilton, Bruce. "Caesarea Philippi." *ABD* 1:803–6.

Christian, Ed. "The Rich Man and Lazarus, Abraham's Bosom, and the Biblical Penalty *Karet* ('Cut Off')." *JETS* 61 (2018): 513–23.

Ciampa, Roy E., and Brian Rosner. *1 Corinthians*. PNTC. Grand Rapids: Eerdmans, 2010.

Clark, John C., and Marcus Peter Johnson. *The Incarnation of God: The Mystery of the Gospel as the Foundation of Evangelical Theology*. Wheaton, IL: Crossway, 2015.

Clement of Alexandria. *The Exhortation to the Greeks; The Rich Man's Salvation; To the Newly Baptized*. Translated by G. W. Butterworth. Loeb Classical Library. Cambridge: Harvard University Press, 1919.

Clowney, Edmund. "The Final Temple." *WTJ* 35 (1973): 156–89.

———. *The Message of 1 Peter: The Way of the Cross*. The Bible Speaks Today. Downers Grove, IL: InterVarsity, 1988.

Coakley, Sarah. "What Does Chalcedon Solve, and What Does It Not? Some Reflections on the Status and Meaning of the Chalcedonian 'Definition.'" Pages 143–63 in *The Incarnation: An Interdisciplinary Study of the Incarnation of the Son of God*. Edited by Stephen T. Davis, Daniel Kendall, SJ, and Gerald O'Collins, SJ. Oxford: Oxford University Press, 2002.

Cole, Graham A. *The God Who Became Human: A Biblical Theology of the Incarnation*. NSBT 30. Downers Grove, IL: InterVarsity, 2013.

Cole, R. Alan. *Exodus: An Introduction and Commentary*. TOTC 2. Downers Grove, IL: InterVarsity, 1973.

Coloe, Mary L., PBVM. "The Garden as a New Creation in John." *The Bible Today* 53 (2015): 158–64.

Confessio fidei in conventu theologorum authoritate Parliamenti Anglicani indicto elaborata; eidem Parliamento postmodum exhibita; quin & ab eodem, deindeque; ab Ecclesia Scoticana cognita & approbata; una cum Catechismo duplici, Majori, Minorique; e sermono Anglicano summa cum fide in Latin versa. Cambridge: Field, 1659.

Cranfield, C. E. B. *A Critical and Exegetical Commentary on the Epistle to the Romans*. 2 vols. ICC. Edinburgh: T&T Clark, 1975–79.

———. *The Gospel according to St. Mark*. 2nd ed. Cambridge Greek Text Commentary. Cambridge: Cambridge University Press, 1963.

Crawford, Matthew R. *Cyril of Alexandria's Trinitarian Theology of Scripture*. Oxford Early Christian Studies. Oxford: Oxford University Press, 2014.

Crisp, Oliver D. *Divinity and Humanity: The Incarnation Reconsidered*. Current Issues in Theology. Cambridge: Cambridge University Press, 2007.

———. *The Word Enfleshed: Exploring the Person and Work of Christ*. Grand Rapids: Baker Academic, 2016.

Cross, F. L., ed. *The Oxford Dictionary of the Christian Church*. 3rd ed. Edited by E. A. Livingstone. Oxford: Oxford University Press, 2005.

Crowe, Brandon D. "'By Grace You Have Been Saved through Faith': Justification in the Pauline Epistles." Pages 239–71 in *The Doctrine on Which the Church Stands or Falls: Justification in Biblical, Theological, Historical, and Pastoral Perspective*. Edited by Matthew Barrett. Wheaton, IL: Crossway, 2019.

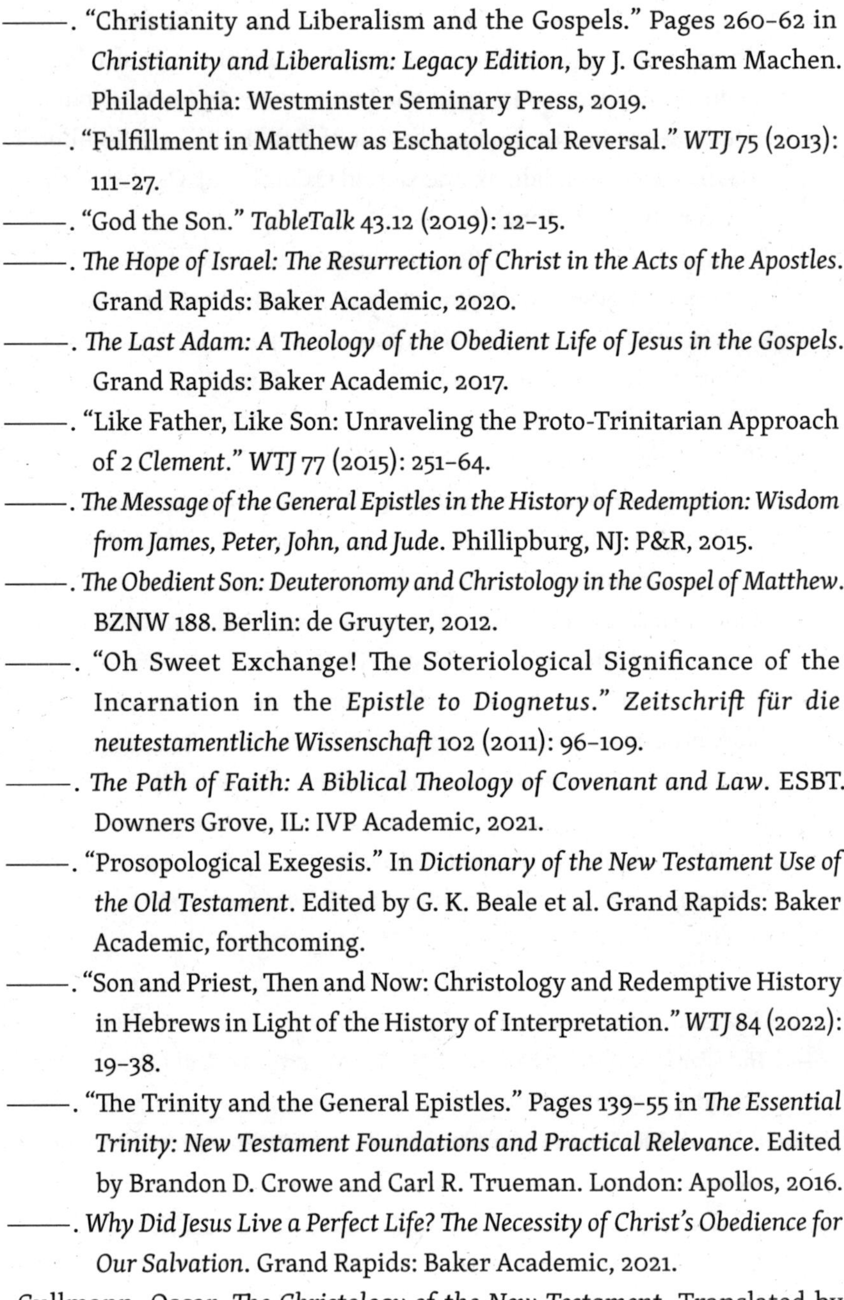

———. "Christianity and Liberalism and the Gospels." Pages 260–62 in *Christianity and Liberalism: Legacy Edition*, by J. Gresham Machen. Philadelphia: Westminster Seminary Press, 2019.

———. "Fulfillment in Matthew as Eschatological Reversal." *WTJ* 75 (2013): 111–27.

———. "God the Son." *TableTalk* 43.12 (2019): 12–15.

———. *The Hope of Israel: The Resurrection of Christ in the Acts of the Apostles*. Grand Rapids: Baker Academic, 2020.

———. *The Last Adam: A Theology of the Obedient Life of Jesus in the Gospels*. Grand Rapids: Baker Academic, 2017.

———. "Like Father, Like Son: Unraveling the Proto-Trinitarian Approach of *2 Clement*." *WTJ* 77 (2015): 251–64.

———. *The Message of the General Epistles in the History of Redemption: Wisdom from James, Peter, John, and Jude*. Phillipburg, NJ: P&R, 2015.

———. *The Obedient Son: Deuteronomy and Christology in the Gospel of Matthew*. BZNW 188. Berlin: de Gruyter, 2012.

———. "Oh Sweet Exchange! The Soteriological Significance of the Incarnation in the *Epistle to Diognetus*." *Zeitschrift für die neutestamentliche Wissenschaft* 102 (2011): 96–109.

———. *The Path of Faith: A Biblical Theology of Covenant and Law*. ESBT. Downers Grove, IL: IVP Academic, 2021.

———. "Prosopological Exegesis." In *Dictionary of the New Testament Use of the Old Testament*. Edited by G. K. Beale et al. Grand Rapids: Baker Academic, forthcoming.

———. "Son and Priest, Then and Now: Christology and Redemptive History in Hebrews in Light of the History of Interpretation." *WTJ* 84 (2022): 19–38.

———. "The Trinity and the General Epistles." Pages 139–55 in *The Essential Trinity: New Testament Foundations and Practical Relevance*. Edited by Brandon D. Crowe and Carl R. Trueman. London: Apollos, 2016.

———. *Why Did Jesus Live a Perfect Life? The Necessity of Christ's Obedience for Our Salvation*. Grand Rapids: Baker Academic, 2021.

Cullmann, Oscar. *The Christology of the New Testament*. Translated by Shirley C. Guthrie and Charles A. M. Hall. Rev. ed. Philadelphia: Westminster, 1963.

Currid, John. *Against the Gods: The Polemical Theology of the Old Testament*. Wheaton, IL: Crossway, 2013.

Cyril of Alexandria. *Commentary on John*. Translated by David R. Maxwell. Edited by Joel C. Elowsky. 2 vols. Ancient Christian Texts. Downers Grove, IL: IVP Academic, 2013–2015.

Davies, John A. *A Royal Priesthood: Literary and Intertextual Perspectives on an Image of Israel in Exodus 19:6*. Journal for the Study of the Old Testament Supplement Series 395. London: T&T Clark, 2004.

Davies, W. D., and Dale C. Allison, Jr. *A Critical and Exegetical Commentary on the Gospel according to St. Matthew*. 3 vols. ICC. Edinburgh: T&T Clark, 1988–1997.

Davis, Leo Donald, SJ. *The First Seven Ecumenical Councils (325–787): Their History and Theology*. Theology and Life 21. Wilmington, DE: Glazier, 1987.

Deissler, Alfons. "Der 'Menschensohn' und 'das Volk der Heiligen des Höchsten' in Dan 7." Pages 81–91 in *Jesus und der Menschensohn: Für Anton Vögtle*. Edited by Rudolf Pesch and Rudolf Schnackenburg. Freiburg: Herder, 1975.

Dempster, Stephen G. *Dominion and Dynasty: A Theology of the Hebrew Bible*. NSBT 15. Downers Grove, IL: InterVarsity, 2003.

Dennison, James T., Jr., ed. *Reformed Confessions of the Sixteenth and Seventeenth Centuries in English Translation, 1523–1693*. 4 vols. Grand Rapids: Reformation Heritage, 2008–2014.

Djuth, Marianne. "Liberty." Pages 495–98 in *Augustine through the Ages: An Encyclopedia*. Edited by Allan D. Fitzgerald. Grand Rapids: Eerdmans, 1999.

Dodd, C. H. "ΙΛΑΣΚΕΣΘΑΙ, Its Cognates, Derivatives, and Synonyms, in the Septuagint." *Journal of Theological Studies* 32 (1931): 352–50.

Drake, K. J. *The Flesh of the Word: The* Extra Calvinisticum *from Zwingli to Early Orthodoxy*. Oxford Studies in Historical Theology. Oxford: Oxford University Press, 2021.

Duguid, Iain M. *Ezekiel*. NIVAC. Grand Rapids: Zondervan, 1999.

Dunn, James D. G. *Jesus Remembered*. Christianity in the Making 2. Grand Rapids: Eerdmans, 2003.

———. *Romans 9–16*. WBC 38B. Dallas: Word, 1988.

Edwards, James R. *The Gospel according to Mark*. PNTC. Grand Rapids: Eerdmans, 2002.

———. *Is Jesus the Only Savior?* Grand Rapids: Eerdmans, 2005.

———. "The Rider on the White Horse, the Thigh Inscription, and Apollo: Revelation 19:16." *Journal of Biblical Literature* 137 (2018): 519–36.

Ehrman, Bart D., and Zlatko Pleše. *The Apocryphal Gospels: Texts and Translations*. Oxford: Oxford University Press, 2013.

Ellingworth, Paul. *The Epistle to the Hebrews*. NIGTC. Grand Rapids: Eerdmans, 1993.

Ellis, Brannon. *Calvin, Classical Trinitarianism, and the Aseity of the Son*. Oxford: Oxford University Press, 2012.

Emerson, Matthew Y. *"He Descended to the Dead": An Evangelical Theology of Holy Saturday*. Downers Grove, IL: IVP Academic, 2019.

———. "The Role of Proverbs 8: Eternal Generation in Hermeneutics Ancient and Modern." Pages 44–66 in *Retrieving Eternal Generation*. Edited by Fred Sanders and Scott R. Swain. Grand Rapids: Zondervan, 2019.

Estelle, Bryan D. *Echoes of Exodus: Tracing a Biblical Motif*. Downers Grove, IL: IVP Academic, 2018.

Evans, Craig A. *Mark 8:27–16:20*. WBC 34B. Grand Rapids: Zondervan, 1988.

Evans, Ernest, ed. and trans. *Tertullian: Adversus Marcionem*. 2 vols. Oxford: Clarendon, 1972.

———. *Tertullian's Treatise against Praxeas*. London: SPCK, 1948.

Fairbairn, Donald, and Ryan M. Reeves. *The Story of Creeds and Confessions: Tracing the Development of the Christian Faith*. Grand Rapids: Baker Academic, 2019.

Fairweather, Eugene R., ed. and trans. *A Scholastic Miscellany: Anselm to Ockham*. Philadelphia: Westminster, 1956.

Fee, Gordon D. *Pauline Christology: An Exegetical-Theological Study*. Peabody, MA: Hendrickson, 2007.

———. *Paul's Letter to the Philippians*. NICNT. Grand Rapids: Eerdmans, 1995.

Ferguson, Everett. *Backgrounds of Early Christianity*. 3rd ed. Grand Rapids: Eerdmans, 2003.

———. *The Rule of Faith: A Guide*. Cascade Companions. Eugene, OR: Cascade, 2015.

Ferguson, Sinclair B. "*Christus Victor et Propitiator*: The Death of Christ, Substitute and Conqueror." Pages 171–89 in *For the Fame of God's*

Name: Essays in Honor of John Piper. Edited by Sam Storms and Justin Taylor. Wheaton, IL: Crossway, 2010.

———. *The Holy Spirit*. CCT. Downers Grove, IL: InterVarsity Press, 1996.

———. *Lessons from the Upper Room: The Heart of the Savior*. Sanford, FL: Ligonier, 2021.

———. *The Whole Christ: Legalism, Antinomianism, and Gospel Assurance—Why the Marrow Controversy Still Matters*. Wheaton, IL: Crossway, 2016.

Ferrara, Dennis M. "'Hypostasized in the Logos': Leontius of Byzantium, Leontius of Jerusalem and the Unfinished Business of the Council of Chalcedon." *Louvain Studies* 22 (1997): 311–27.

Fitzmyer, Joseph A. *The Acts of the Apostles: A New Translation with Introduction and Commentary*. AB 31. New York: Doubleday, 1998.

Frame, John M. *Systematic Theology: An Introduction to Christian Belief*. Phillipsburg, NJ: P&R, 2013.

France, R. T. *The Gospel of Mark: A Commentary on the Greek Text*. NIGTC. Grand Rapids: Eerdmans, 2002.

———. *The Gospel of Matthew*. NICNT. Grand Rapids: Eerdmans, 2007.

Frey, Jörg. *The Letter of Jude and the Second Letter of Peter: A Theological Commentary*. Translated by Kathleen Ess. Waco, TX: Baylor University Press, 2018.

Fullilove, William. "The Representation of Definiteness in Qumran Aramaic: Unsolving the Son of Man Problem." Paper presented at the Annual Meeting of the Society of Biblical Literature, Atlanta, 23 November 2015.

Futato, Mark D. *Interpreting the Psalms: An Exegetical Handbook*. Grand Rapids: Kregel, 2007.

Gaffin, Richard B., Jr. *"By Faith, Not by Sight": Paul and the Order of Salvation*. Waynesboro, GA: Paternoster, 2006.

———. *The Centrality of the Resurrection: A Study in Paul's Soteriology*. Baker Biblical Monograph. Grand Rapids: Baker, 1978.

———. *In the Fullness of Time: An Introduction to the Biblical Theology of Acts and Paul*. Wheaton: Crossway, 2022.

———. *No Adam, No Gospel: Adam and the History of Redemption*. Phillipsburg, NJ: P&R; Philadelphia: Westminster Seminary Press, 2015.

———. "The Priesthood of Christ: A Servant in the Sanctuary." Pages 49–68 in *The Perfect Saviour: Key Themes in Hebrews*. Edited by Jonathan Griffiths. Nottingham, UK: Inter-Varsity, 2012.

———. "The Work of Christ Applied." Pages 268–90 in *Christian Dogmatics: Reformed Theology for the Church Catholic*. Edited by Michael Allen and Scott R. Swain. Grand Rapids: Baker Academic, 2016.

Garland, David E. *1 Corinthians*. BECNT. Grand Rapids: Baker Academic, 2003.

———. *2 Corinthians*. NAC 29. Nashville: Broadman, 1999.

———. *Luke*. ZECNT. Grand Rapids: Zondervan, 2011.

———. *A Theology of Mark's Gospel: Good News about Jesus the Messiah, the Son of God*. Biblical Theology of the New Testament. Grand Rapids: Zondervan, 2015.

Gathercole, Simon J. *The Preexistent Son: Recovering the Christologies of Matthew, Mark, and Luke*. Grand Rapids: Eerdmans, 2006.

Genz, Rouven. *Jesaja 53 als theologische Mitte der Apostelgeschichte: Studien zur ihrer Christologie und Ekklesiologie im Anschluss an Apg 8,26–40*. WUNT 2/398. Tübingen: Mohr Siebeck, 2015.

Gibson, David. "'Fathers of Faith, My Fathers Now!' On Abraham, Covenant, and the Theology of Paedobaptism." *Them* 40.1 (2015): 14–34.

Gibson, David, and Jonathan Gibson, eds. *From Heaven He Came and Sought Her: Definite Atonement in Historical, Biblical, Theological, and Pastoral Perspective*. Wheaton, IL: Crossway, 2013.

Gibson, Jonathan. *Covenant Continuity and Fidelity: A Study of Inner-Biblical Allusion and Exegesis in Malachi*. The Library of Hebrew Bible/Old Testament Studies 625. London: Bloomsbury T&T Clark, 2016.

Gignilliat, Mark S. *Micah: An International Theological Commentary*. International Theological Commentary. London: T&T Clark, 2019.

Gladd, Benjamin L. "An Apocalyptic Trinitarian Model: The Book of Daniel's Influence on Revelation's Conception of the Trinity." Pages 156–74 in *The Essential Trinity: New Testament Foundations and Practical Relevance*. Edited by Brandon D. Crowe and Carl R. Trueman. London: Apollos, 2016.

———. *From Adam and Israel to the Church: A Biblical Theology of the People of God*. ESBT. Downers Grove, IL: IVP Academic, 2019.

Goldingay, John, and David Payne. *A Critical and Exegetical Commentary on Isaiah 40–55*. Vol. 2. ICC. London: T&T Clark, 2006.

Goodwin, Thomas. *Christ Set Forth*. Vol. 4 of *The Works of Thomas Goodwin*. Edinburgh: Nichol, 1862.

Gordon, Bruce. *Calvin: A Biography*. New Haven: Yale University Press, 2011.

Goswell, Gregory. "A Theocratic Reading of Zechariah 9:9." *BBR* 26 (2016): 9–17.

Grant, Robert M. *Greek Apologists of the Second Century*. Philadelphia: Westminster, 1988.

Greer, Rowan A. ed. and trans. "Introduction." Pages 1–37 in *Origen: An Exhortation to Martyrdom, Prayer, First Principles: Book IV, Prologue to the Commentary on the Song of Songs, Homily XXVII on Numbers*. Classics of Western Spirituality. New York: Paulist, 1979.

Grillmeier, Aloys. *Christ in Christian Tradition*. Vol. 1 of *From the Apostolic Age to Chalcedon (451)*. Translated by John Bowden. 2nd ed. Louisville: Westminster John Knox, 1975.

———. *Christ in Christian Tradition*. Vol. 2, part 2 of *From the Council of Chalcedon (451) to Gregory the Great (590–604)*. Translated by John Cawte and Pauline Allen. Louisville: Westminster John Knox, 1995.

Grindheim, Sigurd. *Christology in the Synoptic Gospels: God or God's Servant?* London: T&T Clark, 2012.

Groves, J. Alan. "Atonement in Isaiah 53: 'He Bore the Sins of Many.'" Pages 61–89 in *The Glory of the Atonement: Biblical, Historical and Practical Perspectives*. Edited by Charles E. Hill and Frank A. James III. Downers Grove, IL: InterVarsity Press, 2004.

Gunton, Colin E. *Christ and Creation*. Grand Rapids: Eerdmans, 1992.

Habets, Myk. *The Anointed Son: A Trinitarian Spirit Christology*. Princeton Theological Monographs. Eugene, OR: Pickwick, 2010.

Hafemann, Scott J. "Roman Triumph." Pages 1004–8 in *Dictionary of New Testament Background*. Edited by Craig A. Evans and Stanley E. Porter. Downers Grove, IL: InterVarsity Press, 2000.

Hall, Stuart George, ed. and trans. *Melito of Sardis: On Pascha and Fragments*. Oxford: Clarendon, 1979.

Hamm, Jeffrey. "*Descendit*: Delete or Declare? A Defense against the Neo-Deletionists." *WTJ* 78 (2016): 93–116.

Harmon, Matthew S. *The Servant of the Lord and His Servant People: Tracing a Biblical Theme through the Canon*. NSBT 54. Downers Grove, IL: IVP Academic, 2020.

Harris, Murray J. *Jesus as God: The New Testament Use of Theos in Reference to Jesus*. Grand Rapids: Baker, 1992.

———. *Prepositions and Theology in the Greek New Testament: An Essential Reference Resource for Exegesis*. Grand Rapids: Zondervan, 2012.

———. *The Second Epistle to the Corinthians: A Commentary on the Greek Text*. NIGTC. Grand Rapids: Eerdmans, 2005.

Harrison, R. K. *Jeremiah and Lamentations: An Introduction and Commentary*. TOTC 21. Downers Grove, IL: IVP Academic, 1973.

Harvey, Van A. *The Historian and the Believer: The Morality of Historical Knowledge and Christian Belief*. London: SCM, 1967.

Haykin, Michael A. G. *Rediscovering the Church Fathers: Who They Were and How They Shaped the Church*. Wheaton, IL: Crossway, 2011.

Hays, Richard B. *Echoes of Scripture in the Gospels*. Waco, TX: Baylor University Press, 2016.

———. *The Faithfulness of Jesus Christ: The Narrative Substructure of Galatians 3:1–4:11*. 2nd ed. Biblical Resource Series. Grand Rapids: Eerdmans; Dearborn, MI: Dove, 2002.

Hendriksen, William. *More than Conquerors: An Interpretation of the Book of Revelation*. Grand Rapids: Baker, 1998.

Hengel, Martin. "The Prologue of the Gospel of John as the Gateway to Christological Truth." Pages 265–94 in *The Gospel of John and Christian Theology*. Edited by Richard Bauckham and Carl Mosser. Grand Rapids: Eerdmans, 2008.

———. *The Son of God: The Origin of Christology and the History of Jewish-Hellenistic Religion*. Translated by John Bowden. London: SCM, 1976.

Hill, Charles E. "'He Descended into Hell.'" *Reformed Faith and Practice* 1.2 (2016): 3–10.

———. Regnum Caelorum*: Patterns of Millennial Thought in Early Christianity*. 2nd ed. Grand Rapids: Eerdmans, 2001.

Hodge, Charles. *Systematic Theology*. 3 vols. Reprint, Peabody, MA: Hendrickson, 2008.

Holmes, Michael W., ed. *The Apostolic Fathers: Greek Texts and English Translations*. 3rd ed. Grand Rapids: Baker Academic, 2007.

Hoskyns, Edwyn Clement. *The Fourth Gospel*. Edited by Francis Noel Davey. London: Faber and Faber, 1947.

Hurtado, Larry W. "Christology in Acts: Jesus in Early Christian Belief and Practice." Pages 217–37 in *Issues in Luke-Acts: Selected Essays*. Edited by Sean A. Adams and Michael W. Pahl. Gorgias Handbooks 26. Piscataway, NJ: Gorgias, 2013.

———. *Lord Jesus Christ: Devotion to Jesus in Earliest Christianity*. Grand Rapids: Eerdmans, 2003.

Hyde, Daniel J. *In Defense of the Descent: A Response to Contemporary Critics*. Explorations in Confessional Theology. Grand Rapids: Reformation Heritage, 2010.

Irenaeus. *Irénée de Lyon: Contre les hérésies*. Edited by Adelin Rousseau et al. 10 vols. SC. Paris: Cerf, 1965–2002.

Irons, Charles Lee. "A Lexical Defense of the Johannine 'Only Begotten.'" Pages 98–116 in *Retrieving Eternal Generation*. Edited by Fred Sanders and Scott R. Swain. Grand Rapids: Zondervan, 2017.

Irving, Edward. "The Doctrine of the Incarnation Opened: In Six Sermons." Vol. 5 of *The Collected Writings of Edward Irving*. Edited by G. Carlyle. London: Strahan, 1865.

Jamieson, R. B. "1 Corinthians 15.28 and the Grammar of Paul's Christology." *NTS* 66 (2020): 187–207.

———. *Jesus' Death and Heavenly Offering in Hebrews*. SNTSMS 172. Cambridge: Cambridge University Press, 2019.

———. *The Paradox of Sonship: Christology in the Epistle to the Hebrews*. Studies in Christian Doctrine and Scripture. Downers Grove, IL: IVP Academic, 2021.

Jensen, Matthew D. *Affirming the Resurrection of the Incarnate Christ: A Reading of 1 John*. SNTSMS 153. Cambridge: Cambridge University Press, 2012.

Jeremias, Joachim. *The Eucharistic Words of Jesus*. Translated by Arnold Ehrhardt. Oxford: Basil Blackwell, 1955.

Jobes, Karen H. *Letters to the Church: A Survey of Hebrews and the General Epistles*. Grand Rapids: Zondervan, 2011.

Johansson, Daniel. "*Kyrios* in the Gospel of Mark." *Journal for the Study of the New Testament* 33 (2010): 101–24.

John of Damascus. *Three Treatises on the Divine Images*. Translated by Andrew Louth. PPS. Crestwood, NY: St. Vladimir's Seminary Press, 2003.

Johnson, Adam J. "Theories and *Theoria* of the Atonement: A Proposal." *IJST* 23 (2021): 92–108.

Johnson, Dennis E. *The Triumph of the Lamb: A Commentary on Revelation*. Phillipsburg, NJ: P&R, 2001.

Johnson, Keith E. "Eternal Generation in the Trinitarian Theology of Augustine." Pages 163–79 in *Retrieving Eternal Generation*. Edited by Fred Sanders and Scott R. Swain. Grand Rapids: Zondervan, 2017.

Johnson, Luke Timothy. *Hebrews: A Commentary*. New Testament Library. Louisville: Westminster John Knox, 2006.

———. *Living Jesus: Learning the Heart of the Gospel*. San Francisco: HarperOne, 2000.

Jones, Mark. *Knowing Christ*. Edinburgh: Banner of Truth, 2015.

Kähler, Martin. *The So-Called Historical Jesus and the Historic, Biblical Christ*. Translated by Carl E. Braaten. Philadelphia: Fortress, 1964.

Keating, Daniel. "The Baptism of Jesus in Cyril of Alexandria: The Re-creation of the Human Race." *ProEccl* 8 (1999): 201–22.

Keck, Leander E. "Toward the Renewal of New Testament Christology." *NTS* 32 (1986): 362–77.

Kelly, Douglas F. "Novatian." Page 472 in *New Dictionary of Theology*. Edited by Sinclair B. Ferguson and David F. Wright. Downers Grove, IL: InterVarsity Press, 1988.

———. *Systematic Theology: Grounded in Holy Scripture and Understood in the Light of the Church*. Vol. 2 of *The Beauty of Christ: A Trinitarian Vision*. Fearn, UK: Mentor, 2014.

Kelly, J. N. D. *Early Christian Doctrines*. 5th rev. ed. Peabody, MA: Prince, 2007.

Keener, Craig S. *Acts: An Exegetical Commentary*. 4 vols. Grand Rapids: Baker Academic, 2012–2015.

———. *The Gospel of John: A Commentary*. 2 vols. Peabody, MA: Hendrickson, 2003.

Kidner, Derek. *Psalms 1–72: An Introduction and Commentary*. TOTC 15. Downers Grove, IL: InterVarsity Press, 1973.

Kline, Meredith G. *Kingdom Prologue: Genesis Foundations for a Covenantal Worldview*. Overland Park, KS: Two Age, 2000.

Klink, Edward W., III. *John*. ZECNT. Grand Rapids: Zondervan, 2016.

Koester, Craig R. *Hebrews: A New Translation with Introduction and Commentary*. AB 36. New York: Doubleday, 2001.

Kolb, Robert, and Carl R. Trueman. *Between Wittenberg and Geneva: Lutheran and Reformed Theology in Conversation*. Grand Rapids: Baker Academic, 2017.

Kolb, Robert, and Timothy J. Wengert, eds. *The Book of Concord: The Confessions of the Evangelical Lutheran Church*. Translated by Charles P. Arand. Minneapolis: Fortress, 2000.

Köstenberger, Andreas J. "John." Pages 415–512 in *Commentary on the New Testament Use of the Old Testament*. Edited by G. K. Beale and D. A. Carson. Grand Rapids: Baker Academic, 2007.

Köstenberger, Andreas J., with T. Desmond Alexander. *Salvation to the Ends of the Earth: A Biblical Theology of Mission*. 2nd ed. NSBT 53. Downers Grove, IL: IVP Academic, 2020.

Kruger, Michael J. *Canon Revisited: Establishing the Origins and Authority of the New Testament Books*. Wheaton, IL: Crossway, 2012.

———. *Christianity at the Crossroads: How the Second Century Shaped the Future of the Church*. Downers Grove, IL: IVP Academic, 2018.

Kruse, Colin G. *The Letters of John*. PNTC. Grand Rapids: Eerdmans, 2000.

Lane, William L. *The Gospel according to Mark*. NICNT. Grand Rapids: Eerdmans, 1974.

———. *Hebrews 1–8*. WBC 47A. Nashville: Thomas Nelson, 1991.

———. *Hebrews 9–13*. WBC 47B. Nashville: Thomas Nelson, 2000.

Lee, John J. R. *Christological Rereading of the Shema (Deut 6.4) in Mark's Gospel*. WUNT 2/533. Tübingen: Mohr Siebeck, 2020.

Lessing, G. E., ed. *Fragments from Reimarus*. Edited by C. Voysey. Reprint, Lexington: American Theological Library Association, 1962.

Letham, Robert. *The Holy Trinity: In Scripture, History, Theology, and Worship*. 2nd ed. Phillipsburg, NJ: P&R, 2019.

———. *Systematic Theology*. Wheaton, IL: Crossway, 2019.

———. *The Work of Christ*. CCT. Downers Grove, IL: InterVarsity Press, 1993.

Lincoln, Andrew T. *Born of a Virgin? Reconceiving Jesus in the Bible, Tradition, and Theology*. Grand Rapids: Eerdmans, 2013.

———. *Ephesians*. WBC 42. Nashville: Thomas Nelson, 1990.

Litfin, Bryan M. *Getting to Know the Church Fathers: An Evangelical Introduction*. Grand Rapids: Brazos, 2007.

Litwa, M. David. "Behold Adam: A Reading of John 19:5." *Horizons in Biblical Theology* 32 (2010): 129–43.

———, ed. and trans. *Refutation of All Heresies*. Writings from the Greco-Roman World 40. Atlanta: SBL Press, 2016.

Longenecker, Richard N. *Galatians*. WBC 41. Nashville: Thomas Nelson, 2006.

Lookadoo, Jonathan. "The Role of the Star in Ephesians 18–20: Ignatius of Antioch, Polymorphic Christology, and Second Temple Stars." *Journal of Early Christian History* 7 (2017): 62–88.

Luther, Martin. *Luther's Works*. American Edition. Edited by Jaroslav Pelikan and Helmut T. Lehmann. 55 vols. Philadelphia: Fortress; St. Louis: Concordia, 1955–86.

Machen, J. Gresham. *Things Unseen: A Systematic Introduction to the Christian Faith and Reformed Theology*. Philadelphia: Westminster Seminary Press, 2020.

MacLeod, Donald. *From Glory to Golgotha: Controversial Issues in the Life of Christ*. Fearn, UK: Christian Focus, 2021.

———. *The Person of Christ*. CCT. Downers Grove, IL: InterVarsity Press, 1998.

Marcovich, Miroslav, ed. *Athenagoras: Legatio pro Christianis*. PTS 31. Berlin: de Gruyter, 1990.

———. *Iustini Martyris: Apologiae pro christianis*. PTS 38. Berlin: de Gruyter, 1994.

———. *Iustini Martyris: Dialogus cum Tryphone*. PTS 47. Berlin: de Gruyter, 1997.

———. *Origenes: Contra Celsum libri VIII*. Supplements to Vigiliae Christianae 54. Ledien: Brill, 2001.

———. *Theophili Antiocheni: Ad Autolycum*. PTS 44. Berlin: de Gruyter, 1995.

Marcus, Joel. *Mark 1–8: A New Translation with Introduction and Commentary*. AB 27. New York: Doubleday, 2000.

———. *Mark 8–16: A New Translation with Introduction and Commentary*. AB 27A. New Haven: Yale University Press, 2009.

———. *The Way of the Lord: Christological Exegesis of the Old Testament in the Gospel of Mark*. Studies of the New Testament and Its World. Edinburgh: T&T Clark, 1993.

Maresius, Samuel. *Theologiae elenchticae nova synopsis; sive Index controversiarum fidei ex Sacris Scripturis*. Groningen: Nicolaum, 1646.

Marshall, I. Howard. *Luke: Historian and Theologian*. Grand Rapids: Zondervan, 1970.

———. "Son of Man." Pages 775–81 in *Dictionary of Jesus and the Gospels*. Edited by Joel B. Green, Scot McKnight, and I. Howard Marshall. Downers Grove, IL: InterVarsity Press, 1992.

Martin, Hugh. *The Atonement: In Its Relations to the Covenant, the Priesthood, the Intercession of Our Lord*. Reprint, Edinburgh: Banner of Truth, 2013.

Martin, Ralph P. *James*. WBC 48. Waco, TX: Word, 1988.

Mastricht, Petrus van. *Theoretical-Practical Theology*. Translated by Todd M. Rester. Edited by Joel R. Beeke. 7 vols. Grand Rapids: Reformation Heritage, 2018–.

———. *Theoretico-Practica Theologia*. Rev. ed. Vol. 1. Utrecht: Gerardum Muntendam, 1698.

Matlock, R. Barry. "Detheologizing the ΠΙΣΤΙΣ ΧΡΙΣΤΟΥ Debate: Cautionary Remarks from a Lexical Semantic Perspective." *Novum Testamentum* 42 (2000): 1–23.

Maximus the Confessor. *The Cosmic Mystery of Jesus Christ*. Translated by Paul M. Blowers and Robert Louis Wilken. PPS 25. Crestwood, NY: St. Vladimir's Seminary Press, 2003.

McCartney, Dan G. *James*. BECNT. Grand Rapids: Baker Academic, 2009.

McCormack, Bruce L. "The Person of Christ." Pages 149–73 in *Mapping Modern Theology: A Thematic and Historical Introduction*. Edited by Kelly M. Kapic and Bruce L. McCormack. Grand Rapids: Baker Academic, 2012.

McGraw, Ryan M. and Scott Cook. "Charles Hodge on the Trinity: Personhood and Subordination Language." In *Charles Hodge: American Reformed Orthodox Theologian*. Edited by Ryan M. McGraw. Göttingen: Vandenhoeck & Ruprecht, forthcoming.

McGuckin, John Anthony. *St. Cyril of Alexandria: The Christological Controversy; Its History, Theology, and Texts*. Reprint, Crestwood, NY: St. Vladimir's Seminary Press, 2004.

Meier, John P. *The Vision of Matthew: Christ, Church, and Morality in the First Gospel*. Reprint, Eugene, OR: Wipf & Stock, 2004.

Melito of Sardis. *On Pascha: With the Fragments of Melito and Other Material Related to the Quartodecimans*. Translated by Alistair Stewart-Sykes. PPS. Crestwood, NY: St. Vladimir's Seminary Press, 2001.

Metzger, Bruce M. *The Canon of the New Testament: Its Origin, Development, and Significance*. Oxford: Clarendon, 1986.

Metzler, Karin, ed. *Athanasius Werke*. Vol. 1, part 1, issues 2–3. Berlin: de Gruyter, 1998–2000.

Moffitt, David M. *Atonement and the Logic of Resurrection in the Epistle to the Hebrews*. NovTSup 141. Leiden: Brill, 2011.

———. "It Is Not Finished: Jesus's Perpetual Atoning Work as the Heavenly High Priest in Hebrews." Pages 157–75 in *So Great a Salvation: A Dialogue on the Atonement in Hebrews*. Edited by Jon C. Laansma, George H. Guthrie, and Cynthia Long Westfall. LNTS 516. London: T&T Clark, 2019.

Moloney, Francis J., SDB. *Love in the Gospel of John: An Exegetical, Theological, and Literary Study*. Grand Rapids: Baker Academic, 2013.

Moo, Douglas J. *2 Peter and Jude*. NIVAC. Grand Rapids: Zondervan, 1996.

———. *Galatians. BECNT. Grand Rapids: Baker Academic, 2013.*

———. *The Letter of James*. PNTC. Grand Rapids: Eerdmans, 2000.

———. *The Letters to the Colossians and Philemon*. PNTC. Grand Rapids: Eerdmans, 2008.

Moor, Johannes C. de. *Micah*. Historical Commentary on the Old Testament. Leuven: Peeters, 2020.

Morales, L. Michael. "Atonement in Ancient Israel: The Whole Burnt Offering as Central to Israel's Cult." Pages 27–39 in *So Great a Salvation: A Dialogue on the Atonement in Hebrews*. Edited by Jon C. Laansma, George H. Guthrie, and Cynthia Long Westfall. LNTS 516. London: T&T Clark, 2019.

———. *Exodus Old and New: A Biblical Theology of Redemption*. ESBT. Downers Grove, IL: IVP Academic, 2020.

———. *Who Shall Ascend the Mountain of the Lord? A Biblical Theology of the Book of Leviticus*. NSBT 27. Downers Grove, IL: InterVarsity Press, 2015.

Morris, Leon. *The Apostolic Preaching of the Cross*. Grand Rapids: Eerdmans, 1955.

Moser, J. David. "Tools for Interpreting Christ's Saving Mysteries in Scripture: Aquinas on Reduplicative Propositions in Christology." *SJT* 73 (2020): 285–94.

Motyer, Alec. *The Prophecy of Isaiah: An Introduction and Commentary*. Downers Grove, IL: IVP Academic, 1993.

———. "'Stricken for the Transgression of My People': The Atoning Work of Isaiah's Suffering Servant." Pages 247–66 in *From Heaven He Came and Sought Her: Definite Atonement in Historical, Biblical, Theological, and Pastoral Perspective*. Edited by David Gibson and Jonathan Gibson. Wheaton, IL: Crossway, 2013.

Müller, Paul-Gerhard. *ΧΡΙΣΤΟΣ ΑΡΧΗΓΟΣ: Die religionsgeschichtliche und theologische Hintergrund einer neutestamentlichen Christusprädikation*. Europaïsche Hochschulschriften: Reihe 23, Theologie 28. Bern: Lang; Frankfurt: Lang, 1973.

Muller, Richard A. *Dictionary of Latin and Greek Theological Terms: Drawn Principally from Protestant Scholastic Theology*. 2nd ed. Grand Rapids: Baker Academic, 2017.

Murray, John. *The Epistle to the Romans*. 2 vols. NICNT. Grand Rapids: Eerdmans, 1959–1965.

———. *Redemption Accomplished and Applied*. Grand Rapids: Eerdmans, 1955.

Neill, Stephen. *The Interpretation of the New Testament, 1861–1961*. London: Oxford University Press, 1964.

Nestlehutt, Mark S. G. "Chalcedonian Christology: Modern Criticism and Contemporary Ecumenism." *Journal of Ecumenical Studies* 35 (1998): 175–96.

Niebuhr, Karl-Wilhelm. "One God, One Lord in the Epistle of James." Pages 172–88 in *Monotheism and Christology in Greco-Roman Antiquity*. Edited by Matthew V. Novenson. NovTSup 180. Leiden: Brill, 2020.

Norris, Richard A. *The Christological Controversy*. Sources of Early Christian Thought. Philadelphia: Fortress, 1980.

Novatian. *Notatiani Opera*. Edited by G. F. Diercks. CCSL 4. Turnhout: Brepols, 1972.

O'Keefe, John J., and R. R. Reno. *Sanctified Vision: An Introduction to Early Christian Interpretation of the Bible*. Baltimore: Johns Hopkins University Press, 2005.

Osborn, Eric. *Irenaeus of Lyons*. Cambridge: Cambridge University Press, 2001.

Oswalt, John N. *The Book of Isaiah: Chapters 1–39*. NICOT. Grand Rapids: Eerdmans, 1986.

Owen, John. *The Death of Death in the Death of Christ*. Reprint, Edinburgh: Banner of Truth, 1959.

Packer, J. I. "What Did the Cross Achieve? The Logic of Penal Substitution." *TynBul* 25 (1974): 3–45.

Papandrea, James L. *The Earliest Christologies: Five Images of Christ in the Postapostolic Age*. Downers Grove, IL: IVP Academic, 2016.

———. *Novatian of Rome and the Culmination of Pre-Nicene Orthodoxy*. Princeton Theological Monograph Series 175. Eugene, OR: Pickwick, 2011.

Pass, Bruce R. *The Heart of Dogmatics: Christology and Christocentrism in Herman Bavinck*. Forschungen zur systematischen und ökumenischen Theologie 169. Göttingen: Vandenhoeck & Ruprecht, 2020.

Paulson, Steven D. "Christology." Pages 142–45 in *Dictionary of Luther and the Lutheran Traditions*. Edited by Timothy J. Wengert. Grand Rapids: Baker Academic, 2017.

Petersen, David L. *Zechariah 9–14 and Malachi*. OTL. Louisville: Westminster John Knox, 1995.

Peterson, David G. *The Acts of the Apostles*. PNTC. Grand Rapids: Eerdmans, 2009.

Phillips, Elaine A. "Peter's Declaration at Caesarea Philippi." Pages 286–96 in *Lexham Geographic Commentary on the Gospels*. Edited by Barry J. Beitzel. Bellingham, WA: Lexham, 2016–2017.

Phillips, Richard D. *John*. 2 vols. Reformed Expository Commentary. Phillipsburg, NJ: P&R, 2014.

Pierce, Madison N. "Hebrews 1 and the Son Begotten 'Today.'" Pages 117–31 in *Retrieving Eternal Generation*. Edited by Fred Sanders and Scott R. Swain. Grand Rapids: Zondervan, 2019.

Piper, John. *Jesus the Only Way to God: Must You Hear the Gospel to Be Saved?* Grand Rapids: Baker, 2010.

———. *The Pleasures of God: Meditations on God's Delight in Being God*. Rev. ed. Sisters, OR: Multnomah, 2000.

Plumer, William S. *The Person and Sinless Character of Our Lord Jesus Christ*. Richmond, VA: Presbyterian Committee of Publication; New York: Randolph, 1876.

Polanus von Polansdorf, Amandus. *Symphonia Catholica seu Consensus Catholicus et Orthodoxus*. Basel: Waldkirch, 1607.

———. *Syntagma Theologiae Christianae*. Hanover: Wechel, 1615.

Poythress, Vern S. "Counterfeiting in the Book of Revelation as a Perspective on Non-Christian Culture." *JETS* 40 (1997): 411–18.

———. *The Returning King: A Guide to the Book of Revelation*. Phillipsburg, NJ: P&R, 2000.

———. *Theophany: A Biblical Theology of God's Appearing*. Wheaton, IL: Crossway, 2018.

Pratt, Richard L., Jr. *1 & 2 Corinthians*. Holman New Testament Commentary. Nashville: Holman Reference, 2000.

Rackham, R. B. *The Acts of the Apostles: An Exposition*. 11th ed. Westminster Commentaries. London: Methuen, 1930.

Ramelli, Ilaria L. E. "Origen's Anti-Subordinationism and Its Heritage in the Nicene and Cappadocian Line." *VC* 65 (2011): 21–49.

Rankin, William Duncan. "Carnal Union with Christ in the Theology of T. F. Torrance." PhD diss., University of Edinburgh, 1997.

Ratzinger, Joseph [Pope Benedict XVI]. *Jesus of Nazareth: From the Baptism in the Jordan to the Transfiguration*. Translated by Adrian J. Walker. London: Bloomsbury, 2007.

Rénan, Ernest. *Life of Jesus*. Edited by Joseph Henry Allen. Boston: Roberts Brothers, 1896.

Ribbens, Benjamin J. "Ascension and Atonement: The Significance of Post-Reformation, Reformed Responses to Socinians for Contemporary Atonement Debates in Hebrews." *WTJ* 80 (2018): 1–23.

———. *Levitical Sacrifice and Heavenly Cult in Hebrews*. BZNW 222. Berlin: de Gruyter, 2016.

Ridderbos, Herman. *The Coming of the Kingdom*. Translated by H. de Jongste. Edited by Raymond O. Zorn. Philadelphia: Presbyterian and Reformed, 1962.

———. *The Gospel according to John: A Theological Commentary*. Translated by John Vriend. Grand Rapids: Eerdmans, 1997.

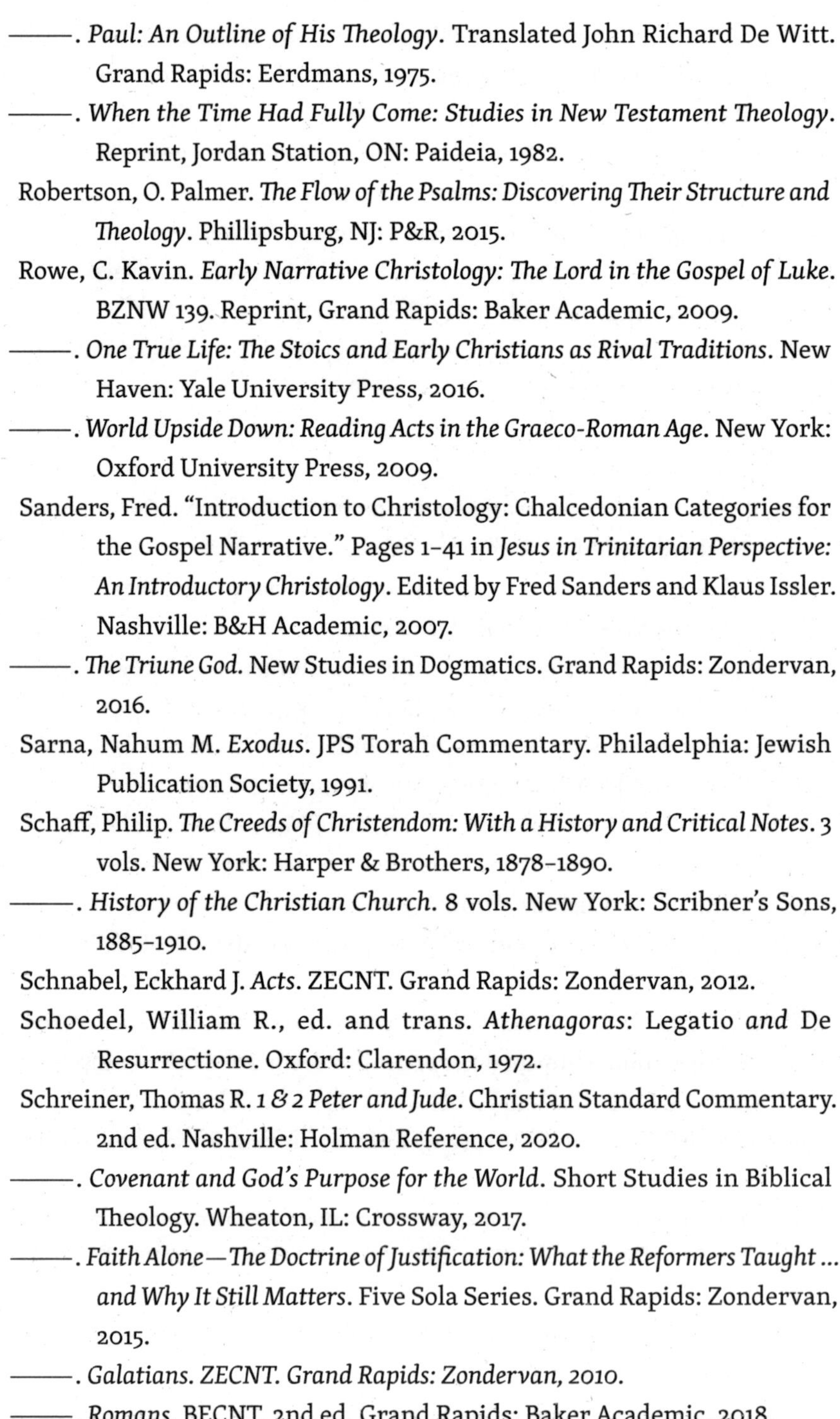

———. *Paul: An Outline of His Theology*. Translated John Richard De Witt. Grand Rapids: Eerdmans, 1975.

———. *When the Time Had Fully Come: Studies in New Testament Theology*. Reprint, Jordan Station, ON: Paideia, 1982.

Robertson, O. Palmer. *The Flow of the Psalms: Discovering Their Structure and Theology*. Phillipsburg, NJ: P&R, 2015.

Rowe, C. Kavin. *Early Narrative Christology: The Lord in the Gospel of Luke*. BZNW 139. Reprint, Grand Rapids: Baker Academic, 2009.

———. *One True Life: The Stoics and Early Christians as Rival Traditions*. New Haven: Yale University Press, 2016.

———. *World Upside Down: Reading Acts in the Graeco-Roman Age*. New York: Oxford University Press, 2009.

Sanders, Fred. "Introduction to Christology: Chalcedonian Categories for the Gospel Narrative." Pages 1–41 in *Jesus in Trinitarian Perspective: An Introductory Christology*. Edited by Fred Sanders and Klaus Issler. Nashville: B&H Academic, 2007.

———. *The Triune God*. New Studies in Dogmatics. Grand Rapids: Zondervan, 2016.

Sarna, Nahum M. *Exodus*. JPS Torah Commentary. Philadelphia: Jewish Publication Society, 1991.

Schaff, Philip. *The Creeds of Christendom: With a History and Critical Notes*. 3 vols. New York: Harper & Brothers, 1878–1890.

———. *History of the Christian Church*. 8 vols. New York: Scribner's Sons, 1885–1910.

Schnabel, Eckhard J. *Acts*. ZECNT. Grand Rapids: Zondervan, 2012.

Schoedel, William R., ed. and trans. *Athenagoras*: Legatio *and* De Resurrectione. Oxford: Clarendon, 1972.

Schreiner, Thomas R. *1 & 2 Peter and Jude*. Christian Standard Commentary. 2nd ed. Nashville: Holman Reference, 2020.

———. *Covenant and God's Purpose for the World*. Short Studies in Biblical Theology. Wheaton, IL: Crossway, 2017.

———. *Faith Alone—The Doctrine of Justification: What the Reformers Taught ... and Why It Still Matters*. Five Sola Series. Grand Rapids: Zondervan, 2015.

———. *Galatians. ZECNT. Grand Rapids: Zondervan, 2010.*

———. *Romans*. BECNT. 2nd ed. Grand Rapids: Baker Academic, 2018.

Schweitzer, Albert. *The Quest of the Historical Jesus*. Translated by W. Montgomery. New York: Collier, 1968.

Silva, Moisés. "Perfection and Eschatology in Hebrews." *WTJ* 39 (1976): 60–71.

———. *Philippians*. 2nd ed. BECNT. Grand Rapids: Baker Academic, 2005.

Sklar, Jay. *Leviticus: An Introduction and Commentary*. TOTC 3. Downers Grove, IL: IVP Academic, 2013.

Smalley, Stephen. *1, 2, and 3 John*. WBC 51. Rev. ed. Grand Rapids: Zondervan, 2008.

Smith, Murray J. "The Book of Revelation: A Call to Worship, Witness, and Wait in the Midst of Violence." Pages 334–71 in *Into All the World: Emergent Christianity in Its Jewish and Greco-Roman Context*. Edited by Mark Harding and Alana Nobbs. Grand Rapids: Eerdmans, 2017.

———. "The Lord Jesus and His Coming in the Didache." Pages 363–407 in *The Didache: A Missing Piece of the Puzzle in Early Christianity*. Edited by Jonathan A. Draper and Clayton N. Jefford. Early Christianity and Its Literature 14. Atlanta: SBL Press, 2015.

Snodgrass, Klyne R. *Stories with Intent: A Comprehensive Guide to the Parables of Jesus*. Grand Rapids: Eerdmans, 2008.

Spence, Alan. "A Unified Theory of the Atonement." *IJST* 6 (2004): 404–20.

Strange, Daniel. *Their Rock Is Not Like Our Rock: A Theology of Religions*. Grand Rapids: Zondervan, 2014.

Strauss, David Friedrich. *The Life of Jesus Critically Examined*. Edited by Peter C. Hodgson. Translated by George Eliot. Reprint, Mifflintown, PA: Sigler, 1994.

Strimple, Robert B. *The Modern Search for the Real Jesus: An Introductory Survey of the Historical Roots of Gospels Criticism*. Phillipsburg, NJ: P&R, 1995.

Stuart, Douglas K. *Exodus*. NAC 2. Nashville: Broadman & Holman, 2006.

Stuckenbruck, Loren T. "The *Book of Enoch:* Its Reception in Second Temple Jewish and in Christian Tradition." *Early Christianity* 4 (2013): 7–40.

Sutanto, Nathaniel Gray. "Herman Bavinck on the Image of God and Original Sin." *IJST* 18 (2016): 174–90.

Swain, Scott R. "B. B. Warfield and the Biblical Doctrine of the Trinity." *Them* 43 (2018): 10–24.

———. "Covenant of Redemption." Pages 107–25 in *Christian Dogmatics: Reformed Theology for the Church Catholic*. Edited by Michael Allen and Scott R. Swain. Grand Rapids: Baker Academic, 2016.

———. "New Covenant Theologies." Pages 551–69 in *Covenant Theology: Biblical, Theological, and Historical Perspectives*. Edited Guy Prentiss Waters, J. Nicholas Reid, and John R. Muether. Wheaton, IL: Crossway, 2020.

Talbert, Charles H. *Reading John: A Literary and Theological Commentary on the Fourth Gospel and the Johannine Epistles*. New York: Crossroad, 1992.

Tanner, Norman P., SJ, ed. *Decrees of the Ecumenical Councils*. 2 vols. Washington, DC: Georgetown University Press, 1990.

Tertullian. *Tertulliani Opera*. Edited by E. Dekkers et al. 2 vols. CCSL 1–2. Turnhout: Brepols, 1954.

Theophilos, Michael P. "ΒΑΣΙΛΕΥΣ ΒΑΣΙΛΕΩΝ (Rev. 17.14; 19.16) in Light of the Numismatic Record." *NTS* 65 (2019): 526–51.

Thiselton, Anthony C. *The First Epistle to the Corinthians: A Commentary on the Greek Text*. NIGTC. Grand Rapids: Eerdmans, 2000.

Thompson, Alan J. *The Acts of the Risen Lord Jesus: Luke's Account of God's Unfolding Plan*. NSBT 27. Downers Grove, IL: InterVarsity Press, 2011.

———. "The Trinity and Luke-Acts." Pages 62–82 in *The Essential Trinity: New Testament Foundations and Practical Relevance*. Edited by Brandon D. Crowe and Carl R. Trueman. London: Apollos, 2016.

Tipton, Lane G. "Christology in Colossians 1:15–20 and Hebrews 1:1–4: An Exercise in Biblico-Systematic Theology." Pages 177–202 in *Resurrection and Eschatology: Theology in Service of the Church; Essays in Honor of Richard B. Gaffin Jr.* Edited by Lane G. Tipton and Jeffrey C. Waddington. Phillipsburg, NJ: P&R, 2008.

Torrance, Thomas F. *Incarnation: The Person and Life of Christ*. Edited by Robert T. Walker. Downers Grove, IL: IVP Academic, 2008.

———. *The Trinitarian Faith: The Evangelical Theology of the Ancient Catholic Church*. Edinburgh: T&T Clark, 1995.

Treier, Daniel J. "Incarnation." Pages 216–42 in *Christian Dogmatics: Reformed Theology for the Church Catholic*. Edited by Michael Allen and Scott R. Swain. Grand Rapids: Baker Academic, 2016.

Trueman, Carl R. *The Rise and Triumph of the Modern Self: Cultural Amnesia, Expressive Individualism, and the Road to Sexual Revolution*. Wheaton, IL: Crossway, 2020.

Turner, Max. "Mission and Meaning in Terms of 'Unity' in Ephesians." Pages 138–66 in *Mission and Meaning: Essays Presented to Peter Cotterell*. Edited by Anthony Billington, Tony Lane, and Max Turner. Carlisle, UK: Paternoster, 1995.

Ussher, James. *A Body of Divinitie, or The Summe and Substance of Christian Religion: Catechistically propounded, and explained, by way of Question and Answer: Methodically and familiarly handled*. London: Downes & Badger, 1645.

Vaillancourt, Ian J. *The Multifaceted Saviour of Palms 110 and 118*. Hebrew Bible Monographs 86. Sheffield: Sheffield Phoenix, 2019.

Van Dixhoorn, Chad. "Post-Reformation Trinitarian Perspectives." Pages 180–207 in *Retrieving Eternal Generation*. Edited by Fred Sanders and Scott R. Swain. Grand Rapids: Zondervan, 2017.

Vidu, Adonis. *The Same God Who Works All Things: Inseparable Operations in Trinitarian Theology*. Grand Rapids: Eerdmans, 2021.

———. "Trinitarian Inseparable Operations and the Trinity." *Journal of Analytic Theology* 4 (2016): 106–27.

Vielhauer, Philipp. "On the 'Paulinism' of Acts." Pages 33–50 in *Studies in Luke-Acts: Essays Presented in Honor of Paul Schubert*. Edited by Leander E. Keck and J. Louis Martyn. Nashville: Abingdon, 1966.

Vincent, Marvin R. *Word Studies in the New Testament*. 4 vols. New York: Scribner's Sons, 1887.

Vos, Geerhardus. *Biblical Theology: Old and New Testaments*. Reprint, Edinburgh: Banner of Truth, 1975.

———. "The Eschatology of the Psalter." *Princeton Theological Review* 18 (1920): 1–43.

———. "The Eschatological Aspect of the Pauline Conception of the Spirit." Pages 91–125 in *Redemptive History and Biblical Interpretation: The Shorter Writings of Geerhardus Vos*. Edited by Richard B. Gaffin Jr. Phillipsburg, NJ: P&R, 1980.

———. "The Priesthood of Christ in the Epistle to the Hebrews." Pages 126–60 in *Redemptive History and Biblical Interpretation: The Shorter Writings*

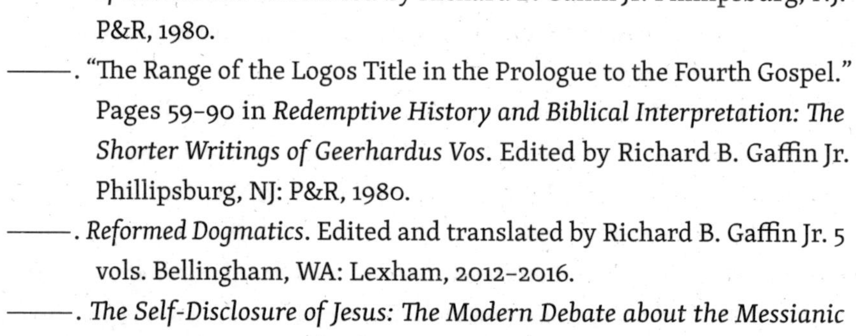

of Geerhardus Vos. Edited by Richard B. Gaffin Jr. Phillipsburg, NJ: P&R, 1980.

———. "The Range of the Logos Title in the Prologue to the Fourth Gospel." Pages 59–90 in *Redemptive History and Biblical Interpretation: The Shorter Writings of Geerhardus Vos*. Edited by Richard B. Gaffin Jr. Phillipsburg, NJ: P&R, 1980.

———. *Reformed Dogmatics*. Edited and translated by Richard B. Gaffin Jr. 5 vols. Bellingham, WA: Lexham, 2012–2016.

———. *The Self-Disclosure of Jesus: The Modern Debate about the Messianic Consciousness*. 2nd ed. Edited by Johannes G. Vos. Reprint, Phillipsburg, NJ: P&R, 2002.

———. *The Teaching of the Epistle to the Hebrews*. Edited by Johannes G. Vos. Grand Rapids: Eerdmans, 1956.

Wallace, Daniel B. *Greek Grammar beyond the Basics: An Exegetical Syntax of the Greek New Testament*. Grand Rapids: Zondervan, 1996.

Waltke, Bruce K. *The Book of Proverbs: Chapters 1–15*. New International Commentary on the Old Testament. Grand Rapids: Eerdmans, 2004.

———. *A Commentary on Micah*. Grand Rapids: Eerdmans, 2007.

Waltke, Bruce K., and James M. Houston with Erika Moore. *The Psalms as Christian Worship: A Historical Commentary*. Grand Rapids: Eerdmans, 2010.

Waltke, Bruce K. *An Old Testament Theology: An Exegetical, Canonical, and Thematic Approach*. Grand Rapids: Zondervan, 2007.

Ware, James P., ed. *Synopsis of the Pauline Letters in Greek and English*. Grand Rapids: Baker Academic, 2010.

Warfield, Benjamin Breckinridge. "The Chief Theories of the Atonement." Pages 351–69 in *The Person and Work of Christ*. Edited by Samuel G. Craig. Philadelphia: Presbyterian and Reformed, 1950.

———. "Christless Christianity." Pages 265–319 in *The Person and Work of Christ*. Edited by Samuel G. Craig. Philadelphia: Presbyterian and Reformed, 1950.

———. "The Emotional Life of Our Lord." Pages 93–145 in *The Person and Work of Christ*. Edited by Samuel G. Craig. Philadelphia: Presbyterian and Reformed, 1950.

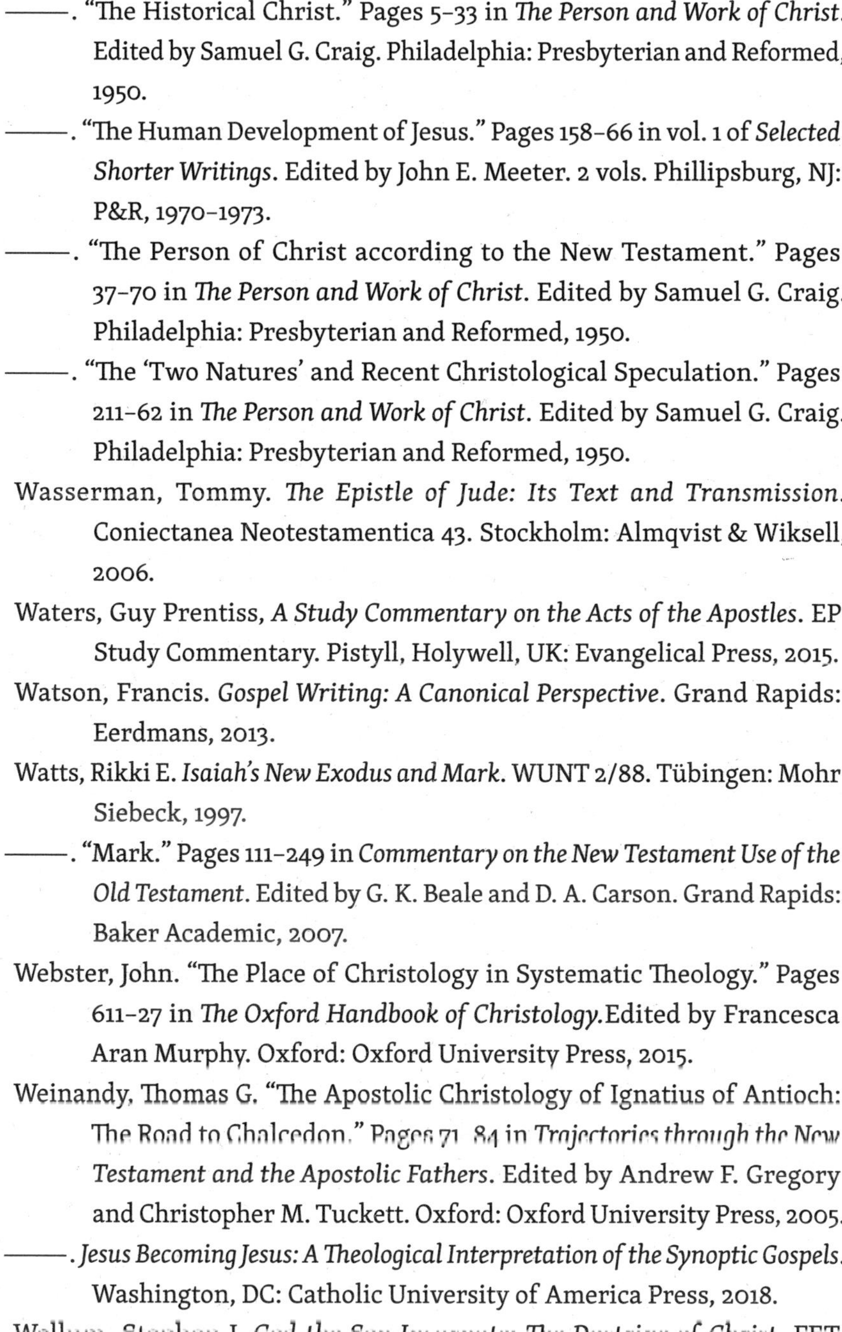

———. "The Historical Christ." Pages 5–33 in *The Person and Work of Christ*. Edited by Samuel G. Craig. Philadelphia: Presbyterian and Reformed, 1950.

———. "The Human Development of Jesus." Pages 158–66 in vol. 1 of *Selected Shorter Writings*. Edited by John E. Meeter. 2 vols. Phillipsburg, NJ: P&R, 1970–1973.

———. "The Person of Christ according to the New Testament." Pages 37–70 in *The Person and Work of Christ*. Edited by Samuel G. Craig. Philadelphia: Presbyterian and Reformed, 1950.

———. "The 'Two Natures' and Recent Christological Speculation." Pages 211–62 in *The Person and Work of Christ*. Edited by Samuel G. Craig. Philadelphia: Presbyterian and Reformed, 1950.

Wasserman, Tommy. *The Epistle of Jude: Its Text and Transmission*. Coniectanea Neotestamentica 43. Stockholm: Almqvist & Wiksell, 2006.

Waters, Guy Prentiss, *A Study Commentary on the Acts of the Apostles*. EP Study Commentary. Pistyll, Holywell, UK: Evangelical Press, 2015.

Watson, Francis. *Gospel Writing: A Canonical Perspective*. Grand Rapids: Eerdmans, 2013.

Watts, Rikki E. *Isaiah's New Exodus and Mark*. WUNT 2/88. Tübingen: Mohr Siebeck, 1997.

———. "Mark." Pages 111–249 in *Commentary on the New Testament Use of the Old Testament*. Edited by G. K. Beale and D. A. Carson. Grand Rapids: Baker Academic, 2007.

Webster, John. "The Place of Christology in Systematic Theology." Pages 611–27 in *The Oxford Handbook of Christology*.Edited by Francesca Aran Murphy. Oxford: Oxford University Press, 2015.

Weinandy, Thomas G. "The Apostolic Christology of Ignatius of Antioch: The Road to Chalcedon." Pages 71–84 in *Trajectories through the New Testament and the Apostolic Fathers*. Edited by Andrew F. Gregory and Christopher M. Tuckett. Oxford: Oxford University Press, 2005.

———. *Jesus Becoming Jesus: A Theological Interpretation of the Synoptic Gospels*. Washington, DC: Catholic University of America Press, 2018.

Wellum, Stephen J. *God the Son Incarnate: The Doctrine of Christ*. FET. Wheaton, IL: Crossway, 2016.

Wengst, Klaus. *Schriften des Urchristentums: Didache (Apostellehre), Barnabasbrief, Zweiter Klemensbrief, Schrift an Diognet: Eingeleitet, herausgegeben, übertragen und erläutert*. Munich: Kösel, 1984.

Wenham, Gordon J. *Genesis 1–15*. WBC 1. Nashville: Thomas Nelson, 1987.

———. *Numbers: An Introduction and Commentary*. TOTC 4. Downers Grove, IL: IVP Academic, 1981.

Wénin, André. "Enracinement vétérotestamentaire du discours sur la résurrection de Jésus dans le Nouveau Testament." Pages 3–23 in *Resurrection of the Dead: Biblical Traditions in Dialogue*. Edited by Geert Van Yen and Tom Shepherd. Bibliotheca Ephemeridum Theologicarum Lovaniensium 249. Leuven: Peters, 2012.

White, Thomas Joseph, OP. *The Incarnate Lord: A Thomistic Study in Christology*. Washington, DC: Catholic University of America Press, 2015.

Wilhite, David E. *The Gospel according to Heretics: Discovering Orthodoxy through Early Christological Conflicts*. Grand Rapid: Baker Academic, 2015.

Wilken, Robert Louis. "St. Cyril of Alexandria: The Mystery of Christ in the Bible." *ProEccl* 4 (1995): 454–78.

Williamson, H. G. M. *Variations on a Theme: King, Messiah and Servant in the Book of Isaiah*. Carlisle, UK: Paternoster, 1998.

Wise, Michael Owen. *A Critical Study of the Temple Scroll from Cave 11*. Studies in Ancient Oriental Civilization 49. Chicago: University of Chicago Press, 1990.

Wise, Michael O., Martin G. Abegg Jr., and Edward M. Cook. *The Dead Sea Scrolls: A New Translation*. Rev. ed. San Francisco: HarperOne, 2005.

Witherington, Ben, III. *The Acts of the Apostles: A Socio-Rhetorical Commentary*. Grand Rapids: Eerdmans, 1998.

Wittman, Tyler R. "The End of the Incarnation: John Owen, Trinitarian Agency and Christology." *IJST* 15 (2013): 284–300.

Wright, Christopher J. H. *Knowing Jesus through the Old Testament*. Downers Grove, IL: InterVarsity Press, 1992.

Wright, N. T. *Colossians and Philemon: An Introduction and Commentary*. TNTC. Downers Grove, IL: InterVarsity Press, 1986.

———. *Jesus and the Victory of God*. COQG 2. Minneapolis: Fortress, 1996.

Young, Frances M. *Biblical Exegesis and the Formation of Christian Culture.* Reprint, Peabody, MA: Hendrickson, 2002.

Zehnder, Markus. "Why the Danielic 'Son of Man' Is a Divine Being." *BBR* 24 (2014): 331–47.

SUBJECT INDEX

G

H

I

J

AUTHOR INDEX

S

T

U

V

SCRIPTURE INDEX

Old Testament

Numbers

Deuteronomy

Joshua

Judges

1 Samuel

2 Samuel

1 Kings

2 Kings

1 Chronicles

Nehemiah

Job

Psalms

Proverbs

Ecclesiastes

Isaiah

New Testament

James

ANCIENT SOURCES INDEX

Dead Sea Scrolls

Old Testament Apocrypha and Pseudepigrapha

Apostolic Fathers

2 *Clement*

Didache

Epistle to Diognetus

Epistle of Barnabas

Ignatius, *To the Ephesians*

Ignatius, *To the Magnesians*